Singing the Self

Northwestern University Press
Studies in Russian Literature and Theory

Singing the Self

GUITAR POETRY, COMMUNITY, AND IDENTITY IN THE POST-STALIN PERIOD

Rachel S. Platonov

NORTHWESTERN UNIVERSITY PRESS / EVANSTON, ILLINOIS

Northwestern University Press
www.nupress.northwestern.edu

This book has been published with the support of the Andrew W. Mellon Foundation.

Arts & Humanities
Research Council

Each year the AHRC provides funding from the UK government to support research and postgraduate study in the arts and humanities. Only applications of the highest quality are funded and the range of research supported by this investment of public funds not only provides social and cultural benefits but also contributes to the economic success of the UK. For further information on the AHRC, please go to: www.ahrc.ac.uk

Printed in the United States of America

10 9 8 7 6 5 4 3 2 1

Library of Congress Cataloging-in-Publication Data

Platonov, Rachel S.
Singing the self : guitar poetry, community, and identity in the post-Stalin period / Rachel S. Platonov.
p. cm. — (Studies in Russian literature and theory)
Includes bibliographical references and index.
ISBN 978-0-8101-2833-0 (cloth : alk. paper)
1. Popular music—Social aspects—Soviet Union. 2. Marginality, Social—Soviet Union. 3. Songs, Russian—20th century—History and criticism. I. Title. II. Series: Studies in Russian literature and theory.
ML3497.P53 2012
782.421640947—dc23

2011050539

∞ The paper used in this publication meets the minimum requirements of the American National Standard for Information Sciences—Permanence of Paper for Printed Library Materials, ANSI Z39.48-1992.

For M.S., who helped inspire me to start this project,
and N.S., who helped inspire me to finish it.

Contents

Acknowledgments

I owe a debt of gratitude to many people who have helped me immeasurably throughout the various stages of this project. I am grateful to my advisory team of Svetlana Boym, William Mills Todd III, and Julie Buckler, and also to Stephanie Sandler, who provided sage advice and constructive criticism on my Ph.D. dissertation, in which this project originated. Likewise, I am deeply indebted to Vladimir Frumkin for sharing his astonishingly broad knowledge of guitar poetry time and again, both while I was working on my dissertation and in the years since.

I also offer my thanks to numerous people in Russia for their friendship, for their unfailing support, both practical and intellectual, and for their enthusiasm as interviewees, unofficial guides to the world of guitar poetry, and traveling companions on fieldwork expeditions. These include Natal'ya Akkuratova, Boris Almazov, Aleksandr Gorodnitsky, Mikhail Kane, Al'fred Tal'kovsky, Valentin Vikhorev, the late Anna Yashunskaya, Sergey Sinel'nikov, Lena Mazalova and her late husband Aleksey, Misha Semenenko, and Lena Demyanova. In Russia, too, Alla and Mark Levitan generously allowed me to work in their remarkable private archive, while Rollan Shipov and Feliks Surkis kindly supplied me with numerous books and other materials about guitar poetry.

Likewise, I am grateful to my family and friends, both for their interest in this project and for being a constant source of good humor and moral support throughout its development.

Last but certainly not least, I gratefully acknowledge the generous financial support that I have received from several institutions: the Davis Center for Russian and Eurasian Studies, which sponsored several summers of fieldwork in Russia; the British Academy, a small research grant from which supported work on chapter 2; and the Arts and Humanities Research Council (AHRC), a matching research leave grant from which provided invaluable support for an intensive period of research, further fieldwork, and writing that allowed me to bring this project to completion.

Author's Note

For transliteration of Russian words and phrases, I have adopted the system of the U.S. Board on Geographic Names (USBGN), but using *yo* in place of the more cumbersome *ë / yë*. Where applicable, however, familiar spellings of Russian terms and proper names have been used (e.g., perestroika, Vysotsky, Mikhailova), even where these deviate from the USBGN system.

In most cases, the texts of guitar poets' songs are now widely available in numerous different editions, and in some cases song titles vary from edition to edition. Wherever possible, I have cited from a single edition of each guitar poet's work. Where appropriate, I have indicated discrepancies between the commonly used titles of songs and those that appear in the editions cited. Unless otherwise indicated, all English translations are my own.

Every effort has been made to obtain the necessary permissions to quote from materials used in this study; if any such permissions have been inadvertently omitted, I would be most grateful to be notified so that they can be included in any future editions. Short sections of several chapters, in particular two song analyses in chapters 6 and 7, appeared previously in *Ulbandus*, vol. 9 (2005–6).

Singing the Self

Introduction

IN THE HEADY DECADE following Joseph Stalin's death in March 1953, public discourse in the Soviet Union acquired not only a new vocabulary but also a new soundtrack. For so many years, the ritual glorification of the "wise father of the Soviet people," the heralding of the "bright and glorious future," and the nearly ubiquitous proclamation that "Party and people [were] united" had been enacted to the tune of countless mass songs, professionally written, loud, choral, and optimistic. By contrast, the "unmasking of the cult of personality," criticism of the "varnishing of reality," and a cautious emphasis on "the all-round development of the individual"[1] played out to a very different kind of background music. Increasingly, the musical repository of the post-Stalin period was filled with the individual efforts of countless urban intellectuals, students, geologists, hikers and campers (*turisty*), and other young people with no more officially recognized musical qualification than something to say and a desire to say it through song.

Far from being a faddish phenomenon that would soon pass, these amateur songs would multiply exponentially throughout the three decades between Stalin and Gorbachev. In the process, they would coalesce into the distinctive, if somewhat amorphous, phenomenon of "guitar poetry." While not a direct translation of any of the genre's customary Russian names—which include, among others, *avtorskaya pesnya* (author's song), *bardovskaya pesnya* (bard song), and *samodeyatel'naya pesnya* (amateur song)—Gerald Smith's felicitous coinage "guitar poetry" succinctly encapsulates two of the genre's chief characteristics while also sidestepping the messy and often contentious debates surrounding the myriad Russian terms for it.[2]

Broadly speaking, guitar poetry was an acoustic singer-songwriter genre typified by the solo performance of one's own lyrics to relatively simple, unobtrusive melodic accompaniment on the Russian seven-stringed guitar. Both thematic, stylistic, and lexical diversity and an unpolished manner of performance were also typical. Few, if any, of guitar poetry's purported generic characteristics are absolute, however, complicating definitions of it considerably. The "triunity" (*triyedinstvo*) of author-composer-performer is often held up as guitar poetry's ideal, for example.[3] Yet various guitar poets ("bards") composed and performed settings of other poets' texts, both classic and contemporary. Moreover, the adoption, adaptation, and popularization of bards' songs by numerous amateur performers were crucial in transforming guitar poetry from an intimate chamber genre into a mass phenomenon—and, in some cases, into "anonymous" folklore as well.

Similarly, an unpretentious or deliberately amateurish style of performance was common. Indeed, many bards openly acknowledged their lack of proficiency and finesse as singers and musicians. Yet, of the major bards alone, several were trained actors; and among the minor bards there were numerous trained composers and musicians, particularly from the 1970s onward. Likewise, it is widely held that the poetic text is guitar poetry's privileged locus of meaning; and that "to [songs' lyrics] are subordinated both the musical side and the manner of performance."[4] At the same time, however, performance has been identified as one of guitar poetry's most distinctive characteristics.[5] Further, it has been argued that if one reads guitar poetry's texts rather than hearing them, songs "sometimes don't make any impression at all, and even become incomprehensible"; concomitantly, it has been suggested that the bard Vladimir Vysotsky, in particular, exists entirely "in sound."[6]

Complicating matters still further is the fact that, from a very early stage, guitar poetry evolved not just as a song genre but also as a sociocultural phenomenon, a medium through which Soviet young people across several generations articulated thoughts, opinions, and identities; recognized and interacted with like-minded individuals; and formed communities that were never entirely within, yet also never entirely outside of, the Soviet *kollektiv* (collective). It is precisely guitar poetry's important social-interactive functions (acknowledged in passing references to songs as "conversations" or "dialogues," but as yet not examined in depth) that are the main subject of this book. In the immediate context, however, guitar poetry's status as a sociocultural phenomenon has terminological consequences as well. Throughout this study, "guitar poetry" is used to designate the song genre itself; and the terms "guitar poet" and "bard" are used synonymously in reference to active practitioners thereof.

In contrast, the broader sociocultural phenomenon of which guitar poetry formed the nucleus is referred to here as the "guitar poetry movement," a term that is understood to include, but not necessarily be limited to, members of amateur song clubs (*kluby samodeyatel'noy pesni,* or KSP). The distinction between genre and movement is important because some bards actively promoted the guitar poetry movement while others distanced themselves from it. Moreover, it is important because not all participants in the movement were bards themselves. For some, that is, active processes of self-fashioning, communication, and community-building through guitar poetry took place at the level of consumption rather than production: through avid and active listening; through organizing song clubs, concerts, and festivals; through producing and distributing homemade tape recordings and "wall newspapers" (*stengazety*); and through meticulously archiving any and all available information, published or unpublished, about guitar poets and guitar poetry.

Since the late 1950s, journalistic and scholarly responses to guitar poetry have been many and varied, revealing (along with emotions ranging from outrage to euphoria) the intense and enduring fascination that this complex phenomenon has provoked. In general terms, the evolution of these responses has described two broad and intersecting arcs. The first arc charts a shift from casting guitar poetry in shades of political conformity versus dissent, to viewing it in somewhat subtler tones of psychological or spiritual oppositionality. The second arc charts a shift from debates about guitar poetry primarily within the context of Soviet song (the Soviet musical establishment having been more vocal than its literary counterpart about guitar poetry's rise and development) to the genre's firm incorporation and celebration within the Russian literary tradition.

From the late 1950s through the 1960s, various accounts published in the Soviet press tended to hew to an assimilate-or-eliminate approach, suggesting guardedly that guitar poetry, like other types of song, could be harnessed in the service of the state; or, in contrast, inveighing against its "anti-Soviet" orientation and its "damaging" influence on Soviet youth.[7] In the 1970s, guitar poetry was widely used in film, television, and theater but was barely discussed in the press, reflecting a concerted attempt to co-opt the genre and the movement broadly, while suppressing specific songs and individual bards through silence; and indicating, perhaps paradoxically, the extent to which guitar poetry had been supplanted as musical threat du jour by the more recent phenomenon of rock and roll. During the same period, various Western and Soviet émigré observers picked up the refrain of guitar poetry as a form of literary-musical "contraband" or "counterculture," and hailed guitar poets themselves as "the modern outlaw minstrels of Soviet society."[8] By and large, though, these responses focused on exceptional cases like the politically outspoken, and eventually outcast, Aleksandr Galich. As a result, they failed to take account of the numerous intersections and interactions between guitar poetry as a whole and fully sanctioned Soviet culture.

Gerald Smith's groundbreaking study *Songs to Seven Strings: Russian Guitar Poetry and Soviet Mass Song* (1984) represented a very important exception to the portrayal of guitar poetry in purely "dissident" terms, a trend that was otherwise dominant in Western sources throughout the 1980s and into the early 1990s.[9] In this study, Smith positions guitar poetry within the spectrum of Soviet popular song and surveys the works of various bards, focusing primarily on Galich, Vysotsky, and Bulat Okudzhava. With a few exceptions, Smith concludes, most of the amateurs who began writing and performing songs in the late 1950s and 1960s "stayed by and large within the tolerated limits of . . . the middle ground" between "what is actively promoted and what is actively persecuted by the authorities."[10] In a sense, though, Smith's study is more descriptive than analytical, a fact that the author himself acknowledges. Introducing guitar poetry to a Western audience then largely ignorant of its existence, Smith focused specifically on "presenting the actual texts of guitar poetry and the song genres most closely related to it"; as a result, Smith observes, "the extensive citing of texts" allowed only limited space for analysis.[11]

Since the collapse of the Soviet Union, guitar poetry has attracted relatively little attention within Western academe, despite ample interest in various forms of Russian and Soviet popular culture;[12] and despite the rising popularity of the late Soviet period as a subject of analysis from a range of disciplinary and interdisciplinary perspectives.[13] Though numerically limited, recent studies by Western scholars have analyzed guitar poetry within a number of different frameworks (including pedagogical, literary, and ethnomusicological).[14] The dominant tone in post-Soviet discussions of guitar poetry has been set within Russian academic and popular discourse, however. Here, guitar poetry has carved out a formidable niche, prompting a flood of scholarly articles and monographs, not to mention collections of bards' works (printed texts as well as audio and video recordings and multimedia CD-ROMs), websites, biographies, personal reminiscences, concerts, festivals, and television specials. Guitar poetry's roots and poetic development have been scrutinized in depth;[15] individual bards' lives (most particularly Vysotsky's) have been examined inside and out, and their lyrics have been studied extensively.[16] Notions of protest and opposition remain significant in various post-Soviet analyses of guitar poetry; but to an extent, an understanding of bards' and songs' opposition to the Soviet regime in psychological or spiritual terms has supplanted broad-based notions of overt anti-Sovietness or political protest.[17]

More prominent among recent Russian approaches to guitar poetry is the second trend mentioned above, namely the interpretation of the genre in purely literary terms. On one hand, this tendency is reflected in many meticulous discussions of linguistic and thematic aspects of individual bards' lyrics, which skirt around issues of musical accompaniment and performance, focusing on the "poetry" at the expense of the "guitar."[18] On the other hand, it is reflected in broad and explicit definitions of guitar poetry as a poetic (rather than song) genre.[19] While such studies are certainly interesting, these approaches reveal a tendency to ignore the complexities and peculiarities generated by guitar poetry's hybridization of text, music, and performance, in favor of narrowly poetic concerns. As such, it may be argued that the prevailing focus on text reveals as much about the intellectual concerns of post-Soviet Russia—including anxieties about the changing roles of the intelligentsia and of literary culture therein—as it does about guitar poetry itself.[20]

It is argued here that, in order to explore guitar poetry's vital functions as a medium of self-fashioning, communication, and community-building, two significant reorientations of approach are necessary. The first of these involves turning from the examination of guitar poetry within an essentially binary paradigm (characterized by oppositions such as official vs. unofficial, conformity vs. dissent, Soviet vs. anti-Soviet, high vs. low/popular culture) to an exploration of the messy and ambiguous interstices between such poles. The second involves moving away from a methodology dominated by textual analysis to a more inclusive approach that, without ignoring guitar poetry's lyrics, emphasizes the significance of and scrutinizes context, accompaniment, and performance as well. Neither of these reorientations is entirely uncomplicated, however, for reasons that will be discussed below.

Rejecting simple binary distinctions in order to focus on the in-between, the present study examines guitar poetry within the theoretical framework of marginality, adapting this diverse body of critical theory to a specifically Russian-Soviet cultural context. Within this framework, guitar poetry is analyzed as a phenomenon that both created and exploited marginality on multiple levels—in the spaces it occupied and the technologies it employed, in the edgy sounds coaxed out of bards' vocal and musical instruments, and in the linguistic, melodic, and generic codes from which their songs were woven. As integral components of marginality, processes of self- and group identification and interaction are considered alongside processes of generating and manipulating marginality itself. Through its marginality-centered approach, this study offers a new paradigm for the interpretation of guitar poetry as a constructive and communicative medium. At the same time, it contributes to a growing body of scholarship that challenges the validity of binary models in the analysis of Soviet reality, especially with respect to the post-Stalin period.[21] Perhaps inevitably, though, it has proven virtually impossible to eradicate all familiar binary pairs from the subsequent discussion. In particular, the distinction between the generally apolitical "romantic bards [*bardy-romantiki*]" (epitomized by Bulat Okudzhava) and the "protest bards [*bardy protesta*]" (including, foremost, Aleksandr Galich) is so firmly entrenched in the discourse on guitar poetry that it is difficult to uproot.[22] Thus, while the rigidity of this distinction is challenged implicitly throughout the subsequent analysis, these monikers have been retained for the sake of convenience.

Likewise, the move away from analyzing guitar poetry's texts in virtual isolation carries its own hazards. From the outset, this approach challenges the notion that lyrics are guitar poetry's most significant component, an axiom that is prevalent in scholarly literature, in popular reception, and in bards' own comments about their work.[23] In part, this prevailing sentiment reflects an assumption (equally common in early scholarship on Western popular music) that "it was through their words" that songs "ma[de] their social mark"; more deeply, however, it reflects a logocentricity that is widespread in Russian culture, what Arlen Blyum describes as "the Russian tradition of venerating . . . the power of the invincible, all-conquering Word, the literary Word in particular."[24] In this context, dissent from a belief in guitar poetry's pure "literariness" can be seen to carry an unspoken challenge to the genre's cultural authority and value as well. No such challenge is implied here. On the contrary, it is argued that guitar poetry's multifaceted marginality and hybridity are the source of its particular and enduring power.

In practical terms, treating guitar poetry as song is no simple matter either. As Gerald Smith has cautioned, daunting "complexities in the perception, description, and interpretation of guitar poetry" arise out of the interrelationships between poetry and music that are inherent in the genre.[25] In an effort to tackle such complexities, the approach adopted here is informed by popular music studies (particularly the work of Simon Frith and Allan Moore) and by folkloristics and performance studies (including Richard Bauman and Charles Briggs's work on poetics and performance). But treating guitar poetry as a form of popular music is also controversial, however; both the genre's status as "music" and its status as "popular" (in the generally pejorative sense associated with that term, especially when used in conjunction with "music" or "culture") are hotly disputed, often rejected outright. Such disputes are particularly acute in light of the extent to which guitar poetry has become enmeshed in post-Soviet debates on the role of high culture in Russian society.

In order to understand guitar poetry's role as a medium of self-fashioning and communication, furthermore, it is necessary to analyze not just guitar poetry's songs but also the people who created, disseminated, and enjoyed them. The primary sources used here in the discussion of bards and audiences include a variety of personal accounts, such as published diaries, memoirs, and interviews; websites devoted to guitar poetry, to particular bards, and to KSPs (what one might call *netizdat* resources); and my own in-depth interviews with bards and guitar poetry fans, most of which were conducted in Russia during three summers of fieldwork between 2000 and 2002. In investigating songs themselves, both printed texts and a range of audio and video recordings have been used. Analysis of interviews and other personal accounts helps to piece together a picture of how bards and audiences experienced guitar poetry and what its role was in their lives. Analysis of performances and song texts helps to illuminate the expressive means by which bards constructed and projected individual identities; how bards and audiences interacted; and how listeners could adopt and adapt guitar poetry into their own (self-)creative and communicative practices.

With these caveats in mind, the overarching questions to be addressed in this study relate to the following intersecting issues: first, the ways in which guitar poetry created marginality on multiple levels (spatial, technological, aesthetic, textual, and generic); second, the ways in which bards and audiences exploited this multifaceted marginality, in performance and reception, as a means of independent self-fashioning, interaction, and community-building; and third, guitar poetry's function as a communicative medium and a means of articulating individual and group identities as underlying motivations for persistent hostility to it within the Soviet political-cultural establishment, a reaction that has long been noted but that is not adequately explained by a focus on text alone.

Part 1 of this study addresses multiple contexts in which guitar poetry is situated and with the help of which it can be analyzed. Looking beyond the confines of the Thaw, chapter 1 establishes the historical and sociopolitical context for guitar poetry's emergence and development. Particular attention is paid to larger cultural processes and cultural-ideological discourses that influenced (and were influenced by) guitar poetry, such as the rise of *khudozhestvennaya samodeyatel'nost'* (amateur creative activity) beginning in the 1940s; the post-Stalin "crisis" in professional Soviet song; and the keen attention paid to "the moulding [*vospitaniye*] of the rising generation," of which song was a key instrument, as part of the complex process of de-Stalinization. A brief survey of guitar poetry's roots, focusing on its relationship to the Russian romance tradition, provides further sociocultural context while also setting the stage for later discussion of guitar poetry's sophisticated generic play.

Chapter 2 considers theories of marginality, (re)envisioning the margins as an interstitial arena, rather than one pole in a binary center-periphery opposition, in which active processes of articulating individual and group identities are fundamental. Discussion and adaptation of marginality theory provide the foundation for an analysis of the interrelated discourses of *lichnost'* (individual, personality) and *obshcheniye* (interaction), both of which were key tropes of the post-Stalin period generally and of guitar poetry more specifically. Exploring both coincidence and conflict between concepts central to guitar poetry and officially promoted discourses, this chapter highlights the need to look beyond a view of marginality as a purely transgressive phenomenon.

In part 2, processes of identity creation and interaction that take place within the margins are analyzed through performance and reception, with a particular focus on the *lichnosti* and *obshcheniye* that guitar poetry fostered. Chapter 3 examines the individual *lichnosti* of a number of well-known bards, focusing on the creation of accessibility and sincerity (*iskrennost'*) through performance; and on the contribution of these qualities to the communicative and metacommunicative functions of guitar poetry. In turn, chapter 4 concentrates on ways in which major bardic *lichnosti* fostered the ideal of *lichnost'* as an abstract force that could be "liberated" by or crafted through guitar poetry, examining how audiences used guitar poetry in their own processes of self-fashioning and community-building.

In part 3, discussion shifts to the exploration of guitar poetry's compositions themselves, exploring ways in which they both manifested and manipulated marginality, but also moved beyond it, through close analysis of song texts, musical accompaniment, and performance. Chapters 5 and 6 explore two types of compositional marginality, termed "overt" and "covert." Overt marginality, which is the subject of chapter 5, focuses on themes that push the boundaries of acceptable public discourse. Encountered in songs that engage with politically sensitive themes, overt marginality comes closest to the notions of resistance and protest often associated with the marginal and equally often attributed to guitar poetry as a whole. Covert marginality, by contrast, involves that which hovers at the margins of noticeability. In chapter 6, covert marginality is discussed as a central feature of numerous songs that focus on "insignificant" themes and minute details of everyday life, underscoring the importance of the "trivial" and, as a consequence, trivializing approved determinations of "importance."[26]

Moving from the levels of theme and style to that of genre, chapter 7 examines guitar poetry's generic multiplicity and flexibility, its ability to encompass songs that seemingly imitate or take inspiration from a wide range of other genres (such as the ballad, the romance [*romans*], and even the fairy tale). The notion of "hypergenericity," defined here as the complex manipulation of generic codes to create multiple, interrelated layers of meaning, is employed in the analysis of the relationships between particular examples of guitar poetry and the other genres to which they claim allegiance in various ways. On one hand, it is argued that, through this hypergenericity, guitar poetry underscored its own generic ambivalence. On the other hand, it is shown that this hypergenericity underpinned guitar poetry's function as a means of communicating about and mediating between the competing realities typical of Soviet everyday experience. Scrutinizing the use of marginal themes, marginal stylistic devices, and ingenious generic ambiguities, these chapters thus illuminate crucial identities, interests, and needs that are defined in and communicated through guitar poetry.[27]

Throughout this study the powerful potential of guitar poetry's multifaceted marginality is underscored, but so, too, is its inherent ambivalence. Points of divergence from officially prescribed norms, values, and attitudes have received significant notice in discussions of guitar poetry (both the genre and the movement). The present study holds that points of intersection are deserving of equally close scrutiny, however. To acknowledge these intersections makes guitar poetry no less radical, no more conformist. Rather, this approach underscores the value of looking beyond reflexive binaries in order to explore the complexities that lie in the spaces between. Moreover, it makes a case for the profoundly disturbing, even destabilizing, effect of such intermediacy within the context of an ideological system that itself was overtly rooted in polarities; and that was struggling to retrofit these paradigms with the aid of new rhetoric, in order to account for the systemic failures of the Stalin period without admitting that the system itself had failed.

PART I

Contexts

Chapter One

Beyond the Soviet Sixties: The Origins and Contexts of Guitar Poetry

GUITAR POETRY'S ORIGINS and development are the subject of an oft-revisited dispute. For some, guitar poetry is an ancient genre that "can be related to the distant past of human culture," and that has functioned throughout history as "a counterweight to official poetry and song."[1] Some adherents of this approach draw analogies between guitar poetry and American folk songs of the 1960s ("political guitar poetry"), seeing both as modern manifestations of a "worldwide" phenomenon that arose "thousands of years ago."[2] For others, guitar poetry is a unique phenomenon that arose "all at once and suddenly" in the Soviet Union in the late 1950s.[3] A more moderate version of this latter view acknowledges guitar poetry's indebtedness to a range of precursors, yet observes that the rise of guitar poetry in the post-Stalin period "nonetheless carried the effect of unexpectedness."[4]

The first of these approaches suggests important commonalities linking guitar poetry to a range of song genres from various cultures and epochs; yet it has the significant disadvantage of obscuring the particular sociopolitical circumstances under which guitar poetry came into being in the Soviet Union. By contrast, the second approach stresses the immediate sociopolitical context for guitar poetry's appearance, yet in doing so detaches it from larger cultural and historical ones. Navigating between these extremes, this chapter charts the origins and development of guitar poetry as a phenomenon that grew out of established practices of popular music-making in Russia; but that was undeniably shaped—both in its performance and in its (official and popular) reception—by the particular political, ideological, and sociocultural climate in which it arose and matured.

THE RISE AND DEVELOPMENT OF GUITAR POETRY

Stirrings of the amateur creative activity that would, in the post-Stalin period, coalesce to form guitar poetry can be traced back at least to the 1940s. Both domestic music-making and various organizations promoting amateur artistic activity (*khudozhestvennaya samodeyatel'nost'*) certainly existed prior to this time. As the Stalinist system of cultural production and administration became increasingly centralized, though, amateur creative organizations lost their relative autonomy and ultimately were liquidated. Alongside the professional creative unions, the establishment of which began in 1932, a parallel system of central organs for the direction of amateur artistic activity was created. By the mid-1930s, amateur artistic activity had been regularized under the umbrella of organizations such as the All-Union House of Popular Creativity (VDNT imeni Krupskoy), the Central House of the Red Army (TsDKA imeni Frunze), the Central House for Children's Artistic Development (TsDKhVD), the Central Children's Artistic Studio of the All-Union Central Soviet of Professional Unions (TsDKhS VTsSPS), and the Central Park of Culture and Leisure (TsPKiO). Guided by such organizations, sanctioned amateur cultural activities developed along much the same lines as their professional counterparts, with a particular emphasis on work of an ideologically edifying (*ideyno-vospitatel'nyi*) and culturally enlightening (*kul'turno-prosvetitel'skiy*) nature.[5]

The experience of World War II had as significant an impact on the development of amateur artistic activity as it did in other areas of life, however. As S. Yu. Rumyantsev and A. P. Shul'pin have chronicled, the mass media and the arts were mobilized in the immediate aftermath of the war in order to "revive the myth of a happy, prosperous socialist society, [and] the trouble-free, sated, settled, festive life of the Soviet people"; and, like its professional counterparts, amateur artistic activity was called upon to participate in this "festive march-parade of postwar life."[6] Determinedly optimistic, official culture ignored the real difficulties and complexities of everyday life in the postwar period, though. In this creative void, various types of "unsupervised art" (*besprizornoye iskusstvo*) began to develop. One especially rich vein of "unsupervised art" was everyday oral creativity, encompassing both a revival of traditional songs (including ballads, "Gypsy" songs, and "cruel" romances) and the creation of new ones (particularly comical song parodies).[7] The Russian seven-stringed guitar quickly gained popularity as a portable and relatively simple accompaniment to such songs, the more so because (having languished in official disfavor for years as an accoutrement of "unenlightened and certainly petty bourgeois everyday life [*byt*]") it was not tainted by association with mass hymns and with the "pseudofolk" repertoire of "official" amateur song.[8]

This general rise in "free," domestic creative activity forms a backdrop against which the immediate pre-history of guitar poetry can be viewed. In fact, it was in the 1940s that a number of individuals who would later rank among the foremost guitar poets began to compose guitar-accompanied solo songs. Mikhail Ancharov began composing guitar-accompanied songs during the war years, for example, and Bulat Okudzhava composed his first well-known song ("Neistov i upryam" ["Frenzied and Stubborn"]) "almost by accident in 1946" while a student of the Philological Faculty at Tbilisi University.[9]

Though individual bards began composing songs in the 1940s, a surge in amateur songwriting and performance would come only in the 1950s. Okudzhava began writing songs in earnest, and performing his songs at private gatherings, during this period; and he gave his first public concert only in 1960. Many of the "second-rank" bards, and numerous minor figures, also date the beginnings of their singer-songwriter careers to this period. A coterie of Moscow bards, including Ada Yakusheva, Yury Vizbor, and Boris Vakhnyuk, began writing songs as students in the early to mid-1950s, for example. Similarly, Leningrader Boris Poloskin began singing at student gatherings in 1956; while fellow Leningrader Aleksandr Genkin began his bardic career in student circles in the mid-1950s, turning to songwriting in 1956 and then taking up the guitar in 1958 after hearing Okudzhava's songs. Likewise, Yuly Kim began composing songs in 1956 and he began giving concerts in the early 1960s. Aleksandr Gorodnitsky began composing songs in the late 1950s, inspired to write by labor camp songs that he heard from ex-convict workers while on expeditions in the Far North; and inspired to sing in order to ease the discomfort he would have felt merely reciting his verse in the decidedly masculine atmosphere of a geologists' field camp.[10]

As the histories of Yakusheva, Vizbor, Poloskin, and others suggest, during the mid- to late 1950s, student circles offered a particularly hospitable climate for the growth of guitar poetry in its earliest manifestations. In Moscow, groupings formed at a number of institutions, including the Moscow Electrotechnical Institute, the Moscow Institute of Engineering and Physics, Moscow State University, and Moscow State Pedagogical Institute (MGPI). By many accounts, MGPI—which numbers among its alumni Kim, Yakusheva, Vakhnyuk, and Vizbor—served as "the center of Soviet student songs" in the late 1950s, boasting such a high concentration of student singer-songwriters that it was informally dubbed Moscow State *Singing* Institute (*Moskovskiy poyushchiy*).[11] In Leningrad, song-oriented student groups arose at Leningrad State University and elsewhere, as evidenced by the "entire volumes of manuscript and rotaprint song collections" that surfaced in and around the city's higher education institutions.[12]

In contrast, Aleksandr Gorodnitsky's account of the circumstances in which he began to compose and sing songs highlights the importance of various outdoor activities in the development of guitar poetry. Recreational pastimes like mountain climbing and "tourism" (i.e., camping, hiking, and walking excursions), and professional activities including geological expeditions and the Virgin Lands campaign, were particularly significant. Such activities took people to the literal fringes and peripheries of the Soviet Union, away from the centers of "powerful, 'industrially' standardizing civilization"; as a result, they offered forums for creative activity that were "less susceptible to [official] organization" than those in urban centers.[13] Other guitar poets who trace their bardic activities to such adventures include Valentin Vikhorev, who began writing songs in 1959 out of a desire to tell others about his expeditions to far-flung regions of the Soviet Union (including the Caucasus and Sakhalin); and Yury Kukin, who wrote his first song while on a geological expedition in 1964.[14]

In the late 1950s and early 1960s, gatherings in private homes—which, like student circles and recreational activities, were natural meeting points for people with common interests—also provided important incubators for the early development of guitar poetry. Indeed, according to Bulat Okudzhava's aphoristic (but not uncontroversial) turn of phrase, guitar poetry "was born in Moscow kitchens in the early 1960s."[15] Both Aleksandr Galich and Vladimir Vysotsky began their bardic careers with "domestic" concerts in Moscow during this period. Throughout Galich's career, moreover, private homes were virtually the only places where he could perform his caustic and outspoken songs. Private gatherings were no less crucial outside Moscow, though: in Leningrad, for example, "Thursdays" (*chetvergi*) held at the homes of Stalina Mishtal', Leonid Nakhamkin, and Valery Sachkovsky in the early 1960s were particularly notable, growing "step by step . . . into evenings of song" held in public venues.[16]

In Leningrad, Moscow, and elsewhere, the public venues into which guitar poetry gained entrance were generally "peripheral" facilities that existed "for leisure activities of a cultural nature" (including clubs, cafes attached to industrial enterprises, and Houses of Culture), but that were somewhat less subject to official control than primary cultural institutions.[17] Such facilities provided the first homes for many Clubs of Amateur Song (*kluby samodeyatel'noy pesni,* or KSP), including two major Leningrad clubs, Vostok (East) and Meridian. Performances in intimate settings—in kitchens, in student circles, around the campfire—were the norm for the early stages of guitar poetry's development. Beginning in the early 1960s, however, the formation and institutionalization of amateur song clubs under the auspices of the Komsomol accompanied an important shift in the live performance of guitar poetry, as concerts began to be held in public settings as well as private ones. This shift is inseparable from increasing official involvement with the genre.

Until the early 1960s, guitar poetry, like other types of largely domestic amateur creativity, received limited attention. In principle, amateur artistic activity was espoused as "an important means of communist upbringing [*vospitaniya*] of the popular masses"; and also as "the best form for the realization of Lenin's legacy—to awaken artists among the masses."[18] Amateur music-making, more specifically, was recognized as "the chief propaganda instrument for music, both Soviet and classical" among young people and outside urban centers.[19] In practice, however, efforts to encourage amateur music-making did not live up to these lofty ideological precepts. According to numerous contemporary critics, the proper development of amateur music-making was inhibited by widespread "musical illiteracy" (hardly surprising, given that sheet music and other instructional materials were hard to obtain); by lack of coherent organization; and also by insufficient support from and oversight by music professionals, including the Composers' Union itself.[20] One manifestation of this lack of attention and oversight was that "professionals either did not notice [bards' songs] at all, or turned them away, as the saying goes, at the doorstep."[21]

As guitar poetry's popularity grew, in large part thanks to circulation via homemade tape recordings (a practice known as *magnitizdat*, "tape-recorder publishing"), it became increasingly difficult for the Soviet cultural establishment to ignore. When official acknowledgment of guitar poetry came, it entailed (quite typically) a combination of limited licensing and extensive monitoring. Dozens of song clubs began to form in cities across the Soviet Union, but the process of obtaining full sanction (and, correspondingly, appropriate meeting space) was often long and arduous; and such clubs inevitably operated under the watchful eye of the KGB and local Party committees. From the very inception of KSP Vostok, for example, club directors were "called in to the appropriate authorities and given a threatening dressing-down or recruited to be stool-pigeons"; and members of other song clubs recount similar experiences.[22] Similarly, Days of Song, concerts, song competitions, and song festivals began to be held regularly, but these took place under the direction of the Komsomol. At public performances, moreover, some seats were invariably reserved for KGB officials and local Party representatives.[23]

Guitar poetry's access to public venues and to the mass media peaked in the mid-1960s. Both song-related events and publications about the genre were more numerous at this time than in the years that preceded or followed. Beginning in 1965, guitar poetry came under particularly close scrutiny from the musical and literary establishments; and leading representatives from both spheres dissected the genre, weighing in with opinionated diatribes on the pages of *Sovetskaya muzyka* (*Soviet Music*), *Literaturnaya gazeta* (*The Literary Newspaper*), and other periodicals, as well as on the radio. The composer Vasily Solov'yov-Sedoy, for example, bemoaned the rise of "amateur musical compositions with primitively selected music and not very coherent text," comprising "monotonously repeating rhythms, poorly rhymed words, [and] an incompetent collection of strings"; similarly, his colleague Ivan Dzerzhinsky fulminated that many bards' songs "provoke in us a feeling of shame and bitter grievance, [and they] deal a serious blow to the upbringing of young people."[24] Yet another critic, echoing rhetoric that condemned the "sickness" of "individualism," lamented that some songs manifested a "maliciously individualistic rejection of all that is sacred."[25]

Not all participants in these debates took an unequivocally negative view, however. The poet and lyricist Lev Oshanin, for example, observed moderately that "as a rule, with people who undertake three forms of art at once, more often than not something gives way [*cho-to khromayet*], something turns out less well"; but he also advocated the need to give serious attention to amateur songs.[26] Musicologist Arnol'd Sokhor was similarly open-minded, noting that bards' songs were "artistic documents of the epoch, which could say much about the tastes and needs of contemporary youth"—and that could also "teach professional songwriters a thing or two," both about how they should *not* write and about how they *should*.[27] Others defended guitar poetry more cautiously, casting the genre's potential merits in terms of functions already approved for officially sanctioned and organized amateur artistic activity. Thus, one commentator argued that songs embodying "the positive ideals of our time" should be promoted on stage and via the mass media, because "each talented song is a weapon in the battle against hack-work, vulgarity, [and] kitschiness"; and, further, that the dissemination of good songs could help to "crowd out both the 'cruel romance' and 'criminal,' vulgar songs."[28] In similarly pragmatic terms, another observer exhorted the Komsomol to take more active interest in the "aesthetic and ideological side" of guitar poetry, so as not to "squander a powerful lever of real moral influence."[29]

By the mid-1960s, however, the political and ideological climate in the Soviet Union was changing inexorably, and the relative liberties of the Khrushchev era were giving way to broadened conservatism. Guitar poetry could not hope to escape the reverberations of such changes. A general shift back to increased restrictions on culture, which began with Khrushchev's crackdown on the arts in 1963–64, accelerated rapidly after the middle of the decade. The 1966 trial and conviction of Andrey Sinyavsky and Yuly Daniel for "anti-Soviet propaganda," on the basis of their literary works, is just one particularly well-known example of a broader phenomenon. In 1966, too, isolated attacks on guitar poetry (including the firing of a journal editor for publishing some of Okudzhava's songs) provided early hints of a broad battle against guitar poetry and its practitioners, which would soon reach a fever pitch.[30]

Marked by the crisis in Czechoslovakia and associated political tensions in the Soviet Union, 1968 was a critical year in the campaign against guitar poetry as well. In the summer of 1967, Vysotsky's starring role in the film *Vertikal'* (*The Vertical*), which also included a number of his songs, had rocketed him to nationwide stardom. But in 1968, unfavorable articles about Vysotsky began to appear in the press, attacking him personally and accusing him of illegal conduct (such as holding public concerts or holding more than the permitted number of concerts in a given time period); and also disparaging his songs (often inaccurately, as some of the songs criticized were attributed to him erroneously).[31]

In March 1968, moreover, a "Festival of Bards" held at the Akademgorodok (Academy Town or Science Village) near Novosibirsk became a rallying point for guitar poetry's opponents. The festival included performances by both major and minor bards, as well as remarks about guitar poetry by insightful and sympathetic commentators (including, notably, Leningrad musicologist Vladimir Frumkin). In the festival's aftermath, the authors of a denunciatory letter to the Central Committee of the Komsomol howled that the festival had been organized "without the knowledge of Party, Soviet and Komsomol organs" and that its "marked political character was kept secret until [its] very opening"; and they lambasted participants for the "clearly tendentious nature" of festival performances, which they claimed were "imbued with a spirit of lack of ideological content [*bezydeynosti*], apoliticality, [and] slander against Soviet reality."[32]

Soon, the Novosibirsk song club Pod integralom (Under the Integral) that had sponsored the festival was shut down and "many people felt the weight of repressions acutely."[33] No performance at the festival excited more outrage than Aleksandr Galich's, which had included a number of songs rich in barbed political statements.[34] Following this performance, which was to be his only public concert in the Soviet Union, Galich became the target of particularly vituperative criticism. He was attacked in the press for "making fun of our most sacred concepts" and for "civic irresponsibility" (*grazhdanskaya bezotvetstvennost'*); and the secretariat of the Writers' Union, of which Galich was a member, asked him "to stop performing publicly."[35] Ultimately, the Novosibirsk festival set Galich on a collision course with the Soviet authorities that culminated in his expulsion from professional creative unions and the Literary Fund (Litfond) of the Writers' Union, which provided financial assistance to writers, depriving him of any means of earning a living; and, in 1974, his forced emigration to western Europe.

1968 was a pivotal year for Yuly Kim as well. Like Galich, Kim wrote openly political songs; and indeed, some of Kim's lyrics had "such a seditious note" that Yury Andropov, then head of the KGB, "wrote separate denunciations about them" for the Central Committee of the Communist Party of the Soviet Union (CPSU).[36] Moreover, Kim was active in the human rights movement in the mid- to late 1960s, signing a number of letters of protest that warned of the dangers of the re-Stalinization of Soviet society and appealed to "members of the Soviet intelligentsia to voice their dissent."[37] While Kim escaped the extreme punishment meted out to Galich, in 1968 he was forced to give up his teaching career and limit his concert activity, and he turned instead to writing plays and composing songs for theatrical spectacles, television, and film. In 1969 he took up the pseudonym Yu. Mikhaylov because he was no longer able to publish under his own name.

It was not just "protest bards" who bore the brunt of official displeasure in the late 1960s, however. Around the same time, the largely apolitical Okudzhava incurred official wrath for volumes of his songs that were published in Berlin by the anti-Soviet publisher Posev in 1964 and 1967, as well as for a recording he made in Paris in 1968. Further, a collection of Okudzhava's song texts with musical notation was denied publication "not on account of the lyrics" but because, as Vladimir Frumkin (the volume's would-be editor) explains, publication of melodies by an amateur composer "would imply official recognition of a doubtful, unofficial genre . . . which was outside any of the norms and rules by which songs [were] composed, selected and distributed in the Soviet Union."[38] In 1972, Okudzhava was expelled from the CPSU for "anti-Party behaviour and refusing to condemn the publication of his works abroad."[39] While he was reinstated fairly quickly, a moratorium on publication of his works in the Soviet Union persisted until the mid-1970s.

By the early 1970s, the Soviet authorities had adopted a two-pronged approach to guitar poetry, simultaneously suppressing and co-opting it. On one hand, certain bards were persecuted and denied the right to publish and attention to guitar poetry in the mass media dropped off sharply. Yet on the other hand, bards' songs featured regularly in the repertoires of Soviet variety stage singers, and lines from songs that KSP members "were not allowed to sing" were routinely used as newspaper headlines.[40] Additionally, various bards were commissioned to write songs for films, television, and theatrical productions. Vysotsky and Vizbor continued their high-profile acting careers, too; and both Vysotsky's starring turn as Hamlet in a long-running (1971–80) production at Moscow's Taganka Theatre and Vizbor's leading role in the now-classic television miniseries *Semnadtsat' mgnoveniy vesny* (1973; *Seventeen Instants of Spring*) rank among their most memorable and best-regarded performances.

In the latter half of the 1970s, official attitudes toward guitar poetry softened perceptibly, but at a price. Amateur song clubs that had been functioning in clandestine fashion were offered the possibility of legalization and material assistance, but this was "unequivocally conditional upon the establishment of a certain ideological control" over them; control measures included both editing of songs (and, in some cases, outright bans on public performance) and "representation of the Komsomol and cultural organs in contest juries."[41] In 1976, for example, the Moscow KSP managed to gain permission to hold a citywide song competition, which had not been possible since 1968; and in the spring of 1977, as longtime organizer Igor' Karimov recalls, "the authorities kept their promise and allocated us [permanent] space for the club on Trofimov Street, house number 33."[42] Some months later, though, it was rumored that one club member was escorted away from a rally (*slyot*) by the KGB, a pointed reminder, notes Karimov, that "all our events were watched intently by their tireless agents."[43]

Such measures were consistent with a general trend toward corralling amateur artistic activity and ensuring its development in appropriate directions. The necessity of managing amateur artistic activity was stressed in a number of Central Committee resolutions at the time, including "On measures for the further development of amateur artistic activity" (1978). Soon there appeared a spate of works oriented at "practitioners occupied with general questions of an organizational [and] administrative nature in the sphere of culturally enlightening work [*kul'tprosvetraboty*] and amateur artistic activity."[44] Such works typically stressed the role of amateur artistic activity as "one of the paths to the mastery of culture, [and] an instrument of moral, aesthetic, [and] ideological influence, a school for the communist upbringing of the masses."[45] They contained explicit instructions that "social significance" was to be a primary criterion by which amateur artistic activity should be judged, furthermore; and that, in assessing social significance, both a work itself and its creators were to be subjected to scrutiny.[46]

On the cusp of the following decade, individual bards' fortunes were mixed. The moratorium on the publication of Okudzhava's works had been lifted in 1976, and in the same year the state recording firm Melodiya released a record of his songs. The following year, a number of Vysotsky's songs were featured on the double album soundtrack for a musical production of *Alice in Wonderland;* but in 1979 Vysotsky tangled with the Soviet authorities once again, this time over his participation in the organization and publication of the controversial almanac *Metropol'* (*Metropolis*).[47] In 1980, though, the first collection of Vysotsky's song texts was published in Moscow, in response to massive and uncontrollable public demand following his untimely death. Similarly, while the late 1970s and early 1980s saw the rise of a new generation of bards, including Oleg Mityayev and the duos of Aleksey Ivashchenko and Georgy Vasil'yev and Vadim and Valery Mishchuk, it also saw singer-songwriters like Aleksandr Rozenbaum, who had once been associated with guitar poetry, turn toward the professional variety stage (*estrada*).[48] On a broader scale, song clubs, rallies, and festivals were again subjected to severe restrictions. The annual Grushin Festival, held outside Kuybyshev (Samara) since 1968,[49] was banned in the run-up to the 1980 Moscow Olympiad and allowed to resume only in 1986. In 1981, the Moscow KSP was shut down following its 24th rally, in response to the political crisis in Poland, and clubs in other cities were targeted as well.[50] It was only during perestroika that guitar poetry at last emerged from the legal half-light, with recordings of bards' songs and collections of their verse being published in significant quantities.

As this brief survey suggests, guitar poetry's fortunes were broadly linked to general shifts in the political-ideological climate that prevailed in the Soviet Union between Stalin's death and the mid-1980s. Guitar poetry's changing fates were also linked to more specific official preoccupations, though. As a predominantly youth-driven song phenomenon that germinated during the Thaw, guitar poetry quickly became entangled in debates on song and its role in the aesthetic, moral, and ideological upbringing (*vospitaniye*) of young people. While youth (*molodyozh'*) and *vospitaniye* had long been catchwords of official discourse, both became key tropes of the post-Stalin period in particular,[51] as the state confronted the dilemma of how to de-Stalinize society without de-Sovietizing it.

GUITAR POETRY AND THE "MOULDING OF THE RISING GENERATION"

The flowering of amateur song in the post-Stalin period was not an isolated cultural phenomenon, but it was an especially important one because of the role accorded to song within the Soviet ideological system. By the 1950s, songs had long been considered particularly effective instruments in the task of creating a new Soviet identity and "a new, joyful mass consciousness," a project that was aimed above all at Soviet youth.[52] The reason for this was a firm belief not just in songs' capacity to express succinctly "ideas and feelings that are shared by millions of people," but also in their superior ability "to influence [people's] will directly, to 'infect' them with an identical mood or impulse to action, to rally them and lead them along."[53] Throughout the 1950s and 1960s, affirmations of "the enormous artistic, ideologically edifying [*ideyno-vospitatel'noye*] significance of song" were a fixture of both professional debates and public discourse about "light music" (*lyogkaya muzyka*).[54]

While certainly not novel, this ideologically colored perception of song took on heightened significance after 1953. In the aftermath of Stalin's death, "the enormous, flawlessly adjusted machinery of the song industry," staples of which had been patriotic mass hymns and paeans to Stalin himself, began to collapse.[55] Not only did the production of new songs from the "gigantic, state song conveyer belt" begin to flag, but old songs also began to disappear from the airwaves; and the "sung codex" of Soviet culture underwent a remarkable shift as mass songs and official hymns increasingly became "the target of a flourishing underground humor."[56] By the mid-1950s, official Soviet song—professionally written and professionally performed—was widely perceived to be in decline; and concern was growing about "vacuous, musically impoverished songs" that were "often heard on the radio, from the television screen, from the variety concert stage, [and] in film."[57]

Within a few years, the "crisis" in Soviet song had become a subject of ongoing debate in the press and at the highest levels of both professional and Party bureaucracy. Throughout the 1950s and early 1960s the pages of *Sovetskaya muzyka*, the official organ of the Union of Soviet Composers, were filled with continual "conversations" about song, in which assessments of the state of contemporary Soviet song formed a constant refrain. In December 1953, a plenary session of the Directorate of the Composers' Union was devoted to problems of Soviet song. Similarly, in the early 1960s, song and other forms of "light music" were the focus of a plenary session of the Directorate of the RSFSR Composers' Union.[58] In 1966, too, the Secretariat of the Central Committee of the CPSU convened a two-day meeting to examine issues of "the aesthetic enlightenment of our youth," at which were discussed "vital problems of the development and propaganda of Soviet song."[59] Throughout these protracted debates, a fundamental understanding of the role of song remained constant and universal: song was to help "shape [*vospityvat'*] patriotic feelings and the communist consciousness of the Soviet people"; and it was to be "a forceful, strategic and sharp musical weapon in the battle for the new citizen of communist society, for our bright future."[60]

Acute concern over the state of professional song thus dovetailed with the larger issue of *vospitaniye*. From the mid-1950s through the 1960s, the discourse of *vospitaniye* was prominent "in the party's dealings with all generations,"[61] and efforts were redoubled to ensure that all Soviet citizens were imbued with the communist spirit. In keeping with this approach, the CPSU issued resolutions calling for increased (and increasingly appealing) propaganda work, in order to ensure that no "population group" was excluded from "daily ideological and political influence."[62] In individual resolutions and in the *vospitaniye* campaign as a whole, however, particular attention was devoted to Soviet youth. In the Third Party Program (1961), the "educat[ion of] all working people in a spirit of ideological integrity and devotion to communism" was declared to be of paramount importance, but "the moulding [*vospitaniye*] of the rising generation" received particular emphasis.[63] Similarly, the Central Committee stressed the importance of educating youth, in particular, and inculcating in them "a correct attitude . . . toward their social obligations"; and it called for improvement in "the functioning of Party organizations and of society as a whole in educating Soviet people, especially the youth."[64]

In this ideological battle, Soviet culture was naturally a key front. Accordingly, the "revitaliz[ation] of Soviet culture" in order to "make it a relevant and exciting means of communication between party and people" was the subject of intense debate.[65] Members of the creative intelligentsia, bearing the heavy mantle of "engineers of human souls," were called upon to produce works that would provide inspiration and guidance; and composers and songwriters were certainly no exceptions to this rule.[66] Given the dire state of professional song in the second half of the 1950s, the rise of amateur song was greeted initially with cautious optimism. However, from an official standpoint, the lack of proper organization and oversight that plagued amateur music-making as a whole carried heightened risks in relation to amateur song.

As articulated in contemporary debates, these risks inhered in certain peculiarities of song as a form. First, songs were seen to be "more directly connected with life than other musical genres"; and relative speed of composition made songs particularly suitable for addressing topical issues and depicting "real-life themes."[67] Second, songs were popular and virtually ubiquitous, "the most widespread [musical genre] among the people."[68] According to this view, songs not only had the potential to reach a broader audience than any other type of music; they could also penetrate more deeply than other musical genres into the lives (and, presumably, psyches) of their audience, thus serving as a "particularly important factor in the ideological and artistic upbringing [*vospitaniya*] of the broad masses."[69] Properly channeled, such immediacy and popularity could be used to great advantage; left unchecked, however, such tendencies could lead to disastrous consequences.

A third, related issue that weighed heavily in debates on song was the relative ease of dissemination. As one critic observed, almost as soon as a song appears, it "immediately becomes the property of a circle of performers and connoisseurs that grows by leaps and bounds, it steps over the boundaries of the professional music sphere."[70] The danger of this lay in the potential it created for unmonitored communication between songwriter and listener: "in song, as in no other genre, a composer can address [the audience] over the heads of professional criticism, so to speak."[71] This situation was vexing enough in regard to professional song, for which the system of evaluation and censorship was muddled and inefficient,[72] but it was still more problematic when songs were written and performed outside monitored professional spheres.

Even in the mid-1950s, it was a matter of some concern that amateur singing was taking place "not just in collectives and not just at competitions," which could be supervised, but also in a range of informal settings (dormitories, parties, at home, on the street).[73] To anxious observers, the contents of homemade songbooks (*pesenniki*) suggested that some songs being performed in these informal settings were "inflict[ing] serious damage on the upbringing of young people"; an examination of provincial students' *pesenniki*, for example, revealed both "good, if not new, songs" and also "low-quality, petty bourgeois and just plain vulgar works" as well as "cynical texts of abominable 'criminal ditties.'"[74] As guitar poetry itself developed into a distinct phenomenon, critics discerned similarly troubling hints of "motley sources" of ideologically problematic pedigree (including "petty bourgeois and criminal song of the NEP period") in bards' lyrics and in their choice of "intonations."[75]

Over the course of the late 1950s and 1960s, however, the combined impact of guitar poetry's immediacy, its "incomparable popularity" in certain circles,[76] and its ability to foster intimate communication seemed to cause greater anxiety than songs' lyrics and "intonations" alone. For example, Tikhon Khrennikov—a professional songwriter and longtime head of the Composers' Union—voiced alarm over guitar poetry's "direct connection" with life, observing that "few new songs by professional composers penetrate into everyday life [*v byt*]" and that "young people live off a supply of time-tested old songs or 'their own' songs."[77] Others fretted that "intimate communication," which was "taken to its logical extreme" in Bulat Okudzhava's songs, presented "a danger of bringing a musical image 'down to earth'"; and worried that "if a composer converses with a listener, addressing him like a friend [*v druzheskom plane*], one on one, then there is a danger of excessive familiarity, sentimentality, [and] cheap emotionalism."[78] Even relatively well-disposed critics reflected on the need to "grasp *why* [people] sing" guitar poetry (emphasis in original); and, recognizing the genre's popularity, emphasized the need to "sort out this complex matter professionally and lead the audience along, rather than pretending that no such problem exists."[79]

This heightened concern over less tangible elements of guitar poetry was motivated by the inextricable link between art and ideology, on one hand, and by issues surrounding *vospitaniye*, on the other. First, the connection between art and ideology was just as potent for "light music" as it was for more elevated artistic forms: as one ideologue stated unequivocally, "light music is always propaganda and agitation. Light music is art coupled with politics."[80] By definition, then, the impact of peccadilloes such as bards' infelicitous choice of "intonations," or "sentimentality" and "cheap emotionalism," was not restricted to the aesthetic sphere. As Tikhon Khrennikov warned sternly, "any manifestation of irregularity in the artistic sphere implies ideological irregularity."[81] Guitar poetry's suspect aesthetics therefore carried the seeds of suspect ideology even when, as was most often the case, songs contained nothing even vaguely political.

Second, because of songs' prominence as instruments of cultural, ideological, and moral *vospitaniye*, there was a logical connection between discerning ideological irregularities in bards' songs and extrapolating their power to shape young hearts and minds in potentially dangerous ways. Where creative activity was conducted in organized institutions or under the aegis of professional creative unions, aesthetico-ideological missteps could be corrected through the usual mechanisms of artistic oversight, censorship, comradely criticism, and self-criticism. Thus, where a bard like Okudzhava (a member of the CPSU and of the Writers' Union) strayed from the ideologically correct path, he might yet be brought back into the fold, as the following comment from the 1963 Plenum of the Directorate of the RSFSR Composers' Union suggests: "it might be possible to explain to Okudzhava that he is on the wrong path, and he would probably understand. But how to explain that to others (his listeners—Ed.)?"[82] This comment is interesting both for its explicit criticism of Okudzhava and for the anxiety it reveals over audiences' possible responses to him: if a measure of ideological control could be exerted over the former, the latter was seen as worryingly out of reach. Taken in the context of a firm belief in songs' power "to influence [people's] will directly," this criticism implies not just the fear that listeners might fail to recognize Okudzhava's "wrong path," but also, and perhaps more seriously, that Okudzhava's missteps might encourage listeners themselves to set out on "wrong paths," creative and otherwise. The threat of unmonitored communication, and the uncontrollable responses it might provoke, was heightened by the fact that bards were, as composer Ivan Dzerzhinsky observed worriedly, "armed with recording tape" in which there lay "a well-known danger: ease of dissemination."[83]

Guitar poetry's ability to foster a sense of intimacy and serve as a medium of communication has been remarked upon variously. This ability is noted not just by anxious official critics but also by bards, fans, and scholars, who have characterized guitar poetry as a "confiding talk," as "a form of dialogue with one another and with the world," and as "intense yet intimate talks among friends."[84] A more extreme view, articulated by Aleksandr Gorodnitsky, holds that songs "are not a goal in and of themselves [*samotsel'*], but above all else [are] a medium of interaction, a sort of identifying code."[85] But the intricacies of this communicative function, as well as guitar poetry's interlinked function as an agent of self-fashioning, are as yet poorly understood. A discussion of guitar poetry's development and immediate sociopolitical environment provides a partial context for a focused analysis of these issues, which will be pursued in subsequent chapters. Additional context is provided by a brief survey of the genre's origins, focusing on both "genetic" and functional links between guitar poetry and a range of nineteenth- and early twentieth-century precursors. Rather than offering a comprehensive study of guitar poetry's lineage,[86] the following discussion deliberately privileges linkages that were particularly significant to the genre's development as a means of self-fashioning and communication in the post-Stalin period.

THE ROOTS OF GUITAR POETRY

Tracing the genealogy of guitar poetry is a complicated affair. On the level of the poetic text, guitar poetry is not terribly distinctive: its "metrical typologies" (principally a slight preference for trochaic and ternary meters and for polymetric structures)[87] align the genre with a broad tradition of "sung poetry as opposed to spoken poetry," but do little to highlight more specific generic connections.[88] Musically, simple melodies in a minor key predominate—whence comes the stereotype of the genre's reliance on three chords—but again this characteristic cannot be linked to a single, unambiguous antecedent. On a stylistic and thematic level, guitar poetry itself is so heterogeneous that connections between precursors and sub-generic branches of guitar poetry (such as "tourist song") are often clearer than links to the genre as a whole. Comparative analysis is further complicated by the fact that various of guitar poetry's predecessors fell into disfavor after 1917 and that, as a result, scholarly studies of such genres are limited and definitions are fluid.

In the broadest sense, guitar poetry continued a tradition of private musical culture that was widespread in Russia in the eighteenth and nineteenth centuries; and that, after a post-revolutionary lull, began to revive as early as the 1930s and to spread with increasing urgency in the 1940s.[89] In a more direct sense, the roots of guitar poetry lie in other synthetic, syncretic genres that flourished in Russia in the nineteenth and early twentieth centuries and that, like guitar poetry, had a strong social function as well as an artistic one. Among these genres, the most notable are the classic romance (*romans*) and the urban romance (*gorodskoy romans*). Guitar poetry should not be viewed as the lineal descendant of either of these genres, however; nor should it be considered a simple hybrid of the two. Rather, guitar poetry drew upon aesthetic, stylistic, thematic, and other features of these genres, with a healthy admixture of additional influences, reflecting and refracting its complex ancestry in distinctive and highly original ways.

The impact of the classic romance on guitar poetry is profound, encompassing facets as diverse as the forums in which the two genres developed and circulated; the range of poetic texts preserved and disseminated through them; the intellectual and aesthetic atmosphere associated with them; and, not least, poetic and musical influences. Having spread to Russia from western Europe in the eighteenth century, by the mid-nineteenth century the classic romance was well established in the spectrum of Russian song. By that time, the formerly confused usage of *romans* had stabilized, and the term was generally understood to refer to "a piece of formally composed (as opposed to folk) music with Russian text" for solo voice, accompanied chorally or instrumentally (on the piano or, to a lesser extent, on the guitar).[90] Both the composition and performance of classic romances were part of a rich culture of domestic music-making, in aristocratic salons, in bourgeois drawing rooms, and on gentry estates, that "fed the musical life of the nation."[91] Musical and musico-literary salons, in particular, were crucial to the development of the classic romance; and these private or semi-private gatherings find reflection in the "Moscow kitchens" and Leningrad "Thursdays" that were central to the development of guitar poetry in the post-Stalin period.

The development of the classic romance in the first third of the nineteenth century is closely linked to the flowering of Russian romantic poetry. In classic romances, poetry and music were rarely composed by the same person, and the works of both major and minor poets were commonly set to music by amateur composers as well as by experienced masters like Mikhail Glinka.[92] Feeding off the works of Russian poets, romance lyrics underwent a period of particular growth during the 1820s. While some of this poetry would have survived without the benefit of a musical setting—numerous romances were written to poems by Alexander Pushkin during his lifetime and after his death, for example, but they are hardly responsible for his continued fame—much of it would not. Thus, as Thomas Hodge argues, the romance played an important role in disseminating and preserving a broad cross-section of nineteenth-century Russian poetry.[93]

With respect to twentieth-century verse, guitar poetry served a similar function, notwithstanding the oft-touted bardic ideal of the "triunity" of author, composer, and performer. Guitar poetry was commodious enough to encompass both great literary talents and lesser ones; and also to include a "composers' branch," represented by Viktor Berkovsky, Yevgeny Klyachkin, Aleksandr Mirzayan, Sergey Nikitin, and others, in which the romance tradition of setting "written" poetry to music found continuation.[94] Various bards composed musical settings for poems by Pasternak, Tsvetayeva, Brodsky, and others, which circulated broadly as songs long before they were admitted into print; and many guitar poetry fans attest that they first became acquainted "with serious poetry [*s vysokoy poeziyey*]" in general, as well as with particular new poets, through guitar poetry.[95]

The strands of influence stretching from Russian romanticism to the classic romance and thence to guitar poetry cover far more than just settings (for performances and of verse), though. Equally important, if not more so, was the particular intellectual and aesthetic atmosphere of progressive Russian romanticism, in which rejection of "the normative aesthetics of classicism" and the defense of individuality and innovation were strongly pronounced.[96] These broad philosophical leanings of nineteenth-century romanticism form a crucial substratum in the romanticism of the 1950s and 1960s, which was itself integral to the development of guitar poetry. In a general sense, the search for "romanticism" in everything was characteristic of the post-Stalin period, becoming one of the central ideological issues raised in critical polemics during the 1960s.[97]

More specifically, guitar poetry's rejection of the normative aesthetics of socialist realism and its valorization of the individual echoed the anti-normative (in this case, anti-classicist) and individualistic orientation of nineteenth-century romanticism. The uniform positivity, homogeneous optimism, and unswerving orientation toward the "bright and glorious future" that characterized socialist realist art were countered by guitar poetry's often elegiac, melancholy quality, by its "ability to be sad and to grieve";[98] and also by bards' profound desire to reflect reality as it was lived and experienced, rather than to replicate the unblemished fictive reality characteristic of official Soviet culture. In addition, post-Stalin official discourse was typified by tension between the "discourse of individual identity" and renewed emphasis on "public initiatives and collective life."[99] Emphasizing the importance of *lichnost'* (both in the sense of "individual" and in that of "personality") and stressing "the correspondence between word and deed"[100] as an important component of *lichnost'*, guitar poetry once again revealed its kinship to the aesthetic and ethical tendencies of nineteenth-century romanticism. Definitions of guitar poetry that hinge on this correspondence (e.g., an explanation of the genre as "that's when you have to live as you sing" [*eto kogda i zhit' nado tak, kak poyosh'*])[101] echo the romantic emphasis on the unity of life and literature. Moreover, Vysotsky demonstrated this credo with exceptional clarity in his fervent poetic declaration that "he who ended his life tragically—he is a true poet" ("Pesnya o poetakh" [1971; "Song About Poets"]); in his fiercely energetic and passionate onstage performances; and in his turbulent private life.[102]

In addition to these broad aesthetic, philosophical, and ethical tendencies, guitar poetry's kinship to the classic romance can be established through poetic and musical features. Both thematically and musically, the classic romance favored a minor mode. Guitar poetry exhibits a similar tendency, and in so doing it not only cleaves close to the romance tradition but also diverges sharply from the ideals of professional Soviet song. Beginning in the early 1960s, criticism of a prevailing "mood of dismal melancholy" became a stock feature of official salvos directed against guitar poetry.[103] In both the classic romance and guitar poetry, love and nature are common themes; and while these are hardly unusual lyric themes, guitar poetry's debt to the classic romance is evident in its approach to them. In the classic romance, love appears in a broad array of guises, most often cast in a negative light: melancholy (*toska*), unhappy liaisons, unrequited passion, and tragic endings are common, as is the depiction of love as a "temporary, fragile retreat from personal turmoil."[104] Representations of love in guitar poetry are similarly heterogeneous and, as often as not, carry a similarly negative tinge.

If guitar poetry's attention to love is indebted to the classic romance (and, as will be discussed below, the urban romance) for its variety and its tonality, it may be argued that bards' frequent invocations of nature are indebted to the romance for their very existence as well. In both genres, nature is laden with symbolism: in classic romances, nature is "invoked as a form of solace" rather than being "celebrated for its beauty,"[105] while in guitar poetry the natural world is often represented as a place of escape, as a symbol of individual freedom, or as a backdrop for acts of personal courage or heroism. Guitar poetry's kinship to the classic romance in its treatment of nature is further underscored by the fact that this theme was virtually absent from official Soviet song of the post-Stalin period.[106]

In both classic romances and guitar poetry, a mournful or minor quality (*minornost'*) in verse is accentuated by a minor mode in melodic accompaniment. In classic romance melodies, the influence of the German *Affektenlehre* code, which "decreed the proper meaning of minor and major modes, as well as fast and slow tempos," was strongly felt: as was deemed appropriate for "the expression of elegiac moods, regret and gentle sorrow," almost all classic romances were written in a minor key.[107] This was the norm for guitar poetry, too; and in some cases "three minor chords" served as the foundation of particular bards' entire musical repertoires.[108] As in classic romances, the minor mode of guitar poetry's melodies reflected (and supported) the minor tonality of its lyrics and a "confessional, lyrico-philosophical nature," especially in the "quiet" strand of guitar poetry (represented by Okudzhava, Novella Matveyeva, and others).[109]

In its more exaggerated manifestations, this *minornost'* also connects guitar poetry to the tradition of the urban romance. As with the classic romance, the influence of this genre on guitar poetry is felt in a number of areas, including modes of composition and dissemination; dominant poetic themes; and aspects of performance. The urban romance arose in the early nineteenth century, seemingly deriving from "everyday songs" (*bytovye pesni*); and it developed alongside, and in interaction with, the classic romance. The popularity of the urban romance grew steadily throughout the nineteenth century, fueled by the growth of Russia's cities; and its heyday in the late nineteenth and early twentieth centuries coincided with a flood of rural poor to urban areas during the period of Russia's rapid industrialization. While it was most strongly connected with the "social psychology of the urban underclass," the genre was broadly popular across a full range of social groups (from workers and peasants to merchants, and even in aristocratic circles and among the progressive intelligentsia).[110]

Delimiting the urban romance with any precision is difficult because it is much less well documented than the classic romance. Maligned even in the nineteenth century for being "art that did not elevate the tastes of the public, but rather lowered itself to them," the urban romance was virtually ignored by Soviet scholars, who referred to it pejoratively (if they mentioned it all) as the "petty bourgeois [*meshchanskiy*] romance," and as "pseudo-folk" (*psevdonarodnyi*), "low-quality" (*niskoprobnyi*), and "criminal" (*blatnoy*).[111] By the 1930s, in fact, the term "petty bourgeois romance" was used in official discourse as a disdainful catchall for most popular urban song genres.[112] Defined loosely, the urban romance is a narrative song about ordinary people that is marked by lexical diversity, combining folkloric and literary elements; and by a narrow focus on a specific event, among which "burning passions" and "violent expressions of emotion" are common.[113] Though the urban romance can be divided into a number of subtypes (such as the "Gypsy romance" [*tsyganskiy romans*] and the "cruel romance" [*zhestokiy romans*]), such distinctions are by no means universally agreed upon, and a great deal of terminological confusion reigns.[114] Forced underground by the late 1920s, the urban romance remained a part of everyday oral tradition throughout the Soviet period.[115]

"Cruel" romances, in particular, continued to be popular throughout the Stalin and post-Stalin periods. In the aftermath of World War II, they "suited people's moods more than artificially cheerful 'Soviet' songs"; and in the mid-1950s they were sung in student circles alongside "'dashing' drinking songs" and "lyric songs from the repertoire of then-forbidden [Pyotr] Leshchenko."[116] The continued appeal of such songs in the 1960s is attested by the fact that some saw guitar poetry as a means of combatting the popularity of the cruel romance and other suspect song genres. Broadly speaking, permutations of the urban romance are significant to the development of guitar poetry because, circulating in domestic settings long after being chased out of public venues, they preserved and presented "alternative models" to official Soviet song.[117] The influence of the urban romance on guitar poetry does not end there, however.

Modes of composition and dissemination offer some of the strongest links joining guitar poetry to the urban romance tradition. Initially, the urban romance was fostered by the efforts of amateurs who typically composed both lyrics and melodies; and it straddled the boundary between oral and literary creativity.[118] During the early nineteenth century, oral dissemination—due to low literacy rates and the orientation of printed songbooks toward a relatively well-educated public—meant that most urban romances were both anonymous and variable, having been subjected to collective "polishing" and "editing" through word-of-mouth transmission.[119]

Likewise, much of guitar poetry was created by singer-songwriters who were amateurs in literature or music (or both), and oral dissemination of songs was common. Moreover, guitar poetry was able to transcend its origins as an intimate, chamber phenomenon and transform into a mass movement because songs were seized upon, performed, and reworked by numerous amateur performers across the Soviet Union. As with the urban romance, this mode of dissemination facilitated the "folklorization" of guitar poetry. In some cases, songs entered the popular repertoire as anonymous creations; and in others, multiple variants of songs developed through such oral transmission. Aleksandr Galich's "Pravo na otdykh" (1965; "Right to a Holiday") and Yuly Kim's "Guby okayannye" (1959; "Accursed Lips") provide two specific examples of this phenomenon, having "become folklore" during guitar poetry's heyday.[120]

While oral transmission was particularly important for the urban romance and guitar poetry early on, both genres later capitalized on new technologies that allowed them to spread with increasing rapidity. After the middle of the nineteenth century, urban romances appeared in inexpensive chapbook song collections (*lubochnye sborniki*), which had a growing audience thanks to improved literacy rates among the lower classes. By the end of the century, the invention of the gramophone and the establishment of regular variety stage seasons provided new outlets for the urban romance.[121]

Like the urban romance, guitar poetry also took advantage of new technology, as the increased availability of portable tape recorders in the 1960s fostered the phenomenon of *magnitizdat* ("tape-recorder publishing"). While guitar poetry was certainly not the only material circulated via *magnitizdat,* homemade tape recordings allowed bards' songs to spread virtually uncontrolled, rapidly reaching a broad and varied audience. Copied and recopied, tapes crisscrossed the Soviet Union "practically at the speed of sound."[122] Aiding in the dissemination of guitar poetry, portable tape recorders simultaneously fostered the rapid "privatization of culture," the "formation of an autonomous, individual artistic sphere" that was difficult to control.[123]

Though both the urban romance and guitar poetry spread rapidly with the help of new technologies, the popularity of both genres was also spurred by the extent to which their themes, moods, and intonations were embedded in the everyday realities of their audiences. For the newly urbanized poor of the late nineteenth century, the appeal of the urban romance lay in its reflection of scenes and situations recognizable from everyday life, the majority of which concerned domestic and romantic relationships.[124] Urban romances depicted a full spectrum of romantic entanglements, from casual intrigues to displays of deep, all-consuming feeling. Yet their human drama was intimately linked to individual struggles within the context of "concrete events in the economic and cultural life of 19th and early 20th-century Russia"; thus, personal encounters were transformed into topical social themes as well.[125]

Unlike the urban romance, guitar poetry had a remarkably broad thematic range (so much so that it has been called "encyclopedic"),[126] but perhaps unsurprisingly, love can be counted among its most popular themes. Depicting a variety of romantic relationships in circumstances specific to everyday life in the post-Stalin period, guitar poetry's topicality recalls that of the urban romance; and as with the urban romance, this was a key factor in its popularity. Similarly, if individual struggles occupied a prominent place in urban romance narratives, in guitar poetry "respect for human individuality" is elevated to the level of a defining philosophy, and the genre itself has been described as a means of self-revelation or individual "emancipation."[127]

Beyond such practical, thematic, and philosophical linkages, a final point of contact between the urban romance and guitar poetry concerns features of performance that derive, in the main, from the late nineteenth- and early twentieth-century variety stage (*estrada*). From the 1890s through the 1910s, urban romances were regularly performed on stage by a pleiad of popular *estrada* stars including Aleksandr Davydov (1850–1911), "the divine" Varya Panina (1872–1911), the Odessan chanteuse Iza Kremer (1889?–1956), and Aleksandr Vertinsky (1889–1957).[128] On the variety stage, manner of performance far outweighed vocal polish. Davydov's voice was "not very strong, but [it was] rich in overtones," for example, while Panina's was "almost coarse, reminiscent of a bass, absolutely un-feminine in timbre."[129] As Isaac Babel wrote, Odessan chanteuses like Iza Kremer "might not have much in the way of a voice, but they have a joy, an expressive joy, mixed with passion, lightness, and a touching, charming, sad feeling for life."[130] Vertinsky—a talented actor, singer, poet, and composer—had a distinctly self-deprecating attitude toward his own abilities, remarking, "I didn't know how to sing! I was a rather modest poet, and even more so a naive composer."[131] Yet his performances were remarkable for their "expressive eurythmics" and "refined quality of gesture," as well as for a spontaneous, improvisational quality that created "the charm of immediacy."[132] Contemporary music critic and composer V. G. Karatygin summarized variety stage performers' special appeal succinctly, noting that the "particular popularity [*obshchedostupnost'*]" of their art derived from its "universal *syncretism* . . . freely combin[ing] elements of singing and declamation, eurythmics [*plastika*] and gesture" (emphasis in original).[133]

Like the turn-of-the-century variety stage, guitar poetry was a syncretic art in which the combined effect of the whole performance was far more significant than the sum of its parts. In guitar poetry, as on the early variety stage, an idiosyncratic singing voice was not merely *not* a drawback, but was even viewed as something of a benefit. Most of the bards who began writing and performing songs in the 1950s and 1960s were not trained musicians, and most sang and played the guitar tolerably though not proficiently. Especially during guitar poetry's heyday, bards' singing and their guitar technique were typically "coarse and unpolished," a fact that bards themselves not only acknowledged but even deliberately underscored.[134] Together, bards' "unpretentious and untrained" singing voices and "unsophisticated" guitar playing were key components in creating guitar poetry's hallmark "atmosphere of immediacy, intimacy, and sincerity."[135]

Russian romance traditions and the turn-of-the-century variety stage contributed much to shaping guitar poetry's aesthetics, its ethical tendencies, its thematics, and its manner of performance. Despite the profound and recognizable impact on guitar poetry of these native Russian traditions, possible foreign influences should not be ignored. Thus, while the urban romance helped to establish a tradition of guitar-accompanied solo singing in Russia, this style of performance was also popularized in the Soviet Union through German cabaret song (particularly the works of Bertolt Brecht); and through French *chansonniers* like Georges Brassens and Yves Montand, whose songs were imported as part of "the opening up of direct cultural relations with the West in the Khrushchev period."[136] But while parallels have been noted between "generic parody" in Brecht's songs and in those of Aleksandr Galich, and stylistic similarities have been observed between Okudzhava's music and French chanson, detailed analysis of possible foreign influences on guitar poetry's development remains to be done.[137]

As soon as guitar poetry emerged, it was at once infused with prerevolutionary Russian cultural traditions and embedded in post-Stalin sociocultural and ideological debates. Evolving as part of a general rise in amateur creative activity, guitar poetry prompted mixed responses from official circles. On one hand, guitar poetry's spontaneous development provided pleasing evidence of the fulfillment of Lenin's desire to "awaken artists among the masses"; while its popularity among young people suggested that, if properly channeled, it could help fill the void left by the crisis in the professional song industry and become a powerful agent of socialist *vospitaniye*. On the other hand, guitar poetry—like various prerevolutionary genres in which it had roots—soon evinced a troublingly individualistic streak that was manifested not just lyrically, but also in its supreme accessibility and in the ease with which it could be produced, disseminated, and consumed in ways that were difficult to control. As anxious critics soon discerned, it was not so much collective *vospitaniye* that was fostered through guitar poetry, as self-fashioning and interaction among like-minded individuals. Deeper exploration of the related issues of self-fashioning, communication, and community-building that took place both in and through guitar poetry will be grounded in marginality theory, which is the central subject of chapter 2.

Chapter Two

Gray Zones: Theories of Marginality in a Russian-Soviet Context

> All margins are dangerous. If they are pulled this way or that the shape of fundamental experience is altered. Any structure of ideas is vulnerable at its margins.
> —Mary Douglas[1]

> Boundaries are where battles take place.
> —Pierre Bourdieu[2]

AS THE PRECEDING DISCUSSION underscores, guitar poetry was a strikingly significant sociocultural phenomenon of the post-Stalin period, but also one that straddled many of the traditionally accepted boundaries of Russian culture and of Soviet sociocultural and political life. Generically, guitar poetry defies easy categorization, combining and synthesizing elements of poetry, music, and, especially in the performances of Galich and Vysotsky, theater as well. Culturally, guitar poetry fails to fit neatly into a paradigm divided along the axis high vs. low, a type of marginality that is realized in the genre's derivation from and relationship to a range of both high- and low-culture antecedents; and that is also reflected in guitar poetry's own uneasy placement within the spectrum of Russian literary and musical activity.

As a form of artistic activity in the post-Stalin period, guitar poetry spanned the juncture between professional and non-professional realms, including among its practitioners both officially recognized poets (like Okudzhava) and amateurs; a number of schooled musicians (such as Boris Almazov and Aleksandr Dol'sky), a greater number of self-taught ones (including Kukin and Okudzhava), and a few who lacked even elementary knowledge of musical notation (Galich, Gorodnitsky); and finally, no small number of professional performers (notably trained actors like Vizbor and Vysotsky). In turn, this heterogeneous artistic ground gave rise to guitar poetry's aesthetic marginality, which is revealed in its simple melodies, self-consciously inexpert guitar playing, and untrained, often highly idiosyncratic, voices; and also in the crackling, hissing, and popping of countless *magnitizdat* tapes. Guitar poetry's predominantly oral circulation (be it in live performance or through *magnitizdat*) highlights, moreover, the genre's stance at the crossroads of oral and literate traditions, an intersection that will be touched upon again below.

In political terms, guitar poetry negotiated a thorny path between the permitted and the prohibited, the official and the unofficial. Despite attempts to characterize the genre as "dissident," "oppositional," or "protest music,"[3] in guitar poetry as a whole explicitly anti-Soviet elements are limited. Indeed, it has been argued variously that the bards "sang pretty much the same thing as Komsomol members"; and that, by and large, the themes of bards' songs were much the same as in professional songs, but with "fresh images [and] pungent words" in place of professional lyricists' "worn-out, commonplace lines" and "insufferable clichés."[4] On balance, most guitar poetry neither actively supported nor actively opposed the official line, instead existing in the gray area between the two. As émigré critics Pyotr Vail' and Aleksandr Genis observed in the late 1970s, moreover, this marginal status applied even to major figures, for "despite the prohibition on Vysotsky, he is not prohibited. He is not permitted, but he is not prohibited."[5]

Issues of permission and prohibition, the figurative spaces guitar poetry occupied in Soviet society, are intimately intertwined with the physical spaces in which it first appeared and later developed. Arising in a range of relatively private settings, and disseminated in ways that proved difficult to censor or control, guitar poetry was nonetheless never entirely free of official scrutiny or involvement. Though guitar poetry flourished on the fringes of urban life and in the literal peripheries of Soviet territory (a type of spatial marginality), the genre's existence in any institutionalized setting was predicated on official willingness to allow its existence—or, at least, on the lack of an unequivocal commitment to stamping it out.[6] Finally, many bards participated in sanctioned, professional creative activity throughout their careers, even in the increasingly difficult climate of the Brezhnev era. To a significant extent, of course, such participation depended on personal involvement with official institutions, including membership in the Communist Party and in various creative unions.

It may seem paradoxical to suggest that one of the central sociocultural phenomena of the post-Stalin period was, in fact, marginal in many ways. Yet guitar poetry thrived in the interstices and gray areas of post-Stalin cultural and social life, as the kinds of ambiguities summarized above indicate. As will be argued here, however, it was in these very ambiguities that guitar poetry's particular power and its particular threat to Soviet officialdom were grounded. The critical framework for exploring guitar poetry's aesthetic, cultural, and political complexities is based on marginality theory, adapted to suit the particular circumstances of post-Stalinist Soviet society. One crucial task in constructing this theoretical framework is to underscore points of contact between marginality theory and views and the vocabulary native to the specific environment in which guitar poetry arose. Beyond simply articulating a framework within which to study a single genre, therefore, this discussion seeks to illuminate ways in which marginality theory offers fruitful analytical tools for approaching Russian and Soviet culture more generally; and thereby to bridge the gap between Russian cultural studies and an important body of critical theory that has yet to be applied rigorously to the study of Russian culture itself.

THE MARGINS AND BEYOND: PARALLEL DISCURSIVE ARENAS

First proposed by the American sociologist Robert Ezra Park in the late 1920s, marginality has proved to be a remarkably productive and elastic concept. Perhaps for this very reason, marginality theory has become as controversial as it has fruitful. In his groundbreaking study "Human Migration and the Marginal Man," Park defined the "marginal man" as an individual situated on the boundary between two different and conflicting cultures, "sharing intimately in the cultural life and traditions of two distinct peoples."[7] According to Park, the marginal man exists in a "relatively permanent" stage of transition and crisis, unable to break fully with one culture yet also not accepted fully into the other; as the site where "changes and fusions of culture" take place, "the mind of the marginal man" thus offers a unique glimpse into processes of cultural change and development.[8] While Park originated the concept of the marginal man, though, it is Everett Stonequist who is most often credited with "fixing and legitimating the concept of marginality in sociology."[9] Drawing on Park's analysis, Stonequist developed the concept of the marginal man further, describing him forcefully as a "key-personality in the contacts of cultures" and as "the crucible of cultural fusion."[10] For Stonequist, as for Park, "the mind of the marginal man" offered potentially revelatory opportunities for studying the processes of "cultural fusion" and cultural change.[11]

Throughout the middle decades of the twentieth century, Park and Stonequist's work aroused intense interest, but it also incited searching critiques.[12] One common thread in these critiques highlights the paucity of rigorous empirical evidence in Park and Stonequist's largely theoretical and highly abstract analyses.[13] A second common feature in these early critiques is a profound uneasiness with Park and Stonequist's slippage between the sociological and the psychological, that is, with the attempt to bring together "at the relatively concrete level of the marginal *man,* the somewhat large components of social situation and personality traits."[14] Indeed, more recent studies have underscored the need to differentiate between "marginal situations" and individuals' responses to them, arguing that individuals occupying marginal positions do not "automatically perceive themselves to be marginals" or view themselves as "blocked, excluded, denied, ineligible aspirants to dominant privilege and power."[15]

Turning away from the marginal *man* and attempting instead to redress the lack of a "clear and comprehensive [sociological] definition of the marginal *situation*" (emphasis added), H. F. Dickie-Clark (1966) proposed a framework based on social hierarchies; and argued that marginal situations were "the result of any departure from complete consistency or congruence among the rankings of an individual or stratum in the various matters regulated by the hierarchy."[16] Dickie-Clark's model is predicated on the existence of subordinate and dominant social strata, the relationship between which is characterized both by unequal distribution of power and by unequal rights of access. Not only does the dominant stratum possess "the power to regulate access to spheres falling within its control," but there also exists "some sort of barrier which maintains the hierarchical nature of the situation."[17] Offering "a means by which strata maintain their separate identities," this barrier is nonetheless (semi-)permeable, preventing the subordinate group from enjoying "the full privileges of the dominant" but not from absorbing "cultural values and outlooks" characteristic thereof.[18] It is the very permeability (or incompleteness) of this barrier that gives rise to marginality; and thus, it is argued, "where barriers are wholly effective, marginal situations cannot occur."[19]

Since the mid-1960s, interest in marginality and marginality theory has scarcely abated within the social sciences. As a result, marginality has been investigated not just as a phenomenon of "cultural and racial hybrids," but also in relation to socioeconomic systems of production and consumption and political participation.[20] Notwithstanding Dickie-Clark's corrective, however, a unified and broadly accepted social scientific definition of marginality still proves elusive.[21] Frequently used, the concepts of marginality and "marginal regions" are subject nonetheless to "varying interpretations and perceptions" in the social sciences; but in the critical literature, "the meaning of these terms is usually assumed, with little effort made to define them."[22] This situation has led some social scientists to deplore marginality as a "Teflon concept" that is "invulnerable to dissent or contrary evidence"; and to argue that, absent an agreed definition and "correlational or convergent support" for any one approach, the concept of marginality "lacks construct validity" and should be discarded from the social scientific vocabulary.[23] A more receptive critical approach allows that Park's original marginal man concept is a "flawed but serviceable instrument," one that deserves continued attention even as it requires more robust development.[24]

While marginality theory has been challenged from within the social sciences, it has also overstepped the boundaries of social scientific inquiry considerably during the past several decades. As Terry Smyth summarizes, despite its "rather chequered history, the notion of marginality has proved . . . to be a powerful and resilient stimulus for many writers from a variety of backgrounds."[25] At least since the 1990s, aspects of marginality theory have been employed productively in fields such as literary and cultural studies, gender studies, and postcolonial studies (including the growing discourse on migration and diaspora). Thus, for example, marginality has been brought to bear in analyses of multicultural literacy, minor(ity) literatures, and postmodern subjectivity;[26] oral literature and performance;[27] and feminist critiques of difference, self-discovery, and modes of writing.[28] More generally, marginality has been invoked as part of the broader cultural studies project of collecting "alternative voices" and mapping "parallel public spheres rarely acknowledged by the mass media."[29] In addition, echoes of marginality theory can be found in numerous discourses that are not necessarily descended directly from Park's marginal man, including examinations of cultural and intellectual "border crossings" and the "border subjects" (artists, litterateurs, cultural critics) who perform them; and explorations of hybridity and "the borderline engagements of cultural difference."[30]

The broad application of marginality theory has generated diverse definitions and interpretations of marginality itself, both within and across disciplines. Though doing so necessitates "conflating quite a few theories," it is nonetheless possible to discern common interests across these widely varying approaches.[31] A fundamental assumption underpinning various concepts of marginality is that of a "lack of fit" between an individual or group, which is referred to as marginal or marginalized, and the dominant (nonmarginal) group in society. The interaction of marginal and nonmarginal is widely construed in hierarchical terms, often expressed through a "Center/Periphery (or Core/Periphery) model."[32] As a consequence of their peripheral situation, the marginal fail to participate in various spheres (e.g., cultural, educational, social, and political) "which are considered to be within the[ir] radius of action and/or access."[33]

This lack of participation suggests a second element shared across definitions of marginality, namely the notion that marginality can be produced both "through coercion . . . [and] through willful estrangement"; thus, it is understood that individuals and groups can not only be marginalized forcibly by the "center," but that they can also marginalize themselves deliberately.[34] The active mode presupposed by "willful estrangement" highlights, in turn, ways in which the margins are not just "a site of deprivation," but also one of "radical possibility."[35] Far from destroying agency and enforcing passivity, then, the margins can serve as a "place of transgression, which in turn subverts hegemonic discourse"; and even as "a central location for the production of counter-hegemonic discourse."[36]

Moving beyond marginality theory specifically, a broader concern with subversion and resistance has also spurred the development of various approaches that posit parallel arenas in which marginal(ized) groups operate and communicate. Particularly relevant among these is the concept of "counterpublics," which theorizes (symbolic) places or bodies in which subordinated social groups can express themselves. Adopting and adapting the vocabulary of marginality, a number of scholars have elucidated counterpublic theory within the framework of recent critiques of Jürgen Habermas's influential work on the public sphere.[37] Challenging the notion of a "monolithic public sphere" that offers a place for discourse independent of (and also potentially critical of) the state, and also challenging the "singular opposition/state model of agitation and control" upon which a unitary notion of the public sphere rests, counterpublic theory acknowledges the existence of multiple sites for the development of "critical oppositional discourses."[38] Counterpublics thus provide discursive arenas in which marginal groups can formulate "interpretations of their identities, interests, and needs"; in so doing, counterpublics "expand discursive space" and thereby "enable marginal groups to overcome the discursive barriers to participation."[39] Identity creation is widely agreed to be a significant component of counterpublic discourse, with some scholars arguing that what happens in counterpublics "in terms of identity creation" may even be more important than "the outward directed rhetoric."[40]

ADAPTING MARGINALITY THEORY TO A RUSSIAN-SOVIET CONTEXT

As well as highlighting key features of marginality theory, the preceding overview also suggests that this body of theory must be approached critically and adapted carefully in order to provide a meaningful framework for the present analysis. The first major problem arising out of existing, cross-disciplinary definitions of marginality is their overwhelming tendency to cleave to a binary analytical model: the value "margin" assumes a corresponding value "center," while notions of opposition and dissent ("counter-" and "anti-") strongly suggest corresponding positions of conformity and support ("pro-"). Some scholars have acknowledged potential drawbacks of this binary conceptual framework, noting critically that "the idea of 'marginality' depends on the notion of a fixed 'center' in relation to which it derives its meaning."[41] In numerous other accounts, however, the polar opposition of margin and center is not simply accepted, but rather underscored. For bell hooks, for example, survival on the margins depends on "ongoing public awareness of the separation between margin and center"; while for Sneja Gunew, "that there should be a marginal allows the center to explain itself."[42]

The underlying binary opposition of "margin" and "center" is an aspect of recent marginality discourse of which we must be particularly aware, and particularly wary, in adapting this body of theory to an analysis of post-Stalin Soviet society and of guitar poetry in particular. As Alexei Yurchak has argued, binary divisions between Soviet state and society, official culture and counterculture, and censored and uncensored discourse are problematic because "many of the common cultural phenomena in socialism that were allowed, tolerated, or even promoted within the realm of the officially censored were nevertheless quite distinct from the ideological texts of the party."[43] Conversely, not everything that circulated within the realm of uncensored discourse could be classified as "dissident" or "oppositional." For example, while homemade tape recordings allowed individuals to circumvent censorship and other "control mechanisms" to a significant extent, *magnitizdat* was "not necessarily something politically subversive," and often "simply reflect[ed] the chronic shortage of consumer goods" in the Soviet Union.[44] In addition, examples of guitar poetry that tacitly supported the official line (on patriotism, for example, or motherhood) were not uncommon.[45] In such circumstances, we are confronted with a situation in which "the separation of things into unlike categories is unattainable," and the consequent mixing of categories "creates liminal zones or spaces of ambiguity and discontinuity."[46]

Intriguingly, the reliance on a binary center/periphery opposition in much recent discourse on marginality represents a significant shift away from Park and Stonequist's original understanding of the marginal man and his sociocultural role. Insofar as it describes the meeting of two conflicting cultures, the Park-Stonequist model does presuppose a binary system. Yet Park and Stonequist's focus lay in the "meet[ing] and fus[ing]" of these two cultures—in the marginal man as a point of contact and overlap between them—not in the diametric opposition of one to the other.[47] This notion of ambivalence must be underscored, because it lies at the heart of a concept of the margins as a space "in between" rather than a space at the edge of or beyond the boundary of that which is defined as the "center."[48] It is this medial, interstitial envisioning of marginality that is most applicable to the study of guitar poetry and the ways in which it defied the binary regularities often imposed on Soviet culture and society.

A second obstacle to applying marginality theory in a Russian-Soviet context is the fact that the connotations attached to marginality in Russia are very different from those current in (or even promoted by) Western academic discourse. Within the latter, value judgements implicit in categories of marginality are hotly contested.[49] In Russia, however, the concept of marginality has long been beleaguered by pejorative connotations. This attitude, which is evident in popular as well as academic discourse, is redolent of the legacy of Marx and Engels, both of whom recognized that "society itself creates marginal populations" but stressed that "marginality is an undesirable and unacceptable condition in society."[50] For much of the Soviet period, marginality was little studied, and seldom evoked except in connection with problems of adaptation and socialization.[51] In these contexts, the term "marginals" (*marginaly*) became virtually synonymous with "hooligans" (*khuligany*) and other terms used to refer to undesirable social groups; and both this usage and its inherent bias still linger in post-Soviet social scientific discourse.[52]

Since the mid-1980s, Russian interest in marginality has grown substantially, with some scholarly investigations concentrating on the rise of "'informal' social movements" (*neformal'nye obshchestvennye dvizheniya*) as vehicles for "express[ing] the interests of marginalized groups."[53] In other studies, most notably the polemical writings of E. Starikov, the creation of marginalized masses through social breakdown has been construed as the antithesis of "a civil society with normal human relations, which was imagined ideally as the main, final goal of perestroika."[54] In the post-Soviet period, the Russian term *marginal'nost'* continues to carry undertones of "alienness, groundlessness, [and] cultural decline"; and individuals or groups labeled "marginal" are still widely considered to be socioculturally inferior, even "cultural vagrants of a sort."[55]

Despite these lingering negative connotations, during the last decade marginality theory has gained greater currency in Russian sociological (and, to a more limited extent, culturological) discourse. Of particular interest here are ways in which recent Russian scholarship emphasizes ambivalent and transitional aspects of marginality. Adopting a largely abstract and philosophical approach, Vladimir Kagansky defines marginality as a "zone of dual belonging [*zona dvuprinadlezhnosti*]" and as a "transitional zone" or position (*perekhodnaya zona, perekhodnaya pozitsiya*), for example.[56] On a somewhat more concrete level, both transitivity (*perekhodnost'*) and intermediacy (*promezhutochnost'*) have been identified as key characteristics of post-Soviet marginality, in accordance with "the specifics of the Russian situation."[57] In this approach, the transitional and ambivalent quality of post-Soviet marginality is seen as symptomatic of the chaotic re-formation of Russian society in the post-1991 period, with the roots of this marginality being traced back to informal movements and groups of the late 1970s and early 1980s.[58] While this implicit challenge to a binary view of marginality is welcome, it falls short, arguably, in tracing the origins of this "in-betweenness" only as far back as the late 1970s. As will be discussed below, a great eruption of the "in-between" into Soviet culture and everyday life began during the Thaw, a period that can itself be regarded as marginal.

With these caveats in mind, marginality theory can nevertheless be adapted as a useful critical tool for analyzing guitar poetry and other hybrid or intermediate phenomena in Russian culture. First, by stripping back the center-periphery distinction that has been superimposed onto marginality, we can recover marginality as a concept and an "in-between" state that challenges binary distinctions and systems—and as a means of exploring cultural and social fusions, mixing, and (inter)change. Within the context of an ideological system the explicit rhetoric of which espoused and promoted binary divisions, moreover, this approach can provide a better understanding of the threat posed by marginal phenomena.[59] As David Sibley argues, "for the individual or group socialized into believing that the separation of categories is necessary or desirable," marginality—reflected in liminal zones or "spaces of ambiguity and discontinuity"—becomes "a source of anxiety."[60]

Having established the "in-betweenness" of marginality, it is possible to undertake an exploration of the interrelated processes of identity creation (or self-fashioning) and communication that take place in the margins. Drawing on notions of identity creation that are central to marginality theory, we can characterize guitar poetry as a sociocultural movement that enabled a broad cross-section of Soviet society to generate independent interpretations of its identities, interests, and needs.[61] This formulation is adapted from Nancy Fraser and Catherine Helen Palczewski, but the emphasis on explicit oppositionality that suffuses their approaches is deliberately elided.[62] This is necessary because, as will be discussed below, the identities, interests, and needs articulated through and promoted by guitar poetry were neither uniformly "oppositional" (or "dissident") nor uniformly "conformist" in nature.

Issues of identity creation are closely linked to communication because of the significant role that language plays in "delineating group boundaries" and serving as "a marker of social identity."[63] As noted above, a broad consensus exists across various approaches to marginality that in-group communication serves the aims of self-fashioning as much as it constitutes an outwardly directed statement of desires, interests, and needs. In situations revolving around oral communication, it is especially important to expand the field of analysis beyond words' literal, denotative meanings because the spoken (or sung) word is pronounced "with a certain intonation, tone, gesture, and facial expression that . . . add to the evaluation"; in turn, these expressive features contribute to the role of oral communication not simply as a means of exchanging information but also as a way of "convey[ing] something about the relationship between communicator and audience."[64]

The intersection of marginality and the everyday represents a final way in which the discourse of marginality will prove useful in the context of this study. What is relevant here is not simply the "marginality of the majority" that Michel de Certeau describes when he argues that "marginality is today no longer limited to minority groups, but is rather massive and pervasive"; or that Phillip Bryan Harper suggests in stating that "marginalized groups' experience of decenteredness is itself a largely unacknowledged factor in the 'general' postmodern condition."[65] What pertains here is, more specifically, the fact that the lived experience of ordinary Soviet citizens was neither addressed nor depicted in any significant way in the media or in the officially mandated and regulated arts. Svetlana Boym stresses that "in Russian intellectual tradition as well as in official Soviet ideology, a preoccupation with everyday life for its own sake was considered unpatriotic, subversive, un-Russian, or even anti-Soviet."[66] Because of this, even during the Thaw, the "reality of people's daily lives" was marginalized, and the surrogate promoted in the official media and represented in the professional arts had a decidedly "fictitious quality."[67]

MARGINALITY, RITES OF PASSAGE, AND SOVIET SELF-FASHIONING

As suggested above, the Thaw itself can be regarded as a marginal period, but not simply because, in retrospect, it was sandwiched between Stalinist dictatorship and the "dictatorship" of Brezhnevian conformity now known as the period of stagnation (*zastoy*).[68] Additionally, we can adapt the Park-Stonequist image of the marginal individual, whose nature is characterized by instability, inner conflict, and tensions between old and new (neither of which can be fully rejected nor fully accepted), as a means of conceptualizing the crises and struggles of the Thaw. One of the overarching dilemmas of the period revolved around the need to shed the legacy of Stalin without fundamentally undermining notions of "Soviet" and "Sovietness" that had become intertwined with Stalin's person, image, and leadership.

The search for a solution to this problem was hardly straightforward. As a result, official policy of the Khrushchev period underwent dramatic and repeated shifts, "as the new leadership attempted to maintain a tense balance between enthusiasm for discarding the past, and uncontrolled iconoclasm . . . between maintaining the Soviet system, and causing its implosion."[69] Debates on the role of song and on the rise of amateur musical activity represented one attempt to negotiate this balance, as did the widespread discourse on *vospitaniye* (particularly in regard to Soviet youth). Such discussions spanned the closely interlinked sociocultural and ideological spheres, providing frequent opportunities for reaffirmation of the far-reaching relationship between culture and ideology; and also for negotiation over "the prerogative to direct and control cultural change."[70]

Official anxiety about major transitions gripping Soviet society at large prompted heightened interest in transitions in the lives of individual Soviet citizens, too. In the late 1950s and early 1960s, debates about *vospitaniye* were complemented by a wave of "socialist ritual-making [*ritualostroitel'stvo*]," focusing on individual "rites of passage," on a level not seen since the 1920s.[71] A general process of "standardizing and simplifying" civic rituals was accompanied by the creation of numerous new rites of passage, which marked the transition from one social status to another.[72] Among the major life events for which new rites of passage were created were the registration of births, marriages, and deaths, entry into the Pioneers or the Komsomol, entry into the labor force, and retirement; and as this list suggests, these new rites of passage were directed predominantly at young people, at stamping the major events in young lives with the indelible mark of Sovietness.[73] Key features of these "new Soviet ceremonies," as contemporary advocates underscored, were a firm grounding in "Marxist-Leninist ideology, communist morality and ethics," a focus on edification (*vospitatel'noye znacheniye*), and the unequivocal expression of "the feeling of collectivism that is inherent in Soviet people."[74]

In promoting the significance of these principles in new rituals and celebrations, no distinction was made between essentially public events (such as graduation from school or enlisting in the army) and more private ones (like wedding celebrations or birthdays). Indeed, as one contemporary commentator stressed, "the entire ritual side of our domestic [and] everyday [*semeyno-bytovykh*] celebrations must be subordinated" to ideology and to communist morality.[75] This was very much in keeping with broad-based efforts to efface distinctions between public and private, to construct the two into a unified bulwark that would allow the Soviet authorities to engage (however gingerly) in a "discourse of individual identity" without condoning (much less encouraging) "a retreat into the private sphere, and disengagement from collective pursuits."[76]

Indicative of such tensions was the discourse of *lichnost'* (individual[ity] or person[ality]) itself, which became prominent in official circles as well as among ordinary Soviet citizens starting in the mid-1950s. While in Stalinist official discourse *lichnost'* was "most frequently used . . . to refer to spectacular heroic persons," by the 1960s this usage competed for currency with *lichnost'* in the sense of the unique, individual features of any person, or the "person as such."[77] Despite this semantic shift, and despite increased attention during the Khrushchev era to "individual well-being and private freedoms," the firm connection between *lichnost'* and *kollektiv* was emphasized continually in official discourse, being articulated with particular clarity in the 1960s.[78] Indeed, the collective was the prime locus in which *lichnost'* was supposed to be shaped, in which "Soviet self-fashioning was supposed to be achieved," and individualism (*individualizm*) was widely criticized as a "sickness."[79]

As a catchword of popular discourse in the post-Stalin period, *lichnost'* was synonymous with "the notion of person(ality) or individuality [that] emerg[ed] amongst the youth who flourished in the wake of the cult of personality."[80] Perhaps nowhere was this more true than in guitar poetry, for which *lichnost'* became both a sine qua non and a raison d'être. On one hand, *lichnost'* is widely cited as a fundamental characteristic of a true bard, as necessary as poetic and (some degree of) musical talent. According to Aleksandr Gorodnitsky, for example, "it is absolutely necessary for [a person] to be a personality [*lichnost'*]" in order to be a bard.[81] In a similar vein, Aleksandr Dol'sky equates guitar poetry with "the author's own personality [*lichnost'*], significant, authoritative, honest, pure, and very talented"; while Natal'ya Akkuratova, a longtime member of KSP Vostok, lists "personality" (*lichnost'*) as one of guitar poetry's essential components, along with "poetry, music, [and] voice."[82] Concomitantly, a number of recognizable *lichnosti*—most frequently Okudzhava, Galich, and Vysotsky—are identified as representing guitar poetry's essence and its apogee.[83] On the other hand, guitar poetry itself has been characterized as valuing "respect for human individuality" and as "asserting the truth of the individual [*pravda lichnosti*]"; and it has been heralded as "a new spiritual [and] practical type of individual revelation [*vyyavleniye lichnosti*]" and as a catalyst for the "emancipation of the individual personality."[84] In short, for bards and audiences, *lichnost'* both *created* guitar poetry and *was created* by it.

As used in reference to guitar poetry, the concept of *lichnost'* preserves a basic dualism that cleaves close to that characteristic of official usage in the post-Stalin period. On one hand, *lichnost'* describes particular bards—spectacular individuals—who achieved significant popular recognition. The appeal and the success of these *lichnosti* is attributed not simply to artistic qualities, not just to the fact that they "elevated 'campfire' song to the level of poetry," but also to personal ones: these are figures whose vision of the world is "interesting to other people, to [their] listeners" and who "have something to reveal to people."[85] On the other hand, *lichnost'* signifies an ideal or aspiration, an espousal of the individual—the "person as such"—as a self-standing entity rather than merely as a constituent part of the *kollektiv*.

What is evidenced by the discourse of *lichnost'* in guitar poetry, then, is not a dramatic break with official discourse, not a schism with official notions of what was meant by *lichnost'*, but rather a subtle shift of emphasis in how it could be created and shaped. Indeed, it would be wrong to say that the notion of *lichnost'* envisioned by bards and their audiences was intractably incompatible with prescribed interpretations of the identities, interests, and needs of a model Soviet citizen. Remarks attributing the success of bardic *lichnosti* to both artistic and personal characteristics echo stipulations that both artistic works and their creators were to be scrutinized in assessing the "social significance" of amateur artistic activity. Furthermore, no less an authority than Bulat Okudzhava opined that guitar poetry

> has a direct relationship to literature, to poetry, and the demand from it should be the same—serious and according to a high standard of reckoning [*po vysokomu schyotu*]. With our creative activity we must expose evil, speak out wrathfully about petty bourgeois [attitudes], [and] philistinism (it is they that oppose the renewal of our society), [and] serve society with the poetic word.[86]

Okudzhava's remarks offer ample evidence of a "civic-minded" approach to art and a firm belief in artists' civic responsibilities that are deeply rooted in Russian culture and that strongly resonate throughout the debates on Soviet song in the 1950s and 1960s. Boris Almazov's reflection that Okudzhava "was not just a gold standard [*etalonom*] of guitar poetry, but also of morals [*nravstvennosti*]" reveals a similar preoccupation; so, too, does Aleksandr Galich's impassioned declaration, made in an open letter following his expulsion from the Writers' Union and the Cinematographers' Union, that while his "literary rights ha[d] been taken away, [his] obligations remained—to compose and sing songs."[87]

As Gerald Smith has argued, to a certain extent guitar poetry "reflects a shared Russian notion of what the arts should concern themselves with and the way they should properly communicate."[88] To this one might add that guitar poets themselves revealed a shared notion of what *artists* should concern themselves with and how *they* should communicate. Instead, what is notably lacking in guitar poetry's discourse on *lichnost'* is the obligatory shackling of *lichnost'* to *kollektiv* that pervades official discourse. Indeed, as Bulat Okudzhava remarked in the mid-1980s, "I value people who respect the individual [*lichnost'*]. Not the collective, but the individual. Because we were taught to respect the collective for a long time, for many years. It is time to begin respecting the individual."[89] The implication of the decoupling of *lichnost'* from *kollektiv*, it would seem, is that both in and through guitar poetry, the individual *lichnost'* was a viable arena in which self-fashioning (or, one might say, self-*vospitaniye*) could take place.

Guitar poetry's "dual belonging" in this respect—its adherence to a discourse of *lichnost'* familiar from official culture combined with a subtle refusal of its underpinnings—reflects a potent feature of popular culture generally, namely its ability "to identify ideas and desires that are relatively oppositional alongside those that are clearly complicit to the official culture."[90] It also reflects a crucial aspect of marginality, the fact that an individual's marginal position does not automatically imply individual perception of oneself as marginal or marginalized. More specifically, such ambivalence also aligns guitar poetry with a broad range of common attitudes and practices of the post-Stalin period. As Alexei Yurchak observes, during this period, "many of the fundamental values, ideals, and realities of socialist life" were genuinely important to great numbers of Soviet citizens, "despite the fact that many of their everyday practices routinely transgressed, reinterpreted, or refused certain norms and rules represented in the official ideology of the socialist state."[91] With respect to guitar poetry, the discourse on *lichnost'* was one arena in which this ambivalence was expressed with particular clarity.

MARGINALITY, LATE SOCIALISM, AND INTERACTION IN THE "IN BETWEEN"

The prominence of *lichnost'* in official discourse of the post-Stalin period and its concurrent centrality in discussions of guitar poetry provide an interesting link between the bard phenomenon and a category of lifestyles and life practices that Alexei Yurchak calls "being *vnye* [outside]."[92] Yurchak has argued compellingly that during late socialism (a period extending from the mid-1950s through perestroika), there was "an explosion of various styles of living that were simultaneously inside and outside the system."[93] As Yurchak observes, various life practices that can be included under the umbrella of "being *vnye*" (from schoolchildren's literary circles to theoretical science) are united by the fact that they "generated multiple new temporalities, spatialities, social relations, and meanings that were not necessarily anticipated or controlled by the state, although they were fully made possible by it."[94] Arguably, it is in guitar poetry and the guitar poetry movement that such styles of living found their earliest expression.

Guitar poetry made use of spaces, hobbies, discourses, and even genres that were not simply made available by the state but also were specifically promoted by it. Yet in so doing, guitar poetry crafted modes of being and modes of interaction that, thanks to its predominantly oral existence and relatively unhindered dissemination via *magnitizdat,* the state could never fully control. The overarching category defining identification and interaction through guitar poetry was the notion of *svoi* ("us," "our people"), as the following assessment by Yury Vizbor illustrates: "All these songs have one common characteristic: they were written amongst *svoi,* sung amongst *svoi* and often addressed only to *svoi.*"[95]

As Vizbor's comment suggests, guitar poetry was not simple entertainment, but rather a medium through which individuals identified, communicated with, and interacted with *svoi.* For guitar poetry's practitioners and fans, songs were a means of self-expression or, as Vysotsky remarked expressively, an opportunity to tell others "about what is bothering me, what grates on my nerves, what tears up my soul [*rvyot dushu*]."[96] In addition, though, guitar poetry's self-expressive songs functioned "as a kind of password" for "in-group members [*dlya 'svoikh'*]"; as a form of communication between members of different social classes, generations, and professions, who shared common views; and as "a medium of interaction, a sort of identifying code."[97]

On one level, this emphasis on communication and interaction was part and parcel of a phenomenon that Pyotr Vail' and Aleksandr Genis have termed the "cult of interaction [*kul't obshcheniya*]" of the 1960s.[98] According to Vail' and Genis, this "cult" emphasized the importance of common understanding and interaction in all spheres of human activity, and valued friendship above all else:

> Be it a builders' brigade, a geological group or a scientific research institute—the atmosphere of friendly mutual understanding seemed much more important than production tasks . . . Friendship became both the essence and the form of leisure. More broadly, even—of life.[99]

Weaving together strands of self-fashioning, in-group identification, and communication, guitar poetry represents a specific kind of communication "with half-words," a practice that is itself "a mark of belonging to an imagined community that exists on the margin" of official public discourse.[100]

While guitar poetry's language was undeniably important, its communication "with half-words" should not be reduced to words alone. Intended for performance to musical accompaniment, however rudimentary, bards' song lyrics did not stand alone as purely verbal acts. Instead, to echo Deborah Tannen, they were marked even in audio recordings by the inflections and intonations of their performers; by paratextual information (performers' asides and commentaries, audience members' deliberate and inadevertent contributions); and, in live performance, by gestures and facial expressions as well. Thus, guitar poetry's communication depended not simply on *what* it expressed but also on *how* it did so; and the *how* of guitar poetry's communication involved an unpretentious performance style, a significant feature of which was what an uncharitable listener might call "bad singing."

Though bad singing may fail to be melodious or even on key, and though it may sometimes grate on the ear, it can be a powerful instrument for the creation of intimacy. As journalist Kelefa Sanneh writes, referring to vocally under-endowed pop singers of the "American Idol" generation,

> At a time when it seems easier than ever to become a celebrity, bad singing can create a seductive illusion of intimacy. To hear a pop star flub a note is to believe, if only for a moment, that you or I could just as easily be onstage, doing no less and no more than our best.[101]

The intimacy created through guitar poetry's "bad singing" was more than just an illusion, however. Initially a form of essentially private, domestic music-making, guitar poetry quickly became a mass phenomenon as bards and their audiences multiplied. In the mid-1980s, for example, Bulat Okudzhava remarked, "now we are used to the fact that all sorts of KSPs exist and all that, but back then [in the late 1950s and early 1960s] none of that existed."[102] Reflecting on his own experiences in Moscow, similarly, Yury Vizbor observed as follows:

> You know, we were young students . . . We wanted to sing songs about us, about how we live, about how we travel, how we feel about life. But there weren't any such songs . . . Because of this, we began to compose our own songs. They circulated on the level of the group . . . but not more than that. In Moscow, two groups formed in this way . . . But then this movement began to spread wider and wider [and] many well-known masters appeared.[103]

If *magnitizdat* was largely responsible for expanding guitar poetry's audiences, then arguably "bad singing" and mediocre guitar playing were largely responsible for expanding the ranks of its bards. Adapting Sanneh's observation, we may say that to hear Okudzhava flub a note was to believe that one could just as easily pick up a guitar and do no less and no more than one's best. Intimacy, like *lichnost'*, was thus both a stimulus for the creation of guitar poetry and a crucial product of its performance.

In a narrow sense, the origins of guitar poetry's hallmark intimacy lay in the kinds of close quarters out of which the genre grew. Intimacy was not a specific product of these settings, however. Rather, the intimacy of these settings reflected ways in which the crafting and expression of individual identities in the margins is interwoven with the formation of group identities and with communication and interaction between in-group members. The marginality-based theoretical framework established here thus provides the basis for subsequent analysis of how *lichnost'* was created in and through guitar poetry; and also of how intimacy and interaction were created with the help of *lichnost'*—not just in what are traditionally thought of as "intimate settings," but in any venue where a bard happened to perform.

PART II

Guitar Poetry's Selves and Communities

Chapter Three

Guitar Poetry and the Creation of *Lichnost'*

> The fundamental nature and meaning of music
> lie not in objects, not in musical works at all,
> but in action, in what people do.
> —Christopher Small[1]

THE PREVIOUS TWO CHAPTERS have concerned themselves largely with guitar poetry's contexts, theoretical as well as historical and sociopolitical. This chapter and the next undertake to examine guitar poetry's performance and reception within these contexts. In guitar poetry, the interplay between bard and audience is considerable, such that a bard's performance is by no means a "one-way system of communication, running from composer to individual listener through the medium of the performer."[2] In guitar poetry, the interaction between performance and reception is heightened not simply because, as Christopher Small argues, "music's primary meanings are not individual at all but social";[3] but also because of the specific emphasis placed on dialogue in guitar poetry and even on guitar poetry *as* dialogue.

The underlying premise of this analysis is that by examining performance and reception, we can learn much about how guitar poetry came to serve as an agent of self-fashioning, communication, and community-building in the post-Stalin period. The common thread linking these two chapters is the notion of *lichnost'*, both as person(ality) and as individual(ity); and, more specifically, ways in which the interplay between the recognizable *lichnosti* of guitar poetry helped to foster the ideal of individual *lichnost'*, and with it a sense of group identity, among guitar poetry's predominantly youthful adherents. In the present chapter, a range of bardic *lichnosti* will be examined in order to draw out key characteristics that helped to establish an atmosphere of sincere, direct interaction between bards and audiences; and, in turn, helped to establish guitar poetry as a means by which bards and audiences could identify and interact with *svoi*.

SOURCES AND APPROACH

In song, as Simon Frith observes, words are "the sign of a voice": for singers, "it is not just what they sing, but the way they sing it, that determines what [they] mean to us and how we are placed as an audience in relation to them."[4] Building on Frith's observation, it is argued here that guitar poetry's power as an instrument of self-fashioning, communication, and community-building derived not simply from what bards sang, but also from how they expressed themselves in performance. Informed by a growing body of popular music scholarship that emphasizes extratextual elements as much as textual ones, the present analysis of guitar poetry's performance and reception explores bardic *lichnosti* through multiple prisms: voice, accompaniment, gesture, and context. In turn, it also draws upon Erving Goffman's dramaturgical metaphor for social interaction (laid out in *The Presentation of Self in Everyday Life*, 1959), which provides a fruitful means of analyzing the communication and interaction embedded in performance.

Of necessity, the source material that forms the basis for the following description and analysis of bardic *lichnosti* is heterogeneous, including personal interviews, secondhand accounts (e.g., reminiscences, written descriptions), formal concerts, casual performances, photographs, video footage, and audio recordings. Such an approach is not without its drawbacks, especially for analyzing a genre in which direct contact between author-performer and audience is accorded special significance. Drawing in part on reproductions of performances and secondary sources, this approach may seem too far removed from the "functional and intimate interaction between performers and audience"[5] that was both cultivated and cherished in guitar poetry. It is important to recall, however, that even contemporary audiences knew the major bards and their songs "directly" (that is, in authorial performance) in large part through *magnitizdat* recordings; and that, absent opportunities for personal contact and verifiable sources of information, such recordings (along with rumor and hearsay) contributed significantly to shaping bards' public personae in the eyes and ears of their audiences.

Among the major bards, for example, Galich gave only one public concert in the Soviet Union; and both his inaccessibility and his untimely death, over which a whiff of conspiracy still hovers, contributed to the "luster of martyrial heroism" that lingers about him.[6] Similarly, Vysotsky's fan base was certainly not limited to those who were able to see him perform live: his early concerts were largely private, while later on the demand for tickets far outstripped the supply. Among Vysotsky's admirers, many knew him through his roles in film and theater (though theater tickets were scarce, too); but, as Vysotsky himself was keenly aware, most knew him through "very poorly re-recorded and often counterfeit tapes [*poddelannykh lentok*]," in other words, through *magnitizdat* recordings.[7] As Christopher Lazarski observes, widespread rumors about Vysotsky's "labor camp past," in particular, support the contention that "the mass audience became acquainted with him mainly through *magnitizdat* editions of his early underworld songs."[8] Indeed, Vysotsky often remarked upon the various rumors to which his songs gave rise:

> People often ask me whether I am the same Volodya Vysotsky who fought at Kursk or at Stalingrad, at Orsha or Vyaz'ma. People think that I went through [*proshyol*] the war. And sometimes people say that I have done time a lot, more than once. According to the sentences I should already be ninety-seven or so. It is not true, it is a fabrication.[9]

Focusing on bards themselves, rather than their fictional guises, this chapter will analyze bardic *lichnosti* as personalities ("spectacular individuals") with the help of Erving Goffman's concept of "front." Goffman defines front as "expressive equipment" that an individual uses during a performance, whether intentionally or not, and that "define[s] the situation for those who observe the performance."[10] Within the category of front, the subcategory of "setting" comprises furniture, decor, physical layout, and other generally stationary background items that "supply the scenery and stage props for the spate of human action played out before, within, or upon it" (22). The locations in which guitar poetry was performed from the late 1950s onward varied tremendously, as did their specific characteristics, such as size, location, or accessibility.

Ostensibly, however, both venue and setting (in the Goffmanian sense) were irrelevant to guitar poetry. Vysotsky's observations about the numerous different locations in which he performed are instructive in this regard:

> I have sung everywhere . . . I wrote and sang my first songs just for a few close friends . . . My songs are an opportunity to converse with you. I have been lucky and now I have the opportunity to tell such a large number of people about what troubles me, what agitates me in this life, what I would like to laugh about. But before I used to sing for five or six people . . . Since then many years have passed. My audience has expanded. I have performed even in Palaces of Sport. I have performed here and abroad. But throughout all the years and venues [*cherez vse vremena i zaly*] I have tried to carry through [*protashchit'*] the atmosphere of absolute trust, uninhibitedness and freedom that we had back then.[11]

Similarly, Vysotsky commented that

> guitar poetry doesn't need any stages, any footlights, any spotlights. I have performed in hangars, in submarines, on landing fields among mechanics black as beetles, while combat aircraft [*boyevye mashiny*] descended, and

> we just went off a little to the side, so the words could be heard; I have sung on the fields of giant stadiums, in rooms, in basements, in attics—anywhere at all, it doesn't matter . . . Guitar poetry doesn't need scenery—it needs atmosphere.[12]

Of course, both of these passages underscore Vysotsky's privileged position among the bards and also, his contentious relationship with the Soviet authorities notwithstanding, within the Soviet cultural esablishment more generally. He could not have gained access to stadiums, Palaces of Sport, and especially foreign travel without a significant level of official complicity: such venues and privileges were certainly not accessible to the Soviet cultural rank and file, still less to bards who were not recognized as composers, poets, or singers. Yet Vysotsky's observations also highlight the particular emphasis placed on the intangibles of atmosphere in guitar poetry, a point that will be examined further below.

The second subcategory of Goffman's front is "personal front," which includes both mutable and immutable features (such as clothing, hairstyle, facial expressions, ethnic or racial characteristics, and sex) "that we most intimately identify with the performer himself and that we naturally expect will follow the performer wherever he goes" (24). More elastic and mobile than setting, personal front can also be more intimately attributed to a specific performer than setting can. Personal front is thus the central theoretical prism through which the individual *lichnosti* of various bards will be examined. In the discussion to follow, aspects of personal front such as appearance, mannerisms, and demeanor will be considered, but voice will receive pride of place. The rationale for this decision is partly pragmatic, voice being an aspect of personal front that is preserved in audio recordings and thus accessible even to those who did not have access to live performances. But it is also justified theoretically by the fact that, as Simon Frith argues, the voice "stands for the person more directly than any other musical device," despite being "easier to change . . . than one's face (or one's body movements)."[13] In relation to guitar poetry, more specifically, it has been observed that "the human voice is one of the most important assets. It is not an instrument of a predetermined tonal quality for eliciting preassigned notes. *It is the person himself*" (emphasis added).[14]

GUITAR POETRY'S "SPECTACULAR INDIVIDUALS"

Selecting individual bards for inclusion in an analysis of bardic *lichnosti* is, in some ways, a complicated task. Three major figures—Galich, Okudzhava, and Vysotsky—are almost universally reckoned to tower above guitar poetry's rank and file, for their popularity, for their uniqueness (or recognizability, or unmistakability), and for their sheer talent. It is they, too, who are most often singled out as having become "folk heroes and celebrities" for several generations.[15] Equally often, though, these same criteria are used to demonstrate that Galich, Okudzhava, and Vysotsky are not representative of guitar poetry proper, but are rather entirely individual, sui generis phenomena.[16] Such claims to exceptionalism are underscored by these bards' own assertions of independence from the broader guitar poetry movement. Guitar poetry's paterfamilias, Okudzhava nonetheless maintained a measured distance from, and even pleaded ignorance of, KSP activities, particularly in later years; and he also observed a hierarchy of talent among other guitar poets, marking Vysotsky and Matveyeva as "phenomena" (*yavleniya*) and figures such as Gorodnitsky, Kukin, and Klyachkin as "talented people," but of lesser stature and significance.[17] Vysotsky was less diplomatic, remarking pointedly, "I never took part in the movement of the so-called bards and minstrels . . . Now there are so many bards and minstrels that I don't want to have anything to do with them."[18]

Regardless of whether the members of this bardic triumvirate considered themselves part of the broader guitar poetry movement, however, they had an enormous role in shaping it. Perhaps only Vizbor—who actively promoted the movement through his work on the radio station *Yunost'* (*Youth*) and through articles in the magazine *Krugozor* (*Horizon*), as well as by performing other bards' songs alongside his own during concerts[19]—can challenge them for breadth and depth of influence. Therefore, Galich, Vysotsky, and Okudzhava, as well as Vizbor, will all be treated in detail. In order to present a fuller picture of bardic *lichnosti*, however, the analysis will be rounded out by the inclusion of several other well-known bards belonging to the so-called "second rank" (*bardy vtorogo polyota*).

The "Romantic Bards"

Educated, poised, and full of quiet reserve, Bulat Okudzhava (1924–1997) is a typical representative of the Soviet urban intelligentsia of which, in his words, guitar poetry was the folklore. By extension, Okudzhava's bardic *lichnost'* is that of a restrained and deferential intellectual, with a dignified appearance (his typical onstage "costume" including a collared shirt, sweater, sport jacket, and, later in life, thick glasses), a furrowed brow, and an air of thoughtful concentration. Okudzhava's natural air of gentle abstraction is heightened by frequent admissions that his entry into the public performance of songs was almost accidental, and by his consequent mild bemusement at his songs' popularity with a broader audience. According to

Okudzhava himself, his first song "appeared completely accidentally" and he began to compose others because "[his] friends liked it"; when he had composed five or six songs, "because everything was recorded on tape recorders and circulated," strangers began to invite him to their homes to perform.[20] "Kitchen" concerts among "thirty or so quiet intellectuals" led to other such concerts, and eventually to invitations to perform in public.[21]

But if Okudzhava's songs were well received in intimate settings, his early public performances were not, as his recollections of his first major public appearance reveal:

> At that time, no one was particularly interested in me or [even] knew me. And there I went out onto that enormous stage [in the Moscow House of Cinema], feeling terribly timid, stood in front of some sort of defective microphone, and began to sing one of my songs. Because I was very nervous, obviously, half the words just disappeared—or so it seemed to me. Suddenly someone in the hall cried out, "Vulgarity! [*Poshlost'*!]"; and the group of people sitting around this person began to applaud. I took my guitar and left the stage. That's how my first big public performance was.[22]

Against the backdrop of official Soviet song, Okudzhava explained such negative reactions as follows: "Immediately after 'the apple trees and pear trees burst into bloom,' all of a sudden I came out and started to sing my boring, sad songs. And, of course, that shocked and worried many people."[23] But Okudzhava's popularity grew because, as he described, "I liked to sing about what troubled me . . . and it turned out that others were moved, not because it was brilliant, but just because most songs in vogue before that were official and semiofficial and cold, without a sense of man's fate."[24]

Okudzhava's early public concerts may have carried particular marks of stage fright, but throughout his career his manner of performance remained "tentative and retiring."[25] As a musician, Okudzhava was a passable guitarist who (by his own admission) "knew only three chords" when he began playing and a grand total of seven more than two decades later; and a self-taught composer who "began to think up some sort of melod[ies]—with one finger on the guitar," melodies that were intended only as "accompaniments, really, well, and to muffle the inadequacies of [his] performance a bit."[26] As a singer, Okudzhava was possessed of decidedly questionable talents, in the form of a weak voice of limited range that was at its most pleasant "on a high tenor note" and when Okudzhava sang "piano-pianissimo."[27] Not infrequently, Okudzhava's inexpert tremolo is so pronounced that a critically minded listener might be tempted to accuse him of warbling.

Also a member of the urban intelligentsia, Aleksandr Gorodnitsky (b. 1933) differs substantially from Okudzhava in physical aspect. Gorodnitsky's erect posture and vaguely military bearing are imbued with a virile strength that reflects years spent on geological field expeditions in the Far North (as Yury Vizbor puts it, Gorodnitsky was "not an armchair geologist, but a working geologist")[28] and on oceanological expeditions all over the world. Gorodnitsky's manner on stage is further marked by the fact that, unlike most of the "classic" bards who got their start in the late 1950s or 1960s, he rarely accompanies himself on the guitar. He explains this habit as follows: "my voice is mediocre, my playing is mediocre, and if everything is mediocre, then that's bad."[29] In the absence of a guitar and not being given to dramatic gesticulation, Gorodnitsky carries himself on stage as though he doesn't quite know what to do with his hands.

With respect to vocal qualities, however, Gorodnitsky is not so different from Okuzhava. Gorodnitsky's voice, too, tends toward the insubstantial, though in his case the risky vibrato of Okudzhava's singing is replaced by a certain breathiness. Lacking in resonance, moreover, Gorodnitsky's voice is slightly strained, as though he is perpetually pushing the very limits of his vocal range—even when performing songs such as his now-classic "Atlanty" (1963; "The Atlases") that barely encompass a one-octave span. On the whole, Gorodnitsky sings hesitantly, almost as if each performance is an experiment the outcome of which is uncertain.

In physical appearance and bearing, Yury Vizbor (1934–1984) represents a marked contrast to the urbanity of Okudzhava and the lean vigor of Gorodnitsky. Stocky, bull-necked, and broad-featured, Vizbor projects physical solidity rather than intellectual refinement, his typical onstage garb of suit and tie notwithstanding. Vizbor's physical presence was neither accidental nor affected, stemming from a passion for mountain climbing and other outdoor activities that provided the "stimulus for writing [his] first song and [his] songs in general," and that is amply reflected throughout his oeuvre.[30] With respect to his musical talents, interestingly, Vizbor is distinctive among the better-known bards for being quite unremarkable. His voice is pleasant, if undistinguished; and he neither strains obviously to reach awkward notes nor slips clumsily off key. Likewise, his guitar playing is generally competent and unobtrusive. In keeping with the familiar bardic "humility topos," though, Vizbor openly downplayed his musical abilities. He was adamant that he "did not have any sort of musical education," and that he did not consider himself "to be in some measure competent . . . in questions of music"; and he was prone to telling audiences not to "expect much" either from his guitar playing or from his singing, as his "vocal qualities . . . [never] really exist[ed] in the first place."[31]

By training a teacher of physical education, Yury Kukin (1932–2011) shares with Vizbor a solid athleticism and a penchant for songs on "outdoorsy" themes. With Okudzhava, Kukin shares a certain sense of surprise at his own popularity, attributing his bardic beginnings to the entirely unexpected success of a single song, "Za tumanom" (1964; "For the Mist"), which he wrote on a geological expedition after hearing songs by Gorodnitsky, Okudzhava, Vizbor, and Novella Matveyeva. As Kukin has explained,

> The song got back to Leningrad before I did, and when I returned, someone knocked on my door unexpectedly, hailed me with the title of laureate of the Leningrad Competition of Tourist Song, and invited me to the prizewinners' concert . . . [At the concert] Bulat Okudzhava pushed me out on stage and said: "Now you sing."[32]

Initially Kukin refused to perform in public, because, as he says, he knew how to play the guitar "only in the key of D minor and only on three strings"; and he concedes, furthermore, that he "cannot sing in the 'proper' sense of the word" (in truth, his singing is entirely adequate, even if his voice is slightly flat and nasal).[33] Ultimately, as Kukin summarizes,

> I was taught [to play the guitar] by my geologist friends, [and] I have not superseded my teachers. And I don't have a voice, I never had one, and there is little hope that I ever will have one. But people put me at ease, saying that now, if a person has a guitar, then the worse his voice is, the better. [And so] I began to sing with what I had.[34]

The "Protest Bards"

Among all the bards, Aleksandr Galich (1918 [1919]–1977) stands out for his outspokenness and his biting satire of Soviet life. He also stands out because of his age: a handful of years senior even to Okudzhava, Galich was nearly two decades older than most bards of the Thaw-era wave and a well-respected and longtime member of the official Soviet literary establishment when he turned, somewhat abruptly, to guitar poetry. Neither of these facts went unnoticed in the polemics against him. As journalist Nikolai Meysak fumed in 1968,

> Who is that bowing on stage? He stands out noticeably from the young people: he's probably about fifty. Why would someone "five minutes away from being a grandfather" perform together with lads who are still wet behind the ears [*s mal'chishkami*]? "Galich, Galich," they whisper in the auditorium. Galich? The author of the magnificent play *Taimyr Is Calling You*, the author of the screenplay for the excellent film *Faithful Friends*? In days past an entirely interesting journalist? Him? It is hard to believe it, but, I repeat,

> precisely this entirely grown-up person is hamming it up, deliberately mangling the Russian language. A fact is a fact: Aleksandr Galich, a member of the Writers' Union of the USSR, sings "in the name of idiots."[35]

Poised and almost courtly in demeanor, like the Stanislavsky-trained actor he was, Galich might indeed have seemed out of place among a crowd of young people at a bard festival, whether or not these were the "untidily dressed" youths with shaggy hair and "unpolished shoes" that Meysak imagined them to be.[36]

Galich's manner of performance, something akin to a growling recitative, is yet another distinctive feature of his bardic *lichnost'*. Indeed, if other bards' singing voices can be described as weak, the way Galich performs can only barely be described as "singing." Commanding a "big, plummy baritone" with a rough edge, Galich sings in a manner that Vladimir Frumkin characterizes superbly as "antivocal."[37] Often, it is only the presence of the guitar accompaniment that identifies Galich's performances as songs rather than (somewhat begrudging) poetic recitations. In addition, Galich's singing is so "ruthlessly dismissive of regular rhythms"[38] that, listening to him perform, one can never be entirely confident that he will actually reach the end of a given phrase, let alone the end of the entire song. Numerous pauses in the vocal line, sometimes oddly timed and sometimes awkwardly elongated, are often identifiable as pauses (and not as the song's end) only by a few barely audible and hesitant notes picked out on the guitar. Overall, Galich's performance is strangely reminiscent of the storytelling of an irritated, yet forgetful and easily fatigued, old man.

Yuly Kim (b. 1936) offers an interesting counterpoint to Galich. Like Galich, Kim had a "tail of . . . anti-Soviet songs behind him"; but in contrast to his older colleague, he has also retained what he calls "a certain inborn flippancy . . . in intonation" throughout his career,[39] a puckishness to Galich's Jovian severity. Similarly, in contrast to the depth and gruffness of Galich's voice, Kim's voice is reedy and nasal, but this does nothing to diminish the gusto of his performance. Given this, it seems fitting that one of Kim's best-known songs contains the exhortation to "Sing—even if you have/Neither talent nor a voice/ . . ./It doesn't matter, however you can do it, just sing!"[40] Like other bards, however, Kim is diffident about his musical background and musical talents and also about his own position in the guitar poetry movement as a whole. As Kim describes,

> Without including myself among the founding fathers [of guitar poetry], I am, I suppose, I can consider myself their younger brother, and just like them, I am neither musically literate nor technically proficient at playing. But I do have significantly more chords.[41]

While each bard examined so far is distinctive in some way, it is widely agreed that the most unusual and the most unmistakable of all the bardic voices belongs to Vladimir Vysotsky (1938–1980). If one examines Vysotsky piecemeal, it is difficult to comprehend both his meteoric rise to fame and his lasting "star power." His physical appearance was decidedly unprepossessing; and individually, his creative talents were hardly extraordinary, including a hoarse voice, inexpert guitar playing, and a modest poetic gift that was elevated occasionally to the level of brilliance by gloriously inventive turns of phrase and an ear for linguistic play. Nonetheless, Vysotsky as a whole is generally acknowledged to be a true phenomenon, "something qualitatively new," as his unprecedented popularity attests.[42]

In sharp contrast to the sternness of Galich, or the quiet dignity of Gorodnitsky and Okudzhava, Vysotsky—who "liked to dress in style," and often appeared on stage in a black turtleneck and fashionably tight pants[43]—exuded restless energy and rakish charm. Vysotsky's performance as a White officer in the film *Sluzhili dva tovarishcha* (1968; *Two Comrades Served*) was so charismatic, for example, that according to theatrical director Yury Lyubimov, it was swiftly decreed that Vysotsky should no longer be allowed to play "negative characters [*otritsatel'nye geroi*]" lest audiences, under the influence of Vysotsky's prodigious charms, feel inappropriate sympathy for them.[44] In concert, both Vysotsky's intensity and his urgent desire to connect with his audiences were expressed not just through his songs but also in direct addresses to his listeners, as the following excerpt highlights:

> It would be good to light a candle in the auditorium, so that I could see [people's] eyes . . . one guy with a guitar is going to be standing here in front of you all night, eye to eye . . . In guitar poetry you count on only one thing, on the fact that exactly the same problems bother both you and me, the same human fates, one and the same thoughts. And injustice and human misfortune tear up your soul and rub your nerves raw, just like they do mine . . . In short, everything is reckoned on trust. That is what is needed for guitar poetry: your eyes and ears, my desire to tell you about something, and your desire to listen.[45]

In a similar vein, Vysotsky urged his listeners not to believe anyone who says that "a person comes out on stage just to express himself," because

> that's not true. All of us who play guitar poetry really count on a response from the auditorium. I'm not pretending and I'm not playing up to you, I'm not groveling, because what's the point?! It's stupid! To me the public is people, not [simply] the public.[46]

Vysotsky's compelling need to forge a sense of connection with his listeners is further emphasized by his own suggestion that "it is possible that I need you [the audience] even more than you need me here on stage."[47]

Arguably, Vysotsky's powerful craving to establish a bond with his audiences was reflected as well in the raw force of his singing. Even more than for other bards, the single most significant component of Vysotsky's *lichnost'* is his voice, unmusical and unmistakable, yet undeniably emotionally powerful.[48] Vysotsky's idiosyncratic baritone has been described as "a throaty semi-shout" marked by "permanent hoarseness"; as "'wracked with despair' [and] straining into a scream"; and as an "unforgettable, low, gruffish voice" that was deemed by the Moscow Art Theater studio school to be "unsuitable for stage or screen."[49] Perhaps the most evocative characterization comes from Yuly Kim, though, who refers lyrically to his fellow bard's "Daring, ruined by drink and by smoke/Staggering voice."[50] Indeed, Vysotsky's singing voice is abundantly rich in what Roland Barthes calls "grain," the signifying of which is defined "by the *friction* between music and . . . the language (and not the message at all)" (emphasis in original).[51]

It has been argued that Vysotsky's characteristic hoarseness was not simply a natural trait, that the singer "strenuously worked over his voice" in order to "increase the drama [of his songs] even further"; and also that he emphasized certain sounds (notably the resonant Russian rolled *r* and the voiced velar fricative *kh*) to produce a particular effect.[52] Vysotsky himself maintained that this was not the case, however. On the contrary, while admitting that he had "broken [his voice] by smoking, drinking and shouting," Vysotsky claimed that his intensified "r-r-r" and "kh-kh" were

> not an added effect. I sing the way I know how. Even more, I don't sing . . . If you want to hear singing, then you'll have to go to a variety stage concert or to the opera. I write poems, which I perform to guitar accompaniment. I come up with a simple melody in order to make reception easier for you. But as far as the "r-r" and "kh-kh" are concerned—that is just how I can do it.[53]

Nonetheless, these characteristic vocal qualities are far more apparent in his later performances than in his earlier ones. In his most extreme moments, as when performing signature songs like "Okhota na volkov" (1968; "The Wolf-Hunt") and "Koni priveredlivye" (1972; "The Capricious Horses"), Vysotsky possesses a "hysterical intensity."[54] But it is precisely these qualities that transform Vysotsky into what Kelefa Sanneh (describing Bob Dylan) dubs "a brilliant croaker who makes you feel sorry for all those hacks content to simply carry a tune."[55] Vysotsky's guitar playing (on a badly tuned guitar) was scarcely more conventional, and he himself admitted that he played "very primitively sometimes, even most of the time."[56]

During Vysotsky's lifetime, the relative lack of reliable biographical information conferred upon him, for the Soviet public at large, an air of mystery and romance that was underscored by what little information *was* available. Vysotsky's "irresponsible, extravagant lifestyle," in particular his marriage to French actress Marina Vlady, made him seem something of a daring rebel.[57] As Vysotsky's son Nikita has observed, people "loved the concept of [Vysotsky]," they loved the image that was created in his songs, regardless of whether this image accorded with his factual biography.[58]

THE BARDIC PERSONA: THE INTERSECTION OF *LICHNOST'* AND *ISKRENNOST'*

Diverse though the *lichnosti* of these various bards are, they nonetheless share certain fundamental characteristics: "bad singing," unpolished guitar playing, "everyman" attire, and a bemused or self-deprecating attitude toward both talent and fame.[59] In a general sense, these characteristics set the bards apart from the canonical model of the Soviet performing star: from the "pompous, stiff" aspect and "smooth and stiff public intonation" of officially promoted singers like Iosif Kobzon, Eduard Khil', Valery Leont'yev, and others.[60] These characteristics of bardic *lichnost'* stand in marked contrast to the rigid posture, immaculate formal attire, and gravity-defying coiffure of the young Kobzon; to the jovially toothy smile and oleaginous charm of Khil'; and, in the 1970s, to the "foot-tapping jollity" of Lev Leshchenko, for example.[61] Likewise, the largely unadorned settings and solo performances of guitar poetry contrast with the elaborate staging typical of the officially approved variety stage (*estrada*), with its massed choirs and orchestras and its complicated backdrops.

More specifically, the cornerstone characteristics of bardic *lichnost'* helped to forge a particular atmosphere of "friendly disposition and mutual trust,"[62] independent of the venue in which any given performance took place. In informal settings—a cramped Soviet kitchen, a packed train car, a circle around a campfire—physical proximity corresponded to and reinforced a sense of psychological proximity between bard and audience. As Liudmila Alexeyeva describes in her memoirs of the Thaw period, bards' "performances were too intimate to be called concerts," while a bard "did not have fans; he had friends."[63] In more formal, public settings, a bard may have been separated physically from his audience by his position on stage, yet a sense of psychological proximity nonetheless suffused concerts in such venues. In part, this sense of spiritual kinship could be fostered by a "lack of fit" between performer and setting: alone on stage, with little other than a guitar, a couple of microphones, and a chair, the bard could seem oddly out of place, just an ordinary person, "one of us," who appears on stage as if by chance. Both Okudzhava's own description of performing on an "enormous stage," standing "in front of some sort of defective microphone," and Vysotsky's pre-concert caveat that "one guy with a guitar is going to be standing here in front of you all night, eye to eye"[64] suggest that even major bards were keenly aware of this "lack of fit."

In addition, though, psychological proximity was forged through interaction between bard and audience. Vysotsky disliked the "clicking" of tape recorders, and disliked being able to see people recording him, specifically because such distractions spoiled the atmosphere in the auditorium, which was "not easy to create" and which, as he stressed, he and his audience "create[d] mutually [*oboyudno*]"; further, he emphasized the importance of a concert's atmosphere above all else, observing that "the most important thing [during a concert] is contact."[65] Yet Vysotsky also recognized that people's desire to record concerts stemmed from just such contact, from the friendly atmosphere of guitar poetry itself: "Guitar poetry is a friendly art. That is why people want to record us on tape recorders . . . People want to hear [us] again."[66] Moreover, Vysotsky attributed the popularity of guitar poetry to its particular aura, observing that the genre

> needs an audience, needs an interlocutor. It seems to me that the reason for its popularity lies in this very amicable orientation [*vot v takom druzhestvennom nastroye*], in the opportunity to converse with people in normal, human language [*normal'nym, chelovecheskim yazykom*], counting on trust in return.[67]

In similar terms, Vysotsky also characterized guitar poetry as "a form of conversation with an audience," attributing its popularity to "a craving for a kind of normal conversation in songs" and to "a yearning for simple human intonation."[68] For Vysotsky, guitar poetry was such a "living thing [*zhivoye delo*]" that, as he expressed it, "you instantly become one organism with the people sitting in the auditorium," and "the kind of pulse that organism has . . . depends on you and me."[69] Though perhaps less effusive in his declarations, Okudzhava viewed guitar poetry analogously, as "one of the means by which people interact with one another."[70]

To foster contact, Okudzhava, Vysotsky, Vizbor, and numerous other bards encouraged their audiences to send notes to them during concerts, to which they would respond, often at great length. Vizbor offered the following invitation to one audience, for example: "If you come up with any questions for me, I will answer your notes with pleasure. Whatever questions there may be—please feel free"; in strikingly similar terms, Vysotsky remarked to an audience, "If something interests you, ask me, please. I will answer your questions with pleasure."[71] Likewise, Okudzhava urged audience members to interact with him during a concert as follows: "Please send your questions [up] here. We will have a chat [*budem obshchat'sya*]. As everyone knows, interaction is cleansing [*obshcheniye ochishchayet*]"; furthermore, Okudzhava observed elsewhere that "one can judge the quality of the audience by the number of notes" sent up on stage.[72]

Such interaction, and the psychological proximity between bard and audience it both represented and encouraged, helped to create the characteristic atmosphere of guitar poetry, which was typified by "immediacy, intimacy, and sincerity [*iskrennost'*]."[73] Among these qualities, sincerity acquires almost totemic significance, being invoked frequently as a defining characteristic and "spiritual core" of guitar poetry; as the single most significant feature distinguishing guitar poetry from Soviet mass song and the variety stage; and as the key to the popularity of individual bards and specific songs.[74] References to *iskrennost'* are so widespread in discussions of guitar poetry, in fact, that some contend the term has become meaningless.[75]

In the broader context of popular music studies and reception, the corollary of *iskrennost'* is "authenticity," a term that is maligned as widely as it is employed. According to Allan Moore, "authenticity"

> has frequently been used to define a *style* of writing or performing, particularly anything associated with the practices of the singer/songwriter, where attributes of intimacy . . . and immediacy . . . tend to connote authenticity . . . It is used to bestow integrity, or its lack, on a performer, such that an "authentic" performer exhibits realism, lack of pretence, or the like.[76]

While acknowledging that such usages are problematic, Moore argues cogently that authenticity need not be abandoned as meaningless if we reconstrue it as a quality that is "ascribed, not inscribed"—that is, as a marker of how we, as listeners, respond to a performer and his or her music, rather than as something that "inhere[s] in . . . [a particular] combination of musical sounds."[77] Teasing out different types of ascription, Moore offers a tripartite model of authenticity that focuses not on songs themselves but rather on audiences' responses to performers: first-person authenticity (or "authenticity of expression"), second-person authenticity (or "authenticity of experience"), and third-person authenticity (or "authenticity of execution").

Moore concedes that, in practice, the divisions between these three types of authenticity are not always clear-cut. Nonetheless, his basic model—and its underlying question of "who, rather than what, is being authenticated" by a performance[78]—provides a fruitful framework for analyzing the interplay between bard and audience in guitar poetry. All three of Moore's subtypes of authenticity may be brought to bear in discussing guitar poetry, but the first subtype has particular relevance here.[79] According to Moore's definition, "authenticity of expression" arises when a performer "succeeds in conveying the impression that his/her utterance is one of integrity, that it represents an attempt to communicate in an unmediated form with an audience."[80] Emphasizing integrity and unmediated communication, authenticity of expression neatly weaves together the characteristic trilogy of *iskrennost'*, intimacy, and immediacy of guitar poetry's atmosphere with the widespread perception of songs themselves as intimate conversations with like-minded people.

This particular emphasis on guitar poetry as conversation suggests that, on a fundamental level, the performance of guitar poetry authenticates the bard not just as a performer, but also as "one of us": through guitar poetry, bard and audience become *svoi*. Within the context of a performance, whether formal or informal, bard and audience together create a "laid-back atmosphere, an uninhibited, friendly, free atmosphere" (to quote Vysotsky once again).[81] The importance of the audience in creating this atmosphere is underscored, for example, by the failure of Okudzhava's first big public performance (before an unreceptive audience); by Vysotsky's frequent complaints about the disruptive effects of listeners who attend concerts just "to record, and . . . [who] are not interested in what is happening here [in the auditorium] at a particular moment"; and also by Vysotsky's observation that "depending on the auditorium, on the mood of people in the auditorium, . . . [he] could change the meaning of a song a bit."[82]

Bards' contributions to creating guitar poetry's atmosphere derived from the key features of bardic *lichnost'* discussed above, among which voice and accompaniment deserve special attention. Weaknesses or flaws of voice and accompaniment in guitar poetry not only contrasted with the smooth professionalism of the Soviet variety stage. More importantly, like bards' willingness to respond to audience members' questions, such imperfections served as hallmarks of immediacy and intimacy. Bards' lack of polish offered confirmation, as it were, that both the content and the style of their self-expression through song were transmitted directly to the audience—unfiltered and unfettered by official restrictions on who could perform, what they could perform, and how they could do it.

Because official celebrities like Kobzon, Khil', and others were manufactured by tightly controlled mechanisms that proscribed as well as prescribed creative activity and public behavior, imperfections of voice and of instrumental accompaniment became unmistakable hallmarks of difference and of independent standing. According to Vizbor, such independence was the very essence and meaning of guitar poetry. Responding to a listener's question about the "meaning of the amateur [song] movement as a whole," Vizbor expressed the following views:

> Its meaning lies in the fact that the movement exists. It is impossible to prohibit it, or to stop it, or to somehow push it forward energetically. This is impossible, too. People are drawn to creative work [*k tvorchestvu*] as such, in general. Its meaning lies in that. Try it yourself—compose something, and you will see that it is very interesting.[83]

In similar fashion, Vizbor attributed guitar poetry's popularity to its independence, to the fact that "it is not popularized by anyone. It exists of its own accord [*sama po sebe*]."[84] As Gerald Smith observes, in a society where cultural resources (like any others) are state-controlled, independent activity of many kinds "is most strongly in evidence in those aspects of human communication where there is least mediation between artist and audience, producer and consumer."[85] For guitar poetry's "publics of *svoi*" (to borrow Alexei Yurchak's term) the independent and unmediated quality of guitar poetry authenticated its expressers, the relative absence of outside controls acting as a barometer of *iskrennost'*, intimacy, and immediacy.

In this sense, guitar poetry is proof par excellence of Erving Goffman's assertion that "individuals, as pieces of expressive equipment, are more effective in some ways than non-human parts of the setting" (220). Massed choruses, elaborate arrangements, and the "stiff, pompous" aspect of variety stage singers like Kobzon are components of a decidedly dramatized type of performance. In Goffmanian terms, these might be called "contrived performances," which the audience "tend[s] to see as something painstakingly pasted together, one false item on another, since there is no reality to which the items of behavior could be a directed response" (70). As the emphasis on *iskrennost'* and interaction suggests, for its adherents guitar poetry exemplified the opposite pole, offering a kind of performance that (as Goffman describes) the audience tends to see as "something not purposely put together at all, being an unintentional product of the individual's response to the facts in his situation" (70).

GUITAR POETRY AND THE ART OF CREATING "BACKSTAGE"

Framed in terms of authenticity, the nature and significance of guitar poetry's intimate and unmediated interaction can be analyzed readily with the help of Goffman's concepts of regions and region behavior. In Goffman's framework, a region is defined as "any place that is bounded to some degree by barriers to perception" (106). The place where a particular performance takes place becomes, for the duration of that performance, the "front region"; while the "back region" or "backstage" is a place, "relative to a given performance, where the impression fostered by the performance is knowingly contradicted as a matter of course" and where "suppressed facts make an appearance" (112). The dividing lines between these regions tend to be quite clear, the attention to decor, order, and proper maintenance of the front region contrasting with the "relatively unprepossessing" nature of backstage; utilitarian in nature and consequently largely untended, certain spaces (back lanes and alleys, service entrances, storerooms, and "behind the counter" areas) almost invariably constitute back regions (123–24). As Goffman argues, the crucial feature of back regions is that their humble nature, "the very fact that an important effect is not striven for," has an impact on individuals' behavior, "set[ting] the tone for interaction, [and] leading those who find themselves [backstage] to act as if they were on familiar terms with one another in all matters" (125–26).

Recalling the unassuming private and semi-private settings in which guitar poetry arose, one may argue that guitar poetry came into being on the "backstage" of Soviet culture. Though the genre was ultimately drawn into more public settings, bards and their audiences nonetheless managed to preserve the confidental, domestic intonations and the amicable, unpretentious atmosphere of kitchen and campfire performances to a significant extent: no matter what the setting, as Vysotsky observed, "there is no flashiness, elevation, staginess, estrangement from the auditorium—[there are] no footlights" in guitar poetry.[86] Just as bards and their audiences picked up on this peculiarity of guitar poetry, so, too, did observers from within the Soviet cultural establishment. Musicologist Arnol'd Sokhor noted, for example, that

> when someone sings such a song out loud or to himself (but in all cases for himself), what is important to him is not the correspondence of the melody directly to the words, but to the mood of the given moment, to which the words correspond in turn . . . While we are theorizing [about this], amateur authors are using this peculiarity of the genre widely.[87]

But while Sokhor held a cautiously favorable attitude toward guitar poetry, appreciating bards' "good lyrics" in spite of their "unoriginal music,"[88] other official critics were not so sanguine. Despite praising Okudzhava's lyrics, for example, composer Matvey Blanter scoffed at bards' music ("excuse me, what kind of music is that?").[89] Even when bards' lyrics were viewed as acceptable, moreover, problems of guitar poetry's "domestic sound" and "everyday intonations" remained vexing, as the following discussion illustrates:

> The question is as follows: striving for an everyday, even somewhat "domestic" sound in song, and using for that purpose various *everyday* intonations, can the composer rise above them, transform them with the strength of his

> talent and mastery? . . . The problem is a *musical* one; one cannot hide behind the expressiveness of the lyric text.[90] (emphasis in original)

Even when guitar poetry's lyrics were not seen as a threat, that is, its "domestic" quality and "everyday" intonations, its intimacy and immediacy, were.

Reconstruing this intimacy and immediacy with the help of Goffman's terminology, we can interpret guitar poetry as the art of creating "backstage," of creating a space in which "suppressed facts make an appearance." In turn, the "atmosphere of friendly disposition," the sense of mutual understanding and trust fostered during a performance, can be construed in terms of the invocation of a "backstage style." This style is interwoven into the bardic *lichnost'* itself, both through qualities of voice and accompaniment (and open admissions of the inadequacy of these) and also through direct, "confidential" addresses to the audience. As Goffman observes, "by invoking a backstage style, individuals can transform any region into a backstage" (128–29). Thus, bards and audiences were able to create an atmosphere of "friendly dialogue" during a performance, irrespective of the setting in which it took place. Following from this, any setting in which guitar poetry was performed—from kitchen to concert stage—became, for the duration of that performance, backstage.

It must be noted, however, that the definition of a particular space as a front region or as backstage is relative, referring (as Goffman stresses) to "the function that the place happens to serve at that time for the given performance" (127–28). In effect, what occurs in guitar poetry is a realignment of regions and a redefinition of the "teams" or "set[s] of individuals who cooperate in staging a single routine" (79). Members of a team are said to be linked by a bond of "familiarity," forced to share certain knowledge and "to define one another as persons 'in the know'" in order to create a particular impression for their audience (82–83). In order to create the particular atmosphere of guitar poetry, in other words, bards and their audiences had to define one another as "persons in the know," as *svoi*.

Within the context of a single performance, the individual bard performs (in the front region) for a particular audience. But through the mode and manner of his performance—through deliberately "not striv[ing] for" an important effect, and by otherwise "invoking a backstage style"—the bard makes the active, responsive members of the audience part of his own team, makes them *svoi;* and, correspondingly, he transforms the entire region of a given performance into a back region in relation to those who are not "in the know," who are not *svoi.* Thus the stage upon which a bard performs in a House of Culture can be characterized as the front region of his performance to responsive members of the audience; but the entire hall can be characterized as the backstage of *another* performance, the performance presented by bard and audience *together* to outsiders (non-fans, government functionaries, representatives of security agencies, etc.). It is out of this particular relationship between bard and audience—teammates, co-performers, *svoi*—that the particular communicative nature of guitar poetry arises.

GUITAR POETRY AS METACOMMUNICATION

As the foregoing analysis reveals, the closeness between performer and audience in guitar poetry at once derives from and contributes to the fact that the genre is a mode of interaction as well as a form of entertainment. From this, in turn, derives the strongly metacommunicative function (Gregory Bateson's term) of guitar poetry's lyrics themselves. The intonations, gestures, and facial expressions that performance adds to the language of guitar poetry not only influence songs' reception, but also establish or "convey something about the relationship between communicator and audience."[91] By virtue of these qualities, guitar poetry participates in a mode of communication that is characteristic of true (primary) orality, despite the fact that it was a product of an overwhelmingly literate society.

It is not infrequently observed that there is little truly novel in guitar poetry—that, for example, most bards were not "interested to any great extent in formal or linguistic experimentation"; that many songs were cobbled together from an "uncomplicated collection of stock phrases"; and that many bards' melodic compositions were limited to "a single motif" or to a very limited number of chords.[92] But such stereotypes about guitar poetry can be seen in a new light if we consider another feature of the communicative model typical of primary orality, namely the fact that familiar or formulaic expressions (such as "sayings, clichés, proverbs and so on") are used as ways of signifying shared knowledge.[93]

In guitar poetry, the use of familiar phrases, both linguistic and musical, in new contexts or with new intonation serves as a kind of shorthand by which members of the guitar poetry movement identify themselves and recognize one another. In Goffman's terms, such familiar or formulaic expressions constitute one kind of "inside secret," the possessing of which "marks an individual as being a member of a group and helps the group feel separate and different from those individuals who are not 'in the know'" (142). Aleksandr Gorodnitsky's reference to guitar poetry as an "identifying code," cited above, anticipates just such a formal analysis.

In this oral communicative model, furthermore, a premium is placed on achieving "a sense of identification with the speaker or characters in the spoken discourse": it is, in fact, this sense of identification that is equated with "knowing."[94] Once again, the foregoing discussion of the importance of intimacy and immediacy, of *lichnost'* and *svoi*, demonstrates the extent to which identification between bard and audience was of paramount importance in guitar poetry. Thanks to technology, however, both the inside secrets carried in guitar poetry's language, music, and intonation, and also the sense of identification with bards and their lyric masks, were accessible even to the multitudes of fans who knew bards and their songs mainly through *magnitizdat* recordings.[95] Yet even indirect oral communication helped to reinforce the role of guitar poetry as social interaction, because even such knowledge of particular bards and their songs became a hallmark of belonging to what has been called variously the "KSP State [*Gosudarstvo KSP*]" and the "amazing country of the KSP."[96] This "amazing country," and the issues of reception, identity creation, and community-building that are intermingled in it, will be the focus of the next chapter.

Chapter Four

The "KSP State": Audience Reception, Self-Fashioning, and "Conversations Between Friends"

INEFFABLE *LICHNOST'* WAS both a defining component of guitar poetry and one of its chief products. A fundamental duality of *lichnost'* in discourse about guitar poetry mapped onto a larger discourse of *lichnost'* in the post-Stalin period. In its official variants, this larger discourse saw subtle competition for currency between *lichnost'* as spectacular individual (a status attainable only by the few) and *lichnost'* as individuality (a characteristic inherent in everyone). In guitar poetry, *lichnost'* identified specific bards, "spectacular individuals," whose talents and personal charisma elevated them above the broad mass of amateur singer-songwriters. Yet in this same context, *lichnost'* was also an abstract quality or force that was "liberated" by guitar poetry; and this second type of *lichnost'* was accessible to anyone, with the help of "bad singing" and a guitar.

Building on the preceding analysis of individual bardic *lichnosti* and their role in fashioning guitar poetry into a means of (meta)communication among *svoi,* this chapter examines the role of bardic *lichnosti* in promoting a broader ideal of *lichnost'*. Particular attention will be paid to patterns of influence, to accounts of how particular bards encouraged others—whether intentionally or not—to fashion their selves, their lives, and their values through and around guitar poetry. In turn, this discussion will help to illuminate the perils (from an official standpoint) inherent in guitar poetry's potency as an agent of self-fashioning, irrespective of the specific characteristics of *lichnost'* that were being fashioned.

Much of this analysis will concentrate on the activities of Clubs of Amateur Song, because KSP activities represented an important forum for the flowering of both individual bardic talents and *lichnost'*. However, the fact that Clubs of Amateur Song never operated entirely free of official interference illustrates the extent to which they were a marginal zone for both creative activity and individual self-fashioning. Similarly, the heterogeneous views and values espoused and expressed by KSP members underscore the extent to which both the individual *lichnosti* and the ideal of *lichnost'* fostered through guitar poetry were neither unambiguously "conformist" nor unambiguously "oppositional" in nature.

LICHNOSTI NURTURING *LICHNOST'*

The interactions described in the previous chapter suggest that in guitar poetry, communication between bard and audience was not perceived by either party as a one-way process, but rather one of mutual engagement. In understanding this process, some of Alessandro Duranti's observations on "the audience as co-author" in verbal communication may be brought to bear. According to Duranti, "speaker and audience are equals . . . because their roles are interchangeable" (the speaker one moment may become the listener the next) and also because "every act of speaking is directed to and must be ratified by an audience."[1] Adapting Duranti's observations to the case of guitar poetry, we may argue that "ratification" took place through the broad-scale consumption and spontaneous redistribution of songs that were, to borrow Vysotsky's description, "intended for . . . close friends."[2] Such redistribution (through secondhand live performance and via *magnitizdat*) may have "deprived listeners of a true picture of the authorship" of songs and even delayed recognition of particular bards' talents,[3] but it also underscores the extent to which songs were accepted as "their own," or ratified, by bards' audiences.

Continuing with this Durantian interpretation, we may argue that bard and audience became equal because active engagement from both was required in order to generate the characteristic atmosphere of guitar poetry; and because ultimately, their places became interchangeable. Perhaps the most basic way in which audiences "changed places" with bards was through the common, informal practice of passing a guitar from person to person around a table or a campfire (*gitara po krugu*). A similar interchange between bard and audience was possible at more formal concerts, too. Introducing the first concert in the 1965 Leningrad series "Youth, Song, Guitar" ("Molodost', pesnya, gitara"), for example, Vladimir Frumkin commented as follows:

> We hope that the goal of these evenings will be achieved: and that both sides—professional and amateur authors—will draw out for themselves much of value, [much that is] fresh. And surely you, the viewers and listen-

ers, will be none the worse off for it, either. Incidentally, not just viewers and listeners; we were very pleased by the telephone calls that have come in over the past few days. A series ticket-holder rings up and asks: "And could we perform, too?" In truth, it was not entirely clear what you wanted to present—poetry, songs, or some sort of words, critiques, analyses. But I must say that you can present anything at all.[4]

Frumkin's comments thus speak to the fact that bards' audiences were "not *just* viewers and listeners" (emphasis added), but rather that they could be active participants in a performance in the most literal sense—even when, as was the case on this particular evening, the list of invited guests included popular and well-known figures like Yevgeny Klyachkin, Boris Poloskin, Valentin Vikhorev, and Aleksandr Dulov. In general terms, Frumkin's comments highlight the fact that, even in a concert hall[5] the boundary between bard and audience was not fixed and impermeable. Returning to a Goffmanian analysis, it can be argued that just as the "backstage" space of guitar poetry was dependent on the context of a particular performance, so, too, were the individual roles of bard and audience.

A description of the same concert by A. Sagalovich, a visiting Moscow KSP member, demonstrates that the context-dependent nature of individual roles was as true for those on stage as it was for those in the hall: "Frumkin opened the series. He presented the comrades [*tovarishchey*] sitting on stage and explained that not everyone would sing during this concert, [but] that he had seated them on stage in order to create an informal atmosphere."[6] As Sagalovich's description demonstrates, the distinction between bard and audience could be a purely nominal one. Moreover, this description underscores the fact that deliberate blurring of the boundaries between bard and audience—whether by seating non-performing (listening, watching) bards on stage, by encouraging audience members to perform, or through less direct means—played a crucial role in fostering the intimate and informal atmosphere that is widely cited as a crucial, perhaps even defining, component of guitar poetry itself.

Instances of bards and audiences literally and metaphorically "changing places" during formal concerts are certainly significant; but the direct influence of particular bards in encouraging others to express themselves through guitar poetry can be identified as a still more dramatic type of "changing places." Many among the first- and second-rank bards acknowledge that hearing other bards prompted them to begin composing and singing their own songs, with Okudzhava and Vizbor being particularly influential in this regard. For example, Vysotsky often explained that he began writing songs (which he persistently referred to as "poems, performed to guitar accompaniment") because

> one day I suddenly heard a tape recorder (at that time they were really bad) . . . of good quality! And then I suddenly heard a pleasant voice, melodies, and lyrics that were remarkable by the standards of the day, which I already knew—it was Bulat (Okudzhava). And suddenly I understood that the impression of lyrics can be strengthened with a musical instrument and a melody. I tried my hand at it right away, took up a guitar right away, as soon as lyrics began to come into my head.[7]

For Yury Kukin, Okudzhava provided a literal push into public peformance at the Leningrad Competition of Tourist Song. Both Okudzhava and other bards gave Kukin a metaphorical push into songwriting as well, though. As Kukin recounts,

> I ended up on a [fieldwork] expedition, [and] there people sang me songs by Okudzhava, Matveyeva, Vizbor, Yakusheva . . . I took it all on board [*vsyo osvoil*], and because I had a good grounding in jazz, I wrote a song myself, as a test, "For the Mist." I thought it up as I went . . . In the end, I wrote a heap of songs. Because I filled up on [*naslushalsya*] Vizbor, Okudzhava, Gorodnitsky, Matveyeva.[8]

Boris Almazov's account of his own bardic beginnings is framed in very similar terms. He began playing the guitar as a teenager in the early 1960s, in part under the influence of an ex-convict named Kostik who came to live in the communal flat shared by the Almazov family and who "played the guitar, having picked one up somewhere along the way."[9] As Almazov recalls, "a couple of weeks later they caught him red-handed [*vzyali na karmane*] and put him in jail again. He disappeared from my life, having fostered in me the firm conviction that I would learn to play the guitar if it killed me."[10] But while Kostik the ex-con inspired Almazov to play the guitar, it was Okudzhava who inspired him to turn his hand to songwriting:

> I remember [Okudzhava's] first concert as a phenomenal success. Though he has talked about a flop . . . I don't remember a flop. I remember success! Tremendous [success]. As far as I was concerned, Okudzhava stunned me for the rest of my life.
>
> A few weeks later . . . my first song appeared, a sort of romance about a fireplace and a dog. Happily, that is all I remember of it.[11]

Acknowledging that Okudzhava's first concert represented a turning point in his own life, Almazov also describes Okudzhava's influence in far broader terms. For Almazov, Okudzhava and his songs defined an entire era:

> And with that memorable concert my life began to turn in a completely different direction. And not just mine: the era of Okudzhava had begun. Within that era Galich and Vysotsky and Kim, and hundreds of us . . . got along easily together . . . The music—what could be heard out of every window where people had a tape recorder—was Okudzhava's songs. Vysotsky started roaring and croaking much later.[12]

Significantly, this description carries clear implications that Okudzhava influenced far more than Almazov's creative activities, in fact changing the entire course of his life.

Interestingly, though, it is not Okudzhava whom Almazov credits as the inspiration for guitar poetry as a mass phenomenon, but rather Aleksandr Gorodnitsky. If Almazov notes that Okudzhava's name (alongside those of Sakharov and Solzhenitsyn) was a kind of "password" repeated by the intelligentsia of the 1960s, he depicts Gorodnitsky as a poster boy, of sorts, for that same generation:

> Aleksandr Gorodnitsky is the gold standard [*etalon*], patriarch, and beginning of mass guitar poetry . . . What's more, the very image of a young fellow in a checked shirt with a guitar and a rucksack on his back—the symbol of the '60s—that is a photograph of Gorodnitsky, Poloskin, and also Kukin, Vikhorev, [Vitaly] Seynov, Genkin, and tens of others like us.[13]

Like Kukin and Almazov, Yuly Kim has acknowledged the influence of a number of bards, including Galich, Vizbor, and Vysotsky, on his own songs. Kim has suggested that "the tragic paradoxes of our time . . . which rang out already, from Vizbor, from Galich" influenced his decision to begin writing politically tinged songs, for example, and he has also remarked that Galich's influence on him was "direct and incontrovertible."[14] Similarly, Kim notes that Vysotsky's "extremely funny song-fairy tales" were a source of inspiration to him as well.[15] The influence of both Galich and Vysotsky is readily apparent, not least, in Kim's stylizations or parodies of their works and also in songs he wrote to melodies borrowed from them.[16]

For his part, Vizbor defers to the influence of Vladimir Krasnovsky (1933–1982) who, like Vizbor himself, was a driving force behind the MGPI student song circle:

> Himself a self-taught guitarist, [Krasnovsky] taught me to play the guitar, Ada Yakusheva, Ira Oltarzhevskaya [as well]. Thanks to his light touch [*s yego lyogkoy ruki*], Yura Koval', Boris Vakhnyuk, [and] Yuly Kim began to play the guitar . . . He was one of the founders of amateur song in that free form in which it exists as a phenomenon of popular [*narodnogo*] art.[17]

But where Vizbor credits Krasnovsky with teaching many future bards to play the guitar, and where Almazov views Gorodnitsky as the initiator of guitar poetry as a mass phenomenon, for many others it is Vizbor himself who set the tone, figuratively and literally, for an entire generation. Yuly Kim argues, for example, that while

> someone else's music turned out a little better, someone else's verse was a little more precise, but still, it was in him, in Vizbor, that everything came together, that everything was reflected and expressed so fully and universally, like in no one else. And our speech, and our humor, and our way of thinking and living. He set the tone for many guitars. And not just guitars . . . In the biography of our generation a minimum of three years were his, Vizbor years . . . When we sang mainly his songs. When . . . we were all *vizbors* a little, each one of us was a *vizbor* in his own way.[18]

As Kim concludes, "the youth of an entire generation was defined by . . . quotations" from Vizbor's songs.[19] Similarly, Lev Anninsky asserts that Vizbor was "the first person (on the cusp of the '50s–'60s) who walked up to a microphone in front of an audience and demonstrated that it was possible to sing poetry, accompanying oneself on the guitar"; and, further, that Vizbor "gave his generation a voice," because "from his voice . . . the craze began, and minstrels of successive generations appeared."[20]

Similar claims are made regarding the breadth and depth of Okudzhava's impact. In addition to directly inspiring Vysotsky, Kukin, Almazov, and others,[21] Okudzhava is credited with having influenced an entire generation or more through his songs. As early as 1967, for example, bard Aleksandr Dol'sky offered the following assessment of Okudzhava's significance:

> It all began with the fact that, at a certain point, the song lyrics of some professional composers stopped satisfying listeners, especially young ones. B[ulat] Okudzhava appeared. Everything was very simple. Three chords on an out-of-tune guitar, but such a rich world of images, philosophical depth and, in addition to that, clarity and naturalness! . . . Obviously, many authors who are now active got their start independently of Okudzhava, but he had an influence on the majority of them, and, particularly significantly, it was with him, really, that audiences' interest in such songs appeared.[22]

Dol'sky's observations that Okudzhava was highly influential both within bardic circles and in popularizing guitar poetry to a broad audience represent early examples of very common responses to the bard.

With the passage of time, though, more and more commentators began to stress Okudzhava's role as both focal point and spokesman for the interests and concerns of his audiences. In the mid-1980s, for example, one commentator remarked that for the generation born in the 1930s and early 1940s, "Okudzhava was the main voice of their sorrows and joys, their poetic vision of reality."[23] Similarly, in a posthumous tribute to his longtime friend, Zurab Kazbek-Kaziyev stresses Okudzhava's particular significance for the intelligentsia, observing that they "received Bulat as one of their own" and that, during concerts, they "were waiting for something from him . . . waiting for him to say everything for them."[24] In her reminiscences, El'mira Kotlyar speaks to Okudzhava's particular significance for ordinary Muscovites: as Okudzhava sang, "the 'Moscow ant' found his voice. And thousands of 'Moscow ants' listened to his songs like a revelation about themselves."[25] For Mikhail Aizenberg, "the sixties began . . . as if with a bell, with [Okudzhava's] guitar fingering [*po yego gitarnomu pereboru*]."[26] Like Kazbek-Kaziyev, Kotlyar, and others, Aizenberg remarks on the powerful effect Okudzhava's songs had on audiences, recalling that "a kind of trance came over all kinds of people, listening to Okudzhava's songs for the first time" and, through these songs, "find[ing] out something significant about themselves, about life."[27]

As Aleksandr Gorodnitsky argues, Okudzhava's influence, and his concomitant stature as the progenitor of guitar poetry, resulted not just from "the scope of his enormous poetic talent," but also

> from the scope of his personality [*lichnosti*], and from the fact that in his songs he was one of the first to replace the pronoun *we*, all too customary for the generations of Soviet youth raised under the Stalinist drumbeat, with the pronoun *I* . . .
>
> It is directly thanks to Bulat Okudzhava's "chamber" works that . . . an individually realized person, a personality [*lichnost'*], "a Moscow ant" appeared in sung (and not just sung) poetry, who showed himself to be an individual and inimitable *I*.[28]

Particularly notable here is the specific emphasis on *lichnost':* according to Gorodnitsky's argument, Okudzhava's own *lichnost'* contributed significantly to his influence, while his songs contributed significantly to the renaissance of *lichnost'* (the "individual and inimitable *I*") in Soviet society at large.

From such accounts of the influence enjoyed by various bards, several important trends emerge. As noted above, the significance of *lichnost'* is emphasized repeatedly: bards' influence is attributed partly to the power of their particular *lichnosti,* and their songs are credited with reviving and encouraging the broader notion of *lichnost'*. Assertions that bards became "spokesmen" for particular groups or generations, effectively speaking on behalf of others or voicing widely held thoughts and concerns through their songs, are similarly widespread. Returning to the earlier discussion of authenticity, these persistent assertions that bards "spoke for" their audiences can be characterized in terms of Allan Moore's category of "second-person authenticity" (or "authenticity of experience"), which arises "when a performer succeeds in conveying the impression to the listener that that listener's experience of life is being validated, that the music is 'telling it like it is' for them."[29]

Guitar poetry became a mass phenomenon in the Soviet Union not just because many people listened to bards' songs, though. In "speaking for" their audiences, bards also encouraged audiences to speak and act for themselves through guitar poetry, as the patterns of influence described above demonstrate. Thus, the crux of the broader guitar poetry movement can be analyzed as the interplay between different types of authenticity: songs' content transformed Okudzhava and others into spokespeople for their audiences (highlighting the importance of authenticity of experience), while their low-tech and accessible form (grounded in "bad singing" and mediocre guitar playing) encouraged those same audiences to "change places" and become bards themselves. Recognizable *lichnosti* like Okudzhava and Vizbor thus helped to authenticate the aspiration of *lichnost'*, the possibility for any audience member to explore his or her own individual identity with the help of stripped-down, readily accessible artistic means.

Against this general backdrop, it is interesting to note which bardic *lichnosti* played the dominant role in fostering self-fashioning, particularly in light of the contemporaneous official obsession with *vospitaniye* and concurrent concerns about the "pernicious" effect that guitar poetry might have on Soviet youth. While opinions are divided on the issue of which bard is responsible for "launching" guitar poetry as a mass phenomenon, in the present context establishing definitive preeminence for any one bard is far less important than noting underlying continuities within seemingly disparate viewpoints. Notably, all of the bards reckoned to have had the most widespread influence on other bards and on audiences more generally are of the largely apolitical "romantic" cast. While Vysotsky remarked that he had "such a colossal number of imitators [*podrazhateli*]" that he "sometimes g[ot] confused—is that me [singing], or isn't it," his name appears relatively rarely in discussions of direct bardic influences.[30] Similarly, while Galich had a profound influence on Yuly Kim, he did not set off a broad wave of anti-Soviet protest music.[31] As will be discussed below, while guitar poetry proved to be a powerful agent of self-fashioning for many Soviet young people, as often as not this self-fashioning was buttressed by familiarly Soviet institutions and expressed in familiarly Soviet terms.[32]

LICHNOST' AND THE "KSP STATE"

If bards like Gorodnitsky, Okudzhava, Vizbor, and others epitomize the role of "spectacular individual" *lichnosti* in guitar poetry, then the guitar poetry movement more generally is emblematic of the broader phenomenon of *lichnost'*, of the "emancipation" of individuality, that was fostered through the genre. While specific concerts, festivals, and gatherings played a role in this movement, the regular activities of Clubs of Amateur Song that blossomed all across the Soviet Union were of still greater significance. Indeed, it may be argued that the "KSP State" or the "remarkable country of the KSP"[33] was the principle "public of *svoi*" for the guitar poetry movement.

The numerous Clubs of Amateur Song that arose beginning in the 1960s varied considerably in size and structure. They also varied in their success at the unavoidable, and often extremely complex, process of negotiation with various official bodies; and at fostering vibrant song-related activities. Nonetheless, they shared certain broad characteristics, being widely perceived as humanizing oases in which guitar poetry was both the common language and, along with self-expression and friendly interaction, the common interest. Writing for the wall newspaper (*stengazeta*) of the Moscow KSP in 1981, for example, M. Zhitomirskaya described the KSP as a "brotherhood [*bratstvo*], the common business of which is song"; and, as she argued, the need for such "brotherhoods" arose because informal groups of young people, "feeling themselves to be a single, unified whole, different from the rest of the world, wanted to sing something of 'their own' [*chto-nibud' 'svoyo'*]" and not the songs played on the radio and in films "that, according to Yuly Kim's apt observation, were addressed to the entire country at once."[34]

As Yury Andreyev has argued, similarly, the KSP were perceived as "a gathering of *normal* people," in which "association . . . around a common interest facilitated the development of a surprisingly harmonious general structure, when everything was decided by *the power of authority* and not *the authority of power*" (emphasis in original).[35] According to Andreyev, the "ancestral foundation" of guitar poetry, which joined KSP members together, was

> sincerity [and] honesty, because in front of one's own people [*pered svoimi*] one does not act against one's conscience, one does not lie, because among one's own people [*v krugu svoikh*] people talk about everything that troubles them, that interests them, that worries them.[36]

Andreyev's interpretation of the KSP as bastions of "normality" resonates strongly with Vysotsky's musings that the secret to guitar poetry's popularity lay in the genre's "friendly orientation, in the possibility to converse with people in normal human language, counting on trust in return."[37] Likewise, both Andreyev's and Vysotsky's emphasis on the "human element" of the KSP (and of guitar poetry itself) finds common ground with Dmitry Sukharev's assertion that the "KSP State [*GKSP*] allowed many people to find a means of human existence on the territory of a country that, on the whole, was not well-suited for such."[38]

More explicitly than these other commentators, Boris Almazov emphasizes a political undercurrent in the development of the KSP, observing that these clubs, "alongside the famed kitchens in small apartments, were the place where the desire for political changes was forged."[39] Yet Almazov also underscores, implicitly, the humanizing role the KSP played in many young lives. As Almazov argues,

> the guitar poetry movement, specifically as a sociopolitical movement, prevented several generations from becoming lost generations, [generations] that perished, that vanished . . . And in general, how many people were saved from God knows what by the KSP movement, which oriented them toward poetry, toward spirituality [*dukhovnost'*]![40]

While there is general agreement that the KSP movement was enormously influential, opinions are divided on the question of which particular KSP played the most significant role in this movement. As is true for individual bards, establishing definitive preeminence for any one KSP is a difficult, even well-nigh futile, task. Below, several major and minor clubs are discussed, in order to provide a better sense of how the KSP operated, and of the opportunities they provided for their members to foster a powerful sense of individuality and an equally powerful sense of community.

The history and development of guitar poetry, both in Leningrad and across the Soviet Union, are tightly bound up with the Leningrad KSP Vostok (East). The club had its origins in a youth cafe of the same name, which opened on December 23, 1961, in the House of Culture of Food-Industry Workers on Pravda Street; and which took its name from the spaceship in which Yury Gagarin made his historic first flight into outer space. According to Aleksandr Gorodnitsky, Vostok was "for many long years and even decades . . . the largest center of guitar poetry in the country"; similarly, Aleksandr Genkin observes that Vostok was not just a club, but also "a unifying principle and, for a long time, the ideological and aesthetic center of tourist-amateur-author's-bard's song [*turistsko-samodeyatel'no-avtorsko-bardovskoy pesni*]."[41]

Initially, the Vostok cafe was simply a meeting place for people with an interest in outdoor sporting activities, such as mountaineering and tourism. But as longtime organizer Irina Kostrits recalls,

> when mountaineers, spelunkers, [and] slalom skiers gathered at Vostok, songs rang out [*zvuchali*] as well on those evenings. Thus, little by little, evenings in the cafe grew into evenings of amateur song. Every first Monday of the month was open for authors and their friends.[42]

According to Vostok's official history, the club's first guitar poetry evening was held on March 4, 1963, with performances by Yevgeny Klyachkin, Vladimir Losev, and Boris Poloskin.[43] These song evenings soon turned into a regular event, quickly becoming so popular that it was necessary to move them from the cafe itself into the House of Culture's 200-seat Small Concert Hall. When the song evenings outgrew even this venue, Kostrits and co-organizer Natasha Smirnova (with support from the administration of the House of Culture) organized the series "Youth, Song, Guitar," which was "the first subscription concert of guitar poetry in the USSR."[44] This series was so heavily oversubscribed that, as Kostrits describes, "it took a lot of effort for people who wanted series tickets to get them. For that reason in the auditorium a collective of people [*kollektiv lyudey*] was formed who knew and loved bard song well, who had been raised [*vospitannykh*] at Vostok."[45]

By the end of the Soviet period, Vostok had organized and hosted over 300 concerts (subscription and non-subscription), featuring performances by various well-known and numerous lesser-known bards including Dulov, Genkin, Valentin Glazanov, Gorodnitsky, Yakusheva, Klyachkin, Kukin, Aleksandr Lobanovsky, Okudzhava, Poloskin, Vikhorev, Vizbor, Vysotsky, and others.[46] In addition to its own song evenings, concerts, and series, Vostok was also closely involved in related events held by other city clubs. By 1964, for example, the youth cafe Rovesnik (Contemporary) was hosting concerts by "well-known Leningrad authors and performers"; and, as Nikolai Kurchev describes, Rovesnik was "the closest [club] to [Vostok] in spirit . . . Not one evening at Rovesnik went by without the participation of Vostok, and at all our evenings kids [*rebyata*] from Rovesnik were present."[47] Likewise, Vostok members, alongside members of what would later become KSP Meridian, participated heavily in a 1965 citywide guitar poetry competition that was organized under the aegis of the regional committee (*obkom*) of the Komsomol.[48]

An interesting peculiarity of Vostok's guitar poetry concerts is the fact that, as described in the club's official history, "they [all] took the form of a discussion. At the end of each part of the concert, the participants entered into a dialogue with the auditorium, either answering notes or calling up to the microphone those who wished to say something."[49] Far from being anomalous, then, the interaction and "changing places" between bard and audience that were key elements of the series "Youth, Song, Guitar" were integral parts of Vostok's guitar poetry activities generally. This assessment is confirmed by numerous firsthand descriptions of evenings at Vostok, which emphasize the friendliness and informality of the club, as well as the free exchange between performers and listeners.

For Valentin Glazanov (b. 1931), for example, performing at Vostok for the first time in 1964 was something of a surprise: "I began to write songs by accident . . . I composed songs for my friends and loved ones . . . But I never imagined that I would sing them on stage"; as a result of his Vostok performances, though, Glazanov had the opportunity to meet and to interact with Gorodnitsky, Kukin, Vikhorev, and even Okudzhava, all of whom had a significant influence on him.[50] Likewise, Yury Kukin's first experience of Vostok was a happy accident that had a marked impact on the course of his life, bardic and otherwise. As Kukin recalls,

> I came to the club Vostok for the first time in 1965, when I unexpectedly became the winner of the first Leningrad song competition. After the concert we all met up, and I became acquainted with authors who have remained my friends to this day. It is they who brought me to Vostok (to the cafe). It was cheerful and noisy there, and very free, and very unofficial. Anyone who wanted to went up to the microphone and sang what he wanted. That is how my life in the club Vostok began, [a club] where I sang for many years, and told stories from the stage and in the cafe.[51]

Kukin's success at Vostok soon earned him accolades well beyond the Leningrad guitar poetry scene. Moscow bard Vladimir Turiyansky (b. 1935) has remarked that Kukin's songs "appeared because people needed them" and that "they flew to all ends of our immense country in a remarkably short time," for example, while fellow Muscovite Leonid Semakov (1941–1988) credited Kukin as his own inspiration for becoming a bard.[52]

Like Kukin, both Boris Almazov and Aleksandr Genkin recall having been drawn into Vostok's activities by friends. Almazov notes simply that "no sooner had I performed my songs somewhere when I was drawn into the circle of personal interaction [*lichnogo obshcheniya*] of the KSP," in large part thanks to a chance introduction to organizer and archivist Mikhail Kryzhanovsky.[53] In Genkin's case, an invitation to Vostok came about because fellow students from the Leningrad Military-Mechanical Institute (Voyenmekh) heard him sing around a campfire. As Genkin recounts,

> I was called straight from that campfire to one of the Vostok "Mondays." With everything that could go numb having become terribly numb, I went up to the microphone, and I was received by the chock-a-block full cafe, and was noticed by authors, and was pestered with questions by the pros. My life in guitar poetry had begun.[54]

In turn, Genkin introduced Vitaly Seynov (1939–2001) both to guitar poetry and to Vostok, as Seynov's own reminiscences make clear:

> How did I get involved with guitar poetry? Sasha Genkin got me involved. We graduated from the institute together . . . Genkin and I went to cafe Vostok together. Then Ira Kostrits was [in charge], I think. We were told: sing not more than one song. And we came at that moment with Sasha Genkin's song "Malen'kiy chyornyi pyos . . ." ("A little black dog . . ."). For some reason that song immediately became a hit, and we were received with [cries of] "hurrah, another song, another, another."[55]

As these various accounts reveal, a pattern of introductions through friends is broadly characteristic of how Vostok developed and expanded; while its friendly, informal atmosphere and the vibrant interaction between performers and audiences were crucial to the crafting of new bardic *lichnosti,* and *lichnost'* more generally, within it.

If the Leningrad KSP scene had its origins in various youth and special-interest clubs, then its Muscovite counterpart arose in large part out of educational institutions. Arguably, the origins of amateur song clubs in Moscow can be traced back at least as far as 1957, to the 6th World Festival of Youth and Students in Moscow. According to Dmitry Sokolov, during this festival "it turned out that people were composing their own songs in all the Moscow institutes and universities [*vuzakh*]";[56] and by the late 1950s, student song circles were active in many major Moscow higher education instutions. The immediate result of these developments was a 1959 song festival organized by students of the Moscow Electrotechnical Institute, in which students from five different universites and institutes participated. However, the Moscow KSP proper began to come together only in October 1966, when two different groups with similar interests (headed by Galina Zakharova and Sergey Chesnokov) joined forces.[57] The club soon began to sponsor regular activities (including concerts, biannual rallies in the forests around Moscow, and a well-known 1967 conference on problems of guitar poetry in Petushki), but it did not receive official sanction until 1975.

Igor' Karimov's detailed account of the Moscow KSP's history and development is interesting both because it demonstrates the extent to which the Soviet authorities attempted to control and intervene in KSP activities; and because Karimov himself provides a clear example of self-fashioning through the consumption of guitar poetry rather than its production. With respect to the former, the history of the Moscow KSP reads like a masterpiece of bureaucratic foot-dragging, with the city committee (*gorkom*) of the Komsomol repeatedly stalling decisions on whether to approve the club, until it became clear that its existence did not depend on official actions alone. As Karimov describes, club organizers

> regularly went to the city committee of the Komsomol to coordinate documentation . . . However, the committee kept putting off confirmation of our club "until later" . . . In April 1967 a day was at last appointed for the Plenum of the committee, at which we would be confirmed as a song club. On the 26th of April we all took off work, put on our white shirts, [and] came to the committee. We wait for half an hour, we wait for an hour. The Plenum is taking place, but we are not being called. And then they tell us that confirmation of the club has been moved to the end of the year. (51, 54)

The countrywide assault on guitar poetry in 1968 complicated the situation of the Moscow KSP still further, though the club did not participate formally in the Novosibirsk bard festival that racheted up the level of these attacks. According to Karimov, the decision to stay away from the Novosibirsk festival was motivated by a desire to remain "clean": "It was clear that the affair would be scandalous, and we were waiting for confirmation of our club by the city committee and did not want to disgrace ourselves, to fall into disfavor" (80). Such circumspectness notwithstanding, the Moscow KSP did not remain free of suspicion; and as a result, its meeting space was revoked and Karimov and others were called into the Central Committee and questioned about their activities (Karimov, *Istoriya,* 90–91).[58]

When questioned as to whether Galich was the club's "ideological inspiration," for example, Karimov "naively attempted to prove to them, to those people, that Galich's songs are interesting, [that they] really help in the development of the individual personality [*razvitiyu lichnosti*]" (90–91). What is notable here is not the fact that Moscow KSP members were questioned about Galich: as Karimov recalls, "We worry them up to a point [*postol'ku, poskol'ku*], but in actual fact they need information about Galich" (90). Rather, it is Karimov's response, in which he frames his attitudes using the phraseology of officialspeak. While this response was not sufficient to remove the taint of suspicion from him,[59] the very fact that he explained his views in familiarly Soviet terms (sincerely, by his own reckoning, if naively) indicates the extent to which the attitudes and values of KSP members were not unambiguously oppositional in nature, even where their actions (such as organizing prohibited guitar poetry rallies or contriving to organize legal concerts for "ideologically unreliable" bards) did defy or subvert official proscriptions.[60]

Despite conflicts with the authorities, official resolutions and restrictions alone were not sufficient to halt the activities of the Moscow KSP. During the early 1970s, the city committee of the Komsomol typically "did not help, but did not interfere [in the club's activities] either" (Karimov,

Istoriya, 97). In the latter half of the 1970s, the Moscow KSP developed a characteristic organizational structure based around small groups (*kusty*). In effect, the impetus for formalizing *kusty* within the club's structure was that the club had become a victim of its own success: so popular had its rallies become that, at the 18th rally (autumn 1975), some 200 different groups of singer-songwriters and song-lovers were present. The formation of *kusty* (on a roughly geographic basis) did not just create a manageable organizational structure within the Moscow KSP as a whole; as Karimov argues, it also "gave the KSP the possibility to exist for many long years" (136–37, 140).

In general terms, the evolution of the Moscow KSP—like that of guitar poetry more broadly—reflects the impact of shifts in the sociopolitical climate of the Soviet Union over the course of the 1960s and 1970s. Significantly, however, the activities and attitudes of individual club members suggest far greater interest in the opportunities for communicating, socializing, and self-fashioning through guitar poetry than in overt political activism.[61] A club activist and organizer rather than a singer-songwriter, Igor' Karimov exemplifies the possibilities that Clubs of Amateur Song provided for the development of individual talents in a variety of non-performing roles (including organizers, archivists and collectors, designers, and others).[62]

But Karimov's views on his own role and responsibilities within the Moscow KSP also underscore a desire to leave politics aside ("that is my personal affair") in order to preserve KSP activities as a "mass oasis in a desert of total prohibitions" (154–55). As Karimov recalls, "it was already a huge victory to give people the possibility to gather together, to interact through songs around the campfire, to find friends and like-minded people, and in that we saw a worthwhile task" (155). At rallies in particular, a central goal was to use this friendly interaction to foster new bardic talents, new bardic *lichnosti:*

> From the very start performances at rallies were arranged in order to give young authors and performers the possibility to try out their talents, to show their worth in front of a small circle of friends [*dobrozhelateley*]. The forest at one's back, kindly eyes in the field, conversations after the performance—all that was to the benefit of beginners. (166)

In addition to regular rallies, in the mid-1970s the club also managed to organize a number of large-scale concerts by adopting the format of "subscription series-lecture-concert," similar to the arrangement employed by KSP Vostok for the series "Youth, Song, Guitar." As Karimov describes, "guitar poetry concerts are, as is well known, always a conversation with listeners as well, so the 'lectures' were received by the audience as completely natural" (144).

Interestingly, though the Novosibirsk KSP Pod integralom (Under the Integral) is best-known for the (in)famous 1968 bard festival that became a flash point for guitar poetry's critics, this club, too, was conceived as an "oasis of openness [*glasnosti*]" rather than as a politically minded fellowship. A. I. Burshtein, a lead organizer of the club Integral (The Integral) of which the KSP formed one wing, describes the club quite explicitly as a point of entry into the "gray area" between the permitted and the prohibited:

> Oral freedom is always broader than the written kind. But what was said and thought out loud in the early 1960s left the printed word far behind. Between what was permitted in the '60s and what was deliberately prohibited lay a broad swath of no-man's land . . . The doors of Integral opened the way into that territory, and there was no lack of people wanting to enter, and to talk, and to listen.[63]

Between 1963 and 1968, continues Burshtein, Integral "won a reputation as a place where you could speak your mind to your heart's content, pour out your soul, open up as far as your courage allowed."[64] An emphasis on both self and community was written into the very statutes of Integral, which proclaimed the club to be an

> original [*samorodnaya*], self-willed, self-made, self-perfecting, self-directed, self-programmed, self-supporting, self-advertising, self-protected . . . self-organization of Akademgorodok-ers.
>
> [The club's] tasks are: to provide members of the club with a free exchange of knowledge and experience. To promote mutual understanding, fellowship and cooperation. To encourage the formation and progressive development of various amateur clubs.[65]

Similar interests are reflected in an extensive discussion held in 1982 at the Vladivostok KSP Poisk (Quest), which was founded in 1977. During the course of this discussion, numerous participants emphasized both self-expression and interaction (*obshcheniye*) as key elements of guitar poetry itself and of the KSP movement. For example, one L. Tsoy observed that

> song is a powerful means of interaction. Despite the fact that amateur songs are highly varied (about nature and about other things), at the same time [*pri etom*] each person distinguishes (or, more precisely, expresses) his own *I* . . . Song educates [*vospityvayet*] a person.[66]

Similarly, highlighting points of contact between the benefits of tourism and those of the KSP, a participant identified only by the initials V. L. stressed the role of amateur song as a means of self-discovery:

> Under industrial conditions there is no time to think, to get inside yourself, to dig deep [*zabrat'sya v sebya, zakopat'sya*], but [on an expedition] all that peripheral, petty stuff is left aside, [and] a person begins to think about why he exists, what he is capable of, and so on. A person discovers himself expressly as an individual, [and] amateur song is the same expression of a person as a person, and not as something general . . . Amateur song is the revelation of oneself [*vyyavleniye sebya*].

Picking up the second strand of L. Tsoy's comments, a certain G. T. expressed the view that "our goal is the upbringing of a person [*vospitaniye cheloveka*]" or, perhaps more precisely, "the upbringing of a person's worldview [*vospitaniye mirovozzreniya cheloveka*]"; while the view that in club activities there is an element of "upbringing through interaction [*vospitaniye cherez obshcheniye*]" is attributed to "everyone (or practically everyone)" present.

Summarizing others' contributions to the discussion, club president Sergey Rybalka also highlighted the significance of interaction—and particularly informal interaction—in KSP activities, as follows:

> The KSP is what gives a particular individual a moment of informal interaction and at least the possibility for answers to vitally important questions, which he cannot find anywhere else . . . Informal conditions give you the possiblity to speak more freely than formal ones about any topic that interests you.

Drawing the discussion to a close, Rybalka reiterated that "guitar poetry and the KSP . . . are a certain concentrated search for the truth [*istiny*]."

What is particularly interesting about Rybalka's comments is the fact that he underscores, explicitly and at some length, the coincidence between the goals and values of the KSP and officially promoted ones:

> And now we will recall a certain document (reads out the "moral codex of a builder of communism"). Do we find any discrepancies with these propositions? Here in our yearning for self-revelation through our own creative activity, in our yearning to search for truth in this narrow, KSP circle, in our yearning to convey to other people that which we consider to be true [*istinnym*]—are there any discrepancies here or not, and if there are, where specifically?
>
> There are none. Simply, we are convinced that the club provides certain additional possibilities to achieve these same goals. Perhaps the main thing that draws people here—it is the realization of significant contradictions between what should be all around us and what is, and a desire not to sit on one's hands when confronted with this.

Given the late date of this particular discussion (1982), the assumption that views expressed by members of KSP Poisk can be attributed to members of the KSP scene at large during the 1960s and 1970s should be approached with caution. Nonetheless, there is a striking similarity between the views expressed here and the emphasis on self-expression, self-discovery, and friendly, informal interaction that runs through participants' comments on KSP Vostok and the other clubs discussed above. A certain emphasis, in both periods, on the extent to which the values and goals of the KSP coincide with official ones—despite the vision of the KSP as a particular circle or "oasis" for the fostering of these values and the pursuit of these goals—is similarly revealing.

"IN-BETWEENNESS" AND *COMMUNITAS* IN THE "KSP STATE"

From the foregoing discussion of specific Clubs of Amateur Song, a clear picture emerges of the KSP as a marginal zone par excellence. Spatially, clubs carved out a marginal existence, making their homes in factory cafes and minor cultural venues or enduring years of peripatetic status and organizing various gatherings and rallies in rural and sylvan settings. Socioculturally and ideologically, they operated largely in the "no-man's land" between the permitted and the prohibited. Officially, clubs' activities were continually monitored, but as often as not the authorities neither helped nor hindered in their development. For KSP members, club activities were widely perceived as islands of normality in a sea of prohibitions. Yet widespread emphasis on clubs' particularity, on the fact that they provided young people with "their own" circle in which to sing "their own" songs; and equally widespread emphasis on clubs' friendliness and informality (an implied contrast to the stilted formality of fully sanctioned activities and organizations) make plain that members perceived the KSP as qualitatively different from other cultural and social circles open to them—and thus as lying somewhere in between what was explicitly prescribed and what was explicitly proscribed. Significant overlap between officially promulgated ideals and ideas and those of the "KSP State," even where KSP members engaged in prohibited activities, serves as further confirmation of this "in between" status.

As discussed in chapter 2, in the margins processes of self-fashioning, communication, and community-building are crucial: the margins provide a much-needed space in which independent identities, interests, and needs can be generated and articulated. All of these processes were integral to the KSP: as the numerous firsthand accounts analyzed above reveal, members were acutely aware of, and indeed specifically drawn to, KSP activities because of the opportunities these clubs provided *for* self-fashioning, communication, and community-building. Members' awareness of, and awareness of the importance of, all these processes is expressed in numerous descriptions of guitar poetry as a means of self-discovery or self-revelation; in frequent references to the possibility of interaction through songs and to concerts themselves as dialogues; in the friendly interaction that expanded club rosters and typified club gatherings; and in the overwhelming embrace of mutual understanding, fellowship, and cooperation.

At a time when the need to reshape Soviet culture as a "relevant and exciting means of communication between party and people" was debated intensely,[67] and when official anxiety about the upbringing of Soviet youth had reached new heights, guitar poetry itself and the guitar poetry movement thus demonstrated a remarkable ability both to foster communication between individuals and to encourage individual self-fashioning through a largely unmediated "backchannel."[68] While official critics' responses to guitar poetry's lyrics and music ranged from cautiously positive to brusquely dismissive and even harshly critical, preoccupation with the genre's ability to reach young audiences, and with its potential to influence listeners, was ever-present. One may argue, then, that Soviet officialdom sensed in guitar poetry not simply "something boding dangerous shifts of social consciousness,"[69] that is, not simply a reflection of nascent trends, but also something that might motivate and inspire such shifts both in individuals and in groups.

In summarizing the threat that guitar poetry and the guitar poetry movement represented for the Soviet establishment, Victor Turner's concept of *communitas* is particularly useful. Turner defines *communitas* as "a modality of social interrelatedness" that arises in interstices and liminal arenas of social structure and social life, and that is typified by an emphasis on "equality and comradeship."[70] Developing on the fringes of Soviet society and promoting an "atmosphere of trust, friendliness, naturalness and unfetteredness," guitar poetry fostered communication between individuals, but it also fostered *communitas*.[71]

According to Turner, central qualities of *communitas* include spontaneity, immediacy, and an emphasis on "personal relationships rather than social obligations."[72] These are precisely the kinds of qualities ascribed to guitar poetry as a genre and emphasized by KSP members as significant and much-needed aspects of KSP life. They are also qualities that conflicted directly with the desire of Soviet officialdom to mediate in communication, to intervene in the private sphere and, even in an era of greater attention to individual well-being, to stress "social obligations" and public engagement over private interests.[73] Similarly, KSP members' emphasis on "possibility" (*vozmozhnost'*) and on "searching" (*poisk*), both of which were central to the appeal of the KSP—that is, an emphasis on a process-oriented rather than goal-oriented approach to identity creation and interaction—may be said to reflect the potentiality of *communitas*, its reliance on the subjunctive mood.[74] In turn, official concern about how listeners might react to guitar poetry may be said to reflect anxiety over this same potentiality; and this, too, is consistent with Turner's observation that "from the perspective of incumbents in positions of command or maintenance in structure, communitas . . . represents a real danger."[75]

Interestingly, in many respects the social function of guitar poetry was not so different from that of official song genres. Like official songs of the post-revolutionary and Stalin periods, guitar poetry did create social cohesion; and, to adapt Anatoly Lunacharsky's oft-cited pronouncement, for many young people guitar poetry was "musical bread that [was] essential for life."[76] But unlike its official counterparts, guitar poetry "[broke] through in the interstices of structure, in liminality; at the edges of society, in marginality."[77] The extent to which this was viewed as problematic is reflected in official anxiety about guitar poetry both as a genre and as a movement, even where individual songs were ideologically unobjectionable or individuals' views were consistent with those promoted by Soviet officialdom.

Moreover, guitar poetry's potential as an agent of self-fashioning challenged the ability of official structures to control *personal* change, a prerogative the continued importance of which was demonstrated by heightened attention to *vospitaniye* after 1953 and by ongoing emphasis on the importance of the collective. Arguably, the creation of alternative identities through guitar poetry—or, more precisely, the *potential* creation of *potentially* alternative identities—represented a far bigger challenge for Soviet officialdom than even an outspoken bard like Galich, with his openly provocative songs. While individual transgressors could be censured and even censored, it was far more difficult for the authorities to deal with the prospect of many individual souls engineering *themselves* through song; with the prospect of many people exploring multiple possibilities for their own *lichnosti* that were fostered through guitar poetry's "conversations between friends."

From the exploration of processes of self-fashioning and interaction, discussion now shifts to guitar poetry's song-conversations themselves. Building on the preceding examination of ways in which the guitar poetry phenomenon was rooted in various types of marginality, chapters 5 and 6 will analyze marginality itself as a compositional element of guitar poetry; and, in turn, ways in which compositional marginality facilitated the articulation of specific identities, interests, and needs through song. Chapter 7 will then examine the nature and function of guitar poetry's own generic diversity. Engaging with a range of works—from explicitly political tirades to quietly philosophical musings, from songs that were castigated in the press to those that were freely published—the next three chapters highlight guitar poetry's heterogeneity on multiple levels. In so doing, they illuminate the extent to which bards' choice of themes, their attention to detail, and their handling of genre helped to craft guitar poetry's central role as an instrument of communication among *svoi*. More broadly, this discussion underscores the complexity of the margins and of the marginal as sites of discourses that are neither simply oppositional nor simply conformist; and as sites of interactions in which the significance of identity creation and in-group communication can be far greater than that of rhetoric directed at an external audience.

PART III

Lyrical Marginalities and Beyond

Chapter Five

Overt Marginality: *Antisovetchina*

Spinu vyaluyu sgorbya,
Ya zh ne prosto khulu,
A grazhdanskiye skorbi
Serviruyu k stolu!

Hunching my limp spine,
I'm serving to table
Not just criticism,
But civic sorrows!
—Aleksandr Galich, "Desire for Fame"

KEENLY ATTUNED TO BOTH cultural and sociopolitical developments, guitar poetry swiftly became an important arena for addressing socially pressing and politically sensitive themes around which public discourse was closely guarded. Emblematic of such engagement is guitar poetry's persistent and highly varied treatment of alcoholism and drunkenness and of the Gulag. Both of these topics featured prominently in Soviet everyday life of the post-Stalin period, but public debate surrounding them was restricted in various ways. By the advent of the Thaw, the Soviet "alcohol problem" was subject to a "soft" taboo. Comedic representations of drunkenness and alcoholism were sometimes possible in official culture; but at the same time, every effort was made to suppress information about the extent of alcohol problems in Soviet society and the severity of their consequences. By contrast, the Gulag was one of the preeminent "hard" taboo themes of the post-Stalin period, admitted to public discourse only in limited and closely monitored forms.

In guitar poetry, by contrast, both topics provided rich material for sustained creative exploration, sometimes deftly humorous and sometimes openly critical, but always closely observed and deeply relevant. In this chapter, guitar poetry's multifaceted treatments of drinking and alcoholism and of the Gulag are analyzed as manifestations of overt marginality. Choosing to sing about politically sensitive topics, bards actively placed certain songs in the margins of acceptable public discourse. As a conseqence, such songs come closest to notions of "resistance" and "protest" that are often ascribed both to the margins and to guitar poetry itself. At the same time, however, it was as much the way the bards handled sensitive themes, the kinds of direct comparisons and indirect associations they drew out, that provoked criticism from and anxiety within the Soviet cultural and ideological establishment—and in not a few cases, complex responses from discomfited guitar poetry fans as well. Ultimately, it is precisely in this tension, in such songs' resistance to easy classification, that their overt marginality is most clearly visible.

DRINKING AND DRUNKENNESS IN OFFICIAL DISCOURSE OF THE POST-STALIN PERIOD

By the late 1950s and early 1960s, official struggles against drunkenness and alcoholism were not new. Statistical information from the annual almanac *Narodnoye khozyaystvo SSSR* (*The Domestic Economy of the USSR*) shows a steady rise in alcohol production over two decades; and both this rise and pointed remarks in the Soviet press support the conclusion that, by the 1960s, there had been "an increase in alcohol consumption and an increase in habitual drunkenness and alcoholism among Soviet citizens."[1] Yet, for a brief period during the Thaw, alcohol consumption, even in flagrant excess, became an acceptable topic for relatively unfettered comedic representation. The early 1960s were the heyday of Leonid Gaidai's enormously popular slapstick comedies, for example, in which excessive drinking and drunkenness play a major comedic role.

Gaidai's rollicking short films *Pyos Barbos i neobychnyi kross* (1961; *The Dog Barbos and the Unusual Race*) and *Samogonshchiki* (1962; *The Moonshiners*), which feature a bumbling trio of petty criminals known collectively as ViNiMor, "brought two important themes from folk culture to the Soviet screen: alcoholism and crime."[2] While drinking is somewhat incidental in *Pyos Barbos* (the plot revolves around an ill-fated fishing trip and the desire of ViNiMor's dog to play fetch with a dynamite-laden stick), it is entirely central to *Samogonshchiki,* the first part of which, as Aleksandr Prokhorov describes, consists of "a series of physical jokes about making and consuming alcohol in a fairy-tale-like hut in the middle of the forest."[3] What is especially notable about these shorts is their affectionately hedonistic bent: far from "engag[ing] in a satire of antisocial behavior," they present ViNiMor as lovable buffoons, "rehabilitat[ing] the ritual of three males consuming a half-liter bottle of vodka."[4]

This relative laxity was short-lived, however. Beginning in 1963, *Na-*

rodnoye khozyaystvo SSSR stopped reporting vodka output as a separate category, instead including it (along with other beverage sales) under "other foodstuffs"; as a result, this new category "immediately became the largest single item in the retail sales statistics, accounting for a third of the total."[5] This shift augured a trend toward statistical sleight-of-hand that increased further under Brezhnev, when alcohol production and consumption became part of a general move toward "resolving" problems "simply by discontinuing the publication of any information about [them]."[6] On the cultural front, even comedic representations of excessive drinking were reined in progressively. Gaidai's films of the mid-1960s still feature the escapades of ViNiMor and other drunken hooligans, but now in situations where they square off against—and are ultimately defeated by—decent and hard-working citizens, including the bespectacled and industrious (if peculiar) student Shurik. In the shorts *Operatsiya Y* (1965; *Operation Y*) and *Naparnik* (1965; *The Partner*) and the feature film *Kavkazskaya plennitsa, ili novye priklyucheniya Shurika* (1966; *Captive of the Caucasus, or Shurik's New Adventures*), for example, Shurik scuttles minor criminal ventures and hooliganish behavior with his integrity and hard work, aided by the inebriated fumbling of his opposites.

By the early 1970s, officially promulgated information about alcohol consumption and abuse had become still more restricted. Drinking binges still made their way into film and television, notably in El'dar Ryazanov's melancholy-tinged comedies (including the two-part miniseries *Ironiya sud'by* [1975; *Irony of Fate*]); but so did explicit warnings about the dangers of drink, such as are found in the satirical comedy shorts comprising *"Sto gramm" dlya khrabrosti* (1976; *"A Hundred Grams" for Bravery*). Complaints about drinking and alcohol abuse still featured in the press as well, but claims that "drunkenness is just another social evil whose eradication is just around the corner" were no longer being advanced.[7] By the end of the decade, media silence on the subject of alcohol and drunkenness was virtually complete.[8]

As public depiction and discussion of drunkenness and alcoholism were increasingly curbed, much effort was expended to ensure that the prevalence of these undesirable behaviors across the social spectrum was likewise hidden from public view. The high incidence of alcoholism among Russia's creative intelligentsia remained a taboo subject, reflecting both an ideologically conditioned view of alcohol abuse as a phenomenon of the lower orders, and also a larger taboo on discussion of deviations from social and behavioral norms.[9] As A. E. Krylov observes, the existence of such taboos meant that "the 'alcoholic' signs" of the post-Stalin period were reflected primarily in works that circulated unofficially.[10]

"LIKE THREE RUBLES FOR VODKA": DRINKING AND DRUNKENNESS IN GUITAR POETRY

While official discourse in the 1960s and 1970s provided a narrowly circumscribed picture of drinking and drunkenness, guitar poetry did just the opposite. What is immediately striking about the "alcohol theme" in guitar poetry is not simply its frequency, but also its social ubiquity. In the bards' songs, virtually all sectors of Soviet society partake of the bacchanalian pleasures; and Galich's songs, in particular, provide a veritable encyclopedia not just of drinking habits and rituals, but also of popular alcoholic beverages themselves. In essence, guitar poetry provides a picture of alcohol consumption—habitual and excessive—not simply as the province of "depraved and inferior people,"[11] not as a comical pastime for bumbling hooligans, but as a pervasive national phenomenon that touched high and low alike. Both the frequency with which drinking is mentioned in guitar poetry and the variety of social types involved thus provide ample illustration that, as one of Galich's protagonists declares, "These days, just like me, / Half the country sits in bars!"[12]

Appearing at much the same time as Gaidai's first film shorts, Vysotsky's early imitations of "criminal songs" (*blatnye pesni*) foreground both drinking and criminal behavior.[13] Yet unlike Gaidai's films, Vysotsky's representations of drunkenness were a "firmly underground" element of his song corpus, and were widely condemned by official critics.[14] The "ritual of three males consuming a half-liter bottle of vodka" that was rehabilitated (publicly, that is) in Gaidai's films features prominently in a number of Vysotsky's early songs as well, including "Skol'ko let, skol'ko let" (1962; "How many years, how many years") and "My vmeste grabili odnu i tu zhe khatu" (1963; "Together we robbed one and the same pad"). Indeed, the latter of these songs features a glorious turn of phrase that has since passed into popular discourse: "My s nimi vstretilis' kak tri rublya na vodku, / I razoshlis' kak vodka na troikh" (We came together like three rubles for vodka, / And went our separate ways like vodka for three people).[15]

The protagonists of these and others of Vysotsky's stylized *blatnye pesni* consume alcohol frequently, in prodigious quantities, and for many different reasons. The protagonist of "Ya v dele" (1962; "I'm on the Job"), a thief, always goes to a bar after robbing someone, declaring, "Kto by chto ni govoril, / Ya sam dobyl—i sam propil" ("No matter what anyone says, / I got it myself, and so I drank it myself") (32). The protagonist of "U menya bylo sorok familiy" (1962 or 1963; "I had forty last names") boasts of his habit of drinking with anyone at all ("Kto-nibud' nakhodilsya— / I ya s nim napivalsya" ["Anyone would turn up— / And I would get drunk with him"]); and he even declares that getting very drunk is the key to enlightenment ("Chtob vo vsyom razobrat'sya—/Nuzhno sil'no napit'sya!" ["In order to work everything out,/You have to get very drunk!]") (34–35). The first lines of another early song (1963) practically speak for themselves: "Esli by vodka byla na odnogo—/Kak chudesno by bylo!" ("If vodka were just for one—/How wonderful it would be!") (38).

Stylized *blatnye pesni* are not the only songs in which Vysotsky refers to drinking and drunkenness, nor are criminals and other lowlifes his only imbibers. Indeed, a host of characters and types can be found among the brotherhood of the bottle in Vysotsky's song corpus. These include, for example, a stool pigeon ("Pesnya pro stukacha" [1964; "Song About a Stool Pigeon"]); a metalworker ("Ya byl slesar' shestogo razryada" [1964; "I Was a Metalworker, Sixth Class"]); a former sniper ("Pesnya pro snaypera" [1965; "Song About a Sniper"]); a militia lieutenant ("Den' rozhdeniya leytenanta militsii v restorane 'Berlin'" [1965; "The Birthday Party of a Militia Lieutenant at the Berlin Restaurant"]); a devil ("Pro chyorta" [1965–66; "About a Devil"]); miners, including a shock-worker ("Sluchay na shakhte" [1967; "Incident at the Mine"]); and a kind simpleton who becomes a ruler but who is ousted for trying to do a good deed ("Zhil-byl dobryi durachina-prostofilya" [1968; "Once Upon a Time There Lived a Kind-Hearted Simpleton"]).

Far from simply mentioning drinking and drunkenness repeatedly in his songs, though, Vysotsky also conveys various states of inebriation adeptly through performance. These talents are amply displayed in renditions of "Oy, gde byl ya vchera" (1967; "Oh, where was I yesterday"), in which Vysotsky's badly hungover protagonist sifts through his hazy recollections of the previous evening:

> Oy, gde byl ya vchera—ne naydu, khot' ubey!
> Tol'ko pomnyu, chto steny—s oboyami,
> Pomnyu—Klavka byla, i podruga pri yey,—
> Tselovalsya na kukhne s oboimi. (141)
>
> Oh, where was I yesterday—I can't figure out to save my life!
> I only remember that the walls had wallpaper,
> I remember that Klavka was there with her friend,
> That I smooched both of them in the kitchen.

For the first few bars, Vysotsky is less a singer than a raconteur, lingering on the song's opening phrase *Oy, gde byl ya vchera-a-a* as if to suggest that his protagonist is playing for time before hazarding a guess as to the details of his evening's entertainment.[16] In subsequent lines, rising intonation and clearer timbre on the initial phrase suggest a flash of recollection, before Vysotsky slides into the lower, gravellier reaches of his vocal range. In the last line of this verse, the deliberate, ungrammatical use of the masculine form *oboimi* (both)—instead of the correct feminine form *obeimi*—not only identifies the protagonist as uneducated, but also adds to the humor of Vysotsky's performance. Vysotsky's pronunciation of both *oboyami* (wallpaper) and *oboimi* is slurred and consequently virtually identical; thus it is unclear, in the absence of the printed text, whether the protagonist was kissing both Klavka and her friend or (in his supremely drunken state) the wallpaper.

As the protagonist's initial hangover-induced disorientation begins to clear, his bravado simultaneously begins to emerge. Vysotsky accentuates the protagonist's boasting about his antics with an aggressive drawl that contrasts sharply with the labored enunciation of the preceding lines:

A nautro ya vstal—
Mne davay soobshchat',
Chto khozyayku rugal,
Vsekh khotel zastrashchat',
Budto golym skakal,
Budto pesni oral,
A otets, govoril,
U menya—general!

And in the morning I got up—
They go and tell me
That I cussed out the hostess,
Wanted to intimidate everyone,
Supposedly I ran around naked,
Supposedly I screeched songs,
And my father, I said,
He's a general!

Here, as so often in his songs, Vysotsky lingers over particular sounds—exaggerating the pronunciation of *g* as *kh* (affecting a provincial, typically southern Russian accent) and rolling each *r* vehemently—so that, for example, *govoril* is transformed into *khovor-ri-i-l* and *general* into *khenerra-a-a-l.*

Like Vysotsky, Yuly Kim depicted drinking and associated antisocial behavior in his songs almost from the very start of his bardic career. In "Khuliganskaya" (1961; "Hooligan's Song"), for example, the song's titular troublemakers are evidently suffering the aftereffects of a drinking binge:

My khodim-brodim, nogi dvizhem ele,
Pokhodka nasha, brattsy, takova,—
Ty ponyal?—

Kak budto sto pudov u nas na tele,
Zato—tuk-tuk-tuk—golova.[17]

We're walking-rambling, legs barely moving,
Our pace, lads, just so,—
Got it?—
As if we're carrying a ton on us,
But—rat-a-tat-tat—go our heads.

Failing to make the desired impression on their audience, whose presence is implied by the interjection *Ty ponyal?*, the hooligans decide to take a shot of courage: "A chtoby byt' strashneye i khrabreye, / Voz'myom da dyornem dvesti gramm" ("In order to be scarier and braver, / We'll up and swig two hundred grams"). This misguided attempt founders, however, when it turns out that their audience is a member of the militia—who summarily sentences them to "ten days and a fine" for "violation of public order."

But like Vysotsky, again, Kim does not depict drinking and drunkenness as the exclusive province of lowlifes and troublemakers, instead drawing his drinkers from across the social spectrum. In Kim's songs, literally all of Russia drinks, from common hooligans to the Party leadership. In "Monolog p'yanogo Brezhneva" (1968; "Drunken Brezhnev's Monologue"), for example, Kim attacks the Soviet leader through verbal caricature, portraying him as an inebriated buffoon who attributes his power (Samson-like) and his bloodthirsty desires to his most memorable facial feature, his bushy eyebrows: "Moi brovi zhazhdut krovi, / Moya sila v nikh odnikh" ("My eyebrows thirst for blood, / My strength is in them alone").[18]

Kim's humorous depiction of Brezhnev also has an undeniably frightening aspect, though. Referring to April 1917, the month "regarded as the birthdate of Soviet ideology,"[19] and to Lenin's speech given from an armored car at Finland Station in Petrograd, Kim's Brezhnev expresses regret that the time is no longer right for *him* to "wordlessly grab a machine-gun" and mow down his enemies. Moreover, he calls upon KGB head Yury Andropov to silence Galich ("Dostavay banduru, Yura, / Konfiskuy u Galicha!" ["Get ahold of a bandura, Yura, / Confiscate it from Galich!"]); and he exhorts the censors to attend to well-known dissidents:

Gde ty tam, tsenzura-dura,
Nu-ka spoy, kak davecha:
Ekh raz, da yeshchyo raz,
Da yeshchyo mnogo, mnogo raz,
Yeshchyo Pashku, i Natashku,
I Larisu Bogoraz![20]

Where are you there, censor-fool,
Well, come on, sing like long ago:
Eh once, and then again,
And many times over again,
And also Pashka, and Natashka,
and Larisa Bogoraz!

The refrain "Ekh raz, da yeshchyo raz,/Da yeshchyo mnogo, mnogo raz" ("Eh once, and then again,/And many times over again") that appears in these final lines also hints at the song's accompaniment. Kim's "Monolog" is set to the melody of a rollicking Gypsy song, and the gaping incongruity between this spirited melody and the gleefully bloodthirsty revelations of the lyrics lend the song a decidedly sinister edge.[21]

Much in this same vein is Kim's "Moya matushka Rossiya" (1974; "My Mother Russia"), in which Mother Russia—personified and expressing herself with numerous slang, substandard, and dialectal expressions—drinks vodka and abuses the song's protagonist in various ways. First, she kicks him for refusing to drink with her:

Moya matushka Rossiya
V [samovar] vodki nalila,
Apel'sinom zakusila,
Mne po zhope poddala:

—Ty chego tam delayesh',
Nos otvoril?
So mnoy vypit' grebuyesh'—
Kto tebya rodil?[22]

My mother Russia
Poured vodka into the samovar,
Chased it down with an orange,
Gave me one on the ass:

—What the heck are you doing there,
Turning up your nose?
You're too squeamish to have a drink with me—
Who gave birth to you?

After having her son put in the infamous Lubyanka prison, this merciless Mother Russia complains, "No matter how I torment him—/He still puffs himself up! . . ." As a result, her only option is to "have at him once . . . [and then] do it again" in an attempt to break his spirit.

If Kim's predilection for comical characterizations of hooligans resonates with Vysotsky's stylized *blatnye pesni,* the specificity and pointedness of his social and political criticisms align him more closely with Aleksandr Galich. But while Kim's lyrics and performance are often infused with a wry irony, Galich's bardic oeuvre is permeated by an air of bitterness. This is as true for songs in which Galich engages with the "alcohol theme" as it is for songs of an even more politically volatile nature. Like both Vysotsky and Kim, Galich took on alcohol and drunkenness early in his career as a bard,[23] and he portrays a vast and varied cast of imbibers in his songs.

Among Galich's myriad drinkers we find former prison camp inmates ("Oblaka" [1962; "Clouds"]); a hospital director who, in a drunken state, babbles about Stalin and has a heart attack as a result ("Bol'nichnaya tsyganochka" [1965; "Hospital Gypsy Song"]); Johann Sebastian Bach ("Po obrazu i podobiyu, ili 'Jedem das Seine'" [1968; "In His Image and Likeness, or 'To Each His Own'"]); Klim Petrovich Kolomiytsev, "holder of many orders, deputy of the town council [*gorsoveta*], workshop foreman, [and] distinguished person" (201), who features in the songs "Istoriya o tom, kak Klim Petrovich dobivalsya, chtob yego tsekhu prisvoili zvaniye 'Tsekha kommunisticheskogo truda,' i, ne dobivshis' etogo, zapil" (1968–70; "Story About How Klim Petrovich Tried to Get His Workshop Awarded the Title of 'Workshop of Communist Labor' and, Not Having Succeeded, Took to Drink") and "Plach Dar'i Kolomiytsevoy po povodu zapoya yeyo supruga" (1968–70; "Dar'ya Kolomiytseva's Lament About Her Spouse's Drinking Binge"); executioners, who drink cognac and sing songs about Stalin ("Plyasovaya" [1969; "Dance Tune"]); and a former labor camp inmate and his former guard, who drink together ("Zhelaniye slavy" [after 1972; "Desire for Fame"]).

Galich's catalogue of popular alcoholic beverages is equally thorough, reflecting the wealth of detail that "thickly stud[s] the texts of [his] songs."[24] In "Ballada pro malyarov, istopnika i teoriyu otnositel'nosti" (1962; "Ballad About House-Painters, a Boiler-Man and the Theory of Relativity"), for example, Galich mentions Zhigulyovskoye beer, Dubnyak (a bitter infusion); and also, in a line that Galich milks for its clever internal rhymes, Stolichnaya vodka: "I lechus' 'Stolichnoyu' lichno ya,/Chtoby mne s uma ne stronut'sya" ("And I, personally, medicate myself with Stolichnaya,/So that I don't go out of my mind") (177–78). In "Ballada o pribavochnoy stoimosti" (1964; "Ballad about Surplus Value"), in which the narrator goes on a monumental bender in celebration of a windfall, Galich mentions both Stolichnaya and Osobaya vodka; and in "Plyasovaya," aged cognac appears alongside other "brand-name" food items like Gvardeyskiy cake and Salyut cookies.

In addition to such verses depicting an impressive array of drinkers, drinking customs, and indisputably Soviet alcoholic beverages, Galich's oeuvre includes songs sung from the point of view of drunks (and imitating the speech patterns thereof), and even songs ostensibly composed while the author was in a drunken state. A particularly interesting example from this last category is part 5 of "Razmyshleniya o begunakh na dlinnye distantsii" (1968–69; "Musings on Long-Distance Runners") which, as its descriptive title indicates, "was written in a very drunken state [*v ochen' sil'nom podpitii*] and which is an authorial digression" (111–13). Though it is more often Vysotsky who is described as a kind of Soviet *skomorokh*, or jester, revealing truths or representing an alternative hierarchy of values through "earthy," debased, or carnivalesque lyric personae,[25] Galich's "drunken" song may also be interpreted in precisely this light. Particularly worthy of comment is the fact that the song's title deliberately effaces the distance between author and narrator: specifically labeled as an "authorial digression," this song presents the author himself, and not a lyric hero or lyric mask, in the quasi-visionary role of the drunk-*skomorokh*.

In the song's first verse, the author-narrator offers what might be called a brief, inverted humility topos. Admitting his ignorance, he declares that he is not ashamed of it, and that he is not capable of being a "great thinker": "Temnoty svoyey ne styzhus',/Ne mogu ya byt' Ptolemeyem,/Dazhe v Engel'sy ne gozhus'" ("I'm not ashamed of my ignorance,/I cannot be Ptolemy,/I'm not even fit to be an Engels"). The particular "great thinkers" the author-narrator mentions are as revealing as his declaration of his own ignorance. Ptolemy's vision of the order of the universe was, of course, ultimately proved wrong; in light of Galich's trenchant opposition to the Soviet system, we understand that the author-narrator considers Engels's vision to be similarly misguided. The fact that the author-narrator declares himself ignorant and unfit to belong to such a company can therefore be interpreted as an inverted expression of an alternative, perhaps more perceptive, vision of the world. In the second and third verses, the author-narrator admits to seeing that "something is not right [*neladno*] in the world," but he expresses resigned hopelessness as to the possibility of real action: he is unable to "get to work" on righting wrongs, because "the age holds [him] firmly/Extinguishes any impulse from the start."[26] This kind of systemic condemnation is typical of an expansive, generalizing approach that is found throughout Galich's oeuvre, especially (as will be discussed below) in his treatment of the Gulag theme.

Part 5 of "Razmyshleniya" also follows a general pattern typical of many of Galich's songs in which the refrain "recurs with slight variations after every third stanza."[27] In the first instance of the refrain, the association between the drunken author-narrator and a *skomorokh*-type figure is underscored as follows:

I vsyo-taki ya, riskuya proslyt'
Shutom, durachkom, payatsyom,
I noch'yu, i dnyom tverzhu ob odnom:
Ne nado, lyudi, boyat'sya!

And nevertheless, running the risk of seeming
A joker, an idiot, a clown,
I repeat one thing both day and night:
There's no need to be afraid!

The author-narrator is fully aware of his position, of the fact that he may seem like an idiot because of the declarations he makes; and in fact, it is precisely this position that allows him to make his declarations openly.

The author-narrator's declarations are not especially subtle, as the second verse and final couplet of the refrain reveal:

Ne boytes' t'yurmy, ne boytes' sumy,
Ne boytes' mora i glada,
A boytes' yedinstvenno tol'ko togo,
Kto skazhet: "Ya znayu kak nado!"

Kto skazhet: "Idite, lyudi, za mnoy,
Ya vas nauchu kak nado!"

Don't fear prison, don't fear beggary,
Don't fear high mortality and hunger,
But fear only this,
The one who says: "I know what's necessary!"

Who says: "Follow me, people,
I will teach you what's necessary!"

Here the author-narrator emphasizes human responsibilty, and specifically the culpability of leaders, for the world's ills. Galich's concept of "leaders" may be interpreted very broadly, however, applying not simply to major figures but also to anyone who claims the very kind of superior knowledge that the author-narrator unequivocally rejects for himself in the song's first verse. As subsequent verses make clear, one who claims such knowledge may curry favor and "declare his love to all of you," but ultimately his actions will have tragic consequences:

On proydyot po zemle zhelezom
I zatopit yeyo v krovi,

I navryot on takiye vraki
I takoy napletyot rasskaz,
Chto ne raz tot rasskaz v barake
Vy pomyanite v gor'kiy chas.

He will tread across the earth with iron
And will drown it in blood,

And he will tell such lies
And will weave such a story,
That you will recall this story more than once
In the barracks in a bitter hour.

The author-narrator thus makes explicit the price of such fallacious omniscience. In the song's final couplet, he exhorts his audience equally explicitly as to how to deal with anyone claiming this omniscience: "Gonite yego! Ne ver'te yemu!/On vryot! On ne znayet kak nado!" ("Chase him away! Don't believe him!/He is lying! He doesn't know what's necessary!").

Where the previous song is framed as having been composed while its author was in a drunken state, in "Zhutkaya istoriya, kotoruyu ya uslyshal v privokzal'nom shalmane" (1969; "A Terrible Story, Which I Overheard in a Train Station Bar") Galich's narrator recounts a bizarre tale, the events of which are set in motion by the protagonist's drunkenness. As with Vysotsky's "Oy, gde byl ya vchera," moreover, performances of this song showcase Galich's facility at mimicking the speech patterns of the inebriated. In an interesting twist, though, this mimicry effectively blurs the distinction between narrator and protagonist: the song's title proclaims the "terrible story" to be a secondhand one, something that the narrator "overheard," yet the narrator's own speech patterns suggest far more direct knowledge of the events he recounts. As voiced by the narrator, both the protagonist's speech and his predilections identify him as a very ordinary, neither cultured nor well-educated, Soviet citizen:

Chto nam Repina palitra!
Chto nam Pushkina stikhi!
My na brata—pó dva litra,
Pó tri portsii ukhi. (315–17)

What is Repin's palette to us!
What are Pushkin's poems to us!
We take two liters per person,
And three portions of fish soup.

Having lost his passport while drunk, the protagonist goes about having the passport reinstated while still hungover and not in full possession of his wits. As "L'vova Klavka" is filling out the appropriate form, he inexplicably ("as if all of a sudden the devil took control") asks her, "for a joke," to indicate his nationality as Jewish ("Ty davay, mol, v punkte pyatom/Napishi, chto ya—yevrey!" ["You go ahead, under the fifth point/Write that I'm a Jew!"]). With the simple stroke of a pen, the protagonist is thus registered as a Jew. As a result, he becomes the target of myriad indignities and injuries that reflect the depth and breadth of anti-Semitism in the Soviet Union. In the end, from being a Russian major and member of the CPSU, he is banished to the provinces, kicked out of the Party, and demoted: ". . . Ya teper' v Kaluge,/Besparteynyi, ryadovoy" (". . . I live in Kaluga now,/Non-Party, rank and file"). Reduced to this sorry state, the protagonist has only one option left: to embrace the identity he adopted as a drunken joke ("Gde tut, brattsy, sinagoga?/Podskazhite, kak proyti?!" ["Where is the synagogue, brothers?/Tell me, how do I get there?"]).

In these two songs, as in songs by Vysotsky and Kim discussed above, references to and portrayals of drinking and alcoholism are troubling, from an ideological standpoint, for multiple reasons. On one hand, these behaviors highlight an obvious and irreconcilable conflict between official values and popular ones. If in the official hierarchy of values both drunkenness itself and the link between drunkenness and other types of antisocial behavior were cause for extreme concern, in the popular mentality frequent and heavy drinking was widely accepted (not to mention practiced) and even tacitly condoned.[28] Moreover, as Walter Connor has discussed, there was a deep-seated official preoccupation with the notion that drunkenness could reveal a person's inner characteristics: "crimes committed in a state of drunkenness are claimed to demonstrate something wrong with the offender beyond the incidental fact that he happened to be intoxicated."[29] Seen in this light, such songs reveal not just a rift between official values and popular ones, but also widespread social breakdown—the failure of *vospitaniye*—not just among the working class to whom problems of drunkenness were most commonly attributed, but throughout Soviet society as a whole.[30] On the other hand, in songs by Kim and Galich in particular, alcoholism and drunkenness do not stand alone as independent themes. Rather, they serve as touchstones through which the bards address some of the most pernicious features of the Soviet system: not just omnipresent and unrestrained drinking, that is, but also equally widespread (and officially promoted) anti-Semitism and the brutal terror of the Soviet regime against its own citizens. This is no less true in songs by Galich and others that confront the Gulag theme, as will be discussed below.

THE GULAG THEME IN PUBLIC DISCOURSE OF THE POST-STALIN PERIOD

In the drive to admit discussion of the Gulag into official public discourse, 1962 was a watershed year. Under the stewardship of editor Andrey Tvardovsky, Aleksandr Solzhenitsyn's *Odin den' Ivana Denisovicha* (*One Day in the Life of Ivan Denisovich*) was published in the progressive-leaning journal *Novyi mir* (*New World*). The novella's publication represented a victory both for open debate about the Gulag and for Tvardovsky, who beat out *Izvestiya* (*News*) editor Aleksey Adzhubey to crack the taboo on publishing accounts of the Gulag. This victory was temporary, however, and a backlash soon followed. As Miriam Dobson has shown, *Odin den'* disturbed many readers because it seemed to challenge deeply felt notions of "Sovietness," heroism, and proper behavior.[31] For the Soviet authorities, the novella's open-endedness, its lack of optimism, and its lack of a clear moral were equally problematic: concisely put, in *Odin den',* "the Party did not triumph in the end, and communism did not emerge the victor."[32]

Almost immediately following the publication of Solzhenitsyn's novella, serious public discussion about the Gulag was attacked on two fronts. In March 1963, Khrushchev issued a speech warning sternly "about the reappearance of the camp experience in recent Soviet literature"; and arguing against "some authors'" focus on "instances of lawlessness, despotism, and abuse of power" that were—according to the official line—the exception, rather than the rule.[33] As a result, strict control was imposed on publications dealing with the Gulag theme, while a swift narrative counteroffensive saw the release of a wave of "true believer" Gulag accounts, written from the point of view of loyal communists, in which the Gulag was presented as a tragic Stalinist anomaly and consigned firmly to the past.[34]

In addition to their firm communist convictions, the protagonists of "true believer" camp narratives shared certain key features: they identified with camp guards (i.e., other loyal communists), not with their fellow prisoners; they fervently believed their arrest and imprisonment to be unfortunate mistakes resulting from simple human error; and they were adamant in dissociating Soviet camps (and the people who ran them) from Nazi concentration camps (and the [by definition inhuman] fascists who ran them).[35] The purpose of such "true believer" camp narratives was, as Dariusz Tolczyk argues, "paradoxically twofold: simultaneously to discover the Soviet camp experience and to provide it with an ideological cover-up."[36] But even the publication of officially approved works on the camp theme was not a sufficient remedy for the crisis spawned by *Odin den'*. Soon, even loyalist narratives could no longer be published. By the end of the 1960s, the labor camp theme had "vanished quietly from a central position within Soviet public discourse" and had again fallen subject to "the only method the Soviet regime could rely on [for control]: the taboo."[37]

"LET THE WHOLE WORLD SIT BEHIND BARBED WIRE!": GUITAR POETRY AND THE GULAG

While publication of *Odin den' Ivana Denisovicha* and the subsequent backlash against it shaped official public discourse about the Gulag theme, these events did far less to define discussion of the Gulag in popular discourse. Information about the labor camps had, after all, trickled out to the Soviet public in oral form for some time before published works appeared, thanks to regular prisoner releases and periodic mass amnesties.[38] In addition to personal accounts, songs provided a particularly rich and easily transmitted vein of information about camp conditions, camp life, and camp values.[39]

Oral accounts of the camps, both personal narratives and songs, provided important inspiration for a number of bards. Aleksandr Gorodnitsky has identified camp songs, which he heard firsthand from ex-convict workers while on expeditions in the Far North in the late 1950s, as his own inspiration for beginning to compose songs.[40] Observing that guitar poetry "was born not just in 'Moscow kitchens,' but on the lumbering camps of the vast GULAG," Gorodnitsky also interweaves camp songs into the origins of guitar poetry itself; this perspective reflects the fact that some songs written in the camps or by former *zeks* (prisoners) were absorbed into, and "became folklore" through, guitar poetry.[41] Inspired by camp songs, Gorodnitsky himself began singing about the Gulag even before published accounts appeared: his first stylized camp songs date to 1960. Yuly Kim began writing camp-themed songs somewhat later, but like Gorodnitsky he cites oral camp narratives as his motivation for doing so. As Kim recounts, "I began to comment upon the stupidities and beastliness of the regime in '63, when I met Pyotr Yakir," who spent seventeen years in the camps, beginning at age fourteen; this meeting was, as Kim describes, the "discovery of a whole world, as if I had read [Solzhenitsyn's] *The Gulag Archipelago* long before it saw the light of day."[42]

Circulating in ways that largely circumvented official organs of censorship and dissemination, guitar poetry could carry "fugitive meanings" (James Scott's term) and express viewpoints that differed sharply from officially accepted norms in relative safety. Depiction and dissection of the labor camps was one of the most notable taboo themes for which this was the case. Both the longevity and the scope of guitar poetry's engagement with the labor camp theme are significant: bards began singing about the Gulag even before published accounts by former prisoners became available, and they continued singing about the Gulag long after former prisoners' memoirs and camp-themed literary prose were no longer admitted into print. Guitar poetry thus helped sustain private debate about the Gulag even after public discourse on the topic had been muzzled thoroughly. In addition, because reproduction of *magnitizdat* tapes was less labor-intensive and less time-consuming than that of *samizdat* manuscripts; and because "acoustic *samizdat* surpassed the manuscript kind in circulation," bards' songs on the Gulag reached a broader audience than even the most assiduously reproduced *samizdat* manuscripts could.[43]

In keeping with guitar poetry's overall generic heterogeneity, the labor camp theme appears in various bards' songs in a broad range of permutations. In Gorodnitsky's songs, for example, the camp experience is presented fleetingly as a backdrop for expressions of personal courage and soul-searching of a type also found in songs focusing on natural settings and outdoor activities (e.g., tourist songs, geologists' songs, mountaineering songs). In Vysotsky's stylized *blatnye pesni,* the labor camp appears in concert with descriptions of or references to criminal behavior. Finally, in both Kim's sardonic ditties and Galich's sung diatribes, the labor camps transcend physical boundaries and become a metaphor for the Soviet system in its entirety.

Aleksandr Gorodnitsky provides an interesting example of a bard who eschews both the criminal and the political in his treatment of the Gulag theme, expressing a dislike of *blatnaya pesnya* and the "romanticization of the criminal world," and also of politicized poetry in general.[44] Praise and admiration are reserved for genuine camp songs (*lagernye pesni*), which Gorodnitsky calls "great songs of a suffering and downtrodden people, frightful accusatory documents of the epoch."[45] Given Gorodnitsky's views, it is not surprising that in his songs the labor camp theme should take on a deeply personal cast.[46] In "Mokroye tsarstvo" (1960; "The Bloody Kingdom"), for example, Gorodnitsky sketches an unforgiving world that is both a time apart and a place apart—but with only the barest indications that this world is a prison camp. Here, "winter will not follow autumn,/The long-awaited summer will not follow spring."[47] Reminders of the outside world are a source of discomfort ("Don't you send parcels, don't you fret about writing"); and the speaker's only confidants are the trees, "because trees know how to be silent,/Because trees live even in unfreedom." The camp itself is mapped synecdochically by "towers in the corners," and camp personnel are indicated metonymically by the mention of "gray wolves in precious collars." In Gorodnitsky's performance, feelings of isolation and melancholy that are refracted through the harsh natural environment are augmented by a simple melodic accompaniment in a minor key, relying heavily on three chords (A minor, D minor, and E), the repetitiveness of which mimics the monotony and absence of change described in the song's lyrics.[48]

Like "Mokroye tsarstvo," Gorodnitsky's "Na materik" (1960; "To the Mainland") is dominated by descriptions of inhospitable and unforgiving nature. Absent references to barbed wire, guard dogs, camp personnel, and other familiar attributes of prison camp descriptions, nature is the most oppressive or imprisoning force in this song, as can be seen in its second verse:

Opyat' purga, opyat' zima
Pridyot, metelyami zvenya.
Uyti v bega, soyti s uma
Teper' uzh pozdno dlya menya.[49]

Again a snowstorm, again winter
Will arrive, ringing with blizzards.
Now it's already too late for me
To take off in flight, to lose my mind.

Here, too, Gorodnitsky evokes the profound isolation and hopelessness that are constant leitmotifs of genuine camp songs,[50] and, as is evident in the song's first stanza (also repeated as its last), a profound sense of melancholy:

Ot zloy toski ne materis',—
Segodnya ty bez spirta p'yan:
Na materik, na materik
Idyot posledniy karavan.

Don't swear out of fierce melancholy,—
You're drunk without spirits:
The last caravan is going
To the mainland, to the mainland.

Gorodnitsky's experiences working in the Far North doubtless aided him in conjuring evocative descriptions of a severe natural world. To judge by the reception of "Na materik," the atmosphere and emotions he conjured in this song were also accurately rendered, ringing true for many who had been through the labor camps themselves. Gorodnitsky recalls hearing the song performed by a group of workers (largely ex-*zeks*) in Turukhan *krai* in 1961, and attempting—because he was "young, stupid, vain"—to convince them that he had written it; as he recounts, "they 'gently' . . . told me that that was impossible, [and certain] individuals were even found who had heard [the song] with their own ears in camps outside of Noril'sk in the 1940s."[51]

Unlike Gorodnitsky, Vysotsky embraced the genre of *blatnaya pesnya.*

A trained actor, Vysotsky excelled in mimicking and manipulating *blatnaya pesnya*—in part because theatricality itself is such an important part of that genre—and many of his songs about the Gulag number among his early stylized *blatnye pesni.* Machismo and irony are central to these songs, which outwardly glorify criminal behavior and an "underworld" lifestyle, and which make liberal use of criminal slang and non-normative grammar. As many have been quick to argue, though, the boastful swagger of songs like "Ya byl dushoy durnogo obshchestvo" (1961; "I was the heart and soul of a bad company") is part and parcel of a particular lyric persona for whom rejection of social norms is obligatory and for whom appearances are crucial, rather than a genuine endorsement of criminal behavior.[52]

The theatrical bravado typical of *blatnye pesni* is much in evidence in songs such as "Vsyo pozadi—i KPZ, i sud" (1963; "It's all behind—the holding cell and court"), in which the protagonist professes not to care what happens to him upon his conviction: "Mat' moya—davay rydat',/A mne zh ved', v obshchem, naplevat',/Kuda, kuda menya poshlyut" ("Mother mine—go ahead and cry,/But me, well, I really don't give a damn/Where, where they send me") (39–40). But though Vysotsky's imitations of criminal songs are certainly permeated with stylistic flair,[53] there is much substance to be found in them as well. Little by little, their protagonists reveal important aspects of the Gulag phenomenon, and also its larger implications for Soviet society as a whole. In "Vsyo pozadi," for example, the protagonist's musings about where he might be sent reveal his poor grasp of Soviet geography (for him, it is of little consequence whether he is incarcerated near the White Sea or the Black Sea), but they also bear witness to the vastness of the labor camp system.[54] In "Zeka Vasil'yev i Petrov zeka" (1962; "Prisoner Vasil'yev and Prisoner Petrov"), Vysotsky alludes to hierarchies of prisoners that operated within the Gulag ("Every day the hardened criminals [*ugolovniki*] torment us"), while also satirizing the common practice of supplying inflated reports: though both Vasil'yev and Petrov are self-described petty criminals, their camp commander is rewarded for "catching two major criminals [*dvukh krupnykh ugolovnikov*]" after their failed escape attempt (42–43).

In "My vmeste grabili odnu i tu zhe khatu" (1963; "Together we robbed one and the same pad"), Vysotsky's protagonist clearly perceives his sentence as time "apart" from his "real life":

> Da eto zh matematika bogov:
> Menya ved' na dvenadtsat' osudili,—
> U zhizni otobrali sem' godov,
> I pyat'—teper' obratno vozvratili! (49–50)
>
> Well, now, that is the mathematics of the gods:
> They sentenced me to twelve years,

Took away seven years of my life,
And now they've given back five!

As various studies have shown, this perception of time is widely attested among prisoners: "Prison time, like prison space, has mythological characteristics: it is 'other' time, not profane, 'inverted,' 'otherworldly.'"[55] For this reason, "psychologically the prisoner does not regard his term as part of his real life . . . He lives in his *srok*, but it is not his life; it has been subtracted from his life."[56]

In the chorus to this same song, as G. I. Cherniyavskiy observes, Vysotsky also satirizes "Soviet propaganda's 'culture of the gift,'" in which "all good things (or all that is deemed to be good)" were attributed to the "'sage stewardship' of the Party and its leaders":[57]

Za khleb i vodu i za prirodu—
Spasibo nashemu soveyskomu narodu!
Za nochi v tyur'makh, doprosy v MURe—
Spasibo nashey gorodskoy prokurature!

For bread and water and for nature
Thank you to our Soviet people!
For nights in jails, interrogations in the Moscow CID,
Thank you to our city public prosecutor's office!

Here, as is so often the case in Vysotsky's songs, the printed text conveys only a shadow of the conversational and nonstandard speech of the protagonist (seen, in part, in the forms *sem' godov* [instead of *sem' let*, "seven years"] and *soveyskomu* [instead of *sovetskomu*, "Soviet"]).[58]

Like Gorodnitsky's "Na materik" and Vysotsky's "My vmeste grabili odnu i tu zhe khatu," Yuly Kim's "Pionerskaya lagernaya pesnya" (1964; "Pioneer Camp Song") reflects labor camp life as if from within. Kim's song is filled not with Gorodnitsky's melancholy or Vysotsky's braggadocio, though, but with a relentless irony that calls to mind Aleshkovsky's "Pesnya o Staline" (1959; "Song About Stalin"). Where Aleshkovsky's song is an unmatched "parody of the genre which had been artificially generated in the 1930s, the 'folk-song' about Stalin,"[59] however, "Pionerskaya lagernaya pesnya" mocks upbeat, youth-oriented mass songs that merrily extol virtues like labor and love of the motherland. Turning ideological set phrases on their heads and juggling neutral and slang meanings of words, Kim quickly destroys any illusions about the identity of the camp referred to in the song's title. Through an artful play on the word *zona* (meaning both "zone" and "prison camp"), the "first-rate lads" and "shock-workers of labor" in whose name Kim sings are soon revealed to live in a camp in which "besides a camp for recreation [*zony otdykha*],/There's a camp [*zona*] just for the heck of it!"[60]

Similarly, the camp leader is revealed to be not simply a *roditel'* (parent), but also a *kum* (meaning both "godfather" and "head of camp operations"):

Nachal'nik nash roditel' nam,
Tochneye skazhem—kum,
I pod yego voditel'stvom
Beryomsya my za um.

Our boss is a parent to us,
Or, more precisely, a godfather,
And under his leadership
We come to our senses.

The song ends with a cunningly ambivalent couplet—"A za kolyuchey provolkoy/Puskay sidit ves' mir!" ("And beyond [or behind] the barbed wire/Let the whole world sit!")—which simultaneously suggests that the "first-rate lads" are content with their lot, but also that the "whole world" might be imprisoned with them. The irony of this song derives both from Kim's wickedly dexterous use of language; and also from the striking contrast between the revelation made in its lyrics and Kim's jaunty, spirited performance, which derisively mimics the incessantly upbeat nature that typified "mass" song.

A similar treatment of the labor camp theme is found in "Skazaniye o Petre Yakire, kotoryi rodilsya v 1923 godu, a sel v 1937–m" (1964; "Tale About Pyotr Yakir, Who Was Born in 1923 and Went to Prison in 1937"). Kim's description of the prison camp experience (here seen from the outside) is no less cutting than in the previous song. Despite being only fourteen, Kim writes, Yakir is already seen as a "political bandit [*politbandit*]."[61] Stalin (called "the caring Father," in a mocking usage of a once-common official epithet) subsequently imprisons many others, in order to ensure that the young inmate "doesn't get bored" and that he "is brought up properly in his stinking cell":

K nemu i podsadil
Zabotlivyi Otets
Odnikh uchyonykh desyat' tyshch,
I neuchyonykh desyat' tyshch,
I neskol'ko mil'yonov—prosto tak, na vsyakiy sluchay.

The caring Father
Put in with him

Ten thousand scholars alone
And ten thousand non-scholars,
And several million—just for the heck of it, just in case.

Nonstandard or quasi-phonetic pronunciations (rendered in the printed text as *tyshch* [instead of *tysyach*, "thousands"] and *mil'yonov* [instead of *millionov*, "millions"]) contribute to a conversational quality of expression. The caustic presentation both of Stalin himself and of the labor camp system as capable of "bringing up" or properly (re)educating people are certainly damning, as are references to widespread anti-Semitism (e.g., "In general they're a talented lot, all those Jews"). What made this song (and others in Kim's oeuvre) particularly subversive was not simply its accuracy, though, but rather its historical specificity, the fact that it contains references to particular people and their experiences. For this reason, in fact, the KGB singled out "Skazaniye o Petre Yakire" and other "seditious ditties" (as Kim called them) for denunciation to the Central Committee of the CPSU.[62]

Even with such "seditious ditties," however, Kim could not match Galich's sustained and uncompromising exploration of the labor camp theme. If in Gorodnitsky's or Vysotsky's songs the Gulag can seem distant from the everyday, a separate time and a world apart, Galich repeatedly insists on spatial and temporal connections, on the many pernicious ways in which the "little zone" (that is, the Gulag itself) leaches into and contaminates the "big zone" (in other words, the country as a whole). He consistently underscores the relationship between, even the identity of, the Gulag and the political system that spawned it. By drawing explicit parallels between the Gulag and Nazi concentration camps, moreover, Galich stresses the fundamental identity of all totalitarian systems while also foregrounding Soviet anti-Semitism. Finally, through the provocative use of "we" and open appeals to conscience and exhortations to action, Galich challenges the notion of the selective responsibility of a depersonalized "system." In so doing, he forces his audience to confront the ways in which, by reason of silent consent and "nonresistance of conscience" (as he writes in "Poyezd" [1966; "The Train"]) ordinary people bear collective responsibility for the horrors inflicted by the regime (305). Insisting on collective guilt and mutual responsibility, Galich openly rejects the official Thaw-era interpretation of Stalinism as "a perversion of Party authority that led to the slaughter of innocent citizens."[63]

The camp theme appears in Galich's songs from the very beginning of his activity as a bard. In "Oblaka" (1962; "Clouds"), which is sung from the point of view of a former camp inmate, the image of clouds floating by "unhurriedly . . . , like in a movie" is used as a spatial and temporal link connecting the camps and the outside world, the past and the present (87–88). Frequent shifts between descriptions of the present and reminiscences about the past strengthen this sense of continuity:

Ya podkovoy vmyorz v sannyi sled,
V lyod, chto ya kaylom kovyryal,
Ved' nedarom ya dvadtsat' let
Protrubil po tem lageryam.[64]

Do sikh por v glazakh snega nast!
Do sikh por v ushakh shmona gam!..
Ey, podayte zh mne ananas
I kon'yachku yeshchyo dvesti gramm!

I froze to the road like a horseshoe,
To the ice that I was digging with a pickax,
It's not for nothing that I spent
Twenty years in those camps.

There's still a thin crust of icy snow in my eyes!
The din of frisking still rings in my ears! . . .
Hey, bring me some pineapple
And another two hundred grams of cognac!

In performance, Galich underscores the inescapability of this past (revealed in the fifth and sixth lines cited above) with a harsh, angry chord that stands out starkly against the song's generally understated musical accompaniment. The narrator's drunkenness is similarly underscored by Galich's hissing concentration on the sibilant *s* of *ananas-s-s* and by his slurring of *kon'yachku.*[65]

While the clouds float toward the campsites of Abakan and Kolyma, the narrator sits in a bar, drinking heavily ("Ya kon'yachku prinyal polkilo" ["I took half a kilo of cognac"]) and reflecting cynically on his life:

Ya i sam zhivu—pervyi sort,
Dvadtsat' let kak den' razmenyav!
Ya v pivnoy sizhu, slovno lord,
I dazhe zuby yest' u menya!

And I myself live—first rate,
Having exchanged twenty years like a single day!
I sit in a bar like a lord,
And I even have my teeth!

In the song's final verse, Galich further underscores the continuity between past and present, between the camps and the country as a whole, by gesturing at the the scope of the labor camp phenomenon as follows:

I po etim dnyam, kak i ya,
Polstrany sidit v kabakakh!
I nashey pamyat'yu v te kraya
Oblaka plyvut, oblaka.

And these days, just like me,
Half the country sits in bars!
And carried by our memories, the clouds,
The clouds float toward those places.

Performing the final verses of "Oblaka," Galich again uses a dramatic shift in musical accompaniment for additional emphasis. Whereas the accompaniment for most of the song consists of a few unobtrusive notes, Galich utters the revelation that "these days, just like me,/Half the country sits in bars" to a series of jarring, repeated chords. This musical shift links this verse acoustically to the earlier revelation of the inescapability of the past. Whereas the narrator had earlier expressed the continuity of his own life (the fact that the camp experience is not forgotten), here he underscores the frightening mundanity of these experiences in Soviet society: half the country sits in bars, just like him, and half the country shares his memories. As was the case with Gorodnitsky's "Na materik," both the relevance and the verisimilitude of Galich's "Oblaka" are confirmed by the fact that the song "became folklore."[66]

In a number of songs, Galich expresses a similar continuity between the camps and the outside world through relationships between camp guards and those they guarded. As Galich illustrates with chilling clarity, the line dividing these two groups is precariously thin; and, moreover, they are locked in mutual dependence. In the camps, *zeks* could be co-opted into guarding their fellow *zeks,* as can be seen in "Fantaziya na russkiye temy" (1968–69; "Fantasy on Russian Themes"): "And now, in the logging operation,/I myself am among the guards" (115–16). Beyond the barbed wire, former guards and former prisoners are reunited in awkward interdependence. In "Zhelaniye slavy" (after 1972; "Desire for Fame"), for example, Galich depicts a "boss [*vertukhay*] and a former number something-or-other" who find themselves in the same hospital room and who "can't get by without one another," until the *vertukhay* dies (129–32). As the former *zek* covers the recently expired *vertukhay* with a sheet, ending one link between this victim and his victimizer, another link is formed: "Vsyo snezhok idyot, snezhok nad Moskvoyu,/I synok moy (po tomu l' po snezhochku?)/Provozhayet vertukhayevu dochku . . ." ("The snow is falling, snow over Moscow/And my sonny boy [through the same snow, is it?]/Is accompanying the boss's young daughter . . ."). Such moments have been interpreted optimistically "in light of the well-known saying that in the Soviet Union half the population did time and the other half stood guard," as representing "universal reconciliation."[67] Arguably, however, one can also interpret moments when the two "halves" meet as signs of the insidious seepage of the Gulag into everyday life.

Outside the Gulag, the position of those in power is perpetually unstable as well: just as *zeks* in the camps can become guards, so, too, can the arbiters and guardians of power become *zeks.* The hypocrisy and danger of shifts in official positions interpenetrate many of Galich's camp and camp-related songs. In "Pesnya o siney ptitse" (1966; "Song About a Blue Bird"), for example, Galich observes that loyalty to the Communist Party was no protection against the harshest of treatments ("Bylo vremya, za krasnyi tsvet/Dobavlyali po desyat' let!" ["There was a time when, for the color red,/They added ten years!"]) (97–98). Similar issues are raised in "Nochnoy razgovor v vagone-restorane" (1969; "Nighttime Conversation in the Cafe Car"), which is part 4 of the six-part cycle "Razmyshleniya o begunakh na dlinnye distantsii" ("Musings on Long-Distance Runners"). The narrator of "Nochnoy razgovor" tells of a camp "godfather" who announces to his charges the occurrence of the 20th Party Congress, with the consequent change in official policy toward Stalin: "Okazalsya nash Otets/Ne ottsom, a sukoyu . . ." ("Our Father turned out to be/Not a father, but a bastard . . .") (108–11).[68]

In "Ave Maria" (1968), which is part 6 of the same cycle, Galich draws an explicit parallel between different manifestations of state-sponsored terror by referring to "the shadows of all Butyrkas and Treblinkas,/Of all treachery, betrayals, and crucifixions" (113–14). In "Pesnya iskhoda" (1971; "Song of Exodus"), similarly, Galich juxtaposes the camp-riddled territories of Kazakhstan and Magadan with sites of Nazi Einsatzgruppen massacres at Ponary and Babi Yar. As these reference suggest, Galich did not stop at the borders of the Soviet Union in his broad interpretation of the camp phenomenon. In numerous songs, Galich draws explicit parallels between Soviet labor camps and Nazi concentration camps, presenting the camp phenomenon as inherent in—and even a direct reflection of—totalitarian systems in general.[69]

Such comparisons are developed further in "Ballada o vechnom ogne" (1968; "Ballad About the Eternal Flame"), in which Auschwitz appears side by side with a broad Gulag landscape bounded by Siberian rivers. Though Galich criticizes mere memorials and ceremonies as insufficient, he notes that sites commemorating other atrocities are both powerful and respected: "I sklonyayut koleni pod grom barabannyi/Pered etoy zagadkoy glavy pravitel'stv!" ("And to thundering drums, heads of state/Go down on bended knee before that mystery!") (309–11). But while fallen soldiers are honored and Nazi atrocities are remembered, Galich cautions, the Gulag remains dangerously obscured and forgotten:

> Pered etoy zemlyoy nikakiye prem'yery,
> Podtyanuvshi shtany, ne pereklonyat koleni!
>
> Nad sibirskoy Okoyu, nad Kamoy, nad Ob'yu
> Ni znamyon, ni venkov ne polozhat k nadgrob'yu![70]
>
> Before this land, not one premier
> Will hitch up his trousers and go down on his knees!
>
> Above the Siberian Oka, above the Kama and the Ob
> Neither banners nor wreaths will be laid on these graves!

While official actions are of great consequence, however, Galich's notion of "camp" does not depend solely on ideology, on impersonal "systems," or on the actions of "heads of state." It also depends on ordinary people, particularly on "people who conform,"[71] and on the choices they make. In songs that span his entire bardic career, Galich asserts repeatedly that guilt for the horrors of the Gulag—and, by extension, for the horrors perpetrated by any repressive system—must be borne collectively; and that only by acts of courage and conscience can this guilt be expiated. As Galich affirms in "Staratel'skiy val'sok" (1963; "Prospectors' Waltz"), silence alone makes us culpable because we "let others cry out in despair," knowing that "silence is more profitable, / Because silence is gold!" (35–36). The same golden silence that brings prosperity and privilege, therefore, also makes us executioners: "Vot kak prosto popast'—v palachi: / Promolchi! / Promolchi! / Promolchi!" ("That's how simple it is to become executioners: / Be silent! / Be silent! / Be silent!"). Morally uncompromising, Galich is adamant that attempts to shirk responsibility are mere acts of self-deception. As he writes in "Ballada o chistikh rukakh" (1968; "Ballad About Clean Hands"), "It's no use pretending—we know what we are doing!" (57).

Such comments on the power of silence and willful self-deception find their counterparts in Galich's declarations of his own personal choice and his willingness to accept the consequences thereof. Perhaps the best-known of these declarations is found in "Ya vybirayu Svobodu" (1971; "I Choose Freedom"):

> Ya vybirayu Svobodu
> I p'yu s ney nynche na ty.
> Ya vybirayu svobodu
> Noril'ska i Vorkuty,

Gde vnov' ogorodnoy tyapkoy
Nad vskhodami plyashet knut,
Gde puleyu ili tryapkoy
Odnazhdy mne rot zatknut. (273–74)

I choose Freedom
She and I are on familiar terms.
I choose the freedom
Of Noril'sk and Vorkuta,

Where once again the knout dances
Above the seedlings like a garden hoe,
Where with a bullet or a rag
One day they'll stop my mouth.

Similar declarations can be found in "Razgovor s Muzoy" (1968; "Conversation with the Muse"), which begins, "I don't give a damn if I disappear in some Inta" (260). Likewise, in "Chernovik epitafii" (1971; "Draft of an Epitaph"), Galich asks,

Skol'ko raz na menya stuchali
I divilis', chto ya—na volye.
Nu a yesli b ya gnil v Suchane,
Vam by legche dyshalos', chto li?! (270)

How many times they ratted on me
And marveled that I was still free.
And what if I had rotted in Suchan,
Would you have breathed easier, really?!

In all of these cases, Galich traces a clear trajectory that leads directly from freedom, from speaking out, to the Gulag, which is identified by references to key labor camp locations. Moreover, Galich's understanding of his own precarious position is combined with a bitter knowledge that many who did speak chose to inform, to speak out against others instead of speaking out against the brutal terrors of the Gulag and other such evils perpetrated in the name of ideology. Through his insistent use of "we" as well as "you," however, Galich implicitly includes both himself and his listeners in the larger community of those responsible for the failings of the Soviet system.

The penetrating directness of Galich's labor camp songs—his "uncompromising civic courage"[72] and frequent, explicit exhortations to the audience—sets them in opposition not just to official ideology and its code of prescriptions and taboos. In many cases, it also sets his views in sharp contrast to those of his fellow bards and of his audiences. Okudzhava, for example, explicitly rejected the notion of collective responsibility for Stalinism and its excesses, musing at length that

> the Party leadership, the organs of mass propaganda, are guilty of [creating] Stalinism, that is, the bosses [*verkhushka*], who create a particular atmosphere in the country, are guilty. After all, I was a Stalinist myself, despite the fact that my parents were repressed . . . Such were the times.[73]

In Galich's songs more than any other bard's, the vast wasteland of the Gulag archipelago becomes a metaphor for all of Soviet society and for repressive political systems in general. In his songs nearly everyone stands accused, by virtue of passivity as much as active involvement, of being among the leaders, the guards, and the executioners responsible for creating and perpetuating repression. Significantly, the very inclusiveness of Galich's critique highlights the drawbacks of coloring even his songs, which are by far the most scathing commentaries on Soviet society to be found in guitar poetry, in the unadulterated shades of protest and dissent. Illustrating the interdependence of victimizer and victim, Galich suggests that, just as the Gulag is an inherent part of the entire Soviet system, so, too, are "they" (the guilty) an inherent part of "us" (the innocent).

With their highly varied songs on drinking and alcoholism and the Gulag, Galich and other bards transformed these politically sensitive topics into quintessentially marginal themes. If at first glance such songs seem like simple "protest music," whether through open challenges to Soviet ideology or simply by their own implicit resistance to restrictions on public discourse, the reality is rather more complicated. On one hand, the overt marginality of bards' songs on the "soft" taboo theme of drinking and alcoholism and the "hard" taboo theme of the Gulag is evident in their manipulation of the boundaries of acceptable public discourse—as well as (particularly in Galich's case) their challenging of the disconnect between public action and private conviction. On the other hand, these songs' overt marginality is reflected in the extent to which they underscore the universality of the phenomena they treat (the impossibility of circumscribing vice socially or spatially, the impossibility of delimiting the Gulag ideologically or geographically) and thereby the extent to which all of Soviet society is a "space of ambiguity." In turn, this ambiguity suggests both the "dual ambivalence" characteristic of marginality and the profound unease that this ambivalence generates—among *svoi* as much as it does among others.

Chapter Six

Covert Marginality: The Significance of Insignificance

Segodnya ne lichnoye—glavnoye
A svodki rabochego dnya.

Today the main thing is not personal matters,
But the totals of the working day.
—Vladimir Kharitonov, "My Address Is the Soviet Union"

WHILE "OVERT" MARGINALITY IS evident in songs on politically sensitive themes, "covert" marginality has subtler and less obvious manifestations in songs that lack explicitly political content. It can be argued that, at a generic level, guitar poetry was political by default because the majority of its songs were apolitical. Political significance could be inferred in bards' songs thanks to the absence of "politics of the customary sort," and songs could be seen as "full of anti-Sovietness [*antisovetchinoy*] in spirit, if not in form"; more broadly, as Aleksandr Gorodnitsky has argued, "in an unfree society, any free expression of feeling is an act of protest."[1] Moving beyond such generalizations, this chapter explores ways in which songs that focus on the "insignificant" constitute small, personal insurrections against Soviet ideology and against the mass culture through which it was promoted.

This approach draws upon Cathy Popkin's concept of the "pragmatics of insignificance," with particular reference to her analysis of insignificance in the works of Mikhail Zoshchenko. Insignificance is defined by contrast to, and is set against the demands made by, the Soviet cultural (and particularly literary) establishment: the very act of directing attention to trifling incidents and mundane objects simultaneously asserts the significance of things deemed "too trivial to merit attention" and trivializes the "larger-than-life icons of Soviet power."[2] According to Popkin, such persistent foregrounding of the insignificant amounts to "an act of insurrection" against the Soviet regime.[3] Here, bards' attention to details and themes that hover at the margins of noticeability is investigated as a means of rejecting, inverting, and subverting official determinations of importance and depictions of the important. In songs that employ covert marginality, insignificance is transformed into an instrument of quiet resistance as marginalized interests and needs become a central point of focus.

WHAT IS "SIGNIFICANT"?

In the post-Stalin period, the tenets of socialist realism continued to shape literary and artistic production, notwithstanding fulsome public declarations of the need for greater "sincerity" in literature and the arts and for the rejection of "rhetoric and the varnishing of reality [*lakirovka deystvitel'nosti*]."[4] Thus we must look to socialist realism for the basic criteria used to determine "significance" not just from the early 1930s until 1953, but also during the Thaw and beyond. The fundamental principles of socialist realism, as they evolved out of the 1930s, demanded the depiction of "the most stern and sober practical work [in combination] with a supreme spirit of heroic deeds and magnificent future prospects."[5] Socialist realist works were to be explicitly didactic in nature, emphasizing "the ideological remoulding and education of the toiling people in the spirit of socialism."[6] In service of this aim, representation of "typical circumstances" and "typical characters" was favored; as Georgy Malenkov explained, however, "typical" did not mean "just that which is encountered most frequently, but that which reflects the essence of a given socialist strength most fully and most pointedly."[7]

These, then, were the basic formulae that effectively "designated significance."[8] People, events, and objects were significant—and therefore worthy of artistic depiction—only insofar as they were officially determined to be significant. Moreover, the right to determine significance rested not with individual authors or other creative professionals, but with Party ideologues and especially with the leadership of the Union of Soviet Writers. According to socialist realist principles, certain topics and themes were highly suspect, considered to be too petty to merit artistic representation. One such theme was the "little man." As Katerina Clark observes, in the 1930s the "little man" was abandoned as "the cornerstone of the new society."[9] In the scripted play of building socialism, ordinary people were shunted aside in favor of a "new cast of high achievers"; and ordinary tasks were overshadowed by the superhuman feats of "spectacular individuals" (in the guise of shock-workers, "zealous Bolsheviks," and other decorated heroes of socialism).[10]

Similarly dubious were mundane situations and occurrences, especially anything touching upon the domestic sphere, which "generally contradict[ed] the aesthetics of the monumental style and the socialist-realist worldview"; indeed, domestic concerns ("a vulgar concept of 'beauty' in art, in life, and in the home") were subsumed into a larger category of "lack of taste [that] should be resolutely combated."[11] Included in the disdained domestic sphere were depictions of personal lives, most especially of romantic relationships that did not conform to a model of premarital chastity and harmonious marital fidelity. Such trivia as "the search for love or the arrangement of [one's] personal life" simply "were not motivating forces of plot" in the culture of socialist realism; as Katerina Clark notes of the Stalinist novel in particular, "love is an auxiliary ingredient" that serves "only to aid [the hero] in fulfilling his tasks and in attaining 'consciousness.'"[12] This attitude toward the personal is summarized succinctly by the patriotic popular song that provides this chapter's epigraph: "Segodnya ne lichnoye—glavnoye, / A svodki rabochego dnya" ("Today the main thing is not personal matters, / But the totals of the working day").[13]

By the mid-1950s the official Soviet song industry was deteriorating rapidly. Even before Stalin's death, serious critiques were leveled at the development of Soviet musical culture generally, with shortcomings attributed, in part, to "a limited and, at times, primitive interpretation of the principles of socialist realism" in music and "an incorrect understanding of the typical."[14] By the middle of the decade, prevailing professional opinion held that mass song had "ceased to play the kind of progressive role" in society that it had during its "golden age" in the 1930s.[15] Concomitantly, lyric song was seen to be hobbled by "petty themes, rampant clichés, hackwork and pandering to bad taste"; and professional songwriters were criticized for "forgetting about the great edifying [*vospitatel'nom*] significance of lyrics," producing instead "puny" works that encouraged "emotional sentimentalism and petty-bourgeois vulgarity."[16]

Thus, notions of "significance" underpinned discussions of official Soviet song throughout the immediate post-Stalin years; and songwriters' failure to address sufficiently "significant" themes was seen as a key factor in the decline of professional song in the 1950s. These discussions had little practical impact, however, as a report released on the eve of the 22nd Party Congress (1961) indicates:

> The voice of Soviet song—mass, lyric, [and] variety stage—has become quieter [and] more monotonous. Critics have expressed alarm many times over the state of this important genre, but so far there have been no significant changes. Obviously, we must begin a serious, major conversation with poets and composers [and] plan avenues for [song's] further development.[17]

By the same time, guitar poetry had become firmly entrenched in the sociocultural life of the Soviet urban intelligentsia and of Soviet young people more broadly. Moreover, the genre's popularity grew in no small part because the bards treated precisely the kinds of "insignificant" themes that were denigrated and ignored in official culture.

Guitar poetry focusing on "insignificant" themes can be categorized by drawing on the "petty" themes noted above, though there is necessarily considerable overlap between categories. Bards' songs dealing with the "little man" are too numerous to count. Various "little men" are a persistent feature of Vysotsky's songs, in particular; and as is observed variously, the characters Vysotsky sang about (and from the perspective of) were often "outcasts, people from the dregs of Soviet society," such as petty criminals, alcoholics, rank-and-file soldiers, and the mentally unstable—all types who "were not allowed to speak out in 'decent' literature."[18] Such characters were provocative simply because turning to "the theme of the 'little' man was a challenge to the official assertion and glorification [*vospevaniye*] of the 'hero of labor,' the 'Stakhanovite,' [and] the 'shock-worker' "; but also because, as depicted in guitar poetry, "little men" were "almost without exception weak, hesitant, and perplexed," and generally alienated from Soviet society.[19]

Equally numerous are songs focusing on mundane concerns and details of everyday life, and on personal and intimate affairs, which figure prominently in the oeuvres of a wide range of bards. It is on these last two categories of "insignificant" song themes that the subsequent analysis will focus. Mundane affairs will be examined through an analysis of bards' songs about Moscow. In socialist realist culture, Moscow was represented as "the symbolic center of the nation" and "a beacon toward which all lesser examples [i.e., cities, towns] . . . should incline"; as the nation's seat of power, moreover, Moscow "came to function as an extraordinarily privileged space."[20] In official culture, then, Moscow was the Soviet Union's ultimate public space. By contrast, in guitar poetry the hyper-public space of Moscow is "privatized," depicted "from below" and "from within" through attention to individual perspectives and private or semi-private spaces and to the particulars of everyday life. Various bards' songs about Moscow therefore provide an opportunity to examine the use of "insignificant" details, the effect of "noticing" that which should not be noticed. More directly, guitar poetry about romantic relationships provides an opportunity to examine bards' heterogeneous explorations of a theme that was itself "insignificant" within official Soviet culture.

A brief overview of canonical depictions of each of these two themes in official Soviet song will be offered as a backdrop for the subsequent analysis. In keeping with socialist realism's emphasis on the "typical," official Soviet songs about Moscow and about love demonstrate a broadly generalizing tendency; they are replete with "high-flown themes and . . . abstract nouns," often employing topoi like Moscow, youth, heart, happiness, and laughter as "ciphers" that "hint at [Soviet myths] in abbreviated form."[21] The human scale is dwarfed both literally and figuratively, a phenomenon that is underscored by the subsumption of the individual into the collective in various ways (e.g., people into crowds, romantic love into patriotic love).

"HEART OF MY MOTHERLAND": MOSCOW IN OFFICIAL SOVIET SONG

As the Soviet Union's symbolic center and exemplary city, Moscow is depicted in official songs in a highly schematized way. The city's topography is conveyed primarily by reference to a few key sites, such as the Kremlin (including its walls and star-topped towers) and the Moscow River. The city's size and grandeur—and, by extension, that of the whole country—are emphasized though frequent use of stock epithets such as "great" (*velikiy*) and "powerful" (*moguchiy*), "broad" (*shirokiy*) and "expansive" (*prostornyi*).[22] In Ol'ga Vysotskaya's "Moskva—velikiy gorod" (1938; "Moscow Is a Great City"), for example, the city is described as "the capital of all capitals" and praised as "our glory/ . . . the country's heart!"[23] Similarly, in Viktor Gusev's "Khorosho na moskovskom prostore" (1941; "It Is Good on a Moscow Expanse"), Moscow's size and openness are emphasized through references to the city's "broad expanses [*shirokiye prostory*]."[24]

Far from making Moscow seem imposing and inhospitable, however, in official song this breadth is linked to openness, optimism, and warm, welcoming commodiousness: despite its vastness, Moscow is nonetheless accessible to all comers.[25] The "heart of the Motherland," Moscow is also "the most beloved"; the "capital of a great universe" that outshines all others, Moscow is also "always near [*blizka*]," inspiring love in her faithful inhabitants:

> Lyublyu ya tebya neizmenno,
> Moy gorod, navek molodoy,
> . . .
> Kogda ya shagayu s raboty,
> Shirokoy, kak more, Moskvoy,
> Poyut moskvichi-patrioty
> Pro gorod vozlyublennyi svoy.[26]
>
> I love you steadfastly,
> My city, forever youthful,
> . . .
> As I stride from work
> Across Moscow, wide as the sea,
> Muscovite patriots are singing
> About their beloved city.

Moscow is personified far more than her populace, described variously as a "dear and beloved city [*rodnoy i lyubimyi gorod*]," as "talkative and vivacious [*govorliva i zhiva*]," and as a youthful beauty (*Moskva-krasavitsa*).[27]

The city's youthful countenance is accompanied by a maternal soul, however, and she receives visitors "like [her] own beloved sons."[28] This is typical of official culture of the 1930s generally, for during this period, as Hans Günther observes, "Moscow became the sacred center of the Soviet motherland, continuing the centuries-old tradition of singing the praises of mother Moscow."[29] Through her maternal embrace, Moscow draws her denizens together with elemental power, transforming residents and visitors alike into joyous crowds of fast friends who flow together "like rivers meet[ing] in the ocean."[30] Indeed, people appear in these and other Soviet mass songs predominantly as groups or collectives, acting—walking, striding, singing, dancing—as one: "poglyadi,—poyot i plyashet/Vsya Sovetskaya strana" ("look, the whole Soviet country/Is singing and dancing").[31] When people do appear individually, they are characterized only minimally, through the use of anonymous epithets (e.g., "dear" or "girlfriend") or through their own enthusiastic self-identification with a larger group (e.g., "guests from the collective farm," or, most commonly, simply "we" [*my, nam s toboy*]).[32]

Such references help to create an "illusion of friendship, a mythologem of intimate, close-knit massiness [*intimno-splochyonnoy massovosti*]."[33] They also serve to blur the boundaries between personal emotion and patriotism. Even in lyrics that purport to be about romantic love, Moscow is presented as the beloved object of unwavering affection. Gusev's "Khorosho na moskovskom prostore" is a love duet,[34] for example, but its would-be lovers are virtually conflated with Moscow through juxtaposition and parallelism:

> Ne zabyt' mne ochey tvoikh yasnykh
> I prostykh tvoikh laskovykh slov,
> Ne zabyt' mne moskovskikh prekrasnykh
> Ploshchadey, pereulkov, mostov.
> . . .
> Golos dal'ney Moskvy mne kazat'sya
> Budet golosom dal'nym tvoim.[35]
>
> I can't forget your clear eyes
> And your simple, tender words,
> I can't forget Moscow's beautiful
> Squares, side streets, bridges.
> . . .
> The voice of far-off Moscow will seem to me
> To be your own far-off voice.

Similarly, Lev Kondyrev's "Moskva-krasavitsa" (1950; "Moscow the Beauty") purports to be addressed to a girlfriend (*podruga*), but it is Moscow that is described as "the beauty [*krasavitsa*]" and as "beloved": "Proydyomsya segodnya, podruga, s toboy/Po nashey lyubimoy Moskve!" ("Today let us stroll together, girlfriend/Around our beloved Moscow!").[36] That this love emanates, through Moscow, to the country as a whole is underscored in official song culture by the persistent trope of Moscow as "the heart of the Motherland [*serdtse Rodiny*]."[37] Parallelism (e.g., rhymes like *Kremlya-zemlya* [Kremlin-earth]) and juxtaposition ("Strana moya,/Moskva moya,/Ty—samaya lyubimaya" ["My country,/My Moscow,/You are the most beloved!"]) serve to strengthen this identification still further.[38] As a synecdoche for the whole country, "Moscow unites and reflects in itself all the best qualities of the motherland in a condensed, heightened form."[39]

"OH, ARBAT, MY ARBAT, YOU ARE MY FATHERLAND": MOSCOW IN GUITAR POETRY

On balance, guitar poetry's Moscow cityscapes differ markedly from the broad generalizations and cheerful vagueness of the scenes described above, though the strategies employed in articulating this difference vary considerably. In various of Galich's songs, for example, Moscow's iconic buildings and spaces are rendered not as a colorful backdrop for a joyous and festive march toward the "bright and glorious future," but rather in deep and haunting shadows that betoken the inescapability of the past, and oftentimes its ominous reemergence as well. In Galich's vision, Red Square and Lenin's tomb frame a military parade evoked as a pointed reminder that "movement to the right/Begins with the left leg"; while at Lobnoye Mesto, a centuries-old platform on Red Square used for both religious ceremonies and political proclamations, a reanimated statue of Stalin "just like in the good old days,/Receives a parade of monsters!"[40] Such depictions are part and parcel of Galich's explicitly politicized approach, however, and thus they are of only passing interest here.

More significant, in terms of the present analysis, are numerous songs in which Moscow's most prominent, ceremonial, public spaces are rejected in favor of workaday, down-at-the-heel, private ones (simultaneously subverting Moscow's symbolic position as the "heart" of the Soviet motherland); and in which Moscow's denizens are presented individually—and as largely ordinary, unremarkable individuals at that. Such depictions feature especially prominently in songs by Vysotsky and Okudzhava; but they can be noted as well in songs by a range of "second-rank" bards like Ada Yakusheva and Aleksandr Gorodnitsky.

Vysotsky's oeuvre provides a useful starting point for discussing the "ordinary" Moscow of guitar poetry, because the titles and first lines of many of his songs read like a map of the city's least spectacular places. Songs like "Bol'shoy Karetnyi" (1962; "Bol'shoy Karetnyi Lane"), "Ey, shofyor, vezi—Butyrskiy khutor" (1963; "Hey, driver, take me to Butyrskiy Khutor"), and "V tyur'me Taganskoy nas stalo malo" (1965; "In the Taganka Prison few of us were left") provide just a few examples. Other Moscow locales that Vysotsky invokes include Savelovsky Station ("Ya byl dushoy durnogo obshchestva" [1961; "By nature I came from bad society,"]); Mar'ina Roshcha ("Gorod ushi zatknul" [1961; "The city plugged its ears,"]); Pervaya Per'yaslavka ("Chto zhe ty, zaraza, brov' sebe podbrila" [1961; "Why did you pluck your brow, bitch"]); Petrovskiye Vorota ("U menya bylo sorok familiy" [1962 or 1963; "I had forty last names,"]); and the Arbat ("Pesnya o gospitale" [1964; "Song About a Hospital"]). Significantly, these locales are associated with average people, more often than not with people from debased or denigrated social groups. Indeed, as L. A. Levina observes, Vysotsky's Moscow comes to life specifically because of "the marginality of details," the ordinary, unofficial, and nonceremonial nature of the streets, buildings, and neighborhoods to which he refers.[41]

Where Vysotsky maps out the general contours of Moscow's underbelly, Okudzhava describes the city with searching attention to detail. In Okudzhava's Moscow songs, mundane minutiae are foregrounded and stock phrases are cleverly reinterpreted. Freed of what he called "primitive, routine rhetorical thoughts about Moscow," Okudzhava depicts a city that has little, if anything, in common with the glittering, expansive metropolis of official song.[42] Unlike that exemplary city, Okudzhava's Moscow revolves not around ceremonial monuments and "broad expanses," but rather around ordinary moments and cozy courtyards (*dvory*); unlike that forever joyful city, furthermore, Okudzhava's Moscow is, as he describes it in "Moskovskiy muravey" (1960; "A Moscow Ant"), "now sad, . . . now cheerful, . . . , but always sublime."[43]

Central to Okudzhava's vision of Moscow is the anchoring motif of the Arbat as what might be called a "local homeland." As Stephen Bittner observes, Okudzhava played a major role in fashioning the potent "animating myth" of the Arbat as "a victim of Soviet power," through his celebrations of the neighborhood as the "intellectual and cultural utopia" of his childhood in the 1920s and early 1930s.[44] Okudzhava's Arbat utopia is far from perfect, however: it is peopled with ordinary individuals and filled with ordinary objects, and despite its seeming autonomy it is buffeted frequently by the vagaries of the world beyond. While Okudzhava's vision of the Arbat did not remain static, as a group his Arbat songs demonstrate genuine closeness to and intimate knowledge of this small corner of Moscow, thus representing a sharp and significant contrast to official songs that simply call Moscow as a whole "dear," "close," or "beloved."

Okudzhava's Arbat emerges as a distinctive world in songs spanning several decades, from the late 1950s through the early 1980s; and key features underpinning these songs echo throughout Okudzhava's other urban renderings as well. In a cluster of songs from the late 1950s, Okudzhava depicts the Arbat as a warren of courtyards the inhabitants of which are joined by youthful loyalties but also touched by tragedies omnipresent in the world outside their *dvory*. For example, in an untitled song commonly known as "Pesenka ob arbatskikh rebyatakh" (1957; "Ditty About Arbat Kids") and in "Korol'" ("The King"), which is also known as "Pesenka o Lyon'ke Korolyove" (1957; "Ditty About Lyon'ka Korolyov"), the Arbat is a place of coziness and timelessness, a place of retreat from a larger and more dangerous world. "Pesenka ob arbatskikh rebyatakh" opens with a reference to Okudzhava's "father, executed by firing squad [*otets rastrelyannyi moy*]," but observes that "there are no dead among the Arbat kids,/it's just that those who needed to have fallen asleep, and those who don't need to have not" (141).

"Korol'" depicts a courtyard where "every evening the radiola was playing," and where the local children call a lad named Lyon'ka Korolyov their "king" (139–40).[45] The lad dies young, killed in battle, but for the author-narrator, "it always seems . . . that just around the next turn/I'll meet the King again." For the author-narrator, Lyon'ka will never truly die because he "can't imagine Moscow/without a king like him."[46] What makes Lyon'ka special, "kingly," and irreplacable is the fact that he is "omnipotent [*vsemogushch*]," ever ready to extend his friends "a faithful hand—and save [them]." Of course, as Lyon'ka's death illustrates, this omnipotence is sadly limited to the little world of the Arbat courtyard.

In "Pesenka ob Arbate" (1959; "Ditty About the Arbat"), Okudzhava elaborates on his intimate and intensely personal vision of his neighborhood by reorienting and reframing clichéd epithets.[47] Here, the Arbat's pedestrians are described as "not grand people [*lyudi ne velikiye*]," who "clatter their heels" as they "rush about their business" (177–78). This simple description is both evocative and *pro*vocative because of the frequent use of the epithet "great" or "grand" (*velikiy*) in official discourse, and the connotations of both size and power with which this epithet was freighted. Calling the Arbat's pedestrians "not grand," and underlining their ordinariness through the banality of their actions, Okudzhava undermines this favorite canonical usage. Unlike the stereotypical positive hero of Soviet fiction and song, who "march[es] upward and onward and peer[s] assiduously into the communist tomorrow,"[48] Okudzhava's Arbat pedestrians are merely noisy little people hurrying about their own affairs.

This recasting of marked vocabulary culminates in the song's final verse, in which Okudzhava exclaims, "Akh, Arbat, moy Arbat, ty—moyo otechestvo" ("Oh, Arbat, my Arbat, you are my fatherland"). In contrast to the expansive notion of Moscow as the "heart of the Motherland," Okudzhava transforms the equally high-flown *otechestvo* (fatherland) into a local, and deeply personal, notion. As in "Pesenka ob arbatskikh rebyatakh" and "Korol'," here the local and the individual, rather than the national and the collective, inspire care, tenderness, and loyalty. Humble though this bustling ordinariness of the Arbat may be, it represents a powerful source not just of loyalty but also of creative inspiration, as Okudzhava suggests in "Zhivopistsy" (1959; "Painters"): "Zhivopistsy, okunite vashi kisti/v suyetu dvorov arbatskikh i v zaryu" ("Painters, dip your brushes/into the bustle of Arbat courtyards and into the sunrise") (178).

Okudzhava was not alone in his ability to upend the stale rhetoric of grand and luminous Moscow, and the tediously predictable celebration of the extraordinary that accompanied it. The intimacy of Okudzhava's early Arbat songs finds echoes, for example, in Ada Yakusheva's "Lyubimyi gorod (Pesnya Moskve)" (1954; "Beloved City [Song to Moscow]"), in which a novel vantage point reveals the inadequacy of hackneyed linguistic formulae to capture the essence of Moscow. "Lyubimyi gorod" is set in a decidedly unprepossessing (one might even say marginal) space, "in the institute, beneath the vaulting of the staircases," where a group of students, "seized by a thirst to create," decide to pen a song in honor of Moscow.[49] The song's chorus suggests that their chosen task is futile, perhaps because so many songs about Moscow already exist ("everything was sung to you long ago") or because they themselves lack the necessary talent ("our gifts are too few").

However, Yakusheva's subsequent verses reveal an originality of vision that belies this claim, while simultaneously exposing as tired and cliché-ridden the very sorts of songs to which the chorus pays tribute. In Yakusheva's rendition, it is not "the whole Soviet country/[that] is singing and dancing [*poyot i plyashet*]" (as in Vasily Lebedev-Kumach's "Moskva mayskaya"); rather, it is "bright drops of rain" that "dance [*plyashut*] along the rooftops." Similarly, while in Lebedev-Kumach's depiction "the morning colors with a gentle tint/The walls of the ancient Kremlin," for Yakusheva "the sunrise stands over Moscow," but "the sun hides its settings/. . . in the crooked lanes of the Arbat." Thus, while the song's final verse observes that "it would seem, we have nothing to give" to Moscow, the perceptiveness and eloquence of Yakusheva's imagery tell a very different story. Like Okudzhava, Yakusheva proves herself adept at making the ordinary sparkle and the "insignificant" more than worthy of notice.

Okudzhava's early Arbat songs focus on ordinary people, detailing everyday concerns, personal loyalties, and personal losses. Both in these songs and in other urban scenes from the same period, Okudzhava's deft handling of detail is readily apparent. In "Korol'," a specific Arbat courtyard is identified by the evening-time playing of a radiola; in "Pesenka ob Arbate," the

Arbat itself is defined by pedestrians' clattering heels. Similarly, in "Pesenka pro Chyornogo kota" (1957–59; "Ditty About a Black Cat"), unpleasant domestic details—the dirty floor and a missing lightbulb—circumscribe the sinister territory of the song's eponymous cat (153–54). In the song generally known as "Akh, Nadya, Naden'ka" (1958; "Oh, Nadya, Naden'ka"), a vivid but almost atemporal cityscape provides the backdrop for the narrator's tale of unrequited love for a female bus driver. The scene is brought to life with just two simple details: "Iz okon korochkoy nesyot podzharistoy,/Za zanaveskami—mel'kan'ye ruk" ("The scent of toasted crusts drifts from windows./Behind curtains, fleeting glimpses of hands") (151–52).[50] The song's pleasantly unstable grip on temporality is achieved through the juxtaposition of hints of the present (the mention of a new bus) and evocative, romantic echoes of the past (repeated references to horses, as though the bus is horse-drawn).

As demonstrated clearly in "Akh, Nadya, Naden'ka," the details Okudzhava employs in such characterizations are, by and large, as timeless as they are mundane: realia, but without a specifically Soviet imprint.[51] In Okudzhava's Arbat songs of the 1960s, this emphasis on timelessness may be said to reflect and simultaneously resist Khrushchev's "campaign to reshape the Arbat neighborhood into his vision of communist modernity," during which much of the old Arbat was destroyed and many residents were displaced in order "to make way for the Novyi Arbat thoroughfare and its concrete and glass skyscrapers."[52] "Na arbatskom dvore" (1964; "In an Arbat Courtyard"), for example, is a bittersweet elegy on the passing of winter in which the narrator muses that "as the March snow dies," wintertime playthings will soon be forgotten: "Po kladovkam po tyomnym porzhaveyut kon'ki,/pozabytye lyzhi po uglam pokorobyatsya . . ." ("In dark closets skates will rust,/forgotten skis will warp in corners . . .") (192). In "Arbatskiy romans" (1969; "Arbat Romance"), the narrator rhapsodizes about the pleasures of drinking from "steamed-up cups" and characterizes his youth as a time when

> Yeshchyo moya pokhodka mne ne byla smeshna,
> yeshchyo podoshvy ne pootryvalis',
> za kazhdym povorotom, gde muzyka slyshna,
> kakie mne udachi otkryvalis'! (318)
>
> My walk was not yet funny to me,
> the soles of my shoes had not yet started to fall off,
> beyond each turn, where there was music,
> what good luck awaited me!

In both "Na arbatskom dvore" and "Arbatskiy romans," everyday objects, entirely commonplace yet brilliant under Okudzhava's close observation, help to create an Arbat that exists outside of a specific time. In other songs from the mid-1960s, though, Okudzhava voices more direct dissatisfaction with the incursions of the present. In "Byloye nel'zya vorotit'" (1964; "You Can't Bring Back the Past"), for example, Okudzhava employs fantastical details to evoke a lost past for which the song's author-narrator yearns wistfully. In the song's first verse, the narrator expresses regret that "it's impossible, even for fifteen minutes,/to stop by for dinner at the Yar with Aleksandr Sergeich [Pushkin]" (284).[53] Pushkin exerts a powerful spiritual presence in this song, providing a specific referent for a general sense of historical awareness,[54] and embodying both an irretrievable past and a vague possibility for the future. But the figure of Pushkin (who reappears only in the final verse) frames decidedly ambivalent descriptions in which the values and achievements of the present are questioned, obliquely and by contrast: "A vsyo-taki zhal'—inogda nad pobedami nashimi/vstayut p'yedestaly, kotorye vyshe pobed" ("But it's a shame, nevertheless, that sometimes above our victories/rise up pedestals that are higher than the victories themselves").

Contrasting sharply with the official image of Moscow as warm, maternal, and welcoming, the city presented by Okudzhava is regrettably merciless, demanding "iron courage, strength and steadfastness in everything"; and prompting the author-narrator to muse that "if you had believed in our tears just once,/Neither we nor you would have had to mourn the past." The sense of regret expressed in this verse permeates the entire song. Frequent repetitions of "but it's a shame [*a vsyo-taki zhal'*]" bring into sharp relief past losses that cannot be offset by present gains, an effect that is underscored by a predominance of conditionals and negatives throughout the song. The pattern of conditionals and negatives is broken only in the song's final verse. Here, Pushkin reappears, strolling "by the Arbat Gates," an occurrence that prompts the narrator to muse, "Well, something will probably happen soon." But while this represents a sharp grammatical contrast to the preceding verses (this line contains the only future-tense verb in the song), this musing promises nothing; instead, it merely opens up an uncertain possibility that is underscored by Okudzhava's melancholy, somewhat tremulous singing.

A strikingly similar yearning for a lost Arbat past can be found in Aleksandr Gorodnitsky's "Arbatskiye starushki" (1974; "The Arbat's Little Old Ladies"). But where Okudzhava's "Byloye" merely alludes to the destruction of the old Arbat, Gorodnitsky bemoans it openly:

> Akh, kak u vremeni nashego norov surov!
> Dnya ne proydyot, chob kakoy-nibud' dom ne razrushit'.
> Skoro ne budet arbatskikh zelyonykh dvorov,
> Skoro ne budet arbatskikh vesyolykh starushek.[55]
>
> Oh, what a stern temperament our age has!
> Not a day passes without some sort of building being demolished.

Soon there will be no more green Arbat courtyards,
Soon there will be no more of the Arbat's cheerful little old ladies.

This keen regret over irrevocable losses is underpinned by a deep ambivalence about the relentless drive toward the future: "Akh, kak stremitel'no my ubegayem vperyod,—/. . ./To, chto samo ne umryot, dolomayut potomki" ("Oh, how impetuously we dash off ahead,/. . ./Whatever does not die on its own, our descendants will finish off").

The undercurrent of antagonism toward the future in Gorodnitsky's "Arbatskiye starushki" prefigures a similar turn in Okudzhava's Arbat verses of the early 1980s, in which the bard's nostalgic vision of the Arbat as a lost "local homeland" crystallizes most fully. In the poem "Arbatskoye vdokhnoveniye, ili Vospominaniya o detstve" (1980; "Arbat Inspiration, or Recollections of Childhood"), Okudzhava returns to the motif of Arbat-as-fatherland ("nadezhdy, sverstnikov moikh,/otechestvo" ["of hope, of my contemporaries,/the fatherland"]), and of his courtyard as a powerful shaping force in his life ("menya vospityval arbatskiy dvor,/vsyo v nyom, ot podlogo do zolotogo" ["the Arbat courtyard raised me,/everything in it, from the base to the golden"]) (384–85). Mundane details ("laundry not yet dry") enrich the scene, but they also lie at the heart of Okudzhava's affection for his private homeland: "Chto mne skazat'? Yeshchyo lyublyu svoy dvor,/yego ubogost', i yego prostor,/i aromat groshovogo obeda" ("What can I say? I still love my courtyard,/its shabbiness, and its expanse, and the aroma of a cheap lunch"). At the same time, though, Okudzhava's reflections are permeated by an acute sense of loss, as a reference to "the bloody scuffle between the past and the future" suggests.

Still, this poem is permeated by a certain ambivalence: the past is represented here not just through recollections of the Arbat itself, but also through references to Stalin ("waggling his smoked-up moustache,/my fellow-tribesman flies past") and Okudzhava's own complicated reaction to him ("I love the Kremlin's man with the moustache,/and I love myself for it"). Both this ambivalence and the associated slippage between past and present relate to the poem's addressee, Okudzhava's son, Anton. Through Anton's voice, Okudzhava interrogates his own nostalgia ("So what is the basis of your love?/you ask with your own inherent skepticism") and it is to Anton's voice that he must explain it. In the poem's closing lines, the ineffable essence of the Arbat is invoked as the answer to the complexities of the past, and as the source of nostalgia even in the face of them: "to, chto ya kogda-to poteryal,/on v vozdukhe arbatskom obnaruzhil" ("he discovered in the Arbat air/that which I had once lost").

In "Nadpis' na kamne" (1982; "Inscription on Stone"), a poem that was later set to music, the ambivalence that characterizes "Arbatskoye vdokhnoveniye" has seemingly dissipated, replaced by a more pronounced sense of grievance over the losses of the past and the ignominies of the future. Referring to himself as "a nobleman from an Arbat courtyard [*dvoryanin s arbatskogo dvora*]" Okudzhava depicts the courtyard itself as life-giving and as imbuing in its children a special sense of kinship:

> Kogda [dvora] ne stanet—ya umru,
> Poka on yest'—ya vlasten nad sud'boyu.
> . . .
> Arbatstvo, rastvorennoye v krovi,
> Neistrebimo, kak sama priroda. (393–94)
>
> When [the courtyard] is no more, I will die,
> But while it exists, I have power over fate.
> . . .
> Arbatness, dissolved in one's blood,
> Is ineradicable, like nature herself.

If in a song like "Byloye nel'zya vorotit'" the future contained only vague possibility, here the future is inevitable and decidedly negative, marked by both destruction and death. What remains is memory and "Arbatness,"[56] which is evoked as a talisman of hope against the unpleasant certainties of the future:

> Kogda kirka, bul'dozer i topor
> spodobyatsya k Arbatu podobratsya
> i pravnuki zabudut slovo "dvor"
> sogrey nas vsekh i soberi, arbatstvo.
>
> When the pick, the bulldozer and the axe
> are considered worthy to steal up on the Arbat
> and our descendents forget the word "courtyard,"
> keep us all warm and gather us in, Arbatness.

In the contemporaneous song "Ya vyselen s Arbata" (1982; "I have been evicted from the Arbat"), Okudzhava's loyalty to his old neighborhood is still more clearly expressed: "I am an Arbat emigre," he writes, "evicted from the Arbat and deprived of my past" (392). Robbed of his local homeland, Okudzhava depicts strangers and newcomers as "foreigners [*chuzhezemtsy*]" and "occupiers [*okkupanty*]"; and observes that while certain features of the landscape may be unchanged, "conversations are uncordial and banquets are cold." With its nobility displaced, the Arbat is fundamentally altered, and that change becomes a mark of suffering for its former inhabitants: "Akh, flora tam vsyo ta zhe, da fauna ne ta . . . / Ya emigrant s Arbata. Zhivu, svoy krest nesya . . ." ("Ah, the flora there is all the same, but the fauna is not the same at all . . . / I am an emigre from the Arbat. I live, bearing my cross . . .").

In official Soviet song, Moscow is both iconic and synecdochic, both the ideal Soviet city and, in its perfection, the ideal microcosm of the motherland as a whole. Broad and expansive, this Moscow emanates boundless charms and bestows upon its denizens boundless love, inspiring in return declarations of boundless affection and devotion. Clad in boilerplate and ornamented with facile tropes of love and joy, the ersatz Moscow of official Soviet song is a poor substitute for the real city in all its glorious imperfection, as guitar poetry about Moscow demonstrates amply. Eschewing the gleam and gloss of official rhetoric, various bards depict a very different Moscow—one made up of seedy neighborhoods, cramped courtyards, and crooked streets, inhabited by ordinary people, and thick with the sights, sounds, and smells of everyday living. In these bards' songs, the insignificant takes on heightened significance, as objects, people, and phenomena that hover on the margins of the noticeable are brought vividly to the center of our attention.

"THANK YOU, HEART, FOR BEING ABLE TO LOVE THUS!": LOVE IN OFFICIAL SOVIET SONG

Like official Soviet songs about Moscow, those about love are marked by a high degree of generalization. As Naum Korzhavin argues, official Soviet love songs lack a "personal principle [*lichnoye nachalo*]" and, consequently, a "personal conception of love."[57] The notion of love presented in Lebedev-Kumach's "Kak khorosho na svete zhit'" (1934; "How Good It Is to Live on This Earth")" (also known as "Serdtse" ["Heart"]), for example, is entirely abstract. The striking peculiarity of this song is the fact that, while ostensibly *about* love, it is not actually a love song: "in it, no one loves [anyone] and no one even pines because of the absence of love."[58] Rather than being endowed with emotional resonance, love is presented in this song as a generic ability: "spasibo, serdtse, chto ty umeyesh' tak lyubit'!" ("thank you, heart, for being able to love thus!").[59] Indeed, one might argue that this song is more about *being in love* than about love itself—a sort of how-to guide to proper romantic behavior.

In light of the "well-known puritanism" of official Soviet culture,[60] it is hardly surprising that this how-to guide stresses both chastity (there is not even the slightest hint of eroticism here) and fidelity to a single person:

Kak mnogo devushek khoroshykh,
Kak mnogo laskovykh imyon!
No lish' odno iz nikh trevozhit,
Unosya pokoy i son,
Kogda vlyublyon.

How many nice girls,
How many tender names!
But only one of them disturbs you,
Carrying away peace and sleep,
When you're in love.

A similar approach is found in Ol'ga Fadeyeva's "Tost za liubimykh" (1950s?; "Toast to Our Loved Ones"), which celebrates both "those whose love is indestructible/Who will preserve fidelity for us!" and those "who know how to love!"[61]

Both of these lyrics are marked by the absence of genuine feelings and of people genuinely capable of feeling, a phenomenon that finds broader reflection in a virtually complete avoidance of negative emotion in official song. Sad circumstances (such as unrequited love and separation) do occur, but they almost invariably serve to deliver a positive moral message (e.g., stoic acceptance, patience, or wisdom gained through unhappy experience).[62] In Mikhail Isaakovsky's "Oy, tsvetyot kalina" (1949; "Oh, the guelder rose is blooming"), for example, a young girl sings of a burgeoning love that she is too timid to voice:

A lyubov' devich'ya s kazhdym dnyom sil'ney
Kak zhe mne reshit'sya rasskazat' o ney
Ya khozhu ne smeyu volyu dat' slovam
Milyi moy khoroshiy dogadaysya sam.[63]

But my maidenly love grows stronger each day
How can I resolve to tell of it
I walk about not daring to give will to my words
My dear, my bonny, guess it for yourself.

Unrequited her love may be, but this maiden's quiet self-sacrifice implicitly underlines her praiseworthy traits of constancy, modesty, and chastity.

A very different lesson is offered by numerous love songs of the late 1930s and early 1940s, in which chaste romance and martial heroism intertwine. In Lebedev-Kumach's "Ya na podvig tebya provozhala" (1937; "I saw you off on your exploits"), for example, a young woman bravely holds back her tears as she encourages her beloved to go off to war "calmly and bravely! / Go, fearing nothing at all!"; and offers her love to him as a protective talisman ("Pust' tebya pomogayet, / Ot pul' sberegayet / Moya molodaya lyubov' " ["Let my young love / Aid you, / And protect you from bullets"]).[64]

A male counterpart to this faithful and courageously stoic heroine is found in Yevgeny Dolmatovsky's "Moya lyubimaya" (1943; "My Beloved"), in which a young man who has gone to war asks his beloved to "smile at [him] from far away" in order that "all [his] dreams come true / In expeditions and in battles."[65] Similarly, in Mikhail Isaakovsky's "Katyusha" (1938; "Katyusha") a soldier's duty to his motherland (*zemlya rodnaya*) and his love for a girl (*devushka rodnaya*) merge into one sanctified whole:

> Pust' on vspomnit devushku rodnuyu,
> Pust' uslyshit, kak ona poyot,
> Pust' on zemlyu berezhyot rodnuyu,
> A lyubov' Katyusha sberezhyot.[66]
>
> Let him recall his own dear girl,
> Let him hear how she sings,
> Let him guard his native land,
> And Katyusha will guard their love.

In the Soviet love song canon, particular emphasis was placed on "the propaganda . . . of high ideals of beauty and humanism" in relationships and on the merging of the lyrical and the patriotic.[67] As a result, however, love devolves into an empty conceptual category, evoking "something pleasant and sensitive" but profoundly detached both from ungovernable passions and from deeply felt losses.[68] The logical continuation of this propaganda of idealized emotion was the deliberate and near-total avoidance of non-normative romantic attachments (such as marital infidelity, love triangles, and one-night stands) in official song;[69] and songs alluding to such entanglements were rare and almost invariably controversial. This was the case, for example, with Yevgeny Dolmatovsky's "Sluchaynyi val's" (1943; "Accidental Waltz"), which describes a fleeting front-line affair ("Your unknown hand / rests in my palm"); and also with Nikolai Dorizo's "Ogney tak mnogo zolotykh" (1953; "So Many Golden Lights"), in which a female protagonist privately confesses her love for a married man but declares that she will be "strong in her resolve not to disturb the marital status quo."[70]

Even after being admitted to public performance, however, songs that depicted unsuccessful, unhappy, or non-normative romantic relationships remained controversial and were widely decried in the press. In 1960, for example, Dmitry Kabalevsky railed against "the microbe of melancholy" that had infected contemporary Soviet song, conjecturing that on the basis of "gloomy, melancholy songs one could compile a kind of encyclopedia of the *insignificant disappointments of everyday life*—unsuccessful loves, rendezvous that did not take place, [and] awkward explanations" (emphasis added).[71] Despite occasional calls for Soviet song to represent a full range of emotions ("gaiety, and joy, and sadness, and sorrow in love"), official Soviet love songs are, on balance, "saccharine, sentimental, extremely vague, and naïve."[72] The distinctions between romantic, familial, and patriotic love are blurred (the latter being, of course, the most noble category to which one can aspire); as a result, love, that most personal of emotions, is depicted as a pure and positive, yet ultimately depersonalized, feeling.

"OUR SECRETS ARE NAIVE . . .": LOVE IN GUITAR POETRY

In sharp contrast to the generalization of the personal that is evident in officially circulated songs about love, in guitar poetry about intimate relationships there is a pronounced interest in personalizing the general. In some cases, this is achieved through a piercing focus on the individual, not infrequently involving subtle reinterpretation and recalibration of ideological slogans and tropes. In this respect, there is significant continuity between strategies and practices evident in the songs to be discussed below and those in bards' songs about Moscow analyzed above. In other cases, this personalization is expressed through the depiction of a full range of (heterosexual) romantic relationships, from passing encounters to abiding love, from marriages of convenience to outright prostitution.

An interesting take on the intensely personal nature of love can be found in Okudzhava's "Pesenka o prisyage" (1958?; "Ditty About an Oath"). This song implies a rejection of the public orientation typical of official Soviet culture by transforming an oath (*prisyaga*) into a declaration of love so private that it cannot be spoken:

> Kakikh prisyag ya ni daval, kakie ne tverdil slova,
> No yest' odna prisyaga—kruzhitsya golova.
>
> Pridu ya k zhenshchine svoyey—vsyu zhizn' k nogam yeyo slozhu,
> no o prisyage etoy ne slova ne skazhu. (153)

> Whatever oaths I have given, whatever words I have repeated,
> There is one oath—my head spins.
>
> I will come to my woman—I will place my whole life at her feet,
> but about that oath not a word will I say.

Oaths are clearly a familiar practice ("Whatever oaths I have given"), yet true power is vested only in the unspoken oath, the one that is passed directly from heart to heart ("by chance someone along the way/will find the words of that oath in his breast").

Okudzhava's "Chasovye lyubvi" (1958; "Love's Sentinels") offers a similar retreat into the private, using martial imagery to a very unmartial end and gently deconstructing aggressive militarism in the process. The song's titular sentinels are "a great, eternal army" comprised entirely of ordinary soldiers (*ryadovye*) because, "after all, love has no marshals" (151). It is these soldiers who guard Moscow faithfully (*neizmenno*), from Smolensk Square to the Arbat, heralding the arrival of spring, with all that season symbolizes. Ultimately, for the song's narrator, "love's sentinels" are the only true soldiers: "Priznayu tol'ko eti voyska! . . ." ("I recognize only these troops! . . .").

Not unlike "Pesenka o prisyage" and "Chasovye lyubvi," Yury Kukin's "Moyo pal'to—moya strana" (1967–68; "My Overcoat Is My Country") rejects public bombast and false cheer, in this case creating a vivid and achingly personal scene of pain and loss. The song's author-narrator has been cast aside, leaving him both bereft and spiritually homeless:

Moyo pal'to—moya strana
Moy vorotnik—moya kvartira.
I ya odin, i ty odna.
Tebe—polmira, mne polmira.[73]

My overcoat is my country
My collar—my apartment.
And I am alone, and you are alone.
Half the world for you, half—for me.

The song does not explore the reasons for this parting, reflecting only its agonizing aftermath. Though the author-narrator has found comfort with another, his world is irrevocably rent in two:

Chuzhogo tela nagota,
I temen' gub, i glaz siyan'ye—
Vsyo tochno tak i vsyo ne tak,
I beskonechnost'—rasstoyan'ye.

The nakedness of another's body,
The darkness of lips, and the sparkling of eyes—
It's all just the same yet not right at all,
And eternity is separation.

The references to nudity and (in colloquial terms) a "rebound fling" themselves test the prescribed boundaries of propriety. However, perhaps a still more profound challenge to approved representations of love lies in the fact that there is no positive lesson to be learned from this unhappy parting. All it brings is "pain, walking in on soft paws," and an icy chill that forestalls explanation, causing unspoken words to fall "to the floor with a dull thud." The "world" of this song is an entirely personal one, shared by only two people. When they separate, this world is cleaved in two "by the door, like a guillotine."

A similarly penetrating depiction of rejection, and the agony that follows it, is found in Yevgeny Klyachkin's "Zachem opasnye slova?" (1964; "Why say dangerous words?"). In this song, Klyachkin sketches out the contours of a delicate emotional dance in which feelings are downplayed ("'love' is banal and irrelevant") in order to mitigate the risk of self-exposure.[74] But while solitude allows for reflection and "reevaluat[ion] of our devotions," time itself "noiselessly corrodes doubts." What results is an inequality of emotion, in which the author-narrator is decidedly the loser:

> Ty ponesyosh' menya vo rtu,
> legko gryzya, kak shokoladku.
> Zametish' fantik na letu,
> a posle skazhesh'—"bylo sladko."
>
> You will carry me in your mouth,
> nibbling lightly, as if on a chocolate.
> You will notice a wrapper in the air,
> and after you will say—"It was sweet."

While his partner will soon forget the affair, recalling afterward only a sweet sensation, the author-narrator, it seems, will be left to endure the bitter taste of being used up and forgotten.

If the previous two songs animate the pain of rejection and loss with visceral clarity, Klyachkin's "Grustnaya pesnya o gorodskikh vlyublyonnykh" (1965; "Sad Song About Urban Lovebirds") casts a harsh light on the indignities of personal life in the public eye. For lack of privacy elsewhere, a young couple are forced to conduct their romance furtively in an entryway (*paradnaya*), in public view: "Kto-to smotrit—nu i pust'!/K chertu ikh, a s nami—Bog!" ("Someone is looking—well let them look!/To the devil with them, God is with us!").[75] This highlights the mortification prompted by private acts conducted in public, but it also underscores the subtle coercion bred of this circumstance. The young man is clearly more eager than his partner (it is he who suggests the entryway, he who brushes off others' gazes), while she complains, "'Oh, anything but the entryway!—/My dear,

I'm feeling queasy . . .'" Klyachkin himself recalls that this song was a constant "stumbling block" for him, frequently criticized as "either pornography or pessimism"; but he rejects such criticism out of hand, calling it "a supremely honest song, a song of protest" over the development of "a noble feeling in ignoble circumstances, because we are given no others."[76]

The warping effect of Soviet *byt* (everyday life) on private lives is foregrounded, similarly, in Yury Vizbor's "Pesenka o naivnykh taynakh" (1979–82; "Ditty About Naive Secrets"). Unlike Klyachkin's lovebirds, Vizbor's couple do have a space of their own, but their relationship to each other is dominated by their differing claims on this space. Both partners are unnamed, referred to only by their residence status: while the man is identified as "one responsible apartment-renter [*kvartiros"yomshchik*]," the woman is described simply as "not having a residence permit for his living space."[77] While she thinks of romance, he is concerned only that they not be seen leaving together:

—Dorogaya, nam luchshe vyyti porozn' . . .
A ona yemu otvetila: Moy drug!
Ya lyublyu, kogda utrom igrayet tikhaya muzyka.
A on yey skazal: . . . inache nas mogut uvidet' sosedi.

—Dear, it's better for us to leave separately . . .
And she answered him: My friend!
I love it when quiet music plays in the morning.
And he said to her: . . . otherwise the neighbors might see us.

This disjointed exchange suggests that the couple's intimacy is inappropriate, in legal terms and in terms of public morality, but it also reveals further fissures in their relationship stemming from the disparity in their status. A sense of domestic discord is underscored by the use of the verbs *otvetit'* (to answer) and *skazat'* (to say, tell) in this exchange: while the woman answers her partner, implying a direct response to him, he simply makes statements, implying no communicative continuity whatsoever. The dissonance between the two partners is highlighted still further by the description, in almost ludicrous detail, of their daily activities. The woman spends the entire day painting the slogan "Sport is health" with water-resistant paint, an activity rendered truly meaningless by the fact that her only athletic pursuit consists in "twisting hair curlers [*zakruchivaniyem bigudey*]." By contrast, her partner spends the day procuring various necessities and, it seems, romancing someone else: "tselyi den' dostaval zapchasti/I dazhe vodil kogo-to v kafe 'Fialka'" ("He spent all day getting spare parts/And even took someone to Cafe Violet").

The couple's late-evening telephone conversation is framed by a weather forecast with obvious symbolic overtones: the promise of sun, when rainclouds are clearly gathering. When she suggests marriage, he responds coolly:

> Ona yemu skazala:—Milyi moy,
> U menya yest' zamechatel'noye predlozheniye:
> Davay my s toboy pozhenimsya!
> A on yey otvetil:—Sozvonimsya . . .
>
> She said to him: My darling,
> I have a wonderful proposition:
> Let's get married, you and me!
> And he answered her: Let's be in touch . . .

This conversation differs from the couple's first exchange in a crucial respect—here he responds directly to her (*on yey otvetil*)—but it offers no resolution. As the song's chorus stresses, "Our secrets are naive, our little secrets are old," yet we continue to deceive, with no end in sight: "Kogda zhe my konchim vrat', na samom dele?" ("When will we stop lying, really?").

Unlike "Pesenka o naivnykh taynakh," which offers only hints at material calculation in affairs of the heart, Aleksandr Galich's "Tonechka (Gorodskoy romans)" (1961–62; "Tonechka [Urban Romance]") lays bare a marriage of convenience in which specifically Soviet material comforts override sincere feeling. As the protagonist's scorned lover reproaches him,

> Tebya zh ne Ton'ka zavlekla gubami mokrymi,
> A chto u papy u yeyo toptun pod oknami,
>
> A chto u papy u yeyo dacha v Pavshine,
> A chto u papy kholui s sekretarshami,
> A chto u papy yeyo payki tsekovskiye
> A po prazdnikam kino s Tselikovskoyu! (215–16)
>
> It isn't Ton'ka who seduced you with her moist lips,
> But the fact that her papa is a real mover and shaker,
>
> The fact that her papa has a dacha in Pavshino,
> The fact that her papa has underlings and secretaries,
> The fact that her papa has Central Committee rations
> And gets to watch movies with Tselikovskaya on holidays!

The comforts that the protagonist finds seem alternately banal and absurd: zippered trousers, wine "as if from a well," an impossibly large bathroom.

But for having chosen material gain over love, the protagonist must sleep in the same bed "with that idiot Ton'ka," unable to forget "her, the other one," but knowing that she has overcome her love for him, "neither betraying nor forgiving."

Contemporary audiences divined in "Tonechka" a satire of social deception for personal and political gain, as its unofficial title "Adzhubeyechka" indicates. Though Galich maintained he did not have anyone particular in mind when he wrote "Tonechka," audiences seized upon this song as a description of Khrushchev's son-in-law Aleksey Adzhubey, who, under Khrushchev's patronage, became editor of *Izvestiya* in 1959 and a member of the Central Committee in 1961.[78] In the absence of a specific, real-life model, the protagonist's actions and attitudes can be viewed somewhat less scathingly, though; and perhaps our impression of the author's attitude toward them can be moderated as well. As Gerald Smith observes, "sexual exploitation for social advancement" was prevalent, if officially ignored, in Soviet society.[79] The fact that the protagonist chooses zippered trousers over love hardly makes him a noble figure; and indeed, because "Russian, and later Soviet, cultural identity depended on heroic opposition to everyday life," such a choice makes him seem decidedly vulgar.[80] But because this choice torments him—he recalls his lost love as soon as he climbs into bed with "that idiot Ton'ka," and he tries to contact his former girlfriend repeatedly—we sense that Galich's song is not simply a critique of the protagonist and his choices, but also of the system that engenders them.

A much more straightforward exchange of "goods" for "services" features in Vysotsky's "Gorodskoy romans" (1964; "Urban Romance"), which plays on the typical urban romance theme of "the young lover in raptures over the beauty of his darling"[81] as well as on the maudlin cliché of love at first sight. Espying a beautiful young girl at a militia office, the protagonist (a self-admitted "hooligan" and a pickpocket) is smitten instantly; he seeks her out, confessing his love and avowing that "life is lost" without her—only to discover, ultimately, that she was not actually at the militia office "to get her passport" (72–73). Vysotsky's descriptions of the protagonist's attempts to romance his ladylove juxtapose affectation and coarseness: he spends money freely on caviar and songs, defends her against others' advances ("I punched one guy in the face/For winking at her"), and promises to reform his own wayward habits ("I haven't robbed anyone for a whole five days"). In response to these torrid demonstrations of love, the young woman replies simply, "I believe you—/And I'll give myself to you for a reasonable price." Understanding at last "what she was doing at the militia/My love-at-first sight . . . ," the protagonist flies into a rage of boiling blood and flying fists. In performance, the mock-pathos of this narrative is heightened by Vysotsky's ill-tuned guitar, periodic irregularities of rhythm, and melodramatic vocal flourishes; in the last instance, both Vysotsky's cracking voice as he hits high notes and his lusty tremolo on the final syllables of alternate lines suggest a man overcome by the deepest of emotions.[82]

While Vysotsky's performance style may recall traditions of the Gypsy romance, the darkly humorous, elliptical revelation that the young woman is a prostitute represents a twist on standard romance themes, as well as a dramatic leap beyond the bounds of propriety of approved Soviet love songs. However, Vysotsky's invocation of romance traditions may not be intended, as one Soviet scholar argued, simply to reveal the falsity and banality of traditional romances.[83] While prostitution was a booming business in the Soviet Union, officially it did not exist until the twilight of the Soviet era. Seen as a "bourgeois" vice that could not exist under socialism, until glasnost prostitution was consigned to official silence along with a host of other social ills (such as drug abuse) of similar putative ideological pedigree. Viewed in this light, then, Vysotsky's coarse narrative of debased "love at first sight" is not simply a rejection of sappy sentiment or a parody of a traditional urban romance, but also an oblique gibe about the stubborn obtuseness of Soviet officialdom and the patent falsity of the pseudo-reality projected by it.

Like Vysotsky's "Gorodskoy romans," Yevgeny Klyachkin's "Fishka No. 2" (1962; "Tidbit No. 2") and "Fishka No. 5" (1962; "Tidbit No. 5") describe fleeting romantic encounters, in the form of casual pickups. The protagonist of "Fishka No. 2" is a self-described "silly boy" who "loves darkness/And also loves girls"—but who swears off nighttime acquaintances (at least without the benefit of illumination) when daylight reveals that his most recent conquest has a face "like a flounder," with "eyes like two black currants" and a "fissure [*shchel'*]" of a mouth.[84] In "Fishka No. 5," Klyachkin adopts a similarly flippant tone. A young man and woman meet by chance in "nighttime Moscow"; and in response to the question, "What time is it?" she answers him "boldly" with her telephone number, "Two-twelve-thirty-six."[85] The young woman declines the young man's invitation to go to a restaurant, but not, as the final couplet makes plain, out of modesty: "A ona: 'Vy zavtra pozvonite,/a seychas menya zhdyot muzh!'" ("And she said: 'Call me tomorrow,/but right now my husband is waiting!'"). Like "Fishka No. 5," Klyachkin's "Pesnya o chestnoy podruge" (1973; "Song About an Honest Girlfriend") addresses the issue of infidelity, and like "Fishka No. 5," this song is full of cunning elisions and sly humor. A short (twelve-line) song performed in a rapid-fire staccato, "Pesnya o chestnoy podruge" constitues a mini-history of the narrator's romance with his "honest" girlfriend. This girlfriend falls in love with the narrator and then out of love again, which precipitates an "honest" betrayal and an "honest" confession: "A kak tol'ko izmenila,/Tut zhe 'chestno' soobshchila" ("And as soon as she cheated,/She confessed 'honestly' on the spot").[86]

Klyachkin's treatments of infidelity are masterpieces of minimalist narrative, laconic, direct, and unsparing in their wry emotional clarity. Given the extent to which fidelity was valorized in official culture, however, even seemingly innocuous declarations could rouse critics to disproportionate reaction. Aleksandr Gorodnitsky's classic "geologist song" "Perekaty" (1960; "Shoals"), for example, angered critics because of two lines that were interpreted as expressing an indecorous lack of constancy: "Lyublyu tebya ya do povorota, / A dal'she kak poluchitsya" ("I'll love you as far as the bend, / And beyond that—we'll see how things turn out").[87] It is hardly surprising, therefore, that Gorodnitsky's "Zhena frantsuzskogo posla" (1970; "The Wife of the French Ambassador")—a humorous account of a passionate extramarital affair—should have "brought its author a great deal of unpleasantness from various official channels."[88]

"Zhena frantsuzskogo posla" opens with an exotic setting and a robust, innuendo-laden exclamation on the wonders thereof:

> Mne ne Tani snyatsya i ne Gali,
> Ne polya rodnye, ne lesa,—
> V Senegale, brattsy, v Senegale
> Ya takiye videl chudesa![89]
>
> I don't dream of Tanyas or Galyas,
> Of native fields, or forests,—
> In Senegal, brothers, in Senegal
> What wonders I saw!

Thence it proceeds to a lusty description of the ambassador's wife that showcases Gorodnitsky's inventive use of language (e.g., rhyming "women [*baby*]" with "baobab trees [*baobaby*]") while leaving little else to the imagination:

> Khot' frantsuzskiy ya ne ponimayu
> I ona po-russki—ni figa,
> No kak vysoka grud' yeyo nagaya,
> Kak naga vysokaya noga!
>
> Though I don't understand French
> And she in Russian—not a thing,
> But how grand her naked breast was,
> How naked her long leg!

The narrator is so enraptured by this encounter that he declares himself ruined for all other women. Thenceforth, one dream comes to him repeatedly, "burning [him] to ash": that of "a bed, the covers thrown wide open,/And the wife of the French ambassador!" Its exotic setting aside, "Zhena frantsuzskogo posla," like the other bards' songs about romantic relationships analyzed above, is firmly grounded in common experiences of Soviet everyday life: not chaste and harmonious pairings that merge romance with patriotism, but casual meetings, lusty affairs, furtive couplings, bruising losses and material gains, all matters of the heart in which the often banal vagaries of circumstance had a decisive role to play.

While Gorodnitsky's song clearly transgressed the boundaries of appropriate artistic representation (as evidenced by the "unpleasantness" he experienced in response to it), in many of the other songs discussed here the transgression is far less clear-cut, hinted at rather than defiantly stated. The articulation of personal values and interests, the expression of individual needs—a shabby and beloved courtyard rather than a pristine socialist metropolis, a romance that satisfies a passing desire rather than epitomizing a patriotic ideal—is carried in slight shifts of emphasis or subtle nuancing of familiar words and phrases; and is embodied in persistent attention to small details and mundane occurrences that hover at the margins of the noticeable, resolutely "refus[ing] to glorify the larger [Soviet] project"[90] but giving life its shape, texture, and variety. Indeed, the covert marginality that is evidenced by the piercing scrutiny to which bards subjected the everyday details of Soviet life, their consistent preoccupation with the "insignificant," provides a rare opportunity to agree with one Soviet critic of the genre, who declared stridently, "All of this is not so very naive as it might seem at first glance!"[91]

Chapter Seven

Genre-Bending and "Hypergenericity"

A fairy tale is a lie, a song is a true story.
—Russian proverb

Fairy tales never capitulate completely to life's truth. Just the opposite. They try at every opportunity to upstage it, to instruct it by way of their own, far superior, solutions.
—Wisława Szymborska[1]

FROM AN ANALYSIS OF overt and covert marginality, with their emphasis on theme and on detail, discussion now turns to issues of form. As has already been discussed, guitar poetry's roots can be traced back to a range of genres of both high and low cultural pedigree. Interestingly, guitar poetry's own generic composition is no less complex, with bards' works including not just songs and ditties (*pesenki*) but also ballads, romances, fairy tales (*skazki*), and quasi-journalistic "song-commentaries [*pesni-reportazhi*]" (pioneered by Vizbor), among others. In turn, this complexity underscores guitar poetry's generic capaciousness, highlighting its productive relationships with multiple musical and literary traditions. Focusing on guitar poetry's generic flexibility and on bards' handling of multiple genres, this chapter explores what will be called the "hypergenericity" of guitar poetry. As used here, the term "hypergenericity" refers to bards' adoption and adaptation of familiar genres (such as the ballad, the romance, and the fairy tale) in their songs, creating a complex and multifaceted dialogue between these songs and other genres to which they do not formally belong.

In its focus on manipulations of genre, this understanding of hypergenericity shares concerns with Jim Collins's analysis of the "hyperconscious textuality" of "eclectic, hybrid genre films" of 1980s and early 1990s Hollywood, which foregrounded a "highly eclectic range of intertexts" and thereby "engage[d] in specific transformation *across* genres" (emphasis in original).[2] Collins emphasizes the destabilizing effect of this "hybridity of conventions" on genre, observing that eclecticism "works at cross-purposes with the traditional notion of genre as a stable, integrated set of narrative and stylistic conventions."[3] Here, however, the primary concern is hypergenericity's destabilizing effect on dominant discourse. As will be discussed below, the noteworthy lack of fit between the expectations created by songs' (implicit and explicit) generic affiliations and their treatment of salient generic traits and characteristics not only underscores guitar poetry's own generic ambiguity; it can also exert a destabilizing effect on official discourse about and approved interpretations of everyday life. Following from this, the key question to be investigated here concerns ways in which hypergeneric guitar poetry fosters a space in which marginal discourses can be carried out and marginal(ized) views expressed; and, in so doing, takes on a very central role as a means of communication and bonding between like-minded people.

HYPERGENERICITY AND (INTER)TEXTUAL PLAY

Before exploring manifestations of hypergenericity in guitar poetry, a few words are needed on the relationship of hypergenericity to other types of textual and intertextual play. On one hand, guitar poetry's hypergenericity is strongly linked to parody, but in a very particular way. In guitar poetry that is seemingly modeled after traditional genres such as the romance, the ballad, or the fairy tale, there is often a profound disjuncture between songs' titles and what is conveyed through text, music, and performance. In such songs, bards manipulate and often undermine salient characteristics and hallmarks of the genres to which they allude. As will be argued here, the parody in these songs is directed not at the chosen "model" genres themselves, but rather extratextually. The disjuncture between generic form and textual, musical, and performative content results in indirect parody or, to borrow A. Morozov's term, "parodic usage." According to Morozov, parodic usage "changes its direction, orienting [parody] toward extra-literary goals"; parody directed toward the "employed ('parodied') original" is secondary at best, or even entirely absent.[4]

The extratextual targets of parody in hypergeneric guitar poetry are varied, but among them Soviet values and Soviet everyday life (or, more properly, aspects of these that diverge sharply from their representation in official discourse and official culture) occupy a prominent position. Focusing on this disjuncture, hypergeneric guitar poetry acts as a form of "narratization" of everyday life, that is, of "narrative representation and transformation of everyday life" into oral communication.[5] According to Klaus Roth, a key function of narratization in socialist societies, alongside entertainment and emotional or social relief, is the interpretation and management of "two different kinds of reality: the promised or faked reality presented by the state through the official media and the harsh reality of socialist everyday life."[6] Consistent with Roth's analysis, in hypergeneric guitar poetry that targets aspects of Soviet everyday experience, "direct opposition or criticism" is generally muted in favor of "unmasking irony and satirizing 'correction'" of the official pseudo-reality.[7] Through irony and satire, hypergeneric guitar poetry symbolically reduces the power that official strictures exercise over bards and their listeners alike and therefore, to quote one longtime guitar poetry fan, "makes officialdom [*ofitsioz*] no longer frightening."[8]

On the other hand, it is necessary to establish a distinction between hypergenericity and various types of intertextuality. Bakhtinian dialogism is not well suited to discussing guitar poetry's play with genres, for a number of reasons. One can hardly help but recall Bakhtin's own firm rejection of the possibility that poetic language could be double-voiced, for example, even though the language of guitar poetry is far removed from the "officialized language of lyric poetry" that Bakhtin had in mind when insisting that "poetic language . . . suppresses the dialogic nature of speech."[9] Leaving aside the open question of whether "the language of the lyric text . . . can be excluded from ambivalent discourse,"[10] a larger stumbling block to construing guitar poetry's hypergenericity in Bakhtinian dialogic terms lies in the latter's emphasis on conflict or competition between voices within a single text. As will be argued here, in drawing upon familiar genres, guitar poetry creates and sustains a communicative model in which dialogue with *extratextual* elements is paramount.

Rooted in Bakhtinian dialogism, the Kristevan model of intertextuality is equally problematic for the present purposes. Emphasizing "three dimensions of textual space," namely "writing subject, addressee and exterior texts," this model is not designed to accommodate the additional dynamics introduced by performance.[11] Both Kristeva's more specific notion of "a permutation of texts, an intertextuality," whereby "in the space of a given text, several utterances, taken from other texts, intersect and neutralize one another"; and Gerard Genette's related view of intertextuality as "a relationship of copresence between two texts or among several texts" are, fundamentally, concerned with text-level phenomena.[12] Both are inadequate, therefore, for discussing cooperation, confrontation, and manipulation at the level of genre.

Taken together, John Frow's observations that "intertextual structures . . . may be of the order of the message or of the order of the code" and that "the conventions of genre" are an important element in constructing texts suggest that genre may play some role in intertextuality; but Frow mutes this suggestion with a subsequent reference to Laurent Jenny's interrogation of "whether one can properly speak of an intertextual relation to genre," with which his limited exploration of genre's role in intertextuality ends.[13] Jenny himself resolves this conflict by introducing the notion of architext (understood as the limited number of structures from which a generic code is realized); and arguing that, if this generic code is closed (as in a "dead" or nonproductive genre), "one can speak of a relation of intertextuality between a specific work and the architext of a genre."[14] While this moves toward a fruitful approach for discussing guitar poetry's engagement with other genres, Jenny's emphasis on architexts as closed generic codes remains an obstacle to adopting his view of intertextuality here. The genres most frequently used in guitar poetry's hypergeneric play, while conventionalized, were by no means nonproductive: ballads and romances thrived in domestic musical culture throughout the Soviet period (even when frowned upon in official circles), while the Soviet authorities devoted considerable resources to promoting the creation of new fairy tales, folk epics (*byliny*), and other traditional folk genres.

Intertextual relations certainly are present in guitar poetry, as bards interweave other texts into their songs through allusion and citation. Moreover, guitar poetry's intertextual relations can be observed not just in verbal texts but also at the level of music and performance (in borrowings of recognizable musical phrases, for example, or in mimicking of characteristic vocal patterns and gestures).[15] But genre-level manipulations in guitar poetry cannot be reduced to such interactions alone. Below, a brief discussion of bards' use of the romance and the ballad will help to establish broad patterns characteristic of hypergenericity; this will be followed by a focused analysis of creative uses of the fairy tale.

NEGOTIATING BETWEEN FORM AND CONTENT: GUITAR POETRY'S "ROMANCES" AND "BALLADS"

Songs that would seem to pay homage to the *romans* (in various permutations) and the ballad are common among the works of a number of bards. This modeling is readily apparent in the titles of songs such as Vysotsky's "Gorodskoy romans" (1964; "Urban Romance"); Galich's "Tonechka (Gorodskoy romans)" (1961–62; "Tonechka [Urban Romance]") and "Teoreticheskiy romans" (1966; "Theoretical Romance"); Mikhail Ancharov's "Ballada o tanke T-34, kotoryi stoit v chuzhom gorode na vysokom krasivom postamente" (1965; "Ballad About a T-34 Tank, Which Stands on a Tall, Beautiful Pedestal in a Foreign City"); and Galich's "Ballada o vechnom ogne" (1968; "Ballad About the Eternal Flame"). Given guitar poetry's historical roots in the romance tradition, one might argue that bards' *romansy*, in particular, are simply contemporary Soviet examples of a prerevolutionary Russian tradition. However, closer scrutiny reveals that the actual relationship between such songs and the genres to which their titles suggest affiliation is far from straightforward.

Because the formal features of the classic romance are only loosely defined, it is at a thematic and emotive level that the genre's conventionality is most pronounced. As Thomas Hodge describes, many common romance themes can be subsumed under the heading of the "lyrical rift," which is "usually expressed as separating freedom and slavery, past and present, life and death, civilization and nature."[16] Qualities associated with the romance include not just lyricism, but also intimacy (a "domestic" or "chamber" quality) and responsiveness to "the most refined nuances of the psyche," with an emphasis on melancholy, "elegiac moods, regret and gentle sorrow."[17] The particular charm of romances is said to rest in their ability to "convey with the greatest fullness an expressive, open, sincere feeling [and] to create an aura of soulfulness."[18]

In the hands of Aleksandr Galich, however, the romance becomes a finely honed instrument for laying bare the baseness and spiritual poverty of the Soviet system. In songs such as "Gusarskiy romans" (1964–66; "Hussar Romance") and "Salonnyi romans" (1966; "Salon Romance"), Galich explores the rift between past and present, between intellectual freedom and ideological enslavement. But though Galich's comparisons are subtly drawn and the emotional register of his performance is often muted, his critiques are harsh and pointed. In "Gusarskiy romans," dedicated to the romantic poet Aleksandr Polezhayev (1804–1838), Galich lashes out at the ruthless destruction of freethinking writers by an oppressive regime. As Galich explained prior to performing this song, Polezhayev "was arrested, demoted and exiled to Siberia because of his satirical poems and songs," after which "he succumbed to alcoholism and ended his days in the madhouse."[19] The parallels between Polezhayev and poets under Soviet rule are unstated, but they are nonetheless abundantly clear: gendarmes who come in the night, "no one to save you," and denunciations that are "more frightening than bullets [*kartech'*]" (135–36).

In "Salonnyi romans," Galich turns his attention to the early twentieth century, specifically to the "romantic world of the songs of Aleksandr Vertinsky," to whom the song is dedicated.[20] Here Galich evokes not just Vertinsky's songs but also Gogol and Akhmatova (with references to an "old overcoat [*staroy shinel'koy*]" and a "gray-eyed king [*seroglazyi korol'*]"); and he articulates the sad fate of romantic dreams and of beauty itself, symbolized by Helen of Troy, in contemporary society (139–40).[21] With his eyes closed, "in the oblivion of grandfathers' armchairs," the narrator can see wondrous things, such as the "copper-colored . . . cruiser" from Brazil that "sails into a muslin harbor" (a reference to Vertinsky's song "Brazil'skiy kreyser" ["Brazilian Cruiser"]). The chief agent in this song is not the narrator, however, but rather the capricious and temperamental "age" (*vek*), which "cannot help but interfere" and which "crumples fates like candy wrappers" because chaos and confusion suit it.

The debasement of the romantic dreams of a bygone age is epitomized by the fact that the "grandson of the lilac negro" (a reference to Vertinsky's song "Lilovyi negr" ["The Lilac Negro"]) comes "to Moscow for a loan," thus identifying the corrosive "age" as contemporary and Soviet. The discovery that the celebratory "farewell dinner" has now been replaced with "a hundred-fifty [grams of vodka] with Borzhomi [mineral water]" serves as further evidence of disgrace. Ultimately, the age intervenes decisively, turning dreams to dust and stealing away beauty itself:

Vsyo predano prakhu i tlenu,
Ni dat ne ostalos', ni vekh.
A nashu Yelenu, Yelenu
Ne greki ukrali, a vek!

Everything is betrayed to dust and rot,
Not a date has remained, not a milestone.
And our Helen, Helen
Stolen not by the Greeks, but by the age!

Galich underscores this dispiriting revelation vocally, delivering *Yelenu* as a wistful sigh before dropping into a weighty and measured rumble to enunciate the verse's (and song's) final line.[22]

Like the romance, the ballad proved to be a versatile and productive genre with which Galich and other bards experimented liberally. Differentiating the ballad from the romance at a generic level is not a simple task, however. Often treated as a subgenre of the romance, the ballad is characterized by relatively simple stanzaic structure (iambic lines, alternating rhymes, and repeated refrains); a lyrical atmosphere; and, most notably, a strong narrative element (often focusing on historical or heroic-epic themes).[23] In songs by various bards, the ballad's emphasis on narrative provides the richest material for creative reworking. Mikhail Ancharov's "Ballada o tanke T-34," for example, is a short narrative on a traditional heroic theme (war), for example, but with an interesting slant.[24] Ancharov's "ballad" is actually a "character song," a first-person confession told by the titular tank itself (a medium-weight model first produced in 1940), and the view of war presented through the tank's confession is far from wholeheartedly heroic.

Ancharov's tank characterizes itself as an "iron elephant" that mercilessly crushes all in its path, until it is stopped in its tracks by the sight of an abandoned doll, "the symbol of someone else's love, someone else's family."[25] Unable to bring itself to step on the doll, the tank "is therefore slain" and takes up its place on a pedestal, "Like Christ,/Having righted death by death." In the song's final verse, the tank asks, "And now do you recognize me?/I am love,/Frozen for evermore." The contrast between the song's conclusion and its earlier descriptions of grinding, crushing violence is jarring, indeed, and seems to indicate a highly ambivalent attitude toward World War II. Because World War II was one of the preeminent "sacred" themes of official Soviet culture, demanding glorious depictions of heroic feats performed by brave Soviet soldiers, even a vaguely uncertain attitude toward the war was ideologically questionable.

Unlike Ancharov's "Ballada o tanke T-34," Vysotsky's "Ballada o gipse" (1972; "Ballad About a Cast") eschews traditional ballad thematics entirely, though in its alternating rhyme scheme, repeated refrain, and fairly detailed narrative it does adhere to the formal structure typical of a ballad. The narrative in question borders on the absurd, however, being the first-person tale of an ordinary man who ends up in a full-body cast after "a thirty-thousand kilo dump truck/crushed [his] skeleton to pieces"; and who declares that, even though he has been "well for a long time since, [he] doesn't intend to take the cast off" because it is "more comfortable for [him] to seem like an elephant/and to feel thick-skinned" (302–4). Vysotsky's "Ballada o korotkoy sheye" (1973; "Ballad About a Short Neck") is hardly less absurd, though certainly more pointed. Here, Vysotsky observes that a commander ought to have a "short, unobtrusive neck," because "it's significantly more difficult to strangle,/And there's nothing for a lasso to catch on" (351). Successive verses emphasize that "sticking one's neck out [*vytyagivat' sheyu*]" is dangerous, because doing so leaves one's "neck exposed for a noose"; and explain that while "one can see farther, it is not far-sighted/To live among people with an exposed neck."

Galich likewise combines the absurd and the deadly serious in a number of ballads the names of which are virtually narratives unto themselves. Examples include "Pravo na otdykh, ili Ballada o tom, kak ya yezdil naveshchat' svoyego starshego brata, nakhodyashchegosya na izlechenii v psikhbol'nitse v Belykh Stolbakh" (1965; "The Right to a Holiday, or Ballad About How I Went to See My Older Brother, Who Was in a Psychiatric Hospital in Belye Stolby for Treatment"); "Ballada o starikakh i starukhakh, s kotorymi ya vmeste zhil, lechilsya i otdykhal v kardiologicheskom sanatorii oblastnogo Soveta profsoyuzov v 110 kilometrakh ot Moskvy" (1967; "Ballad About Old Men and Women with Whom I Lived, Underwent Treatment, and Vacationed in the Cardiological Sanatorium of the Regional Union Council 110 Kilometers from Moscow"); and "Ballada o tom, kak edva ne soshyol s uma direktor antikvarnogo magazina No. 22 Kopylov N. A., raskazzanaya im samim doktoru Belen'komu Ya. I." (1968; "Ballad About How N. A. Kopylov, Director of Antique Store No. 22, Almost Went Crazy, Told by Him to Doctor Ya. I. Belen'ky").

Like Vysotsky's "Ballada o gipse," Galich's "Pravo na otdykh" is a "character song" sung from the point of view of an ordinary and rather coarse man, in which the alternating rhyme scheme and repeated refrain characteristic of the ballad provide the framework for a humorous narrative with serious undertones. Having gone to a mental hospital to visit his brother, the narrator of "Pravo na otdykh" ends up staying:

> A bratan i govorit mne: "Sen', a Sen'!
> Ty pobud' tut za menya denyok-drugoy!
> I po vykhodke, i po rozhe my
> Zavsegda s toboy byli skhozhimi,
> Tebe zh net v Moskve vzdokha-prodykha,
> Pozhivi zdes', kak v dome otdykha!" (183–84)
>
> And my brother, he says to me: "Zan, hey Zan!
> Stay here in my place for a day or two!
> In the way we walk, and in our looks we
> Have always been similar, you and I,
> You don't have any R & R in Moscow,
> Live here for a bit, like in a rest home!"

The implications of the brother's "invitation" are made especially sinister by the fact that *dom otdykha,* literally "rest home," also carries the slang meaning of "prison" or "prison camp." Somewhat ominously, the brother's robe fits the narrator "to a tee—/Like it had been specially made" for him.

Ultimately, the playful and slightly singsong character of the lyrics (which Galich emphasizes in performance) is belied by the song's revealing refrain:

> Akh, u psikhov zhist'—
> Tak by zhil lyuboy:
> Khochesh'—spat' lozhis',
> Khochesh'—pesni poy!
> Predostavleno
> Nam vrode litera:
> Komu—ot Stalina,
> A komu—ot Gitlera!
>
> Oh, a nutso's life—
> Anyone would live like that:
> Wanna sleep? Lie down,
> Wanna sing? Sing songs!
> We're all granted
> Something like a travel pass:
> Some of us by Stalin,
> Some by Hitler!

As so often in Galich's songs, the attack launched in this refrain is not monofocal. On one hand, Galich mocks the "privileges" of (psychiatric) incarceration. On the other hand, he draws an explicit parallel between Stalin's regime and Hitler's; and his telling use of "we" suggests that, just as the whole Soviet Union might be considered a vast Gulag, so, too, might it be considered a vast mental hospital.

As in "Pravo na otdykh," in the more succinctly titled "Ballada o soznatel'nosti" (1967; "Ballad About Consciousness"), Galich demonstrates his masterful talent for "conveying the speech rhythms" of social types far removed from his own;[26] but conversational and at times playful language does nothing to dull the barbs hidden in this song. The song's protagonist, one Yegor Petrovich Mal'tsev, is a diabetic who is expiring quietly, only to be revived by a remarkable announcement. Closer to death than to life, Yegor has a "miraculous dream," in which he is visited by "a chorus decorated with the Order of the Red Banner" (151–53). The chorus exhorts Yegor to "stand up," because *Pravda* has proclaimed that "diabetes is no more / In the Soviet land" and so, by dying from it, he is "disgracing / [His] own media." Duly chastened by these words, Yegor rises—not only brought back from the brink of death, but also cured of his diabetes. The song ends with Yegor's triumphant promenade through Moscow:

Po ploshchadi po Tribunoy
Idyot on, milyi drug,
I vsyo yemu dostupno,
Chto vidit on vokrug:

Dostupno kushat' slasti
I gazirovku pit' . . .
Lish' pri Sovetskoy vlasti
Takoye mozhet byt'!

Across Tribune Square
He walks, dear friend,
And he can have everything
That he sees around him:

He can eat sweets
And drink sparkling water . . .
Only under Soviet power
Could such a thing happen!

Detailing the "polyphonic dissonance [*razlad*] between the verbal and melodic lines" in this song, Vladimir Frumkin describes "Ballada o soznatel'nosti" as a virtuoso example of Galich's "generic parody [*zhanrovaya parodiya*]."[27] Frumkin's analysis of Galich's "motley verbal-musical collages" is highly astute; but arguably the designation "generic parody" is imprecise when applied to "Ballada o soznatel'nosti," for the ballad itself is not, or not primarily, the target of Galich's parody here. Rather, "Ballada o soznatel'nosti" exemplifies Morozov's "parodic usage," in which parody is oriented at an extratextual target, as the song's direct references to preposterous declarations in *Pravda* and the miraculous effects thereof make clear. Pivoting on the conflict between the "faked reality" presented through the Soviet media and the experienced reality of Soviet everyday life, this parodic usage, in turn, represents a telling example of hypergeneric guitar poetry as "narratization" of everyday life, as a means of carving out an alternative discursive space in which to manage competing visions of reality.

"IN A CERTAIN KINGDOM . . .": USES OF THE FAIRY TALE IN GUITAR POETRY

Of all possible genres that could be employed in guitar poetry's "narratization" of Soviet everyday life, the fairy tale (*skazka*) is perhaps the ideal candidate. The reasons for this relate both to characteristics of fairy tales themselves and to the status of folklore within official Soviet culture. First, it is widely agreed that, throughout history and across cultures, fairy tales have played a significant role in civilizing and socializing processes, whether by "reflect[ing] upon mores, norms, and habits" of a particular society or by encouraging self-reflection leading to self-discovery.[28] As a powerful instrument of socialization, the fairy tale could be used to promote a particular set of values or a particular type of self-discovery and, just as easily, to challenge these; in the Soviet Union fairy tales "proved to be an excellent means both to propagate . . . and to question the official dogmas."[29] Moreover, the fact that the fairy tale is generally considered to be a children's genre can provide a built-in disguise for such challenges, an outward veneer of "fantasy" that partially masks the critique of reality lying beneath.[30]

Second, the traditional fairy tale represents a combination of opposites on various levels, a conscious coupling of the ordinary and the fantastical, the optimistic and the terrifying. As a rule, readers of fairy tales "do not believe in the reality of what is told [*raskazannogo*]," firmly understanding the tales to be "something invented"; yet unusual and even fantastical characters and plots are couched in a matter-of-fact terms, with "even the most remarkable encounters [being] related in casual, everyday ways."[31] Likewise, fairy tales balance the positive and the negative, expressing an overall optimism and a promise of resolution and fulfillment, "no matter how terrifyingly serious some features of the story may be."[32] This coupling of opposites, in turn, provides an ideal context in which to perform the navigation between and management of competing realities that are characteristic of narratization practices in socialist societies.

Third, "the idea of 'life as a fairy tale'" became one of the "vital tropes of 'Sovietness'" in the 1920s,[33] while folklore itself (including fairy tales and heroic epics [*bylini*]) acquired a privileged position in official culture beginning in the 1930s. Following Maksim Gorky's keynote address at the first All-Union Congress of Soviet Writers (1934), which included remarks on "the relations between folklore and labor," folklore was recognized as "a powerful force to advance communism" and as "a significant factor in the formation of . . . 'socialist culture.'"[34] Having recognized the "strong social and political function of folklore," the Soviet authorities moved to promote "ideologically correct" folklore and folklore studies.[35] This was brought about both by gathering "any item of traditional folklore that might demonstrate the people's positive attitude toward the Revolution" and the government; and also by publishing "new folklore works" based on traditional genres but featuring new Soviet heroes and new Soviet contexts.[36] In new Soviet fairy tales, for example, traditional folktale heroes were replaced with "heroes of science and technology," Arctic explorers, aviators, and other figures drawn from the Soviet heroic pantheon, while folktale villains were replaced by familiar Soviet bad guys such as noblemen, capitalists, and kulaks.[37]

Folktale motifs and situations were updated as well, in order to provide these new tales with a specifically Soviet ideological context. Thus, in I. F. Kovalyov's "Tale of Three Falcons," the traditional introductory formula "in a certain kingdom [*v nekotorom tsarstve*]" is used to establish the tale's setting and message in no uncertain terms: "In a certain kingdom, in a certain land, namely the one in which we live, there reigned a weak and lifeless, almost mindless, tsar, who loved landowners, capitalists, kulaks, and priests."[38] Similarly, the anonymous tale "The Chuvash Peasant and the Eagle" (1937) ensures that there can be no mistaking *its* context or meaning. For completing typical folkloric trials (killing a series of animals), the tale's hero is granted happiness: his impoverished village is miraculously transformed into a well-provisioned, "clean and wonderful" new village, which is identified explicitly as a collective farm (*kolkhoz*).[39] The tale's final lines provide an equally unambiguous interpretation of its heroes and villains: the animals killed by the hero are "unmasked" as the tsar, the landlord, and the kulak, while "the eagle who showed the poor Chuvash the way was—Stalin!"[40]

The emphasis on transformation in "The Chuvash Peasant and the Eagle" is broadly typical of new Soviet fairy tales, in which, as Catriona Kelly writes, "sentimental elves, fluffy kittens, and gnomes (not to speak of fairies) were banned, but . . . astonishing stories of self-transformation were *de rigueur.*"[41] While newly manufactured Stalin-era folklore fell out of favor after 1953, both specific tales and the overall politicization of folklore remained embedded in the public consciousness long after this time. Thus, alongside traditional folklore, new Soviet folklore forms an important backdrop for guitar poetry's uses of the fairy tale.

In songs by various bards, numerous aspects of the fairy tale are subjected to dramatic reinterpretations. The customary relationship between reality and fantasy, and between optimism and terror, is reversed; formal elements (such as the introductory phrases "once upon a time" [*zhili-byli*] and "in a certain kingdom" [*v nekotorom tsarstve*]) are appropriated and transmuted; and fairy-tale characters, situations, and themes are introduced and induced to serve new functions. In many cases, there is significant overlap between these categories: a song that adopts and transforms fairy-tale characters, for example, will often do so in the context of a fairy-tale-like situation. In short, the fairy tale represents an extremely productive form that various bards manipulated creatively and to great effect.

Fairy-Tale Characters, Russian and Foreign

The simplest and most widespread approach to the use of fairy tales in guitar poetry involves the incorporation of folkloric characters into songs. This technique is evident in songs by numerous bards, in which various fairy-tale heroes and villains, foreign as well as Russian, play a decisive role. Novella Matveyeva's "Letuchiy gollandets" (1960; "The Flying Dutchman") provides an interesting starting point for discussion of this technique because while Matveyeva's works normally evince a "strong escapist element,"[42] this song seems to deny the possibility of folklore in an ambiguous world. In the song's chorus Matveyeva asks,

> Kto nam pesni spoyot,
> Kto nas uverit, chto ne vsyo proydyot,
> Kto pered nami fonaryami vpot'makh
> Zasvetit nebylitsy?[43]
>
> Who will sing us songs,
> Who will assure us that not everything will pass by,
> Who will illuminate fables before us
> in the dark with lanterns?

The unfortunate answer is "No, no one will sing." Instead, the famed ghost ship "will be used for firewood" and over a fire built from its wood, "The cook will prepare . . . / Paté out of the blue bird." (The bird in question is the fabled "bluebird of happiness.") This resolution suggests both the debasement of folklore itself, the ephemeral made physical; but it also hints that the promise of happiness will never be realized, and so its delicate symbol might better be put to a crudely utilitarian use.

Not unlike Matveyeva's "Letuchiy gollandets," Klyachkin's "Pesnya Chudy-yudy bezzakonnogo" (1967; "Song of the Lawless Chudo-Yudo") uses a timeless setting as the backdrop for a critique with clear relevance to contemporary Soviet circumstances. The song was commissioned for a regional children's theater production called *Tayna Chyornogo Ozera* (*Secret of the Black Lake*), in which Chudo-Yudo is given the responsibility of guarding a trunk containing the truth.[44] As he sits on the trunk, Chudo-Yudo is assailed by the "black snake of doubt": he begins to wonder if his work isn't merely a way of passing time, and if the trunk he guards contains any truth at all.[45] But, he concludes,

> . . . somnevat'sya mne nelz'ya:
> yesli uzh ya stanu somnevat'sya,
> znachit, rushitsya zemlya,
> i v nashem tsarstve strashno ostavat'sya
> vsem nachal'nikam.
>
> I can't doubt:
> for if I begin to doubt,
> that means that the world will collapse,
> and it will be scary for all the bosses
> to remain in our kingdom.

The political statement here is, of course, quite transparent. Indeed, Klyachkin himself remarks that, in this song, he wanted "to be a little naughty [*poshalit'*] politically" and that it is not a children's song at all; not surprisingly, the song "didn't make it into the show" for which it was commissioned.[46]

In contrast to the two songs discussed above, Galich's "Vesyolyi razgovor" (1964; "Cheerful Conversation") sees an archetypal figure transported from the misty realm of folklore to the gray banality of the everyday. Here, Galich uproots Little Red Riding Hood from her traditional sylvan setting and thrusts her into a modern, urban, Soviet one: she is taught to be a cashier in a food store, where she sits "as in a place of public punishment" (220–21). Her life is presented matter-of-factly as a series of events: advances from a wolfish boss, a lover who is taken off to war and never returns, the birth of a daughter; a brush with the law ("They found that she was short,/They charged her according to article one hundred thirty five"); jail, amnesty, her daughter's marriage to her boss, and the birth of a granddaughter. The passage of time is conveyed laconically through references to her changing hair color (from black to salt-and-pepper, to [dyed] ginger, to white).

These changes are accompanied by the "cheerful conversation" of clacking cash register keys, culminating in the gloomy verdict that this clacking measures not monetary change, "not kopecks," but "life's account!" In its bleak ending, Galich's tale of a contemporary Soviet Little Red Riding Hood is closer to Charles Perrault's version of the tale, which ends with the wolf devouring the girl, than to the more familiar version popularized by the Brothers Grimm, in which the girl is ultimately rescued. But where Perrault offers an explicit moral, warning "that young children/Especially pretty girls" should beware of talking to strangers because "the sweetest tongue has the sharpest tooth,"[47] Galich provides no such guidance on how to avoid the fate to which his heroine has succumbed. Offering neither a happy ending nor consolation nor an edifying moral, Galich's song suggests instead that neither the fairy tale nor innocence itself can survive the grim realities of the Soviet present unscathed.

Yet another song in which the collision between fairy tale and reality results in the corruption or even destruction of the former is Vysotsky's "Pesnya-skazka pro dzhinna" (1967; "Song–Fairy Tale About a Genie"). In this song, Vysotsky borrows the figure of the genie in a bottle from Middle Eastern folkloric tradition and transplants him into an entirely recognizable, contemporary Soviet context.[48] The narrator is an alcoholic who craves a drink, and who is disturbed to find a genie inside his wine bottle instead of the expected libation:

> U vina dostoinstva, govoryat, tselebnye,—
> Ya reshil poprobovat'—butylku vzyal, otkryl . . .
> Vdrug ottuda vylezlo chtoy-to nepotrebnoye:
> Mozhet byt', zelyonyi zmey, a mozhet—krokodil! (132–34)
>
> Wine has healing properties, so they say—
> I decided to try—I took a bottle, opened it . . .
> Suddenly something obscene crawled out of there:
> A green snake, perhaps, or perhaps—a crocodile!

Unfortunately for the narrator, the "green snake" (a play on the phrase *dopit'sya do zelyonogo zmiya,* "to get drunk to the green snake," i.e., to the point of hallucination) turns out to be no mere figment of an alcohol-hazed mind. Rather, he is a genie, whom the protagonist finally identifies as such after recalling Lazar' Lagin's socialist realist fairy tale *Starik Khottabich* (1938; *The Old Genie Khottabych*), and who possesses a certain physical prowess but no actual magic powers.

The alcoholic begins to suspect that this "rude bumpkin [*grubyi muzhuk*]" had been hiding out in the bottle: "Kto zagnal tebya syuda, v vinnuyu posudinu, / Ot kogo skryvalsya ty i chego skryval?" ("Who chased you in here, into the wine bottle, / Who were you hiding from, and what were you hiding?"). In response, the genie quells his rescuer's fears by announcing that he is neither a thief nor a spy and promising to fulfill the narrator's commands (after a fashion) by beating up a person or two. As it turns out, the genie is devoid of all powers *but* this ("Krome mordobitiyev—nikakikh chudes!" ["Aside from face-pounding—no miracles!"]). After the genie demonstrates his "powers" on his unfortunate rescuer, the narrator summons the police, who summarily arrest the genie and cart him off to parts unknown. That Vysotsky's genie turns on his rescuer is not, in itself, remarkable: in Middle Eastern folklore, after all, genies appear as both benefactors and malefactors. Rather, what is noteworthy is the genie's utter degradation: he appears from a wine bottle (no magic lamps here) and his gifts amount to petty thuggery, but "versus the militia he couldn't do a thing." Equally striking is the tale's lack of a meaningful lesson. In defiance of traditional fairy-tale convention, the narrator's greed (both for wine and for riches) goes unpunished, while in defiance of Soviet fairy-tale convention, neither the narrator nor the genie undergoes an astonishing self-transformation.[49]

In Vysotsky's "Skazka o neshchastnykh skazochnykh personazhakh" (1967; "Fairy Tale About Unhappy Fairy-Tale Personages"), traditional fairy-tale settings and characters are debased in similar fashion. The traditional fairy-tale castle is replaced by "an awful building, / From far away reminiscent of the U.N," for example, while the villain Koshchey the Deathless becomes an "unhappy little old man" and the "hero Ivan [*Dobryi molodets Ivan*]" occupies himself with "idle feats" (151–53). Ultimately, Koshchey turns out *not* to be immortal, and his humiliation is heightened by the fact that Ivan slays him with mere insults rather than heroic deeds—and insults that have a decidedly Soviet accent, at that ("you vile factory-owner! / Look how many rooms you built over there, / And you hid the girl, you schemer!"). An analogous deflation of heroic strength and of magic words is found in Vysotsky's "Pro dvukh gromilov—brat'yev Prova i Nikolaya" (1970; "About Two Thugs—the Brothers Prov and Nikolai"). Here, the rapine of the titular thugs is stopped neither by the local menfolk (*muzhich'yo*) nor by a charm (*zaklatiye*), but rather by the simple words of a "useless person" and a "victim of misfortune [*goremyka*]," who cries, "Brothers, / You should be ashamed of yourselves!" (238–39).

Perhaps the finest example of the pointed transformation and transposition of folkloric characters is to be found in Vysotsky's "Lukomor'ya bol'she net (Antiskazka)" (1967; "The Sea-Cove Is No More [An Anti-Fairy Tale]"), however.[50] As in "Pesnya-skazka pro dzhinna," in "Lukomor'ya" Vysotsky draws upon multiple sources, including traditional folklore; classic Russian literature, particularly the prologue to Pushkin's *Ruslan i Lyudmila* (1820; *Ruslan and Lyudmila*); and also Soviet urban folk culture, in the form of "parodic variations on the theme of the Sea-Cove" that began to appear in the 1930s.[51] The folkloric characters, images, and settings that appear in "Lukomor'ya" are thus filtered through multiple antecedents, but their transformation is no less astonishing for this.

In "Lukomor'ya," both the landscape of the sea-cove and its denizens are subjected to Vysotsky's penchant for "lower[ing] and ground[ing] his chosen theme," through seemingly minor grammatical and lexical alterations as well as through major changes to their traditional roles and characteristics.[52] In Vysotsky's verse, for example, the "green oak" that spreads its branches over Pushkin's sea-cove[53] is multiplied into many oaks—and then chopped down to be used as lumber:

Lukomor'ya bol'she net,
Ot dubov prostyl i sled,—
Dub goditsya na parket—
  tak ved' net:
Vykhodili iz izby
Zdorovennye zhloby—
Porubili vse duby
  na groby. (147–50)

The sea-cove is no more,
Even the trail of the oaks has gone cold,—
The oak's good for parquet—
  but no:
Burly louts
Came out of the hut—
They chopped down all the oaks
  for coffins.

Similarly, Pushkin's "thirty fine knights" become Vysotsky's "thirty-three bogatyrs,"[54] a disgruntled bunch who abandon their heroic calling to become petty landholders. Most arrestingly, the "scholarly cat" (from whom Pushkin's narrator hears the fairy tale told in *Ruslan i Lyudmila*) is utterly transformed, becoming a heavy-drinking jokester who tells anecdotes instead of fairy tales and who pawns his gold chain in order to buy liquor. The cat's drinking binges are such that, far from Pushkin's idyll in which "there is the Russian spirit . . . there it smells of Rus'," in Vysotsky's despoiled sea-cove "it reeked of alcohol across a whole hectare!"

In addition, a number of figures with decidedly minor roles in Pushkin's prologue are given rather more substantial and significantly more scandalous roles in Vysotsky's "Lukomor'ya." For example, the virginal mermaid (*rusalka*) of Russian folk tradition is transformed into a light-skirted wench whose many lovers refuse to claim her bastard child; while Pushkin's sorcerer (*koldun*) becomes "a liar, a chatterbox, and a joker," who offers to take in the disgraced mermaid along with her child, an offer that she accepts with great reluctance ("I poshla ona k yemu/kak v t'yurmu" ["And she went to him/as if to jail"]). For his part, the wood-goblin (*leshii*), who simply wanders around Pushkin's sea-cove, becomes a violent alcoholic who "[beats] his wood-gobliness [*leshachikha*]" and threatens to "flatten" her if she does not give him the money to buy more booze. Vysotsky's lyrical evisceration of the sea-cove and its folkloric inhabitants concludes with the terse observations that "the sea-cove is no more" and that "everything the poet wrote/is nonsense."

The utter degradation of the fairy-tale world of the sea-cove is effected not just at the level of characters and images, but also at a linguistic level. In the song's printed text, linguistic coarsening and rustication is evident in nonstandard forms such as *kazhnyi* (instead of *kazhdyi,* "each"), *v yom* (instead of *v nyom,* "in it"), *ikhniy* (instead of *ikh,* "their"), and *leshachikha* (instead of *lesovikha,* "wood-gobliness"). Vysotsky's dynamic performance adds another layer to the linguistic richness of the song, though, revealing a polyphonic composition in which numerous voices intertwine.[55] Chief among these voices is the narrator, who intones the song's first line, announcing gravely that "the sea-cove is no more," and who then shifts abruptly to a strained, high-pitched whine to plead, "Abate, abate, melancholy/In my breast."

The introduction of the cove's folkloric figures brings about a dramatic shift, as Vysotsky imbues the narrator's voice with a rough edge. Vysotsky's signature rolled *r*'s and throaty *kh*'s are present alongside clipped word endings and a varied palette of dialectal pronunciations. In the narrator's description of the cat's antics, for example, the hard g and *k* of *peregar* (hangover) and *gektar* (hectare) are rendered as a typically south Russian *kh* and the final *r*'s reverberate exuberantly (*V Lukomor'ye perekharrrr na khekhtarrrrr*). In the narrator's description of "bearded Chernomor,/The sea-cove's first thief," moreover, can be found phonetic phenomena representative of entirely separate dialects. These include the *okan'ye* typical of the Volga region (evident in the full, rounded prononciation of both unstressed and stressed *o*'s in *kovyornyi samolyot* [flying carpet]) alongside the *akan'ye* of Muscovite Russian (heard in the pronunciation of unstressed *o*'s as *a*) and also the *yakan'ye* characteristic of some south Russian dialects (heard in the pronunciation of *letat'* [to fly] as *lyatat'*). At a basic level, these heterogeneous dialectal features evident in Vysotsky's performance, which "are incompatible in the speech of a real person," serve to create "a generalized portrait of [Vysotsky's] countryman."[56]

"Lukomor'ya" has been described as an "outrageous parod[y] of Russian folklore" that is "almost childish in the level of its humor."[57] But as with Galich's "Ballada o soznatel'nosti," Vysotsky's parody is indirect: as has been observed variously, the target of the criticisms implied in the song is neither folklore nor *Ruslan i Lyudmila,* but rather contemporary Soviet socioeconomic and cultural circumstances.[58] Arguably, the dialectal mixing noted above both deepens and broadens these criticisms. On one hand, like the geographical speculation of Vysotsky's uneducated criminal protagonist in "Vsyo pozadi," it suggests the all-encompassing scope of the malaise illustrated in "Lukomor'ya." The destruction of the fairy-tale world and the disrespect for its values are omnipresent in a Sovietized society, and so the narrative of this destruction is delivered through the speech of a pan-Soviet everyman. On the other hand, and perhaps paradoxically, this "advertised anonymity" increases verisimilitude by allowing virtually any audience member to discern something familiar and true to his or her experience in the tattered, no longer magical world that Vysotsky describes. The characters and phenomena therein are born of shared knowledge and experience, and so a listener might well recognize him or herself somewhere in them—with a wince as well as with a laugh.

Fairy Tale Situations and Motifs

A second common strategy in bards' uses of the fairy tale, already glimpsed in a number of the songs discussed above, involves the adaptation of fairy-tale situations and motifs. In some cases, these are evoked simply through the use of standard fairy-tale formulae. In "Chekharda s bukvami" (1968; "Leap-Frog with Letters"), for example, Galich integrates the fairy-tale opening *zhili-byli* ("once upon a time") and the fairy-tale "magic number" three into the reworking of a popular children's riddle ("A, I, B sideli [igrali] na trube. A upalo, B propalo, chto ostalos' na trube?" ["A, I, B were sitting [playing] on a pipe. A fell, B disappeared, what was left on the pipe?"]).[59] Galich's use of *zhili-byli* introduces neither a timeless setting nor fantastical events, however, but rather a sinister and all-too-familiar tale of arrests, disappearances, and imprisonments from the not-too-distant Soviet past (54–55).

In other cases, typical fairy-tale plots, tasks, or quests provide raw material for the creation of original, and often highly idiosyncratic, sung "fairy tales." In "Bumazhnyi soldatik" (1959; "Little Wooden Soldier"), for example, Okudzhava freely adapts the theme of Hans Christian Andersen's tale "The Brave Tin Soldier." Okudzhava's paper soldier is an idealist who "wanted to remake the world,/so that each person was happy," and whose readiness to sacrifice himself for his ideals compels him to forget his own vulnerability (177).[60] Okudzhava's song-parable ends with the paper soldier going "into the fire," where he perishes "for nothing:/for he was a paper soldier." Here, as in "Korol'," Okudzhava questions the value of war by underlining its terrible costs. In addition, he muses on the sad fate of well-meaning idealists from whom the truth is kept hidden ("You did not trust him/With your important secrets") and who are swallowed up by the very ideals they dedicate themselves to pursuing. While Okudzhava's parable lacks a specific setting, the song's date (1959) underscores its relevance to the process of reexamining Stalinism and its aftermath.

Similarly, Vysotsky's "Zhil-byl dobryi durachina-prostofilya" (1968; "Once Upon a Time There Lived a Kind-Hearted Simpleton")—which is likewise an original sung "fairy tale" based on an archetypal plot—is widely interpreted as a commentary on Nikita Khrushchev's expulsion from power and "about the power grab that led to his removal."[61] In "Zhil-byl dobryi durachina-prostofilya," the traditional figure of the idiot (*durak*), who in Russian fairy tales invariably triumphs over whatever obstacles are set before him, is thoroughly undermined. The song's titular hero undergoes a familiar folkloric trial, as follows:

> Posredi bol'shogo polya—glyadi—tri stula,—
> Durachinu v oblast' pecheni kol'nulo,—
>   Sverkhu—nadpis': "Dlya gostey,"
>   "Dlya knyazey,"
> A na tret'yem—"Stul dlya tsarskikh krovey." (173–75)
>
> In the middle of a large field—look—three chairs,—
> The ninny felt a prick in the region of his kidney,—
>   On top—an inscription: "For guests,"
>   "For princes,"
> And on the third—"Chair for royal blood."

As the simpleton moves from chair to chair, both his power and his ego grow until finally, having climbed onto the chair for kings, he feels an overwhelming urge to exercise his power. While his initial impulses are childish and unflattering ("he began to stamp his feet and shout"), eventually he takes it into his head to do good by "issuing an order about surplus." But the simpleton's desire is thwarted by the chair itself—"Tol'ko stul podobnikh del/Ne terpel:/. . . yasno, tot ne usidel" ("But the chair such matters/Did not tolerate:/. . . it's clear, that one didn't keep his seat")—a turnabout that constitutes a thinly veiled jab at the propensity of political institutions to thwart individual good intentions.

In "Pro dikogo veprya" (1966; "About a Wild Boar"), Vysotsky adapts the familiar plot of a king offering his daughter's hand in marriage to the man who performs a particularly heroic feat (such as saving his kingdom from some sort of monster). In Vysotsky's version, however, the young hero has no interest in the princess, stating his preference for "a tub of port" instead and snorting derisively, "I wouldn't take the princess even as a gift/I'll defeat Chudo-Yudo anyway!" (106–7). Far from being Prince Charming, this "once leading marksman, now disgraced" is both an alcoholic and an uneducated boor. Details like the "tub of port" (a drink notorious in the Soviet Union for being both cheap and strong) and the king's threat to throw the marksman in jail (instead of a dungeon) mark out a world that is vaguely, though nonetheless recognizably, modern; and that is populated by a heterogeneous cast of characters.[62] The end result is tragicomic, as the marksman "wrangled [away] the port,/Put down Chudo-Yudo, and ran off . . . ," shaming both the princess and the king. Ultimately, though, the tragedy is not that of the poor princess, unwanted by her asthmatic father and her drunken and unwilling suitor. Rather, it is the tragedy of the fairy tale itself, debased by a modern world in which the values it represents are no longer honored.

In "Strannaya skazka" (1970; "Strange Fairy Tale"), Vysotsky employs both standard fairy-tale formulae and motifs to offer a very contemporary, politically tinged critique. The song's first verse introduces the first of three troubled realms:

> V Tridevyatom gosudarstve
> (Trizhdy devyat'—dvadtsat' sem')
> Vsyo derzhalos' na kovarstve—
> Bez problem i bez sistem. (239–40)
>
> In a Thrice-nine state
> (Three times nine is twenty-seven)
> Everything was supported by perfidy—
> Without problems and without systems.

The innocent opening formula "in a Thrice-nine state" transforms, slowly but inexorably, into something quite different: its magical property to transcend time and to efface distance by evoking the land of make-believe is undermined by the "solving" of its magical formula, as though this is no more than a banal and trivial math problem. Next, the realm evoked by this formula is dragged still closer to earth by the revelation that in it, "Everything was supported by perfidy."

This technique becomes the pattern for the song, which plays on the common fairy-tale motif of three kingdoms. Successive verses introduce new realms that are identified by magical formulae, and then bring these realms abruptly back to earth by making their "magic" trite. The third verse introduces the "Thrice-ten kingdom," followed immediately by the parenthetical question, "Three times ten is thirty, isn't it?"; while the fifth verse introduces the "Thrice-eleven tsardom," followed by the pedantic explanation, "That would be in tsardom Thirty Three."[63] All three kingdoms are further disgraced by their singularly unattractive rulers: the Thrice-nine state is ruled by an argumentative drunkard, the Thrice-ten kingdom by a brutal tyrant, and the Thrice-eleven tsardom by "a militarist and a vandal" who sends offensive missives to his neighbors every Saturday.

Unlike the progression from kingdom to kingdom in traditional Russian fairy tales, the progression from realm to realm in "Strannaya skazka" does not offer increasing wealth and fortune: all three are equally dismal, though in different ways. Similarly, unlike the optimistic ending characteristic of traditional fairy tales, the ending of Vysotsky's "Strannaya skazka" offers no respite and bodes only ill. The various realms have lost their "magic names" entirely (being called, simply, the Twenty-Seventh, Thirtieth, and Thirty-Third); the three rulers virtually come to blows; and the Thirtieth kingdom is wracked by purges ("the commanders/Have all drowned in the well") and incipient rebellion, with ellipses suggesting that further chaos is to come. The Thrice-ten kingdom, with its tyrannical ruler and its political strife, might be interpreted as a narrow reference to the Stalinist 1930s. Yet the fact that all three realms are equally troubled, despite their superficial differences, allows one to infer a sidelong comment about the fundamental sameness of all political regimes, their outward trappings notwithstanding.

By contrast, the political critique underpinning Galich's "Pesnya o neshchastlivykh volshebnikakh" (1966; "Song About Unhappy Sorcerers") is of a far less ambiguous nature. Following the introductory phrase "Once upon a time . . . [*Zhili-byli* . . .]," this song depicts an unhappy scene of "unhappy sorcerers" at odds with their environment; this is broadly in keeping with the traditional fairy-tale pattern in which this formula is followed by some kind of "but," by the revelation of something unexpected or sad.[64] However, the environment into which these unfortunate, pseudo-folkloric characters have been transplanted is a decidely un-fokloric place in which magic is only an illusion. Eschewing subtle comparisons and vague allusions, Galich situates his tale firmly and explicitly within a Soviet context, commenting bitterly on official control of creative activity and also on popular complicity in supporting a repressive regime.

Considered to be "scholars," the unhappy sorcerers try (unsuccessfully) to learn how to be happy from "magical textbooks [*volshebnye uchebniki*]" (255–56). However, their sorcery comprises no more than showy magic tricks (e.g., releasing doves, turning cards into dice), which they perform under the direction of the banal (and yet vaguely Gogolian) maestros Skripochkin (from *skripka,* "violin") and Lampochkin (from *lampa,* "lamp, light"); and they perform for an adoring public that cries "Bravo! Encore!" *before* their act has even begun. The magic words of old have been replaced by the militaresque *German* phrase "Ein! Zwei! Drei!"; and this phrase is further debased by explicit translation and unrestricted use:

I otrezannye golovy
U zhelayushchikh iz publiki,
Ulybayas' i podmigivaya,
Govorili: "Raz! dva! tri!"
Chto v doslovnom perevode
Oznachaet: "Ein! tsvey! drey!"

And the cut-off heads
From those desirous among the public,
Smiling and winking,
Said: "One! two! three!"
Which in literal translation
Means: "Eins! zwei! drei!"

The parallel use of Russian and German throughout the song, along with repeated statements that these two phrases are interchangeable, suggest the same comparison between communism and fascism that Galich makes elsewhere.

After the performance, even the sorcerers' physical appearance is revealed to be a mere façade. Having peeled off their false mustaches and slunk off to a cafe "to forget about the unpleasantness for a time," the so-called sorcerers are unmasked as nothing more than "two tired sages" who are disenchanted with their own performance. In a parallel to their stage performance, their meager dinner ("two glasses of milk and two noodles") is presided over by banal restaurant musicians: the maestro Balalayechkin (from *balalayka,* "balalaika") and the singer Doremikina (from Do, Re, Mi), who rounds out the cliché by singing "something about the moon [*chto-to . . . pro lunu*]." The sorcerers initially despair of their situation, "quietly, thoughtfully/Saying: 'How do you like that!'" Watching warily as maestro Balalayechkin drinks and flings around his batons, the sorcerers eventually fall in line and, like the severed heads of audience members in the second verse, obediently take up the refrain "One! two! three!"

An abrupt shift to first-person narration interrupts the unhappy sorcerers' tale, at the same time bringing the song's Soviet context into sharp focus. The narrator is "summoned to Semichastnyi," that is, to the KGB, where "Textbooks proved to [him], like two times two,/That the sorcerers are happy sorcerers!"[65] Thus, the narrator is swiftly brought to heel—suggesting that while magic cannot be learned from textbooks, obedience can. This suggestion is underscored in the song's final verse, which demonstrates the narrator's full awareness of the creative restrictions imposed upon him:

I ne nado by, ne nado by
Radi krasnogo slovtsa
Sochinyat', chto ne polozheno
I ne nuzhno nikomu!

And one shouldn't, one shouldn't
Compose something unacceptable
And not needed by anyone
Just for the sake of eloquence!

Fully aware that he cannot control his own fate, the narrator labors under his restraints "like a dog rattling its collar," having mastered the necessary art of self-censorship:

Ya idu, povesiv golovu,
Ne tuda, kuda mne khochetsya,
A tuda, gde: "At'! dva! tri!,"
Chto ni kapli ne pokhozhe
Na volshebnoye "Ein! tsvey! drey!"

I walk along, having hung my head,
Not going where I want to go,
But going to that place where: "Hep! two! three!,"
Which isn't at all similar
To the magical "Eins! zwei! drei!"

It is tempting to see "Pesnya o neschastlivykh volshebnikakh" as a response to Lev Oshanin's "Ya rabotayu volshebnikom" ("I Work as a Sorcerer") which was recorded by variety stage singer Mark Bernes in 1964. In this song, which exemplifies the cheerful banality of the Soviet variety stage, the narrator attributes his various powers (flying to various lands, bringing rain to the desert, giving sunshine to good people) to the fact that he has not studied life "from textbooks," but rather "works as a sorcerer."[66] However, his "simple sorcery" comes in the form of rather Boy Scout-ish acts, such as making someone's journey a little easier or "think[ing] a little about others"; and the song ends with a syrupy request for the listener to help with such "sorcery." But such everyday acts are no more "magic" than the parlor tricks of Galich's "Pesnya o neshchastlivykh volshebnikakh," and when analyzed against this backdrop Galich's song becomes a bitter lament not just about creative restrictions but also, and more broadly, about the hollowness of values and ideals promoted through official Soviet culture.

Metaliterary Uses of Fairy Tales

Yury Kukin's songs "Skazochnik" (1964–65; "Teller of Fairy Tales") and "Volshebnik" (1964; "Sorcerer") provide an interesting counterpoint to the songs already discussed, both because they are more narrowly intertextual than many of the other songs analyzed here, and because they are at the same time metaliterary. While both songs borrow from the discourse of the fairy tale in the range of characters mentioned in them, they are, more importantly, about the telling of and the belief in fairy tales. Perhaps as a consequence of this, they are characterized by a tone that is less caustic, and far more melancholy, than that of Vysotsky and most especially Galich. The melancholy of "Skazochnik" comes through most clearly in its final verses, in which the "old teller of fairy tales" admits,

> Ya sam sebe rasskazyvayu skazki
> I zhdu, kogda oni nachnut sbyvat'sya.
>
> A sbyvshimisya skazki ne byvayut,
> Nesbyvshiyesya skazki—zabyvayu.
> I bol'no mne, no ya ne unyvayu—
> Ya staryi skazochnik, ya mnogo skazok znayu.[67]
>
> I tell myself fairy tales
> And wait for them to begin coming true.
>
> But fairy tales that come true never happen,
> And fairy tales that don't come true—I forget.
> And it's painful for me, but I am not dejected—
> I am an old teller of fairy tales, I know a lot of fairy tales.

Here, then, the telling of fairy tales becomes a type of willing self-deception: the teller waits for the tales to be realized, all the while knowing that they never will be, and thus he takes comfort only in the telling.

"Volshebnik," in which the author-narrator entreats a "kind wizard" for help, is similarly forlorn in tone. The author-narrator's wishes (to fly, to become invisible, to have a never-ending supply of money) have not been fulfilled, despite his entreaties, and he is left with the sad knowledge that he himself dreamed up the sorcerer.[68] The simple melody, Kukin's unassuming playing, and his quiet, wistful singing lend this song a poignancy that sets it apart from the other songs discussed in this chapter:

Gde zh ty, moy dobryi volshebnik?
Ya do sikh por ne letayu.
Vidish', stoyu na kolenyakh,
Khot' sam pridumal tebya ya . . .[69]

Where are you, my kind sorcerer?
I am not flying as yet.
You see, I am standing on my knees,
Though I thought you up myself . . .

When we juxtapose Kukin's songs with those discussed above, however, we are reminded once again that in the contemporary Soviet context the magic of old has lost its power. Throughout these "fairy-tale" songs by various bards, wizards are revealed to be mere figments of a wishful imagination, heroic fighters devolve into cowards, drunkards, and thuggish brawlers, and fearsome and unconquerable villains are reduced to ineffectual old men. Similarly, wondrous and eternal landscapes are laid waste through laziness and greed, or are simply replaced with the gritty homogeneity of the everyday. Finally, magic words are either supplanted by ordinary ones, implying the uselessness of traditional magic; or these magic words (in the form of traditional fairy-tale formulae) are decoded or explained, implying that they are no longer potent in their own right.

As L. G. Kikhney and T. V. Safarova have noted, in oral folk culture every element is a kind of sign "in which one or another aspect of the popular attitude [*narodnogo mirooshchushcheniya*] has crystallized."[70] Arguably, then, the fact that various fairy-tale signs need to be decoded indicates that the knowledge they represent is no longer shared. However, the fairy-tale characters, formulae, and motifs used by Vysotsky and others form a significant part of the cultural knowledge shared across different strata of Soviet society and therefore *would* have been familiar to their audiences.[71] In this light, it seems all the more reasonable to conclude that through hypergeneric "fairy-tale" songs, Vysotsky, Galich, Kim, and others comment not so much on fairy tales or folklore itself, but rather on a sociopolitical system that destroys their meaning and value. It only deepens the debasement of these once-sacred signs that trite modern words have gained power over the fairy-tale world of old, and that the denizens of the fairy-tale world are correspondingly reduced in status.

HYPERGENERICITY, NARRATIZATION, AND METACOMMUNICATION

Diverse though the songs discussed here are, the attitude toward the particular genres from which they co-opt salient characteristics forms a common undercurrent. Galich's "romances" depicting the destruction of romantic dreams by the contemporary "age"; Ancharov's "ballad" of a guilt-ridden military machine; and Vysotsky's strange "fairy tale" of political ineptitude and self-interest, to name just a few, are not aimed at discrediting the respective genres themselves. Rather, they satirize, and in some cases even boldly unmask, the artificiality and spiritual poverty of official Soviet reality. Moreover, they do so not simply by making use of "traditions of song that the official world had tried to ignore, discourage, or suppress,"[72] but also by manipulating genres that were specifically promoted by the Soviet cultural establishment. Romances and ballads were well suited to such narratization because they remained entrenched in domestic musical culture during the Soviet era even when they were frowned upon officially.[73] But fairy tales were, perhaps, even better suited because the Soviet system defined its own ideals in terms of the fairy tale and generated new and specifically Soviet fairy tales. Yet, as the bards' songs show, this same system also made it impossible to believe in any fairy tale at all.

While offering ironic and corrective narratization, hypergenericity also highlights guitar poetry's orality-centered mode of communication. As well as being universally familiar to bards' audiences, the genres most widely used in this hypergeneric play are also highly conventionalized. This combination of familiarity and conventionality gives rise, in turn, to certain expectations for guitar poetry's audiences: knowledge of what is *supposed* to follow "Once upon a time . . . [*Zhili-byli* . . .]" in a fairy tale, in other words, provides essential (if implicit) context for what *does* follow that stock phrase in guitar poetry. Bards' references to and borrowings from familiar, conventionalized genres therefore serve a function similar to that of formulaic or ritual expressions in traditional oral culture: they are a way of mapping out common ground, of signifying "knowledge that is already shared."[74]

Defining common ground, guitar poetry's borrowings from familiar genres reflect not simply communication between bard and audience, but also metacommunication. Using generic borrowings to convey shared attitudes about Soviet life, society, and values, guitar poetry does not so much transmit new information; rather, it "convey[s] something about the relationship between communicator and audience,"[75] identifying bards and their listeners as members of the same (imagined) community, the same "public of *svoi.*" As a result, hypergenericity is a central component of guitar poetry's function as both a "conversation between friends" and an "identifying code."

Conclusion

On the cusp of the 1950s and 1960s, guitar poetry was poised to become one of the central sociocultural phenomena of the post-Stalin period. Bards quickly became emblematic of an entire generation and beyond, as more and more young people turned to guitar poetry as singer-songwriters and as listeners; and, in doing so, drew together into communities around their common interest in bards' eminently accessible songs. As this study has shown, though, in many ways guitar poetry was also a phenomenon of the margins and of the marginal. On one hand, guitar poetry was rooted in various types of marginality, from the generic (in its diverse roots and its musico-poetic hybridity) and the aesthetic (in the sounds of "bad singing," amateurish guitar technique, and poor-quality *magnitizdat* tapes); to the physical (in the spaces in which it developed and flourished) and the sociopolitical (in its uneasy interactions with fully sanctioned cultural activities and its delicate negotiation of the gray area between the permitted and the prohibited). For several generations of Soviet young people, moreover, guitar poetry was an important means of self-fashioning, communication, and community-building, all processes that are integral to marginality. On the other hand, marginality was also embedded in guitar poetry itself as an element of composition, in the selection and treatment of specific themes, in the use of seemingly trivial details, and in the deft handling of multiple generic codes.

Grounded in an understanding of the margins as interstitial arenas of social and cultural fusion, instability, and change, this analysis offers both a new approach to guitar poetry and also a new way of conceptualizing the crises and struggles of the immediate post-Stalin period as complex manifestations of a marginal state. In so doing, it firmly situates the great eruption of the "in between" into Soviet life in that same period, rather than (as is more widely argued) in the 1970s and 1980s. Among the ideological quandaries that were precipitated by Stalin's death and the dismantling of his legacy, issues surrounding the cultural, moral, and ideological *vospitaniye* of Soviet youth—the problem of reshaping essential "Sovietness" and a concomitant sense of Soviet identity while removing the Stalinist foundation on which these had long depended—occupied an extremely prominent place. But the simultaneous "crisis" in Soviet song deprived ideologues of a key instrument of *vospitaniye,* one that was felt to be particularly important for reaching Soviet youth.

Thus, the Soviet cultural establishment initially greeted amateur singer-songwriters' efforts with tentative praise, viewing them as a wellspring of popular creativity that could be channeled in service of the state, not least as a much-needed aid to *vospitaniye.* But this early approbation faded rapidly as the impossibility of corralling guitar poetry permanently and definitively became increasingly obvious. The standard weapons of institutionalization and oversight, cajoling and co-opting, threats and censorship were deployed; but they were of limited utility in combatting guitar poetry's popularity and its relatively unhindered spread across the entire Soviet Union.

The formation of Clubs of Amateur Song provided structures in which Party organs, the Komsomol, and the KGB could scrutinize bards' and fans' activities, for example. But bards' and fans' willingness to operate simultaneously within and outside such constraints—and even more, their adeptness at doing so—meant that KSP activities were never fully controllable. Even as particular bards were struck off approved concert lists, clever organizers contrived to enter them into song competitions on an entirely legal basis. Even as urban concerts and festivals were restricted or banned, guitar poetry enthusiasts continued to organize rallies in sylvan settings and to carry songs with them on expeditions to the far-flung reaches of the Soviet Union. Similarly, while censuring and censoring could be effective in targeting the most outspoken bards, such heavy-handed tactics were impractical against legions of guitar-strumming young people and scores of songs that lacked explicitly anti-Soviet content.

The discourse of *vospitaniye* and the related discourse of *lichnost'* underpinned official concerns about the wildfire spread of guitar poetry and its particular popularity among young people. For Soviet youth of the post-Stalin period, guitar poetry—perhaps especially guitar poetry of an apolitical cast—appealed not just as a means of entertainment; but also, as attested by the numerous firsthand accounts analyzed here, as a means of self-discovery, self-fashioning, and communication with like-minded individuals. That is, *lichnost'* was as much a part of the discourse about guitar poetry and the guitar poetry movement as it was of official discourse. Indeed, *lichnost'* was so fundamental to guitar poetry that it (rather than the poetic text) can be seen as the foundation on which the entire guitar poetry phenomenon rests.

Where guitar poetry's discourse of *lichnost'* diverged from the official line was not in an understanding of what it was: for bards and their audiences, as in contemporaneous official usage, *lichnost'* referred both to spectacular individuals or personalities ("Personalities," even) and to the more nebulous notion of individuality or personality (the "person as such"). Rather, the point of divergence was an understanding of where and how *lichnost'* could be fashioned. In official discourse, the collective was firmly held to be the primary, indeed the only appropriate, site for the development of *lichnost'*. But guitar poetry, musically accessible, intimate, and unmediated, opened up vast possibilities for an individual to craft his or her own, independent *lichnost'* with nothing more than an idea and a guitar. As contemporary debates illustrate, critics, ideologues, and members of the musical establishment were keenly attuned to the possibilities that song provided for essentially private, unmonitored communication between songwriter and listener. Espousing a firm belief in the inseparability of art and ideology, as well as in the role of song as an ideological weapon, these same circles expressed profound anxiety that the "backchannel" of communication that guitar poetry created between bards and audiences also created the possibility for the former to induce the latter to set out on cultural and ideological "wrong paths"—that is, in a most basic sense, to engage in independent self-fashioning and self-expression.

To an extent, these concerns were not unfounded: as discussed here, the spectacular *lichnosti* of guitar poetry played a crucial role in fostering the quest for *lichnost'*, both through what they sang and through how they sang it. Crucially, though, the figures who were most influential in spurring guitar poetry's popularity and sparking the broader guitar poetry movement—becoming the voices of their contemporaries and encouraging their contemporaries to find their own voices—were largely apolitical "romantic" bards who remained engaged in wholly sanctioned creative pursuits and ideologically acceptable (even laudable) professional activities throughout their bardic careers. Like many of their fans, among whom KSP members occupied a particularly significant place, these bards negotiated a delicate balance between the prescribed and the proscribed in their lives and in their creative works. In other words, both the bardic *lichnosti* who helped most in transforming guitar poetry into a mass movement and the particular ideal of *lichnost'* that they helped to shape were neither vehemently oppositional nor ardently conformist, but quietly marginal.

Admittedly, describing guitar poetry and its most eminent proponents as "marginal" is controversial, both because of the negative connotations that attach to marginality in Russian and because, since 1991, guitar poetry has become a prism through which are refracted post-Soviet cultural and intellectual concerns, not least among which are anxieties about the (perceived) decline of high culture. As has been argued here, however, during the late Soviet period guitar poetry's multifaceted marginality was both its greatest strength and the source of its most potent threat to Soviet officialdom. Guitar poetry's sociopolitical marginality—the fact that the authorities never prohibited it wholesale and indeed tried to co-opt both the genre and the movement—ensured its continued existence after the end of the Thaw; while its aesthetic marginality, rooted in the power of "bad singing," helped to transform it into a mass phenomenon by offering an eminently accessible means of self-expression. Similarly, its compositional marginality—overt, covert, and hypergeneric—provided means to explore issues that were largely ignored in, and sometimes excised from, official public discourse. Taken together, these different kinds of marginality made guitar poetry a powerful force for self-fashioning, communication, and community-building. Because the overt rhetoric of the post-Stalin Soviet system was still underpinned by binary distinctions, guitar poetry's inherent ambivalence had a profoundly destabilizing effect, even when the identities, interests, and needs expressed through it were consonant with officially promoted norms and values.

Because so much of guitar poetry is bound up with the marginality of the post-Stalin period, it is not surprising that it has been profoundly affected by the dramatic social, political, and technological changes of the post-Soviet period. Indeed, guitar poetry as it exists today in Russia is very much altered from the low-tech, semi-clandestine, predominantly oral affair that it once was. As a cultural artifact, guitar poetry enjoys popularity across all possible media, old and new. As an object of study, it has found firm footing within Russian academe and in school curricula. As a living, evolving phenomenon, guitar poetry continues to be represented, at least in part, by the efforts of solitary singer-songwriters, including both "classic" figures like Aleksandr Gorodnitsky and Yuly Kim; and individuals like Mikhail Shcherbakov and Timur Shaov, who began their bardic careers in the late 1980s and early 1990s. In addition, however, guitar poetry now also encompasses complicated orchestral arrangements, choral performances, and cover versions of classic songs by honey-voiced performers such as Galina Khomchik.

Moreover, many of the bards who came to prominence in the late 1970s and 1980s have become driving forces in the (re)development of guitar poetry in the post-Soviet period. For example, Oleg Mityayev, Aleksey Ivashchenko, Georgy Vasil'yev, and Vadim and Valery Mishchuk are all involved with Pesni nashego veka (Songs of Our Century), an ensemble formed in the late 1990s that performs guitar poetry with elaborate orchestral accompaniment and that has released a popular series of self-titled recordings. As projects like Pesni nashego veka demonstrate, however, in both performance style and presentation, guitar poetry as an oral/aural genre is becoming less and less distinct from other popular music genres like the variety stage (*estrada*). Major guitar poetry festivals, which continue to grow and flourish, reflect a similar trend toward increasing professionalism and even flashiness, complete with sophisticated audiovisual equipment and commercial sponsorship.

These transformations are so profound that, as Vladimir Frumkin has observed, what exists is no longer "guitar poetry" so much as "guitar variety stage [*gitarnaya estrada*]."[1] Similarly, Aleksandr Gorodnitsky has remarked, with no small amount of regret, that most festival performances now resemble the variety stage more closely than guitar poetry; and that the Grushin Festival, in particular, has become a "show" filled with "first-rate performers" instead of true bards.[2] The post-1991 commercialization of guitar poetry is, perhaps, wearyingly inevitable. No longer targeted for official scrutiny or persecution, and no longer constrained by the vagaries of third-rate tape recording technology, guitar poetry has become a means by which singer-songwriters (as well as composers, performers, and others) can and do make money—however much its ardent supports may insist that it "remains an unmistakable characteristic of guitar poetry . . . that it is never composed, in the first instance, for sale."[3]

However, while guitar poetry is increasingly indistinguishable from the variety stage in performance, in its textual existence the genre is being pulled further into the realm of high culture. Scholarly works that define guitar poetry as a poetic genre or that position bards' works explicitly within the confines of high literary culture are one indication of this trend. Collections of bards' works that omit identification of which texts were written to be sung and which were not; or that include poetic texts written by authors far removed (culturally, geographically, and temporally) from the context of the post-Stalin Soviet Union are similarly telling. Among the latter, perhaps the most remarkable is a "guitar poetry" anthology of some 700 poetic texts in which works by Galich, Okudzhava, Vysotsky, and other luminaries of the genre are vastly outnumbered by the works of Konstantin Bal'mont, Aleksandr Blok, Ivan Bunin, Langston Hughes, Mikhail Kuzmin, Mikhail Lermontov, Pablo Neruda, Boris Pasternak, Alexander Pushkin, William Shakespeare, Marina Tsvetayeva, and others.[4]

On one hand, new recording projects and festivals are evidence of the continued evolution (or, many would argue, degeneration) of guitar poetry, of explorations of its present and possible trajectories for its future. Publications that deliberately entrench guitar poetry within the exclusive province of (high) literary culture, on the other hand, seem not merely to readdress the genre's past but also to attempt to rewrite it. In turn, these divergent lines of development in the post-Soviet period demonstrate that guitar poetry is still very much alive in the arena of cultural politics, changed sociocultural and political circumstances notwithstanding. In this arena, furthermore, guitar poetry is still contested territory for the confrontation of opposing poles in the kind of binary system into which, ironically, it fits so uneasily.

Notes

INTRODUCTION

1. The "all-round development of the individual" received special attention at the 22nd Party Congress (1961). See KPSS, *The Road to Communism: Documents of the 22nd Congress of the Communist Party of the Soviet Union (October 17–31, 1961)* (Moscow: Foreign Languages Publishing House, 1961), 260ff.

2. Gerald Stanton Smith, *Songs to Seven Strings: Russian Guitar Poetry and Soviet "Mass Song"* (Bloomington: Indiana University Press, 1984). In addition to the Russian terms already mentioned, *menestrel'naya pesnya* (minstrel song), *molodyozhnaya pesnya* (youth song), and *studencheskaya pesnya* (student song) are also common, especially in contemporary official sources. A range of other terms indicating affiliation with specific leisure activities or professions—e.g., *geologicheskaya pesnya* (geologist song) and *turistskaya pesnya* (tourist song)—are also encountered, though generally in reference to particular thematic or sub-generic strands of guitar poetry. Following Smith's coinage, *gitarnaya poeziya* has also passed into limited usage in Russian; see, e.g., Rosen Dzhagalov, "Avtorskaya pesnya kak zhanrovaya laboratoriya 'sotsializma s chelovecheskim litsom,'" *Novoye literaturnoye obozreniye,* no. 6 (2009); Vladimir Frumkin and Boris Kushner, "Tsvetok ili sornyak na skale? Sud'ba pesni pri totalitarizme," *Zametki yevreyskoy istorii,* no. 5 (96) (May 2008), http://berkovich-zametki.com/2008/Zametki/Nomer5/Frumkin1.php; Vladimir Kovner, "Zolotoy vek magnitizdata [part 3]," *Vestnik Online,* no. 9 (346) (April 28, 2004), http://www.vestnik.com/issues/2004/0428/koi/kovner.htm. For discussions of the history and usage of various terms, see Yu. A. Andreyev, *Nasha avtorskaya . . . Istoriya, teoriya i sovremennoye sostoianiye samodeyatel'noy pesni* (Moscow: Molodaya gvardiya, 1991), 57–58; James Martin Daughtry, "The Intonation of Intimacy: Ethics, Emotion, Metaphor and Dialogue Among Contemporary Russian Bards" (Ph.D. thesis, University of California at Los Angeles, 2006), 47–59; I. A. Sokolova, "Avtorskaya pesnya: Opredeleniya i terminy," in *Mir Vysotskogo: issledovaniya i materialy IV* (Moscow: GKTsM V. S. Vysotskogo, 2000), 439–46.

3. See, e.g., Svetlana Biryukova, *Spasite nashi dushi* (Tambov: Tambovskiy

filial Serpukhovskogo otdeleniya Fonda Akademii tvorchestva SSSR, 1990), 4; B. M. Dobrovol'sky, "Sovremennye bytovye pesni gorodskoy molodyozhi," in *Fol'klor i khudozhestvennaya samodeyatel'nost'*, ed. N. V. Novikov (Leningrad: Nauka, 1968), 198; Yekaterina Lebedeva, "Traditsii i istoki pesen Bulata Okudzhavy," in *Tvorchestvo Bulata Okudzhavy v kontekste kul'tury XX veka: Materialy Pervoy mezhdunarodnoy nauchnoy konferentsii, posvyashchyonnoy 75–letiyu so dnya rozhdeniya Bulata Okudzhavy* (Moscow: Sol', 2001), 77; Aleksandr Orlov, "Avtorskaya pesnya: Vchera, segodnya . . . zavtra (po materialam sotsiologicheskikh issledovaniy)," in *Voprosy sotsiologii muzyki: Sbornik trudov III* (Moscow: Gosudarstvennyi muzykal'no-pedagogicheskiy institut imeni Gnesinykh, 1990), 77; B. A. Savchenko, *Avtorskaya pesnya*, vol. 7, Novoye v zhizni, nauke, tekhnike: Seriya "Iskusstvo" (Moscow: Znaniye, 1987), 4; Gerald Stanton Smith, "The Metrical Repertoire of Russian Guitar Poetry," *International Journal of Slavic Linguistics and Poetics* 30 (1984): 131; G. S. Smith, *Songs to Seven Strings*, 119; Sokolova, "Avtorskaya pesnya: Opredeleniya i terminy," 449; Richard Stites, *Soviet Popular Culture* (New York: Cambridge University Press, 1992), 134; D. A. Sukharev, "Vvedeniye v sub"yektivnuyu bardistiku," *Znamya* 10 (2000): 184.

4. V. I. Novikov and E. N. Basovskaya, *Avtorskaya pesnya* (Moscow: Olimp, 2000), 8. See also N. E. Kuteynikova, "Iskusstvo bardov kak organichnoye yedinstvo fol'klora i literatury," in *Natsional'naya dukhovnaya kul'tura i obrazovaniye* (St. Petersburg: ?, 1994), 71; Lebedeva, "Traditsii i istoki," 77; Savchenko, *Avtorskaya pesnya*, 4; Sokolova, "Avtorskaya pesnya: Opredeleniya i terminy," 449; and others. A welcome counterpoint to this trend is offered by a handful of scholars, including Anatoly Vishevsky (see Anatoly Vishevsky, *Soviet Literary Culture in the 1970s: The Politics of Irony* [Gainesville: University Press of Florida, 1993], 47).

5. Biryukova, *Spasite nashi dushi*, 52; Smith, *Songs to Seven Strings*, 6.

6. Yury Mal'tsev, "Menestreli," in *Mir Vysotskogo: Issledovaniya i materialy III.1* (Moscow: GKTsM V. S. Vysotskogo, 1999; reprint of *Vol'naya russkaya literatura: 1955–75*), 298; Savchenko, *Avtorskaya pesnya*, 28–29. See also Andrey V. Skobelev and Sergey M. Shaulov, "Menestreli nashikh dney," *Literaturnaya Gruziya* 4 (1986): 159; Vladimir Vysotsky, *Sochineniya v dvukh tomakh*, 2 vols. (Moscow: Lokid-Press, 2001), 1:473.

7. Contemporary Soviet debates on guitar poetry are discussed at length in chapter 1.

8. Hedrick Smith, "Intellectual Life: The Archipelago of Private Culture," in *The Russians* (New York: Quadrangle/New York Times, 1976), 411. See also Argus, "Zoshchenko v stikhakh," in *Mir Vysotskogo: Issledovaniya i materialy III.1* (Moscow: GKTsM V. S. Vysotskogo, 1999; reprint of *Novoye russkoye slovo* [May 18, 1968]); Rosette C. Lamont, "Horace's Heirs: Beyond Censorship in the Soviet Songs of the Magnitizdat," *World Literature Today* (Spring 1979);

Mal'tsev, "Menestreli"; Gene Sosin, "Aleksandr Galich: Russian Poet of Dissent," *Midstream* 20, no. 4 (1974); and Gene Sosin, "Magnitizdat: Uncensored Songs of Dissent," in *Dissent in the USSR: Politics, Ideology, and People,* ed. Rudolf L. Tokes (Baltimore: Johns Hopkins University Press, 1975).

9. Works from the 1980s and early 1990s that further the "dissident" view of guitar poetry include Rosette C. Lamont, "The Subcontinent of the 'Magnitizdat': The Soviet Bards," in *New Literary Continents, 5th NDEA Seminar on Foreign Area Studies* (Whitestone, N.Y.: Griffon House, 1984); and Katja Lebedewa, *Komm Gitarre, mach mich frei! Russische Gitarrenlyrik in der Opposition* (Berlin: Collection BuchPlus, 1992). See also Helene Blanc, *Les Auteurs du printemps russe: Okoudjava, Galitch, Vyssotski* (Montriche: Les Éditions Noir sur Blanc, 1991). David Lerner's characterization of Vysotsky as an "outlaw troubadour" is also worth noting ("Vysotsky: The Revival of a Russian Pop Icon," *Mother Jones,* November 1987, 23).

10. G. S. Smith, *Songs to Seven Strings,* 91, 33.

11. Ibid., 2–3.

12. Recent studies of various forms of Russian popular music include, for example, Thomas Cushman, *Notes from Underground: Rock Music Counterculture in Russia,* SUNY Series in the Sociology of Culture (Albany: State University of New York Press, 1995); Polly McMichael, "'After All, You're a Rock and Roll Star (At Least, That's What They Say)': *Roksi* and the Creation of the Soviet Rock Musician," *Slavonic and East European Review* 83, no. 4 (2005); Yngvar B. Steinholt, "You Can't Rid a Song of Its Words: Notes on the Hegemony of Lyrics in Russian Rock Songs," *Popular Music* 22, no. 1 (2003); and Michael Urban, *Russia Gets the Blues: Music, Culture, and Community in Unsettled Times* (Ithaca, N.Y.: Cornell University Press, 2004). More broadly, Russian popular culture has been surveyed in works such as Adele Marie Barker, ed., *Consuming Russia: Popular Culture, Sex, and Society Since Gorbachev* (Durham, N.C.: Duke University Press, 1999); and Birgit Beumers, *Pop Culture Russia!: Media, Arts, and Lifestyle,* Popular Culture in the Contemporary World (Santa Barbara, Calif.: ABC-CLIO, 2005).

13. Relevant works include Stephen V. Bittner, *The Many Lives of Khrushchev's Thaw: Experience and Memory in Moscow's Arbat* (Ithaca, N.Y.: Cornell University Press, 2008); Polly Jones, ed., *The Dilemmas of De-Stalinization: Negotiating Cultural and Social Change in the Khrushchev Era* (London: Routledge, 2006); and Alexei Yurchak, *Everything Was Forever, Until It Was No More: The Last Soviet Generation* (Princeton, N.J.: Princeton University Press, 2006).

14. See, e.g., Ruby Jean Jones, "Echoing Their Lives: Teaching Russian Language and Culture Through the Music of Vladimir S. Vysotsky" (Ph.D. thesis, University of Texas, 2008); Magdalena Romanska, "Bulat Okudzhava: Bard and Voice of a Waking Russian Nation" (Ph.D. thesis, McGill University, 2003);

and Gerald Stanton Smith, "Polyusa russkoy poezii 1960–1970–kh: Brodskii i Vysotsky," in *Mir Vysotskogo: Issledovaniya i materialy III.2* (Moscow: GKTsM V. S. Vysotskogo, 2000). Heather Lynn Miller examines issues of identity and "Russianness" in Vysotsky's songs in her Ph.D. thesis ("'Vysotsky's Soul Packaged in Tapes': Identity and Russianness in the Music of Vladimir Vysotsky" [University of Maryland, 2006]). In his Ph.D. thesis, J. Martin Daughtry explores the relationship between Soviet guitar poetry and its post-Soviet émigré counterparts ("Intonation of Intimacy").

15. Relevant studies include L. A. Levina, *Grani zvuchashchego slova: Estetika i poetika avtorskoy pesni* (Moscow: Neft' i gaz, 2002); and I. A. Sokolova, *Avtorskaya pesnya: Ot fol'klora k poezii* (Moscow: GKTsM V. S. Vysotskogo, 2002).

16. Numerous monographs exist, including Vsevolod Chubukov, *Vysotsky: Vova, Volodya, Vladimir* (Moscow: GKTsM V. S. Vysotskogo, 2000); Anatoly Kulagin, *Poeziya V. S. Vysotskogo: Tvorcheskaya evolyutsiya* (Moscow: Knizhnyi magazin Moskva, 1997); A. E. Krylov, *Galich—"Soavtor"* (Moscow: Blagotvoritel'nyi fond Vladimira Vysotskogo, 2001); V. I. Novikov, *Vladimir Vysotsky: Zhizn' i tvorchestvo* (Moscow: [Vagant], 2000); Valery Perevozchikov, *Pravda smertnogo chasa: Posmertnaya sud'ba* (Moscow: Politburo, 2000); Valery Perevozchikov, *Neizvestnyi Vysotsky* (Moscow: Vagrius, 2005); Fyodor Razzakov, *Vladimir Vysotsky: Po lezviyu britvy* (Moscow: Yauza, Presskom, 2004); R. A. Shipov, ed., *Pyat'desyat rossiyskikh bardov: Spravochnik* (Moscow: Vagant, 2001); Pyotr Soldatenkov, *Vladimir Vysotsky* (Moscow: Olimp, 1999); Irena Vysotskaya, *Moy brat Vysotsky: U istokov* (Moscow: Rizalt, 2005); and S. N. Zubrilina, *Vladimir Vysotsky: Stranitsy biografii* (Rostov-on-Don: Feniks, 1998). Relevant articles are too numerous to list individually, though focused periodic editions such as the series Mir Vysotskogo: Issledovaniya i materialy (Moscow: GKTsM V. S. Vysotskogo) and Golos nadezhdy: Novoye o Bulate Okudzhave (Moscow: Bulat) deserve particular mention.

17. See, for example, N. Bogomolov, "Bulat Okudzhava i massovaya kul'tura," *Voprosy literatury* 3 (2002): 12; Georgy Chernyavsky, "Politika v poezii velikikh bardov: 'Neistov i upryam, gori, ogon', gori': Bardovskaya pesnya protiv vlastey," *Kaskad,* no. 195 (August 6, 2003), http://kackad.com/kackad/?p=3727; E. N. Khomutova, "Avtorskaya pesnya kak kul'turno-istoricheskiy fenomen v Rossii XX veka," in *Nauchnye trudy Nizhnevartovskogo gosudarstvennogo pedagogicheskogo instituta: Seriya "Kul'turologiya" 1* (Nizhnevartovsk: Izdatel'stvo Nizhenevartovskogo pedagogicheskogo instituta, 2000), 168–69; Kuteynikova, "Iskusstvo bardov," 73–74; Aleksandr Mirzayan, "V nachale byla pesnya," *ApArt* 1 (1996): 4; Novikov, *Avtorskaya pesnya,* 10; Vladimir Novikov, "Avtorskaya pesnya kak poeziya soprotivleniya," *Vestnik Online* 5 (290) (February 28, 2002), http://www.vestnik.com/issues/2002/0228/koi/novikov.htm; and Sokolova, "Avtorskaya pesnya: opredeleniya i terminy," 437.

18. These include M. V. Antonova, "Osobennosti sozdaniya skazochnogo mira v poezii V. S. Vysotskogo," in *Vysotskovedeniye i vysotskovideniye: Sbornik nauchnykh statey,* ed. M. V. Antonova, V. P. Izotov, et al. (Orel: Ministerstvo obrazovaniya Rossiyskoy federatsii; Orlovskiy gosudarstvennyi pedagogicheskiy universitet, 1994); S. S. Boyko, "'Novoyaz' v poezii Bulata Okudzhavy i Vladimira Vysotskogo," in *Mir Vysotskogo: Issledovaniya i materialy III.1* (Moscow: GKTsM V. S. Vysotskogo, 1999); A. V. Borzenko, "Neudachlivyi antikhrist: Stalin-bog v poezii Aleksandra Galicha," in *Galich: Novye stat'i i materialy,* ed. A. E. Krylov (Moscow: Yupaps, 2003); Chernyavsky, "Politika v poezii velikikh bardov: 'Neistov i upryam, gori, ogon', gori': Bardovskaya pesnya protiv vlastey"; L. G. Frizman, *"C chem rifmuyetsya slovo istina . . .": O poezii A. Galicha* (St. Petersburg: Oreol, 1992); Kulagin, *Poeziya V. S. Vysotskogo;* I. B. Nichiporov, *Avtorskaya pesnya v russkoy poezii 1950–1970-x gg. Tvorcheskiye individual'nosti, zhanrovo-stilevye poiski, literaturnye svyazi* (Moscow: Maks-Press, 2006); Vladimir Novikov, *Roman s literaturoy* (Moscow: Intrada, 2007), 86–113; M. L. Rogatskina, "Obraz liricheskogo *ya* v poezii Vysotskogo," in *Mir Vysotskogo: Issledovaniya i materialy III.1* (Moscow: Komitet po kul'ture Moskvy; GKTsM V. S. Vysotskogo, 1999); and T. D. Sokolovskaya, "Zhanrovo-stilevoye mnogoobraziye rechevykh sredstv poezii Vladimira Vysotskogo," in *Mir Vysotskogo: Issledovaniya i materialy* (Moscow: Komitet po kul'ture Moskvy; GKTsM V. S. Vysotskogo, 1997).

19. See, e.g., D. N. Kurilov, "Avtorskaya pesnya kak zhanr russkoy poezii sovetskoy epokhi (60–e—70–e gg.)" (Ph.D. thesis, Literaturnyi institut im. Gor'kogo, 1999); and Novikov, "Avtorskaya pesnya kak poeziya soprotivleniya." For a brief discussion of debates concerning the definition of guitar poetry as a poetic genre, see also Sokolova, "Avtorskaya pesnya: opredeleniya i terminy."

20. In extreme cases, guitar poetry has been interpreted in quite chauvinistic terms as the "foundation of the Russian national idea" (Aleksandr Mirzayan, "Avtorskaya pesnya kak baza russkoy natsional'noy idei," http://www.bard.ru/esse.htm.) and as a counterweight to the "pestilential, aggressive scum that reigns on our screens" and the "narcomusic that aims point-blank at our children" (Sukharev, "Vvedeniye," 200). A discussion of Mirzayan's view of guitar poetry is presented in Daughtry, "Intonation of Intimacy," 68–70.

21. Representative of this line of criticism are works including Miriam Dobson, "Contesting the Paradigms of De-Stalinization: Readers' Responses to 'One Day in the Life of Ivan Denisovich,'" *Slavic Review* 64, no. 3 (2005); Juliane Fürst, "Friends in Private, Friends in Public: The Phenomenon of the *Kompaniia* Among Soviet Youth in the 1950s and 1960s," in *Borders of Socialism: Private Spheres of Soviet Russia,* ed. Lewis H. Siegelbaum (New York: Palgrave Macmillan, 2006); Polly Jones, "Introduction: The Dilemmas of De-Stalinization," in *The Dilemmas of De-Stalinization: Negotiating Cultural and Social Change in the Khrushchev Era,* ed. Polly Jones (London: Routledge, 2006); and Yur-

chak, *Everything Was Forever.* As Yurchak observes, "certain problematic assumptions about Soviet socialism" are reflected in the widespread use of "binary categories" to describe Soviet reality (4–5).

22. A similar scheme divides the bards into the categories "loud" and "quiet." See Deming Brown, "'Loud' and 'Quiet' Poets of the Nineteen Sixties," in *Papers in Slavic Philology,* ed. Benjamin A. Stolz (Ann Arbor: University of Michigan Press, 1977); and Tat'yana Cherednichenko, "'Gromkoye' i 'tikhoye' v massovom soznanii: Razmyshlyaya o klassikakh-bardakh," *Sovetskaya muzyka* 11 (1991).

23. See, e.g., Kuteynikova, "Iskusstvo bardov," 71; Lebedeva, "Traditsii i istoki," 77; Novikov, *Avtorskaya pesnya,* 8; Savchenko, *Avtorskaya pesnya,* 4; and Sokolova, "Avtorskaya pesnya: Opredeleniya i terminy," 449. Among the bards themselves, Okudzhava asserted, "I never wrote songs. I always wrote poetry, [and] there is a small difference," noting that "some [songs] began to turn into poems of their own accord"; while Vysotsky remarked that "the most important thing in guitar poetry is text, information, poetry" (quoted in Biryukova, *Spasite nashi dushi,* 17. See also Vladimir Vysotsky, *Sobraniye sochineniy v chetyrekh tomakh, Tom 4: Proza,* e-book ed. [Moscow: Vremya, 2010], 106).

24. Simon Frith, *Music For Pleasure: Essays in the Sociology of Pop* (Cambridge, Eng.: Polity, 1988), 105; Arlen Blyum, *A Self-Administered Poison: The System and Functions of Soviet Censorship,* trans. I. P. Foote, European Humanities Research Centre Special Lecture Series (Oxford: Legenda, 2003), 19.

25. G. S. Smith, *Songs to Seven Strings,* 2.

26. In its analytical framework, this chapter builds upon Cathy Popkin's concept of the "pragmatics of insignificance," which is developed in *The Pragmatics of Insignificance: Chekhov, Zoshchenko, Gogol* (Stanford, Calif.: Stanford University Press, 1993).

27. This formulation draws on Nancy Fraser's critique of the Habermasian view of the public sphere and Catherine Helen Palczewski's discussion of counterpublics, both of which will be discussed further in chapter 2. See Nancy Fraser, "Rethinking the Public Sphere: A Contribution to the Critique of Actually Existing Democracy," in *Habermas and the Public Sphere,* ed. Craig Calhoun (Cambridge, Mass.: MIT Press, 1996), 123; and Catherine Helen Palczewski, "Cyber-Movements, New Social Movements, and Counterpublics," in *Counterpublics and the State,* ed. Robert Asen and Daniel C. Brouwer (Albany: State University of New York Press, 2001), 168–69.

CHAPTER ONE

1. Khomutova, "Avtorskaya pesnya," 168. See also Lev Anninsky, "Shyopot i krik," in *Natyanutyi nerv struny: Stikhi i pesni bardov 50–80 godov,* ed. Aleksandra Nikolashina and Maria Shmakova ([Khabarovsk]: Khabarovskoye kni-

zhnoye izdatel'stvo, 1991), 8; Lev Anninsky, *Bardy* (Moscow: Soglasiye, 1999), 12; A. M. Gorodnitsky, *I zhit' yeshchyo nadezhde . . .* (Moscow: Vagrius, 2001), 347; Lev Kopelev, "Pamyati Aleksandra Galicha," *Kontinent* 16 (1978): 340; Ye. Ya. Lianskaya, "A. N. Vertinsky i predystoriya bardovskoy pesni: Vzglyad muzykanta," in *Mir Vysotskogo: Issledovaniya i materialy III.2* (Moscow: GKTsM V. S. Vysotskogo, 1999), 396–97; S. P. Rasputina, "Sotsial'naya motivatsiya sovetskogo bardovskogo dvizheniya: Filosofsko-sotsiologicheskiy aspekt," in *Mir Vysotskogo: Issledovaniya i materialy III.2* (Moscow: GKTsM V. S. Vysotskogo, 1999), 378; and Andrey V. Skobelev and Sergey M. Shaulov, *Vladimir Vysotsky: Mir i slovo* (Voronezh: MIPP Logos, 1991), 155.

2. Andreyev, *Nasha avtorskaya,* 11.

3. Sukharev, "Vvedeniye," 187. See also Dobrovol'sky, "Sovremennye bytovye pesni," 177.

4. Biryukova, *Spasite nashi dushi,* 11. See also S. Yu. Rumyantsev, "Lyubitel'skiy muzykal'nyi teatr: Avtorskaya pesnya," in *Samodeyatel'noye khudozhestvennoye tvorchestvo v SSSR: Ocherki istorii, Konets 1950–kh—nachalo 1990–kh godov* (St. Petersburg: Gosudarstvennyi institut iskustvoznaniya, 1999), 52.

5. S. Yu. Rumyantsev and A. P. Shul'pin, "'Nizovoy' sloy narodnogo tvorchestva," in *Samodeyatel'noye khudozhestvennoye tvorchestvo v SSSR: Ocherki istorii, 1930–1950 gg.* (Moscow: Gosudarstvennyi institut iskustvoznaniya, Ministerstvo kul'tury RF, 1995), 94; S. Yu. Rumyantsev and A. P. Shul'pin, "Samodeyatel'noye tvorchestvo i 'gosudarstvennaya' kul'tura," in *Samodeyatel'noye khudozhestvennoye tvorchestvo v SSSR: Ocherki istorii, 1930–1950 gg.* (Moscow: Gosudarstvennyi institut iskustvoznaniya, Ministerstvo kul'tury RF, 1995), 21, 45.

6. Rumyantsev and Shul'pin, "'Nizovoy' sloy," 79–80.

7. Ibid., 87–89; F. M. Selivanov, "Introduction," in *Gorodskiye pesni, ballady, romansy* (Moscow: MGU, 1999), 7. See also S. Yu. Rumyantsev, "Muzykal'naya samodeyatel'nost' poslevoyennykh let," in *Samodeyatel'noye khudozhestvennoye tvorchestvo v SSSR: Ocherki istorii, 1930–1950 gg.* (Moscow: Gosudarstvenyi institut iskustvoznaniya, Ministerstvo kul'tury RF, 1995), 126–27.

8. Anninsky, "Shyopot i krik," 6; Rumyantsev, "Muzykal'naya samodeyatel'nost'," 912. See also Katja Lebedewa, "Russische Gitarrenlyrik und die Tonbandrevolution des 'Magnitizdat' nach 1956—kulturelle Voraussetzungen und Quellen," *Zeitschrift fur Slawistik* 36, no. 2 (1991): 234; G. S. Smith, *Songs to Seven Strings,* 61, 63; and Richard Stites, "The Domestic Muse: Music at Home in the Twilight of Serfdom," in *Intersections and Transpositions: Russian Music, Literature, and Society,* ed. Andrew Baruch Wachtel (Evanston, Ill.: Northwestern University Press, 1998), 192.

9. Novikov and Basovskaya, *Avtorskaya pesnya,* 16. See also Vladimir Frumkin, "Ne tol'ko slovo: Vslushivayas' v Galicha," *Obozreniye* 9 (1984): 16. Ancharov, in whose early songs can be found hints of the "thematic, linguistic and intonational possibilities" of guitar poetry, is considered by some to be the

genre's "true" patriarch. See, e.g., I. A. Sokolova, "V nachale byl Ancharov . . . O poeticheskom tvorchestve Mikhaila Ancharova i yego vklade v razvitiye zhanra avtorskoy pesni," in *Mir Vysotskogo: Issledovaniya i materialy II* (Moscow: GKTsM V. S. Vysotskogo, 1998), 357–58, 375. However, Ancharov did not achieve widespread popularity until the mid-1960s, after Okudzhava's songs were already in broad circulation.

10. A. [M.] Gorodnitsky, "Istoriya odnoy pesni," (2001), http://writer.fio.ru/news.php?n=6950&c=1351; Vladimir Frumkin, "Liberating the Tone of Russian Speech: Reflections on Soviet *Magnitizdat,*" in *The Soviet Union and the Challenge of the Future, Volume 3: Ideology, Culture, and Nationality,* ed. Aleksandr Shtromas and Morton A. Kaplan (New York: Paragon House, 1989), 282.

11. Lebedewa, *Komm Gitarre,* 118; Georgy Lepsky, "V flibust'erskom dal'nem sinem more . . . ," *Vol'nyi veter,* no. 40 (1999), http://veter.turizm.ru/40/lepskiy.shtml.

12. Anna Yashunskaya, quoted in A. Levitan and M. Levitan, eds., *Ot kostra k mikrofonu: Iz istorii samodeyatel'noy pesni v Leningrade* (St. Petersburg: Respeks, 1996), 132.

13. Kopelev, "Pamyati Aleksandra Galicha," 340; G. S. Smith, *Songs to Seven Strings,* 43.

14. Sergey Kalinin [webmaster], *Bards,* www.bards.ru; Shipov, ed., *Pyat'desyat Rossiyskikh bardov,* 97; Yury Kukin, *Dom na polputi* (Moscow: Sovetskiy fond kul'tury, 1991), 118.

15. This statement is widely known in guitar poetry circles, cited frequently and in a number of variants, but often without a specific reference. According to one version of events, it comes from a 1988 article in *Pravda,* while a competing account suggests a much later date (circa 1995). See Boris Gordon, "Prosto pesnya," *Ogonek* 23 (2002): 37.

16. Valentin Vikhorev, "Raznoobrazny i samobytny," in *Bereg nadezhd: Pesni leningradskikh avtorov: 1950–1960–e,* ed. A. Levitan and M. Levitan, *Gitara vremeni* (St. Petersburg: Boyanych, 2002), 5; Levitan, ed., *Ot kostra,* 311ff. See also A. Timofeyev, "Pesni Vikhoreva," in *Ya by skazal tebe mnogo khoroshego . . .* ed. A. Levitan and M. Levitan (St. Petersburg: Boyanych, 1996), 6.

17. G. S. Smith, *Songs to Seven Strings,* 43.

18. "Smotr muzykal'noy samodeyatel'nosti," *Sovetskaya muzyka* 8 (1950): 6; T. Khrennikov, "Muzykal'no-esteticheskoye vospitaniye detey i yunoshestva," *Sovetskaya muzyka* 5 (1961): 20.

19. Khrennikov, "Muzykal'no-esteticheskoye vospitaniye," 19.

20. See, e.g., A. Abramsky, "Puti muzykal'noy samodeyatel'nosti," *Sovetskaya muzyka* 5 (1959): 81; S. Aksyuk, "O sovremennoy russkoy pesne," *Sovetskaya muzyka* 11 (1953): 32; T. Khrennikov, "Na puti k muzykal'noy kul'ture kommunizma," *Sovetskaya muzyka* 6 (1962): 22; A. Morov, "O durnykh vkusakh i nedostatkakh vospitaniya," *Sovetskaya muzyka* 7 (1955): 116, 120; "Smotr," 67.

21. A. Sokhor, "Massovaya, bytovaya, estradnaya . . . ," *Sovetskaya muzyka* 10 (1965): 21–22. See also Biryukova, *Spasite nashi dushi,* 5.

22. Gorodnitsky, *I zhit' yeshchyo nadezhde . . . ,* 390. See also A. M. Gorodnitsky, "'. . . Nam ne khvatalo Okudzhavy'," in *Golos nadezhdy: Novoye o Bulate Okudzhave,* ed. A. E. Krylov (Moscow: Bulat, 2005), 78; Igor' Karimov, *Istoriya Moskovskogo KSP: Sub"yektivnyi vzglyad na ob"yektivnuyu real'nost'* (Moscow: Yanus-K, 2004), 90; Sergey Sinel'nikov, personal communication to Rachel S. Platonov, June 23, 2001.

23. Vikhorev, "Raznoobrazny i samobytny," 6; Gorodnitsky, *I zhit' yeshchyo nadezhde . . . ,* 390.

24. Reprinted in Novikov, *Avtorskaya pesnya,* 427; Levitan, ed., *Ot kostra,* 244.

25. Khrennikov, "Na puti," 10; Yu. A. Andreyev, "Chto poyut?" *Oktyabr'* 1 (1965): 191.

26. Reprinted in Novikov and Basovskaya, *Avtorskaya pesnya,* 243–44.

27. Sokhor, "Massovaya, bytovaya, estradnaya . . . ," 22. See also E. Ol'khovich, "Kogda molodyozhi interesno . . . ," *Sovetskaya muzyka* 8 (1966): 126.

28. Reprinted in Levitan, ed., *Ot kostra,* 243. See also Il'ya Suslov, "Pesni, nashedshiye svoikh avtorov," *Yunost'* 11 (1963): 4.

29. Yu. A. Andreyev, "Problemy molodyozhnoy pesni," *Oktyabr'* 1 (1967): 217–18.

30. The journal in question was *Sel'skaya molodyozh'* (*Rural Youth*), a Komsomol-sponsored publication with a not-inconsiderable monthly circulation of some 150,000 copies. (On this journal, see Arthur E. Adams, "Informal Education in Soviet Agriculture," *Comparative Education Review* 11, no. 2 [1967]: 227.) One of the offending songs was "Pesenka pro Chyornogo kota" (1957–59; "Ditty About a Black Cat"), which is often interpreted as anti-Stalinist; for relevant analyses, see Novikov and Basovskaya, *Avtorskaya pesnya,* 34; Klaus Dieter Seemann, "Bulat Okudzavas 'Cernyj kot' als antistalinistische Parodie," *Welt der Slaven-Halbjahresschrift fur Slavistik* 31, no. 1 (1986).

31. G. S. Smith, *Songs to Seven Strings,* 152–54; Novikov and Basovskaya, *Avtorskaya pesnya,* 61.

32. Reprinted in Aleksandr Galich, *Aleksandr Galich,* Antologiya Satiry i Yumora Rossii XX veka (Moscow: Eksmo, 2003), 550.

33. Karimov, *Istoriya Moskovskogo KSP,* 81.

34. Among the songs Galich performed at the festival was "Pamyati Borisa Leonidovicha Pasternaka" (1966; "In Memory of Boris Leonidovich Pasternak"), which contains scathing references to the Soviet regime's extermination of numerous writers and other creative professionals: "Kak gordimsya my, sovremenniki, / Chto on umer v svoyey posteli" ("How proud we are, contemporaries, / That he died in his own bed") (Aleksandr Galich, *Sochineniya v dvukh tomakh,* 2 vols. [Moscow: Lokid, 1999], 1:147).

35. Nikolai Meysak, reprinted in Aleksandr Galich, *Pesni, Stikhi, Poemy, Kinopovest', P'yesa, Stat'i* (Ekaterinburg: U-Faktoriya, 1998), 608, 611; Galich, *Aleksandr Galich,* 558–59.

36. Yuly Kim, *Sochineniya* (Moscow: Lokid, 2000), 535.

37. Il'ya Gabai, Pyotr Yakir, and Yuly Kim, "K deyatel'yam nauki, kul'tury i iskusstva SSSR," *Radio Liberty Research Paper* 21 (1968): 1a.

38. "Liberating the Tone," 286–87. See also G. S. Smith, *Songs to Seven Strings,* 118.

39. Quoted in G. S. Smith, *Songs to Seven Strings,* 117.

40. Quoted in Andreyev, *Nasha avtorskaya,* 227. For a pertinent discussion focusing on lines taken from Vysotsky's songs for *Vertikal',* see A. E. Krylov, "Bytovaniye i transformatsiya krylatykh vyrazheniy Vysotskogo v gazetno-zhurnal'nykh zagolovkakh," in *Mir Vysotskogo: Issledovaniya i materialy IV* (Moscow: GKTsM V. S. Vysotskogo, 2000).

41. Andreyev, *Nasha avtorskaya,* 229. On prohibitions against Moscow bards Aleksandr Mirzayan and Viktor Luferov, for example, see Karimov, *Istoriya Moskovskogo KSP,* 146. According to Aleksandr Gorodnitsky, of the dozens of clubs that were formed in the 1960s, for many years KSP Vostok was "the only authorized club in all of Russia" ("Kontsert 40–letiya 'Vostoka,'" http://www.dkgaza.spb.ru/cocert%2040%20let.html.) The fact that the club *was* authorized, however, underscores its complicated political status—and, by extension, that of guitar poetry as a whole—on the boundary between the permitted and the prohibited.

42. Karimov, *Istoriya Moskovskogo KSP,* 142, 145.

43. Ibid., 152, 154.

44. E. V. Bykova, A. S. Zubatkin, and N. G. Mikhailova, eds., *Sotsial'nye i tvorcheskiye problemy khudozhestvennoy samodeyatel'nosti* (Moscow: Nauchno-issledovatel'skiy institut kul'tury, 1981), 4.

45. N. G. Mikhailova, "Perspektivy izucheniya khudozhestvennoy samodeyatel'nosti kak sotsial'no-kul'turnogo yavleniya," in *Sotsial'nye i tvorcheskiye problemy khudozhestvennoy samodeyatel'nosti,* ed. E. V. Bykova, A. S. Zubatkin, and N. G. Mikhailova (Moscow: Nauchno-issledovatel'skiy institut kul'tury, 1981), 5. See also N. G. Mikhailova, ed., *Problemy otsenki khudozhestvennoy samodeyatel'nosti (v praktike raboty zhyuri)* (Moscow: Nauchno-issledovatel'skiy institut kul'tury, 1980), 4–5; N. G. Mikhailova, "Kriterii otsenki khudozhestvennoy samodeyatel'nosti i rabota zhyuri smotrov i konkursov (Osnovnye rezul'taty i prakticheskiye vyvody issledovaniya)," in *Problemy otsenki khudozhestvennoy samodeyatel'nosti (v praktike raboty zhyuri),* ed. N. G. Mikhailova (Moscow: Nauchno-issledovatel'skiy institut kul'tury, 1980), 8–9.

46. Mikhailova, "Kriterii otsenki," 14, 19.

47. For a detailed explanation of the "*Metropol'* affair," see G. S. Smith, *Songs to Seven Strings,* 154–55.

48. Indeed, in the post-Soviet period, Rozenbaum (who "requests categorically that he not be counted as a bard") has become one of the best-known singer-songwriters associated with *shanson* (chanson), an "amorphous genre" that is heavily indebted to *blatnaya pesnya* (criminal song) and that is sometimes called "the soundtrack of contemporary Russia" (S. Istomin and D. Denisenko, *Samye znamenitye bardy Rossii* [Moscow: Veche, 2002], 171; Sophia Kishkovsky, "Notes from a Russian Musical Underground: The Sounds of Chanson," *New York Times,* July 16, 2006).

49. The festival was inaugurated to honor Valery Grushin (1944–1967), an avid *turist* and performer of guitar poetry who died tragically during a camping expedition while trying to save several of his companions from drowning.

50. Andreyev, *Nasha avtorskaya,* 230.

51. Juliane Fürst, "The Arrival of Spring? Changes and Continuities in Soviet Youth Culture and Policy Between Stalin and Khrushchev," in *The Dilemmas of De-Stalinization: Negotiating Cultural and Social Change in the Khrushchev Era,* ed. Polly Jones (London: Routledge, 2006), 136; P. Jones, "Introduction," 10.

52. V. S. Tyazhel'nikova, "Sovetskaya pesnya i formirovaniye novoy identichnosti," *Otechestvennaya istoriya* 1 (2002): 178–79.

53. Quoted in Vladimir Frumkin, *Pevtsy i vozhdi* (Nizhny Novgorod: Dekom, 2005), 25.

54. V. Zakharov, "O sostoyanii i zadachakh pesennogo tvorchestva," *Sovetskaya muzyka* 2 (1954): 4, compare 14. Similar sentiments can be found in numerous articles from *Sovetskaya muzyka* during this period, including T. Khrennikov, "Bol'shoy i slavnyi put'," *Sovetskaya muzyka* 2 (1969): 17–18; Morov, "O durnykh vkusakh," 120; A. Novikov, "O pesne," *Sovetskaya muzyka* 4 (1957): 16–17, 21; M. Sergeyev, "I sporit' i deystvovat': Vmesto otchyota," *Sovetskaya muzyka* 2 (1963): 17; A. Sokhor, "Nashe oruzhiye—nashi pesni," *Sovetskaya muzyka* 10 (1957): 16; V. Solov'yov-Sedoy, "Za podlinnuyu massovost'," *Sovetskaya muzyka* 5 (1956): 35; "Za ideynuyu chistotu i podlinnuyu massovost'," *Sovetskaya muzyka* 7 (1966): 17.

55. Frumkin, "Liberating the Tone," 280.

56. Gorodnitsky, *I zhit' yeshchyo nadezhde . . . ,* 346; Frumkin, "Liberating the Tone," 280.

57. G. Pavlova, "Pesni, rozhdyonnye v vuzakh," *Muzykal'naya zhizn'* 10 (1959): 4.

58. See D. Kabalevsky, "Poiski i zabluzhdeniya," *Sovetskaya muzyka* 2 (1963): 10.

59. "Za ideinuyu chistotu," 7. Following this trend, the 24th Congress of the CPSU (1971) reaffirmed Party control over the production of songs and other artistic works. Resolutions from this congress were later used in *Pravda,* the Party mouthpiece, to promote songs' development as "a means for the ideological-

political and moral-aesthetic education of the broad masses" (quoted in G. S. Smith, *Songs to Seven Strings*, 9).

60. Zakharov, "O sostoyanii," 4; Khrennikov, "Na puti," 12.

61. P. Jones, "Introduction," 10.

62. Grey Hodnett, ed., *Resolutions and Decisions of the Communist Party of the Soviet Union*, vol. 4: *The Khrushchev Years, 1953–1964* (Toronto: University of Toronto Press, 1974), 143.

63. Ibid., 245–46.

64. Ibid., 135, 311.

65. P. Jones, "Introduction," 10.

66. The phrase "engineers of human souls" is attributed to Stalin, who applied it to Soviet writers. By the early 1950s, though, it was commonly used in reference to artists and composers as well. See, e.g., "K novomu pod"yomu muzykal'nogo obrazovaniya," *Sovetskaya muzyka* 8 (1950): 4; G. Khubov, "Muzyka i sovremennost' " *Sovetskaya muzyka* 3 (1953): 3.

67. D. Kabalevsky, "Muzyka i sovremennost'," *Sovetskaya muzyka* 3 (1960): 15; Novikov, "O pesne," 15. See also T. Khrennikov, "Sostoyaniye i zadachi sovetskogo muzykal'nogo tvorchestva," *Sovetskaya muzyka* 5 (1957): 33.

68. Zakharov, "O sostoyanii," 14.

69. Ibid.

70. "Diskussiya o pesne," *Sovetskaya muzyka* 3 (1954): 54.

71. Ibid.

72. Because of songs' "hybrid" nature, professional songwriting typically involved composer-lyricist duos. This hybridity also meant that, technically, songwriting fell within the purview not just of the Composers' Union, but also of the Writers' Union. As professional lyricist and poet Lev Oshanin complained, though, "questions of song" were rarely discussed seriously by the Writers' Union and there was a lack of real and consistent cooperation between the two unions ("Iz pesni slova ne vykinesh'," *Sovetskaya muzyka* 2 [1954]: 28–29). Moreover, lack of communication between different directorates within the Ministry of Culture meant that it was possible for "a song accepted for the radio [to be] performed, but not published; and, on the contrary, [for] a song rejected for the radio [to be] published trouble-free, but never heard on the air" (Zakharov, "O sostoyanii," 21. Compare Sergeyev, "I sporit' i deystvovat'," 20).

73. Morov, "O durnykh vkusakh," 116.

74. Ibid., 117.

75. Sergeyev, "I sporit' i deystvovat'," 19; Sokhor, "Massovaya, bytovaya, estradnaya . . . ," 22.

76. Sokhor, "Massovaya, bytovaya, estradnaya . . . ," 21–22.

77. Khrennikov, "Muzykal'no-esteticheskoye vospitaniye," 17.

78. Sergeyev, "I sporit' i deystvovat'," 19.

79. Sokhor, "Massovaya, bytovaya, estradnaya . . . ," 22; Ol'khovich, "Kogda molodyozhi interesno . . . ," 126.

80. Sergeyev, "I sporit' i deystvovat'," 17.

81. "Za ideynuyu chistotu," 9. See also Khrennikov, "Bol'shoy i slavnyi put'," 17.

82. Quoted in Sergeyev, "I sporit' i deystvovat'," 19. Leonid Bakhnov has argued that Okudzhava enjoyed relative freedom as a bard precisely because he belonged to the Soviet literary establishment: "Okudzhava wasn't just lucky: as we all know, socialism is registration and control, and he had been 'registered' in the capacity of poet before he began to compose his songs . . . A cook makes stewed fruit, a pilot flies airplanes. And a poet? That's right—he composes poems. So he *had the right*" ("V kontekste sovetskoy deystvitel'nosti," in *Tvorchestvo Bulata Okudzhavy v kontekste kul'tury XX veka: Materialy Pervoy mezhdunarodnoy nauchnoy konferentsii, posvyashchyonnoy 75–letiyu so dnya rozhdeniya Bulata Okudzhavy* [Moscow: Sol', 2001], 31).

83. Reprinted in Levitan, ed., *Ot kostra,* 244.

84. Andreyev, "Chto poyut?" 188; Mirzayan, "V nachale byla pesnya," 4; Vishevsky, *Soviet Literary Culture,* 46. For similar descriptions, see also Biryukova, *Spasite nashi dushi,* 5, 13, 15; Karimov, *Istoriya Moskovskogo KSP,* 144, compare 155; L. G. Kikhney and T. V. Safarova, "K voprosu o fol'klornykh traditsiyakh v tvorchestve Vladimira Vysotskogo," in *Mir Vysotskogo: Issledovaniya i materialy III.1* (Moscow: GKTsM V. S. Vysotskogo, 1999), 75; Kuteynikova, "Iskusstvo bardov," 75; Sokolova, "Avtorskaya pesnya: Opredeleniya i terminy," 437.

85. Quoted in Andreyev, *Nasha avtorskaya,* 134. See also Savchenko, *Avtorskaya pesnya,* 23.

86. Guitar poetry's roots have been discussed by a number of scholars. For the fullest treatments, see Lebedewa, *Komm Gitarre,* 13–109; and Sokolova, *Avtorskaya pesnya: Ot fol'klora k poezii,* 53–149. Sokolova's discussion is particularly strong in highlighting links between guitar poetry and "low" cultural forms (like criminal song [*blatnaya pesnya*]), a topic that remains controversial in scholarly and popular discourse surrounding the genre.

87. Trochee is a binary (two-syllable) meter, in which each metrical unit, or foot, consists of a stressed syllable followed by an unstressed syllable. The most common ternary (three-syllable) meters are dactyl (stress on the first syllable only), amphibrach (stress on the middle syllable only), and anapest (stress on the final syllable only). In polymetric structures, more than one type of metrical foot is used.

88. G. S. Smith, "Metrical Repertoire," 140, 148. On the use of specific metrical categories in song texts and in poetry generally, see also Thomas P. Hodge, *A Double Garland: Poetry and Art-Song in Early-Nineteenth-Century Russia,*

Studies in Russian Literature and Theory (Evanston, Ill.: Northwestern University Press, 2000), 35.

89. A. Ogarkova, "Avtorskaya pesnya: Istoriya, sovremennost', budushcheye," in *Gorizonty kul'tury* (St. Petersburg: Institut, 1992), 51; Rumyantsev, "Muzykal'naya samodeyatel'nost'," 145.

90. Hodge, *Double Garland,* 15.

91. Stites, "Domestic Muse," 199.

92. Russia had few professional music schools, and no major concert organizations or conservatories, until the second half of the nineteenth century. By default, then, amateur composers dominated the early stages of the romance's development. The prolific and often highly skilled work of such amateurs was made possible, however, by the prominence of music in domestic education—among the bourgeoisie as well as in gentry families. See G. G. Soboleva, *Russkiy romans* (Moscow: Znaniye, 1980), 13. See also Hodge, *Double Garland,* 221; T. Vladyshevskaya et al., *Istoriya russkoy muzyki* (Moscow: Muzyka, 1999).

93. Hodge, *Double Garland,* 13–14.

94. See Biryukova, *Spasite nashi dushi,* 11.

95. Viktoriya Fomenko, "Iosif Brodsky i avtorskaya pesnya," in *Iosif Brodsky i mir: Metafizika, antichnost', sovremennost'* (St. Petersburg: Zvezda, 2000), 222; Sokolova, "Avtorskaya pesnya: Opredeleniya i terminy," 438.

96. Vladyshevskaya, *Istoriya russkoy muzyki,* 229–30.

97. Ogarkova, "Avtorskaya pesnya," 54–56. In these polemics, some participants pursued a distinction between "active" and "passive" romanticism—between, as David MacFadyen sumarizes, "prospective doers and retrospective dreamers" (*Songs for Fat People: Affect, Emotion, and Celebrity in the Russian Popular Song, 1900–1955* [Montreal: McGill-Queen's University Press, 2002], 264).

98. Ogarkova, "Avtorskaya pesnya," 56. See also Kuteynikova, "Iskusstvo bardov," 80.

99. P. Jones, "Introduction," 9.

100. Andreyev, *Nasha avtorskaya,* 10.

101. O. Marinicheva, "Chtob dushi i glaza svetali," *Komsomol'skaya pravda,* October 22, 1986, 4.

102. Vitaly Korotich, "Slushat' i slyshat' vremya," *Sovetskaya muzyka* 12 (1987): 5; Christopher Lazarski, "Vladimir Vysotsky and His Cult," *Russian Review* 51 (1992): 63; G. S. Smith, *Songs to Seven Strings,* 150; Vysotsky, *Sochineniya,* 275–76.

103. Kabalevsky, "Muzyka i sovremennost'," 15. See also Khrennikov, "Na puti," 11.

104. Hodge, *Double Garland,* 74.

105. Ibid., 90.

106. As musicologist Arnol'd Sokhor remarked in the mid-1960s, "of late

it seems our [professional] songsters have forgotten about [nature]" (Sokhor, "Massovaya, bytovaya, estradnaya . . . ," 22).

107. Stites, "Domestic Muse," 189.

108. Cherednichenko, "'Gromkoye' i 'tikhoye,'" 20–21.

109. Ibid., 20.

110. Ya. I. Gudoshnikov, *Russkiy gorodskoy romans* (Tambov: Tambovskiy Ordena "Znak pocheta" gosudarstvennyi pedagogicheskiy institut, 1990), 5–6.

111. Ibid., 27; V. G. Smolitsky and N. V. Mikhailova, eds., *Russkiy zhestokiy romans: Sbornik* (Moscow: Gosudarstvennyi respublikanskiy tsentr russkogo fol'klora, 1994), 3.

112. Selivanov, "Introduction," 7.

113. Gudoshnikov, *Russkiy gorodskoy romans,* 30, 68–69, 19; I. Nest'yev, *Zvyozdy russkoy estrady (Panina, Vyal'tseva, Plevitskaya): Ocherki o russkikh estradnykh pevitsakh nachala XX veka,* 2nd ed. (Moscow: Sovetskiy kompozitor, 1974), 24.

114. Gudoshnikov, *Russkiy gorodskoy romans,* 12. Indeed, "Gypsy" romance and "cruel" romance are widely used as synonyms for urban romance in general, rather than as designators of particular subtypes within urban romance. See, e.g., E. B. Nikanorova and S. A. Prokhvatilova, eds., *Russkiy romans* (St. Petersburg: Lenizdat, 1993).

115. See Levitan, ed., *Ot kostra,* 42; Selivanov, "Introduction," 7; S. G. Shulezhkova, *Krylatye vyrazheniya russkogo yazyka, ikh istochniki i razvitiye* (Moscow: Azbukovnik, 2001), 129.

116. Selivanov, "Introduction," 7; Levitan, ed., *Ot kostra,* 42. See also Robert A. Rothstein, "Popular Song in the NEP Era," in *Russia in the Era of NEP: Explorations in Soviet Society and Culture,* ed. Sheila Fitzpatrick, Aleksandr Rabinowitch, and Richard Stites (Bloomington: Indiana University Press, 1991), 279.

117. G. S. Smith, *Songs to Seven Strings,* 86.

118. Gudoshnikov, *Russkiy gorodskoy romans,* 8–9; Smolitsky, ed., *Russkiy zhestokiy romans,* 4.

119. Selivanov, "Introduction," 6, 11; Gudoshnikov, *Russkiy gorodskoy romans,* 25, 17, 19.

120. Aleksandr Galich, *Aleksandr Galich* (Moroz Records, 2001), track 11; Kim, *Sochineniya,* 530. More recently, several of Vysotsky's songs were submitted, as anonymous lyrics and in several different variants, for a post-Soviet collection of "urban folklore"; and Aleksandr Gorodnitsky's "Na materik" (1960; "To the Mainland") was published in an anthology of "criminal" songs as anonymous labor camp folklore (Kikhney, "K voprosu," 82; I. Toporkova, ed., *Blatnye pesni: Tsyplyonok zharenyi,* Zolotaya seriya poezii [Moscow: Eksmo, 2005], 104).

121. Quoted in Shulezhkova, *Krylatye vyrazheniya,* 122; B. A. Savchenko, *Aleksandr Vertinsky,* vol. 6, Novoye v zhizni, nauke, tekhnike: Seriya "Iskusstvo" (Moscow: Znaniye, 1989), 19–21.

122. For a brief account of materials circulated via *magnitizdat,* see G. S. Smith, *Songs to Seven Strings,* 95–96; Kovner, "Zolotoy vek magnitizdata [part 2]."

123. Rumyantsev, "Lyubitel'skiy muzykal'nyi teatr," 57. Boris Almazov recalls attempts to control the use of portable tape recorders through registration with the local militia (*Ne tol'ko muzyka k slovam: Memuary pod gitaru* [Moscow: Tsentropoligraf, MiM-Del'ta, 2003], 300–301). Such attempts did not seem to stem the flood of *magnitizdat* tapes in circulation, however.

124. Gudoshnikov, *Russkiy gorodskoy romans,* 24.

125. Ibid., 34–37, 53.

126. E. A. Tarlysheva, "Avtorskaya pesnya: problema zhanra," in *Problemy slavyanskoy kultury i tsivilizatsii* (Ussuriysk: Ministerstvo obshchego i professional'nogo obrazovaniya Rossiyskoy Federatsii; Ussuriyskiy gosudarstvennyi pedagogicheskiy institut, 1999), 82.

127. Novikov, *Avtorskaya pesnya,* 10; Anninsky, "Shepot i krik," 11; Frumkin, *Pevtsy i vozhdi,* 165. See also Anninsky, "Shepot i krik," 8.

128. For discussions of Vertinsky's influence on guitar poetry, in particular, see Anatoly Kulagin, "'Snachala on, a potom my . . .': Krupneyshiye bardy i naslediye Aleksandra Vertinskogo," in *Golos nadezhdy: Novoye o Bulate Okudzhave* (Moscow: Bulat, 2005); Lianskaya, "A. N. Vertinsky"; and E. A. Tarlysheva, "Vertinsky i bardy shestidesyatykh," in *Mir Vysotskogo: Issledovaniya i materialy III.2* (Moscow: GKTsM V. S. Vysotskogo, 1999).

129. Savchenko, *Aleksandr Vertinsky,* 16–18.

130. Isaac Babel, *The Complete Works of Isaac Babel,* trans. Peter Constantine (New York: Norton, 2002), 76.

131. Aleksandr Vertinsky, *Dorogoy dlinnoyu* (Moscow: Pravda, 1991), 96.

132. Savchenko, *Aleksandr Vertinsky,* 27; Lianskaya, "A. N. Vertinsky," 392.

133. Paraphrased in Nest'yev, *Zvyozdy,* 14–15.

134. Gerald Stanton Smith, "Modern Russian Underground Song: An Introductory Survey," *Journal of Russian Studies* 28 (1974): 6. In the 1970s, the musical profile of guitar poetry was altered by the appearance of a number of bards (including, notably, Boris Almazov and Aleksandr Dol'sky) who were professionally trained as musicians. By the 1980s, significant numbers of bards—including Aleksandr Rozenbaum, Viktor Luferov, and Sergey Nikitin—had "a magnificent command of all the subtleties of guitar playing" (Savchenko, *Avtorskaya pesnya,* 45).

135. Frumkin, "Liberating the Tone," 282.

136. Vishevsky, *Soviet Literary Culture,* 45; G. S. Smith, *Songs to Seven Strings,* 86–87.

137. For a brief discussion of such connections, see Frumkin, "Ne tol'ko slovo," 18–19; Frumkin, "Liberating the Tone," 287. Peter Hawkins's study of mid-twentieth-century French singer-songwriters (*Chanson: The French*

Singer-Songwriter from Aristide Bruant to the Present Day [Burlington, Vt.: Ashgate, 2000]) provides the basis for some intriguing comparisons between chanson and guitar poetry (e.g., generic hybridity, ambiguous cultural status, reverence accorded to particular performers), but a close comparative study of the two genres has yet to be undertaken.

CHAPTER TWO

1. Mary Douglas, *Purity and Danger: An Analysis of the Concepts of Pollution and Taboo* (London: Ark Paperbacks, 1984), 121.

2. Pierre Bourdieu, *The Logic of Practice,* trans. Richard Nice (Stanford, Calif.: Stanford University Press, 1990), 228. On the potential dangers of "hybrid" zones, see also Bourdieu, *Distinction: A Social Critique of the Judgement of Taste,* trans. Richard Nice (London: Routledge, 2010), 158.

3. See, e.g., Kuteynikova, "Iskusstvo bardov," 73–74; Lebedewa, *Komm Gitarre;* Novikov, *Avtorskaya pesnya,* 10; H. Smith, "Intellectual Life," 411; Sosin, "Magnitizdat." Compare Sokolova, "Avtorskaya pesnya: Opredeleniya i terminy," 436. As an interesting counterbalance, Pyotr Vail' and Aleksandr Genis characterize much of guitar poetry (Vysotsky's oeuvre, in particular) as "pseudoprotest" that "provid[es] a necessary outlet for negative emotions, but at the same time [does] not obligate [its audience] to serious contemplation, still less to action" ("Shampanskoye i politura," *Vremya i my* 36 [1978]: 141). See also Gorodnitsky, "'. . . Nam ne khvatalo Okudzhavy,'" 79.

4. Pyotr Vail' and Aleksandr Genis, *60–e—mir sovetskogo cheloveka* (Moscow: Novoye literaturnoye obozreniye, 2001), 126; Sokhor, "Massovaya, bytovaya, estradnaya . . . ," 22. See also Andreyev, "Chto poyut?" 184–87.

5. G. S. Smith, *Songs to Seven Strings,* 91, 33, 110; Vail' and Genis, "Shampanskoye i politura," 140.

6. Of the development of the Moscow KSP, for example, Igor Karimov notes that at various points the authorities "did not exactly give us permission [to organize events], but they didn't really bother us [either]" (*Istoriya Moskovskogo KSP,* 142).

7. Robert E. Park, "Human Migration and the Marginal Man," *American Journal of Sociology* 33, no. 6 (1928): 892.

8. Ibid., 892–93.

9. I. P. Popova, *Marginal'nost': Sotsiologicheskiy analiz* (Moscow: 1996), 8; *Marginal'nost' v sovremennoy Rossii: Kollektivnaya monografiya* (Moscow: Moskovskiy obshchestvennyi nauchnyi fond, 2000), 8, 11.

10. Everett V. Stonequist, *The Marginal Man: A Study in Personality and Culture Conflict* (New York: Charles Scribner's Sons, 1937), 221.

11. Ibid., 222; Park, "Human Migration," 893.

12. See, e.g., H. F. Dickie-Clark, "The Marginal Situation: A Contribution

to Marginality Theory," *Social Forces* 44, no. 3 (1966); D. I. Golovensky, "The Marginal Man Concept—An Analysis and Critique," *Social Forces* 30, no. 3 (1952); A. W. Green, "A Re-examination of the Marginal Man Concept," *Social Forces* 26, no. 2 (1947).

13. For one empirically based challenge to some of Park and Stonequist's key claims, see Golovensky, "The Marginal Man Concept," 334. See also Green, "A Re-examination," 168; Terry Smyth, "Marginality and the Role of the Clinical Teacher," *Journal of Advanced Nursing* 13 (1988): 622. As Dickie-Clark observes, however, some of the early challenges to the "marginal man" concept were themselves "purely conceptual" (364).

14. Dickie-Clark, "Marginal Situation," 363.

15. Leo Spitzer, *Lives In Between: The Experience of Marginality in a Century of Emancipation* (New York: Hill and Wang, 1989), 135.

16. Dickie-Clark, "Marginal Situation," 366, 367.

17. Spitzer, *Lives In Between,* 130.

18. Smyth, "Marginality," 623; Spitzer, *Lives In Between,* 130.

19. Dickie-Clark, "Marginal Situation," 366. Dickie-Clark himself was uneasy with the concept of a "permeable" barrier, regarding it as "logically rather dubious" and proposing hierarchical "consistency" or "congruence" as more precise alternatives thereto (366–67). In works that draw on Dickie-Clark's hierarchical model, however, the barrier concept has proved more accessible than his proposed alternatives.

20. Popova, *Marginal'nost',* 11; Gino Germani, *Marginality* (New Brunswick, N.J.: Transaction Books, 1980), 3.

21. For recent overviews of the widely varying ways in which marginality is understood and used in the social sciences, see Bradley T. Cullen and Michael Pretes, "The Meaning of Marginality: Interpretations and Perceptions in Social Science," *Social Science Journal* 37, no. 2 (2000); Jose A. Del Pilar and Jocelynda O. Udasco, "Marginality Theory: The Lack of Construct Validity," *Hispanic Journal of Behavioral Sciences* 26, no. 1 (2004). A more sympathetic reading of this profusion of definitions is offered by I. P. Popova, who identifies within the overarching concept of marginality three subtypes of cultural marginality, structural marginality, and "marginality of social role" (*Marginal'nost',* 17).

22. Cullen and Pretes, "Meaning of Marginality," 215, 26.

23. Del Pilar and Udasco, "Marginality Theory," 3, 11.

24. Adam Weisberger, "Marginality and Its Directions," *Sociological Forum* 7, no. 3 (1992): 428.

25. Smyth, "Marginality," 621.

26. Sneja Gunew, *Framing Marginality: Multicultural Literary Studies* ([Carlton, Victoria]: Melbourne University Press, 1994); Phillip Brian Harper, *Framing the Margins: The Social Logic of Postmodern Culture* (New York: Oxford University Press, 1994).

27. Graham Furniss and Liz Gunner, "Introduction: Power, Marginality and Oral Literature," in *Power, Marginality and African Oral Literature,* ed. Graham Furniss and Liz Gunner (Cambridge, Eng.: Cambridge University Press, 1995).

28. Janet Wolff, *Resident Alien: Feminist Cultural Criticism* (New Haven, Conn.: Yale University Press, 1995).

29. Susan Herbst, *Politics at the Margin: Historical Studies of Public Expression Outside the Mainstream* (New York: Cambridge University Press, 1994), 16.

30. Mae G. Henderson, "Introduction: Borders, Boundaries, and Frame(work)s," in *Borders, Boundaries, and Frames: Essays in Cultural Criticism and Cultural Studies,* ed. Mae G. Henderson (New York: Routledge, 1995), 3, 5; Homi Bhabha, *The Location of Culture* (London: Routledge, 1994), 2. Adam Weisberger argues that "most of the current feminist and poststructuralist investigations of marginality and social knowledge do not trace their lineages to Park's discussion," but that Park's ideas nonetheless "remain viable as a theory of the sociocultural determinants of marginality" ("Marginality and Its Directions," 425–26).

31. Sneja Gunew, "Framing Marginality: Distinguishing the Textual Policies of the Marginal Voice," *Southern Review* 12, no. 2 (1985): 144.

32. Cullen and Pretes, "Meaning of Marginality," 221.

33. Germani, *Marginality,* 9.

34. Lesley D. Harman, *The Modern Stranger: On Language and Membership,* Contributions to the Sociology of Language 47 (New York: Mouton de Gruyter, 1988), 93. Similarly, in describing the paradoxes of hybridity, Homi Bhabha notes that "the borderline engagements of cultural difference may as often be consensual as conflictual" (*The Location of Culture,* 2).

35. bell hooks, "Marginality as a Site of Resistance," in *Out There: Marginalization and Contemporary Cultures* (Cambridge, Mass.: MIT Press, 1995), 341. See also Cullen and Pretes, "Meaning of Marginality," 217.

36. Gunew, "Framing Marginality: Distinguishing the Textual Policies," 144–45; hooks, "Marginality," 341.

37. See especially Fraser, "Rethinking the Public Sphere." For a brief discussion of guitar poetry in the context of a Habermasian public sphere, see Dzhagalov, "Avtorskaya pesnya kak zhanrovaya laboratoriya," 205–8.

38. Palczewski, "Cyber-Movements," 161. Palczewski's discussion of counterpublics is strongly influenced by Nancy Fraser's definition of "subaltern counterpublics" as "parallel discursive arenas where members of subordinate social groups invent and circulate counterdiscourses" ("Rethinking the Public Sphere," 123).

39. Fraser, "Rethinking the Public Sphere," 123; Palczewski, "Cyber-Movements," 168–69.

40. Palczewski, "Cyber-Movements," 166. Compare M. A. K. Halliday on the significance of self-expression in "antisocieties" ("Antilanguages," in *Language as Social Semiotic: The Social Interpretation of Language and Meaning* [London: University Park, 1978], 182, 72). See also Richard Gregg on the rhetoric of protest and the "*constituting* of self-hood through expression" ("The Ego-Function of the Rhetoric of Protest," *Philosophy and Rhetoric* 4, no. 2 [1971]: 71, 74).

41. Harper, *Framing the Margins,* 12.

42. hooks, "Marginality," 341; Gunew, "Framing Marginality: Distinguishing the Textual Policies," 142. Cullen and Pretes draw on hooks and others in a brief description of "relative marginality," which derives from a "postmodern perspective [that] provides a multiplicity of reference points among which we are free to move" ("Meaning of Marginality," 217). They do not challenge the notion that these reference points are opposed to each other in a center/periphery relationship, however.

43. Yurchak, *Everything Was Forever,* 5–6.

44. G. S. Smith, *Songs to Seven Strings,* 95–96.

45. Ibid., 110.

46. David Sibley, *Geographies of Exclusion: Society and Difference in the West* (New York: Routledge, 1995), 32–33.

47. Park, "Human Migration," 881. See also Stonequist, *Marginal Man,* 221–22. Building on the Park-Stonequist model, Adam Weisberger recognizes the ambivalence inherent in the marginal position. Echoing Victor Turner's phraseology of "betwixt and between," Weisberger characterizes "the marginal person" as being "caught in a cross-current, located within a *structure of double ambivalence*" (emphasis in original), unable to reject either the native culture or the "host" culture completely in favor of the other ("Marginality and Its Directions," 429). See also Victor Turner, "Betwixt and Between: The Liminal Period in Rites de Passage," in *The Forest of Symbols: Aspects of Ndembu Ritual* (Ithaca, N.Y.: Cornell University Press, 1967).

48. Lesley Harman conceptualizes the "in between" as a suspension between ways of seeing (*Modern Stranger,* 94). Other relevant concepts include Victor Turner's "space of 'liminality'" (defined as a mediating space or "border zone" that is "sometimes characterized by . . . the 'blurring and merging of distinctions'") and Jacques Derrida's notion of *parergon* (something that is "neither simply outside nor simply inside") (Henderson, "Introduction," 5; Jacques Derrida, *The Truth in Painting,* trans. Geoff Bennington and Ian McLeod [Chicago: University of Chicago Press, 1987], 54). See also Homi Bhabha on hybridity and "in-between" spaces as "the terrain for elaborating strategies of selfhood" (*The Location of Culture,* 116, 2); and Pierre Bourdieu on networks of oppositions and their relationship to social status and social order (*Distinction*).

49. See, e.g., Del Pilar and Udasco, "Marginality Theory," 11; Leela Ghandi,

Postcolonial Theory: A Critical Introduction (New York: Columbia University Press, 1998), 42–45, 55; Golovensky, "The Marginal Man Concept," 335; Gunew, *Framing Marginality: Multicultural Literary Studies*, 27; Wolff, *Resident Alien*, 1–2.

50. Ephraim H. Mizruchi, *Regulating Society: Marginality and Social Control in Historical Perspective* (New York: Free, 1983), 9, 10.

51. Popova, *Marginal'nost'*, 22.

52. See, e.g., V. A. Kozlov, *Massovye bezporyadki v SSSR pri Khrushcheve i Brezhneve (1953–nachalo 1980–kh gg.)* (Novosibirsk: Sibirskiy khronograf, 1999), 184–216. In other post-Soviet studies of marginality and marginal groups, the term *marginaly* also encompasses "the remnants of [prerevolutionary] privileged social classes," including "priests, merchants, [and] the nobility," and "'innovations [*novoobrazovaniya*]' of the Stalin epoch—special settlers, logistical guardsmen [*tyloopolchentsy*], etc." (S. A. Krasil'nikov, *Na izlomakh sotsial'noy struktury: Marginaly v poslerevolyutsionnom rossiyskom obshchestve [1917–i-konets 1930–kh godov]* [Novosibirsk: Novosibirskiy gosudarstvennyi universitet, 1998], 8). See also L. I. Pystina, "'Spetsy' kak sotsial'naya gruppa v strukture rossiyskogo obshchestva 1920–nachala 1930–x gg. (problemy izucheniya)," in *Marginaly v sovetskom obshchestve 1920–1930–x godov: Istoriografiya, istochniki: Sbornik nauchnykh trudov* (Novosibirsk: Rossiyskaya akademiya nauk, Sibirskoye otdelenyie; Institut istorii, 2001).

53. Popova, *Marginal'nost'*, 22. See also *Marginal'nost' v sovremennoy Rossii*, 32. For a detailed analysis of informal youth groups (*neformaly*) in particular, see Hilary Pilkington, *Russia's Youth and its Culture: A Nation's Constructors and Constructed* (London: Routledge, 1994). A more personal account is offered by I. P. Smirnov, "Mikrorevoliutsiya, ili Traktat o neformal'nykh kollektivakh (Pochti vospominaniya)," *Zvezda* 11 (2001).

54. *Marginal'nost' v sovremennoy Rossii*, 33.

55. A. A. Oganov, "Fenomen marginal'nosti v kul'ture," in *Marginal'noye iskusstvo* (Moscow: Izdatel'stvo Moskovskogo universiteta, 1999), 64.

56. Vladimir Kagansky, *Kul'turnyi landshaft i sovetskoye obitayemoye prostranstvo* (Moscow: Novoye literaturnoye obozreniye, 2001), 533, 529.

57. *Marginal'nost' v sovremennoy Rossii*, 44. See also Krasil'nikov, *Na izlomakh*, 4; Popova, *Marginal'nost'*, 5.

58. *Marginal'nost' v sovremennoy Rossii*, 44.

59. Discussions of binary divisions in totalitarian systems are numerous, including Hannah Arendt, *The Origins of Totalitarianism* (New York: Harcourt, Brace and World, 1966); Boris Groys, "The Art of Totality," in *The Landscape of Stalinism: The Art and Ideology of Soviet Space*, ed. Evgeny Dobrenko and Eric Naiman (Seattle: University of Washington Press, 2003); Tomas Venclova, "Two Russian Sub-Languages and Russian Ethnic Identity," in *Ethnic Russia in the USSR: The Dilemma of Dominance*, ed. Edward Allworth (New York: Perga-

mon, 1980). As Polly Jones observes, however, after Stalin's death "never again could state-society relations [in the Soviet Union] be meaningfully described as totalitarian" ("Introduction," 14).

60. Sibley, *Geographies of Exclusion*, 33.

61. Compare Alexander Gershkovich's more general assertion that alternative art "shows the artist the possibility of finding his own path, even under conditions of non-freedom" ("The Alternative Messages in Recent Soviet Art and Literature," in *The Soviet Union and the Challenge of the Future, Volume 3: Ideology, Culture, and Nationality*, ed. Alexander Shtromas and Morton A. Kaplan [New York: Paragon House, 1989], 252).

62. As discussed above, Fraser accentuates the role of counterpublics in promoting the formulation of "oppositional interpretations of . . . identities, interests, and needs"; similarly, Palczewski focuses on counterpublics as sites "that develop critical oppositional discourses" (Fraser, "Rethinking the Public Sphere," 123; Palczewski, "Cyber-Movements," 161).

63. Magda Stroinska, "Introduction: Beyond Language and Culture: Relative Points of View," in *Relative Points of View: Linguistic Representations of Culture*, ed. Magda Stroinska (New York: Berghahn Books, 2001), 2.

64. Deborah Tannen, "The Oral/Literate Continuum in Discourse," in *Spoken and Written Language: Exploring Orality and Literacy*, ed. Deborah Tannen, Advances in Discourse Processes vol. 9 (Norwood, N.J.: Ablex, 1982), 9, 2–3.

65. Michel de Certeau, *The Practice of Everyday Life*, trans. Steven Rendall (Berkeley: University of California Press, 1988), xvii; Harper, *Framing the Margins*, 4. Compare E. Rashkovsky's assertion that marginality is "not so much the exception, but rather the norm of existence of millions and millions of people" in the contemporary world (quoted in Popova, *Marginal'nost'*, 23).

66. Svetlana Boym, *Common Places: Mythologies of Everyday Life in Russia* (Cambridge, Mass.: Harvard University Press, 1994), 2.

67. Magda Stroinska, "Forbidden Reality: The Language and Function of Propaganda," in *Secret Spaces, Forbidden Places: Rethinking Culture*, ed. Fran Lloyd and Catherine O'Brien (New York: Berghahn Books, 2000), 122–23; Arendt, *Origins*, 413.

68. Alexei Yurchak points out that "the term stagnation (*zastoi*), which features prominently as a tag for the period of Brezhnev's rule . . . , emerged only in retrospect, during the time of Gorbachev's reforms" (*Everything Was Forever*, 7).

69. P. Jones, "Introduction," 1. Yurchak argues that the disappearance of Stalin's authoratitive "metadiscourse on ideology" played a decisive role, leading to "a major transformation of the Soviet discursive and cultural regime"; and that this transformation marked the beginning of "the epoch of late socialism" (*Everything Was Forever*, 47).

70. P. Jones, "Introduction," 5.

71. V. V. Glebkin, *Ritual v sovetskom obshchestve* (Moscow: Yanus-K, 1998), 121, 130. As Glebkin summarizes, "the 1920s were characterized by active attempts at creating specifically 'communist' ritualism, in the 1930s–50s 'rites of passage' simply disappeared from official social practice . . . , and the 1960s were marked by a new burst of socialist ritual-making" (121).

72. Yurchak, *Everything Was Forever,* 59; Glebkin, *Ritual,* 130.

73. Glebkin, *Ritual,* 130. On the Komsomol's involvement in establishing new rituals for young people, see *Ritual,* 130–31.

74. Quoted in Glebkin, *Ritual,* 132.

75. Quoted ibid.

76. P. Jones, "Introduction," 9.

77. Oleg Kharkordin, *The Collective and the Individual in Russia: A Study of Practices* (Berkeley: University of California Press, 1999), 189–90, 199.

78. P. Jones, "Introduction," 9; Kharkordin, *The Collective and the Individual,* 211.

79. Kharkordin, *The Collective and the Individual,* 191. See also Feliks Kuznetsov, "K zrelosti: Konets 'chetvertogo pokoleniya,'" *Yunost'* 11 (1966): 88. In theory, this was true of socialist societies more generally (see Kazimierz Zygulski, "Leisure and Personality," in *Personal Activity in the Socialist Society,* ed. N. S. Mansurov et al. [Moscow: Institute for Sociological Research (Academy of Sciences of the USSR), Institute of Philosophy and Sociology (Polish Academy of Sciences), 1974], 431). On the "sickness" of individualism, see, e.g., Khrennikov, "Na puti," 10; Kabalevsky, "Muzyka i sovremennost'," 13; F. V. Konstantinov, ed., *Lichnost' pri sotsializme* (Moscow: Nauka, 1968), 90.

80. David MacFadyen, *Red Stars: Personality and the Soviet Popular Song 1955–1991* (Montreal: McGill-Queen's University Press, 2001), 9.

81. Quoted in Andreyev, *Nasha avtorskaya,* 136. See also Aleksandr Gorodnitsky, "Tol'ko Avtor i Slushatel'," *APArt* 3 (1996): 10; Savchenko, *Avtorskaya pesnya,* 4.

82. Aleksandr Dol'sky, "Ya ne chervonets, chtoby vsem nravit'sya!," *Rossiyskaya gazeta* (2002), http://www.rg.ru/Anons/arc_2002/0205/hit.shtm; Natal'ya Akkuratova, interview by Rachel S. Platonov, May 30, 2002.

83. See, e.g., Cherednichenko, "'Gromkoye' i 'tikhoye,'" 26; Istomin, *Samye znamenitye bardy Rossii,* 31.

84. Novikov, *Avtorskaya pesnya,* 10; Anninsky, "Shyopot i krik," 11, 8; Frumkin, *Pevtsy i vozhdi,* 165. See also Khomutova, "Avtorskaya pesnya," 173; Mirzayan, "V nachale byla pesnya," 4; Sokolova, "Avtorskaya pesnya: Opredeleniya i terminy," 437; Tarlysheva, "Avtorskaya pesnya," 80; Vikhorev, "Raznoobrazny i samobytny," 5.

85. Lev Anninsky, "Togda ya yemu sovsem drugoye skazal," *APArt* 2 (1996): 4; Gorodnitsky, "Tol'ko Avtor," 10.

86. Quoted in Andreyev, *Nasha avtorskaya,* 154–55.

87. Almazov, *Ne tol'ko muzyka k slovam,* 265; Galich, *Pesni, Stikhi,* 504.

88. G. S. Smith, *Songs to Seven Strings,* 110.

89. Bulat Okudzhava, *Ya nikomu nichego ne navyazyval* (Moscow: Knizhnyi magazin "Moskva," 1997), 51.

90. Quoted in Henderson, "Introduction," 19.

91. Yurchak, *Everything Was Forever,* 8. This held even for participants in human rights campaigns of the late 1960s, which saw the circulation of numerous letters of protest (various of them prompted by the Sinyavsky-Daniel trial). Significantly, the protests articulated in these letters were "explicitly nonoppositional in character, . . . stress[ing] the appeal to legality"; while warning about the dangers of re-Stalinization, "the 'signers' did not want to be seen as an opposition faction and did not consider themselves as such" (Mikhail Heller and Aleksandr M. Nekrich, *Utopia in Power: The History of the Soviet Union from 1917 to the Present,* trans. Phyllis B. Carlos [New York: Summit, 1986], 615–16).

92. In conceptualizing "being *vnye,*" Yurchak draws upon Mikhail Bakhtin's concept of *vnenakhodimost',* which "emphasizes a *relationship between* inside and outside" (*Everything Was Forever,* 133, 128).

93. Ibid., 4, 128, 127.

94. Ibid., 128.

95. Quoted in Rumyantsev, "Lyubitel'skiy muzykal'nyi teatr," 46. Similarly, Yurchak identifies the practice of characterizing "in-group" members as *svoi* (a shifting and context-dependent category that reflected not "a binary opposition between 'us' [*svoi,* common people] and 'them' [the state]," but rather a sense of like-mindedness, mutual understanding, and "a particular ethic of responsibility to others") as crucial to the particular social relations attached to "being *vnye*" (*Everything Was Forever,* 131, 109, 112).

96. *Vladimir Vysotsky* (32-CD collection) ([Moscow]: Moroz Records, 2000), disc 15, track 1.

97. Kurilov, "Avtorskaya pesnya"; Kuteynikova, "Iskusstvo bardov," 75. Quoted in Andreyev, *Nasha avtorskaya,* 134. See also Biryukova, *Spasite nashi dushi,* 5, 13; Vysotsky, *Sobraniye sochineniy v chetyryokh tomakh, Tom 4: Proza,* 119. On Vysotsky as a catalyst for "a mutual recognition of *svoi,*" see Yurchak, *Everything Was Forever,* 123–24.

98. Vail' and Genis, *60–e,* 181. On *obshcheniye* as a form of "being *vnye,*" see Yurchak, *Everything Was Forever,* 148–51.

99. Vail' and Genis, *60–e,* 69–70. Compare Svetlana Biryukova's assertion that friendship was "the ethical basis of guitar poetry" (*Spasite nashi dushi,* 15).

100. Boym, *Common Places,* 1.

101. "The Sweet Sounds of Really Bad Singing," *New York Times,* January 18, 2004, 26.

102. Okudzhava, *Ya nikomu,* 41.

103. Yury Vizbor, *Monologi so stseny: O sebe, o kino, o pesne* (Moscow: Gud'yal-Press, 2000), 96.

CHAPTER THREE

1. Christopher Small, *Musicking: The Meanings of Performing and Listening*, ed. George Lipsitz, Susan McClary, and Robert Walser (Hanover, N.H.: University Press of New England, 1998), 8.

2. Ibid., 6.

3. Ibid., 8.

4. Frith, *Music For Pleasure*, 120–21.

5. Michael Dowdy, "Live Hip Hop, Collective Agency and 'Acting in Concert,'" *Popular Music and Society* 30, no. 1 (2007): 79.

6. Cherednichenko, "'Gromkoye' i 'tikhoye,'" 18. Galich directly acknowledged the portable tape recorder's importance to guitar poetry both as an intentional means of dissemination and, in the hands of a "stool-pigeon neighbor," as a threat—in songs such as "My ne khuzhe Goratsiya" (1966; "We Are No Worse than Horace") and "Zhelaniye slavy" (1972 or later; "The Desire for Glory") (Galich, *Sochineniya*, 46, 129). Moreover, by various accounts, Galich's expulsion from the Union of Soviet Writers came about because *magnitizdat* tapes of his performances fell into the wrong hands (see Galich, *Pesni, Stikhi*, 504; Sosin, "Magnitizdat," 299).

7. Kseniya Marinina, dir., *Monolog* ([Moscow]: [Gosteleradiofond], 2002). See also Vladimir Vysotsky, *Monologi so stseny* (Moscow: AST, 2000), 142.

8. Christopher Lazarski, "Vladimir Vysotsky," 64. See also Vysotsky, *Sobraniye sochineniy v chetyryokh tomakh. Tom 4. Proza*, 122.

9. Vysotsky, *Monologi so stseny*, 136. It is interesting to note that the kinds of histories attributed to Vysotsky and others (while erroneous in their particulars and certainly lacking in socialist realist positivity) were nonetheless broadly in keeping with the contemporary dual discourse of *lichnost'*: the "spectacular individual" (such as soldiers and athletes of extraordinary courage, or even criminals of extraordinary brazenness) and the "person as such" (in the guise of numerous "little men," or "everymen," often trapped by circumstances beyond their control). As in Vysotsky's case, Galich's labor camp songs gave rise to the widespread (and erroneous) belief that he himself was a Gulag survivor. See Georgy Chernyavsky, "Politika v poezii velikikh bardov: 4. 'Smeyesh' vyyti na ploshchad' v tot naznachennyi chas?': Aleksandr Galich," *Kaskad*, no. 200 (October 23, 2003), http://kackad.com/kackad/?p=4099; G. S. Smith, *Songs to Seven Strings*, 195.

10. Erving Goffman, *The Presentation of Self in Everyday Life* (New York: Anchor/Doubleday, 1990?), 23. All subsequent references to this source will be given parenthetically.

11. Vysotsky, *Monologi so stseny,* 139, 150–51, compare 137. See also Vysotsky, *Vladimir Vysotsky* (32-CD collection), disc 15, track 1.

12. Vysotsky, *Sobraniye sochineniy v chetyryokh tomakh, Tom 4: Proza,* 108, compare 106.

13. Simon Frith, *Performing Rites: On the Value of Popular Music* (Cambridge, Mass.: Harvard University Press, 1996), 191, 197. Frith notes that "this argument has legal sanction," as demonstrated by "cases of musical theft" in which imitation of a star singer's voice has been deemed equivalent to "steal[ing] their 'personality'" (191).

14. N. A. Bogomolov et al., "Ot redkollegii," in *Golos nadezhdy: Novoye o Bulate Okudzhave* (Moscow: Bulat, 2004), 3. Compare Biryukova, *Spasite nashi dushi,* 19–20.

15. Liudmila Alexeyeva and Paul Goldberg, *The Thaw Generation: Coming of Age in the Post-Stalin Era* (Boston: Little, Brown, 1990), 103. For a detailed discussion of the Vysotsky "cult," see Lazarski, "Vladimir Vysotsky."

16. See, e.g., Bogomolov, "Bulat Okudzhava i massovaya kul'tura," 4; Kopelev, "Pamyati Aleksandra Galicha," 353; Dmitry Suvorov, "Ocherki o Vysotskom," *Ural,* no. 7 (2002), http://magazines.russ.ru/ural/2002/7/suv-pr.html.

17. Okudzhava, *Ya nikomu,* 219–20, 25.

18. Vysotsky, *Sobraniye sochineniy v chetyryokh tomakh, Tom 4: Proza,* 115. Compare Vysotsky, *Monologi so stseny,* 191.

19. *Krugozor* was an illustrated monthly magazine with a literary and musical orientation. Its main distinguishing feature (and attraction) was the flexible records that were included with each issue. On Vizbor as a popularizer of guitar poetry, see I. A. Sokolova, "Mnogogolos'ye Yuriya Vizbora: Zhanry, formy, stilistika," in *Mir Vysotskogo: Issledovaniya i materialy III.2* (Moscow: GKTsM V. S. Vysotskogo, 1999), 405–6.

20. Okudzhava, *Ya nikomu,* 29, 31.

21. Ibid., 37; compare 42.

22. Ibid., 30; compare 37.

23. Ibid., 41. The lyrics Okudzhava cites here come from Mikhail Isakovsky and Matvey Blanter's classic patriotic song "Katyusha" (1938; "Katyusha").

24. Quoted in Sosin, "Magnitizdat," 279. See also Okudzhava, *Ya nikomu,* 51–52.

25. G. S. Smith, *Songs to Seven Strings,* 120.

26. Okudzhava, *Ya nikomu,* 33, 29.

27. R. Pletnyov, "O pesenkakh B. Okudzhavy," in *Golos nadezhdy: Novoye o Bulate Okudzhave,* ed. A. E. Krylov and O. Ya. Batrakova (Moscow: Bulat, 2004), 264. Compare Gerald Smith, who observes that Okudzhava sounds "like somebody singing to himself," with a voice that "continually threatens not to be able to manage its owner's own melodies," precarious pitching, and an "unsound, even querulous" tone (*Songs to Seven Strings,* 120).

28. Vizbor, *Monologi so stseny,* 102.

29. A. M. Gorodnitsky, "Concert" (Kontsertnyi zal u Finlyandskogo vokzala [St. Petersburg, Russia]: May 16, 2002); Gorodnitsky, "'I zhit' yeshchyo nadezhde . . .' (concert)" (Temple Israel [Boston]: March 16, 2002). An alternative explanation, likewise offered by Gorodnitsky himself, is that he never learned to play the guitar properly because a guitar would never have survived in the Far North, where he spent some seventeen years (interview by Rachel S. Platonov, June 10, 2002).

30. Vizbor, *Monologi so stseny,* 136. Vizbor is considered one of the founders and foremost exponents of the "tourist" and "mountaineering" subgenres of guitar poetry.

31. Ibid., 155, 5.

32. Kukin, *Dom na polputi,* 118–19.

33. Ibid., 119; Yury Kukin, *Traktat o pesnyakh* (Moscow [?]: MP "Bit," 1999), 22.

34. Kukin, *Dom na polputi,* 119.

35. Reprinted in Galich, *Pesni, Stikhi,* 607.

36. Reprinted ibid., 604. Meysak made his assessments after "listening to a recording of performances by 'bards'" (as the article's subtitle states), which is in itself telling. It seems that for Meysak, who was not just a journalist but also a veteran and staunch communist, violation of one set of norms automatically implied violation of others as well.

37. Valery Lebedev, "Blazhen muzh, ne idushchiy na sobraniye nechestivykh (K 20–letiyu so dnya smerti A. Galicha)," http://www.bard.ru/galich/galich3.html; Frumkin, "Ne tol'ko slovo," 16.

38. MacFadyen, *Songs for Fat People,* 90. Though MacFadyen is referring to Aleksandr Vertinsky's performance, his description is well suited to Galich, too. Yury Mal'tsev comments, similarly, on the "comical expressiveness of unexpected rhythms" in Galich's songs ("Menestreli," 301).

39. Yuly Kim and Valentina Soroka, "Lyuboy bard—grafoman," *Gazeta pokiyevski Online* (November 15, 2007), http://www.pk.kiev.ua/interview/2007/11/15/090052.html; Yuly Kim, *Na sobstvennyi motiv* (Moscow: Lokid, 1998), 12.

40. Kim, *Sochineniya,* 53–54.

41. Kim, *Na sobstvennyi motiv,* 8.

42. Suvorov, "Ocherki o Vysotskom." As Christopher Lazarski notes, by the 1970s, Vysotsky had become a true "superstar of Soviet popular culture" ("Vladimir Vysotsky," 66).

43. "Vladimir Vysotsky: People Shone When They Stood Next to Him," *Spotlight with Al Gurnov* (January 25, 2008), http://www.russiatoday.com/spotlight/release/1066/video; Vadim Roshin, dir., *Vsenarodnyi Volodya,* ed. Yelena Roshina (Moscow: Soyuz-Video, 2000).

44. Pavel Leonidov, "Do svidaniya, Volodya!" *Novoye Russkoye Slovo,* August 14, 1980, 3.

45. Vladimir Vysotsky, "Khorosho by zazhech' svet," *Pskovskaya guberniya*

3, no. 322 ([2007]), http://gubernia.pskovregion.org/number_322/12.php. See also Vysotsky, *Vladimir Vysotsky* (32-CD collection), disc 31, track 6; Valery Perevozchikov, "Vladimir Vysotsky: 'Vot esli by magnitofony byli pri Pushkine,'" *Izvestiya* (January 24, 2008), http://www.izvestia.ru/news/332667.

46. Vysotsky, *Sobraniye sochineniy v chetyryokh tomakh, Tom 4: Proza,* 119.

47. Vysotsky, *Vladimir Vysotsky* (32–CD collection), disc 15, track 1. See also Vysotsky, *Sobraniye sochineniy v chetyryokh tomakh, Tom 4: Proza,* 119.

48. Fittingly, Vysotsky's voice has been discussed in scholarly literature much more so than those of other bards (see, e.g., Yu. Karyakin, "O pesnyakh Vladimira Vysotskogo," *Literaturnoye obozreniye* 7 [1981]: 94; Novikov, *Avtorskaya pesnya,* 67; Skobelev, *Vladimir Vysotsky,* 159; Savchenko, *Avtorskaya pesnya,* 29; Vysotsky, *Sochineniya,* 473). Given that Vysotsky was an actor, it is perhaps not surprising that he seems to emphasize the complete performance (visual as well as aural aspects) when speaking about his songs. In *Monolog* (dir. Marinina), for example, Vysotsky quite consistently speaks about "showing" or "demonstrating" his own songs, using the verb *pokazat'.*

49. Lazarski, "Vladimir Vysotsky," 62; Skobelev, *Vladimir Vysotsky,* 162–63; "Ot golosa Vysotskogo damy padali v obmorok," *Interfax* (2008), http://www.rambler.ru/news/culture/ inmemoriam/554772566.html.

50. Kim, *Sochineniya,* 151.

51. "The Grain of the Voice," in *The Responsibility of Forms* (Berkeley: University of California Press, 1985), 273.

52. Lazarski, "Vladimir Vysotsky," 62; Karyakin, "O pesnyakh Vladimira Vysotskogo," 96; Vysotsky, *Monologi so stseny,* 197.

53. Vysotsky, *Monologi so stseny,* 197. See also Vysotsky, *Vladimir Vysotsky* (32-CD collection), disc 14, track 2.

54. G. S. Smith, *Songs to Seven Strings,* 174.

55. "Sweet Sounds," 1.

56. Quoted in Zubrilina, *Vladimir Vysotsky,* 185. See also Suvorov, "Ocherki o Vysotskom."

57. Lazarski, "Vladimir Vysotsky," 65.

58. "Vladimir Vysotsky: People Shone."

59. Arguably, this latter characteristic applies even to Vysotsky, though many sources attest to the fact that he hungered for recognition (see, e.g., Vizbor, *Monologi so stseny,* 150). Despite craving fame, Vysotsky often remarked that he never expected to fill large auditoriums or stadiums, and that his songs were "intended for [his] close friends" (Marinina, *Monolog.*) See also Zubrilina, *Vladimir Vysotsky,* 187.

60. G. S. Smith, *Songs to Seven Strings,* 31; Frumkin, "Ne tol'ko slovo," 16. The quiet lyricism of Okudzhava and others also stands in marked contrast to "a vocal style oriented towards crushing volume" that was characteristic in performances of Stalin-era civic songs (quoted in MacFadyen, *Red Stars,* 44).

61. MacFadyen, *Red Stars,* 176.

62. Savchenko, *Avtorskaya pesnya,* 3. This is, of course, very similar to the "studious avoidance of glamour" and "deliberate informality of presentation" characteristic of (Western) folk music concerts, in which "stages are generally small and unpretentious, and amplification, if it is used at all . . . is discreet," and in which performers tend to "fraternize with the audience when not performing" (Small, *Musicking,* 48–49).

63. Alexeyeva, *The Thaw Generation,* 230, compare 103. See also Vysotsky, *Sobraniye sochineniy v chetyryokh tomakh, Tom 4: Proza,* 119.

64. Okudzhava, *Ya nikomu,* 30, compare 37; Vysotsky, "Khorosho by zazhech' svet." See also Perevozchikov, "Vladimir Vysotsky: 'Vot esli by magnitofony byli pri Pushkine.'"

65. Vysotsky, *Sobraniye sochineniy v chetyryokh tomakh, Tom 4: Proza,* 121, compare 108, 119. See also Vysotsky, *Monologi so stseny,* 132.

66. Vysotsky, *Monologi so stseny,* 142.

67. Vysotsky, *Sobraniye sochineniy v chetyryokh tomakh. Tom 4. Proza,* 106.

68. Vysotsky, *Vladimir Vysotsky* (32-CD collection), disc 14, track 2.

69. Vysotsky, "Khorosho by zazhech' svet."

70. Okudzhava, *Ya nikomu,* 227.

71. Vizbor, *Monologi so stseny,* 135, 142. See also Vysotsky, *Sobraniye sochineniy v chetyrekh tomakh, Tom 4: Proza,* 122.

72. Okudzhava, *Ya nikomu,* 5, compare 227.

73. Frumkin, "Liberating the Tone," 282. Svetlana Boym suggests that there is a certain intrinsic synergy between these concepts, because "the Russian word *iskrennost'* suggests kinship, proximity, closeness" (*Common Places,* 97).

74. See, for example, Yu. A. Andreyev, "Chto poyut?" 188; Yu. A. Andreyev, "Problemy molodyozhnoy pesni," 214–15; Yu. A. Andreyev, *Nasha avtorskaya . . . ,* 7; L. P. Belen'ky, *Voz'myomsya za ruki, druz'ya!, Rasskazy ob avtorskoy pesne* (Moscow: Molodaya gvardiya, 1990), 9; Orlov, "Avtorskaya pesnya: Vchera, segodnya . . . zavtra (po materialam sotsiologicheskikh issledovaniy)," 82; Pletnyov, "O pesenkakh B. Okudzhavy," 264; Savchenko, *Avtorskaya pesnya,* 5; and many others. Pyotr Vail' and Aleksandr Genis comment that *iskrennost'* is the most significant characteristic of Vysotsky's songs in particular ("Shampanskoye i politura," 135). Analogously, Christopher Lazarski attributes the popularity of Vysotsky's songs to the fact that they were "authentic and genuine" ("Vladimir Vysotsky," 62).

75. Valentin Vikhorev, interview by Rachel S. Platonov, July 6, 2001.

76. Allan Moore, "Authenticity as Authentication," *Popular Music* 21, no. 2 (2002): 210–11.

77. Ibid., 210. David Tetzlaff puts forward a similar argument, observing that "authenticity is not created by performers, nor embodied in their character. It is created by fan cultures and embodied in the sign systems they use to articu-

late their sense of the real. A star's image is just another part of this signifying system" ("Music for Meaning: Reading the Discourse of Authenticity," *Journal of Communication Inquiry* 18, no. 1 [1994]: 111).

78. Moore, "Authenticity," 220.

79. The relevance of Moore's second subtype, "authenticity of experience," will be taken up in chapter 4. The relevance of Moore's third subtype, "authenticity of execution," can be seen in the popularity and effectiveness of *rolevaya lirika* (literally "role [or role-playing] songs," but loosely parallel to "character songs" of Anglophone popular song traditions), in which a bard donned a lyrical mask and projected a persona that was distinct from his own; however, detailed discussion of *rolevaya lirika* lies beyond the scope of this study. Problems of *rolevaya lirika* in guitar poetry are treated in works such as V. N. Babenko, "Svoyeobraziye rolevoy liriki Vysotskogo," in *Mir Vysotskogo: Issledovaniya i materialy III.1* (Moscow: GKTsM V. S. Vysotskogo, 1999), 201; N. V. Fedina, "O sootnoshenii rolevogo i liricheskogo geroyev v poezii V. S. Vysotskogo," in *V. S. Vysotsky: Issledovaniya i materialy* (Voronezh: Izdatel'stvo Voronezhskogo universiteta, 1990); Kulagin, *Poeziya V. S. Vysotskogo,* 65ff.; T. P. Tilipina, "O sootnoshenii rolevogo i liricheskogo geroyev," in *Mir Vysotskogo: Issledovaniya i materialy III.1* (Moscow: GKTsM V. S. Vysotskogo, 1999); M. V. Voronova, "Stilisticheskiye sredstva markirovki liricheskogo i rolevykh geroyev V. S. Vysotskogo," in *V. S. Vysotsky: Issledovaniya i materialy* (Voronezh: Izdatel'stvo Voronezhskogo universiteta, 1990), 118. For a brief but illuminating discussion of "character song" in British popular music, see Frith, *Performing Rites,* 171.

80. Moore, "Authenticity," 214.

81. Vysotsky, *Sobraniye sochineniy v chetyryokh tomakh, Tom 4: Proza,* 106, compare 102, 121.

82. Ibid., 121, 107; Vysotsky, *Monologi so stseny,* 146. See also Vysotsky, *Vladimir Vysotsky* (32-CD collection), disc 31, track 6.

83. Vizbor, *Monologi so stseny,* 143.

84. Ibid., 140. As a testament to guitar poetry's popularity, furthermore, Vizbor observed that 100,000 people had attended the 12th Grushin Festival (1979), and that they had "come at their own expense, on their own dime [*za svoi den'gi*] from all cities and from across the whole country . . . I don't know another event that would attract a hundred thousand [people] in similar conditions. Maybe if they were giving out free kielbasa, but even then it's not likely" (*Monologi so stseny,* 140).

85. G. S. Smith, *Songs to Seven Strings,* 92–93.

86. Vysotsky, *Sobraniye sochineniy v chetyryokh tomakh, Tom 4: Proza,* 106.

87. Sokhor, "Massovaya, bytovaya, estradnaya . . . ," 22.

88. Ibid.

89. Quoted in Vladimir Frumkin, " 'Mezhdu schast'yem i bedoy . . . ,' " *Vestnik Online* 2003, no. 19 (330) (September 17, 2003), http://www.vestnik.com/issues/2003/0917/koi/v_frumkin.htm.

90. Sergeyev, "I sporit' i deystvovat'," 18.

91. Tannen, "Oral/Literate Continuum," 9, 2–3.

92. G. S. Smith, *Songs to Seven Strings*, 110; Andreyev, "Chto poyut?" 189; Vizbor, *Monologi so stseny*, 144; Cherednichenko, "'Gromkoye' i 'tikhoye,'" 20.

93. Tannen, "Oral/Literate Continuum," 1.

94. Ibid., 2.

95. The production and consumption of *magnitizdat* recordings underscores, in turn, the "secondary orality" (Walter Ong's term) of guitar poetry, its dependence on indirect (and technology-driven) oral communication as well as direct, face-to-face performance. On primary and secondary orality, see Walter Ong, *Orality and Literacy: The Technologizing of the Word* (New York: Routledge, 1997), especially chapter 1.

96. Sukharev, "Vvedeniye," 185, Karimov, *Istoriya Moskovskogo KSP*, 7.

CHAPTER FOUR

1. "The Audience as Co-Author: An Introduction," *Text* 6, no. 3 (1986): 243.

2. Marinina, *Monolog;* Vysotsky, *Vladimir Vysotsky* (32-CD collection), disc 15, track 1. See also Zubrilina, *Vladimir Vysotsky*, 187.

3. Sokolova, "V nachale byl Ancharov," 358.

4. Levitan, ed., *Ot kostra*, 272, compare 74. Describing this series later, V. Suslov observed that "it became clear that the listeners have a burning desire to meet with the singer-songwriters as often as possible, and the latter [to meet] with the listeners" (*Ot kostra*, 286). Again, this emphasizes the sense of mutual interaction and two-way communication between bard and audience that is so central to guitar poetry.

5. The concert series was held in the Great Hall of the House of Culture of Food-Industry Workers, which was home to the Leningrad KSP Vostok.

6. Levitan, ed., *Ot kostra*, 290.

7. Quoted in Zubrilina, *Vladimir Vysotsky*, 185. See also G. S. Smith, *Songs to Seven Strings*, 152.

8. Kukin, *Traktat o pesnyakh*, 7, 9.

9. Almazov, *Ne tol'ko muzyka k slovam*, 186.

10. Ibid., 187.

11. Ibid., 195–96.

12. Ibid., 264–65.

13. Ibid., 266, 330.

14. Kim, *Sochineniya*, 535; Vladimir Baburin, "25 let so dnya smerti Aleksandra Galicha: Interv'yu s Yuliyem Kimom," *Radio Svoboda* (December 17, 2002), http://www.svobodanews.ru/content/transcript/24199562.html.

15. Kim, *Sochineniya*, 540.

16. "U Mosgorsuda" (1968; "At the Moscow City Court") is an imitation (*podrazhaniye*) of Vysotsky, for example, while "Nachal'stvo slushayet magito-

fon" (1968; "The Bosses Are Listening to a Tape Recorder") is an imitation of Galich written to the melody of Galich's own "Staratel'skiy val'sok" (1963; "Prospector's Waltz"). See Kim, *Sochineniya,* 115–16, 118, 539.

17. Quoted in Rumyantsev, "Lyubitel'skiy muzykal'nyi teatr," 50. Kim claims, however, that his aunt "showed [him] a few chords on a seven-stringed guitar with an amateur fingering [*stroyem*], where you press on strings with your thumb—for professionals that is the first sign of 'amateurism' [*lyubitel'shchiny*]" (Baburin, "25 let so dnya smerti Aleksandra Galicha: Interv'yu s Yuliyem Kimom").

18. Kim, *Sochineniya,* 386–87.

19. Ibid., 385, compare 388. Igor' Karimov and others make similar reference to the 1960s and 1970s as the "epoch of Vizbor." See Igor' Karimov, Nikolai Lisunets, and Galina Khomchik, "Opros ofitsial'nogo sayta Yuriya Vizbora," http://www.vizbor.ru/index.php?chrazdel=9 &chmenu=18&r=opros.

20. Quoted in Sokolova, "Mnogogolos'ye Yuriya Vizbora," 405; Anninsky, "Togda," 5.

21. Among the other bards who cite Okudzhava's influence are Aleksandr Genkin (b. 1938), Valentin Glazanov (b. 1931), Al'fred Solyanov (1930–2002), and Al'fred Tal'kovsky (b. 1935). See Levitan, ed., *Ot kostra,* 96, 105, 294; Kalinin, *Bards*.

22. Aleksandr Dol'sky, "Gitary protiv meshchanstva," *Za industrial'nye kadry* (December 28, 1967), http://bard-cafe.komkon.org/Ural/text/Dolsky/t002 .html

23. Marran, "Bulat Okudzhava i yego vremya," *Kontinent* 36 (1983): 331, 53.

24. "Vospominaniye," *Literaturnoye obozreniye* 3 (1998): 9.

25. "Pamyati Bulata Okudzhavy," *Literaturnoye obozreniye* 3 (1998): 17. "I am a Moscow ant!" is a quote from Okudzhava's song "Moskovskiy muravey" (1960; "A Moscow Ant"). Similar imagery also features in Okudzhava's "Mne nuzhno na kogo-nibud' molit'sya" (1959; "I need to pray to someone").

26. "'. . . I novyi plashch odenu,'" *Literaturnoye obozreniye* 3 (1998): 17.

27. Ibid. Compare Igor' Karimov's recollection that, while listening to Okudzhava's songs, "for us a completely different world opened up, [a world] with astonishing images and concepts, which burned themselves into our memories for the rest of our lives" (*Istoriya Moskovskogo KSP,* 24).

28. Gorodnitsky, "'. . . Nam ne khvatalo Okudzhavy,'" 74. Such sentiments are representative of the wave of tributes that have poured in since Okudzhava's death in 1997. See also Valentin Berestov, "Vesyolyi barabanshchik," *Literaturnoye obozreniye* 3 (1998): 15; Aleksandr Borisov, "K godovshchine konchiny Bulata Shalvovicha Okudzhavy," *Literaturnoye obozreniye* 3 (1998): 29–30; Georgy Yans, "Neistov i upryam," *Odintsovo Info* (May 8, 2008), http://www.odintsovo .info/news/?div_id=54&id=16735; Yelena Kamburova, "On zashchishchal nas ot grubosti i nevezhestva," in *Golos nadezhdy: Novoye o Bulate Okudzhave,* ed.

A. E. Krylov (Moscow: Bulat, 2005), 6–7; Yevgeny Kiselyov, "Nashe Vsyo," *Ekho Moskvy* (June 8, 2008), http://www.echo.msk.ru/programs/all/519168–echo/; Nikolai Petrov, "Sovest' rossiyskoy kul'tury," *Literaturnoye obozreniye* 3 (1998): 39.

29. Moore, "Authenticity," 220.

30. Vysotsky, *Vladimir Vysotsky* (32-CD collection), disc 14, track 2. See also Vysotsky, *Sobraniye sochineniy v chetyryokh tomakh, Tom 4: Proza,* 121.

31. Kim himself notes that "among the bards there were two dissidents. Or, more precisely, one and a half: Galich, of course, was a complete dissident . . . And I was half [a dissident]" ("Lyuboy bard—grafoman").

32. As Boris Gladarev observes, "for 'tourists' and participants in the bard movement the Soviet system itself did not seem antipathetic, and there was a significant cultural gap between the KSP and the dissident movement" ("Zhiznennye miry 'osoboy' leningradskoy molodyozhi," *Neprikosnovennyi zapas* 4, no. 36 [2004], http://magazines.russ.ru/nz/2004/4/glad6.html).

33. Sukharev, "Vvedeniye," 185; Karimov, *Istoriya Moskovskogo KSP,* 7.

34. M. Zhitomirskaya, "Avtorskaya pesnya i fol'klor," *Menestrel'* 2 (1981).

35. Levitan, ed., *Ot kostra,* 6.

36. Ibid.

37. Vysotsky, *Sobraniye sochineniy v chetyryokh tomakh, Tom 4: Proza,* 106.

38. Sukharev, "Vvedeniye," 193.

39. Almazov, *Ne tol'ko muzyka k slovam,* 372, compare 381.

40. Ibid., 372, 384.

41. Levitan, ed., *Ot kostra,* 117, 96.

42. Ibid., 148. Stalina Mishtal' emphasizes the fact that the song-oriented "Mondays" at Vostok grew out of similar "Thursdays" held at her apartment on Liteynyi Prospect, while Valery Sachkovsky recalls tape-recording Vostok "Mondays" and playing the tapes at Mishtal's "Thursdays." See Levitan, ed., *Ot kostra,* 86–87, 159–60.

43. R. Bekreneva et al., "Istoriya sozdaniya i deyatel'nosti kluba pesni 'Vostok,'" *Klub pesni Vostok* (2009), http://ksp-vostok.spb.ru/history.par. See also Levitan, ed., *Ot kostra,* 311.

44. Levitan, ed., *Ot kostra,* 149; Bekreneva, "Istoriya sozdaniya i deyatel'nosti kluba pesni 'Vostok.'" The regional committee (*obkom*) of the Komsomol gave its approval for the subscription series on the condition that each concert would consist of two parts, one of which would feature performances by professional artists (Bekreneva, "Istoriya sozdaniya i deyatel'nosti kluba pesni 'Vostok'"). For Vladimir Frumkin's discussion of how this stipulation worked out in practice, see Levitan, ed., *Ot kostra,* 272–73.

45. Levitan, ed., *Ot kostra,* 149.

46. Vysotsky's performance during Vostok's 13th subscription concert, held on January 18, 1967, is considered to be his first-ever public concert (Bekreneva, "Istoriya sozdaniya i deyatel'nosti kluba pesni 'Vostok'").

47. Levitan, ed., *Ot kostra,* 39, 117.

48. KSP Meridian had its origins at the Youth Club of the Petrograd Side, founded in 1956 as the first youth club in the Soviet Union. By 1964, a group of guitar poetry fans had coalesced around this club; and various members of this group helped to organize the 1965 song festival. Among these was Solomon Rabinov, later an active leader of Meridian, who apparently proposed the idea for the festival to Nikolai Kurchev and Stalina Mishtal'. See Bekreneva, "Istoriya sozdaniya i deyatel'nosti kluba pesni 'Vostok' "; Levitan, ed., *Ot kostra,* 36.

49. Bekreneva, "Istoriya sozdaniya i deyatel'nosti kluba pesni 'Vostok.' "

50. Levitan, ed., *Ot kostra,* 105.

51. Ibid., 249.

52. Kukin, *Dom na polputi,* 10, 93, compare 96–97.

53. Almazov, *Ne tol'ko muzyka k slovam,* 373–74.

54. Levitan, ed., *Ot kostra,* 96–98.

55. Ibid., 237–38.

56. Sokolov, "Samodeyatel'naya (avtorskaya) pesnya."

57. D. Sokolov, "Klub samodeyatel'noy pesni (KSP)," in *Neformal'naya Rossiya: O "neformal'nykh" politizirovannykh dvizheniyakh i gruppakh v RSFSR (opyt spravochnika),* ed. V. Berezovsky and N. Krotov (Moscow: Molodaya gvardiya, 1990), 266. Igor' Karimov offers a more detailed—and self-confessedly subjective—discussion of the Moscow KSP's founding, detailing at some length the power struggles and personal conflicts that swirled around the club in its early stages (see *Istoriya Moskovskogo KSP,* 45–49). All subsequent references to Karimov's *Istoriya* will be given parenthetically.

58. See also Sokolov, "Klub samodeyatel'noy pesni (KSP)," 267.

59. In 1970, Karimov was denied a place on a scientific-research expedition to Cuba—and thenceforth all possibility to travel outside the Soviet Union—because "a negative reply came from the KGB in response to our institute's query about my loyalty" (*Istoriya,* 91).

60. As Karimov recounts, Aleksandr Mirzayan and Viktor Luferov were considered "ideologically unreliable" because they set poems by prohibited poets to music. Invited to participate in an approved citywide guitar poetry competition, however, both Mirzayan and Luferov then "began to give concerts on a legal basis, as laureates of the Moscow City Competition of Amateur Song" (ibid., 146).

61. Valery Abramkin (b. 1947), a KSP member with openly dissident views, is arguably an exception who proves the rule. Having been very active in the founding and early development of the Moscow KSP, in 1975 Abramkin withdrew from the club in the face of increasing official involvement in it and began to organize "his own, separate, mini-rallies" (which came to be called "Revivals" [*Voskreseniya*]). From 1976 onward, Abramkin was keenly watched by the KGB, interrogated, and arrested multiple times because of his involvement in the dissident movement. Abramkin's activities are described ibid., 136, 54–55 and in

"Pisateli-dissidenty: Biobibliograficheskiye stat'i," *Novoye literaturnoye obozreniye,* no. 66 (2004), http://magazines.russ.ru/nlo/2004/66/pisat29–pr.html.

62. Levitan, ed., *Ot kostra,* 6.

63. "Rekviyem po shestidesyatym, ili Pod znakom integrala," in *Nauchnoye soobshchestvo fizikov SSSR: 1950–1960–e gody,* ed. V. P. Vizgin and A. V. Kessenikh (St. Petersburg: Izdatel'stvo Russkoy Khristianskoy gumanitarnoy akademii, 2005), 575.

64. Ibid.

65. Ibid., 577.

66. Sergey Kalinin, "Diskussiya kluba samodeyatel'noy pesni 'Poisk' g. Vladivostok (16 noyabrya 1982 goda)," http://www.bards.ru/press/press_show.php?id=335&page=1. All subsequent quotations from this discussion are taken from the same source.

67. P. Jones, "Introduction," 10.

68. Herbst, *Politics at the Margin,* 28–29.

69. Stanislav Rassadin, "Vremya Okudzhavy?" *Novaya gazeta* 2 (January 14, 2002), http://www.novayagazeta.ru/data/2002/02/26.html.

70. Victor Turner, *Dramas, Fields, and Metaphors: Symbolic Action in Human Society* (Ithaca, N.Y.: Cornell University Press, 1974), 231–32. See also Victor Turner, *The Ritual Process: Structure and Anti-Structure* (London: Routledge, 1969), 95.

71. Marinina, *Monolog.* Interestingly, Turner himself remarked that it is "fascinating to consider how often expressions of communitas are culturally linked with simple wind instruments . . . and stringed instruments"; he does not analyze this connection in depth, however, simply conjecturing that "perhaps, in addition to their ready portability, it is their capacity to convey in music the quality of spontaneous human communitas that is responsible for this" (*Ritual Process,* 165).

72. Turner, *Ritual Process,* 127, 12–13.

73. Hodnett, ed., *Resolutions,* 135.

74. Turner, *Ritual Process,* 128.

75. Turner, *Dramas, Fields, and Metaphors,* 245.

76. Quoted in E. Kolmanovsky, "Sovetskaya pesnya—nashe ideynoye oruzhiye," *Sovetskaya muzyka* 11 (1979): 45.

77. Turner, *Ritual Process,* 128.

CHAPTER FIVE

1. Walter D. Connor, *Deviance in Soviet Society: Crime, Delinquency, and Alcoholism* (New York: Columbia University Press, 1972), 37–38. As Connor explains, "most Soviet sources make no clear distinction between 'drunkenness' and 'alcoholism,' the drunkard and the alcoholic, and seem to use the terms in-

terchangeably" (*Deviance,* 36). The use of these terms here reflects this terminological slippage.

2. Aleksandr Prokhorov, "Cinema of Attractions versus Narrative Cinema: Leonid Gaidai's Comedies and El'dar Ryazanov's Satires of the 1960s," *Slavic Review* 62, no. 3 (2003): 462.

3. Ibid., 464.

4. Ibid., 462.

5. Vladimir G. Treml, *Alcohol in the USSR: A Statistical Study* (Durham, N.C.: Duke Press Policy Studies, 1982), 4; Stephen White, *Russia Goes Dry: Alcohol, State and Society* (Cambridge, Eng.: Cambridge University Press, 1996), 32.

6. White, *Russia Goes Dry,* 31–32.

7. Connor, *Deviance,* 35.

8. For contemporary responses to this silence, see White, *Russia Goes Dry,* 33; Treml, *Alcohol in the USSR,* xi. According to Boris Segal, "Soviet officials explained the absence of national statistics by declaring that the social roots of alcoholism had been destroyed, and the number of alcoholics had been permanently diminished by the advent of Communism" (*The Drunken Society: Alcohol Abuse and Alcoholism in the Soviet Union* [New York: Hippocrene, 1990], 171).

9. See Connor, *Deviance,* 44–45, 50. See also Efim Etkind, "Sovetskiye tabu," *Sintaksis* 9 (1981): 10–11.

10. *Ne kvasom zemlya polita . . . : Primechaniya k 'chelovecheskoy tragedii' Aleksandra Galicha* (Uglich: Promdizayn, 2001), 7.

11. Quoted in Argus, "Zoshchenko v stikhakh," 323. In the late 1960s, as Argus notes, Vysotsky was attacked in the press for singing "in the name of" various "unworthy" types, including alcoholics, criminals, hooligans, and the nonspecific "depraved and inferior people" (323).

12. Galich, *Sochineniya,* 88. All quotations from Galich's song lyrics are from this source; hereafter, all such references will be given parenthetically.

13. *Blatnaya pesnya* is a problematic term, and one that Vysotsky himself alternately employed and rejected in reference to his early songs. As used here, *blatnaya pesnya* refers to songs with "criminal" thematics (and, correspondingly, abundant use of underworld slang) that feature a markedly theatrical attitude toward their subject matter. (See, e.g., Sokolova, *Avtorskaya pesnya: Ot fol'klora k poezii,* 111; Abram Terts, "Otechestvo: Blatnaya pesnya . . . ," *Sintaksis* 4 (1979): 85). Thus, *blatnaya pesnya* is regarded here as a subcategory of "songs of unfreedom"—which also include labor camp/Gulag songs, prerevolutionary prison songs, songs of exile, etc.—rather than a synonym thereof. Problems of terminology and classification of "songs of unfreedom" are discussed more extensively in Stefano Garzonio, "Tyuremnaya lirika i shanson: Neskol'ko zamechaniya k teme," *Toronto Slavic Quarterly,* no. 14 (2005), http://www.utoronto.ca/tsq/14/ garzonio14.shtml; and Sokolova, *Avtorskaya pesnya: Ot fol'klora k poezii,* 104–21.

14. G. S. Smith, *Songs to Seven Strings,* 150.

15. Vysotsky, *Sochineniya,* 49. All quotations from Vysotsky's song lyrics are from this source; hereafter, all such references will be given parenthetically.

16. Vladimir Vysotsky, *Pesni lyubimye narodom* (Retro, 2000), 3 CDs, disc 1, track 15. An apt parallel among anglophone singer-songwriters would be Tom Waits's performance of "The Piano Has Been Drinking (Not Me)," from his 1977 album *Small Change.*

17. Kim, *Sochineniya,* 29–30.

18. Ibid., 121–22.

19. Heller, *Utopia,* 31.

20. On August 25, 1968, the three dissidents named by Kim—Pavel Litvinov, Natal'ya Gorbanevskaya, and Larisa Bogoraz—and several others were arrested on Red Square for protesting the Soviet invasion of Czechoslovakia. See Kim, *Sochineniya,* 539.

21. Kim names this song specifically as one of the "twenty or so anti-Soviet songs" in his oeuvre. See Kim and Soroka, "Lyuboy bard—grafoman."

22. Kim, *Sochineniya,* 134–35.

23. A. E. Krylov observes that Galich's characters drink starting with "Lenochka" (1961; "Lenochka"), which was his "very first [bard] song" (*Ne kvasom zemlya polita . . . ,* 9).

24. G. S. Smith, *Songs to Seven Strings,* 192.

25. See, e.g., Mikhael' Ben-Tsadok, "Trubadury protiv obskurantov: Zametki o sovremennoy sovetskoy pesennoy poezii," in *Mir Vysotskogo: Issledovaniya i materialy III.1* (Moscow: GKTsM V. S. Vysotskogo, 1999), 317; Cherednichenko, "'Gromkoye' i 'tikhoye,'" 21–22; Kikhney, "K voprosu"; Suvorov, "Ocherki o Vysotskom."

26. See also Galich's "Salonnyi romans" (Salon Romance, 1966), which is discussed in chapter 7.

27. G. S. Smith, *Songs to Seven Strings,* 194.

28. Indeed, as Walter Connor observes, "in no other case of deviance is the gap between official and unofficial or public attitudes so great as in that of drunkenness" (*Deviance,* 42–43, see also 39).

29. Ibid., 47.

30. See ibid., 44; Etkind, "Sovetskiye tabu," 10–11.

31. See Dobson, "Contesting the Paradigms."

32. Anne Applebaum, *Gulag: A History* (New York: Doubleday, 2003), 522–23. Compare Dariusz Tolczyk, *See No Evil: Literary Cover-Ups and Discoveries of the Soviet Camp Experience* (New Haven, Conn.: Yale University Press, 1999), 257–58.

33. Tolczyk, *See No Evil,* 307–8.

34. Examples include Yury Piliar's "Lyudi ostayutsya lyud'mi" (1963; "People Remain People"), Andrey Aldan-Semenov's "Barele'f na skale" (July 1964; "Bas-Relief in the Rock"), Boris D'yakov's "Povest' o perezhitom" (July 1964; "Tale of

What I Went Through"), and Georgy Shelest's "Kolymskiye zapisi" (September 1964; "Kolyma Notes").

35. For a more detailed analysis of these features, see Tolczyk, *See No Evil,* especially 221, 226, 239. For specific instances, see, e.g., Boris D'yakov, "Povest' o perezhitom," *Oktyabr'* 7 (1964): 54, 66–69; Georgy Shelest, "Kolymskiye zapisi," *Znamya* 9 (1964): 179.

36. Tolczyk, *See No Evil,* 220.

37. Ibid., 308–9.

38. See also Frumkin, "Liberating the Tone," 281; Tolczyk, *See No Evil,* 185. Interviews conducted with Soviet refugees between 1949 and 1953 reveal, for example, fairly specific knowledge of camp conditions, including details of the organization of camp hierarchies, the nature and quantity of food rations ("norms"), and the treatment of political prisoners by criminal ones (*urki*). Relevant interviews from the Harvard Project on the Soviet Social System include: Schedule A, Vol. 2, Case 22 (interviewer H.B., type A2): http://nrs.harvard.edu/urn-3:FHCL:939743; Schedule A, Vol. 3, Case 27 (interviewer H.D., type A2): http://nrs.harvard.edu/urn-3:FHCL:939725; Schedule A, Vol. 30, Case 487 (NY) 1693; Schedule B, Vol. 1, Case 136 (interviewer S.H.): http://nrs.harvard.edu/urn-3:FHCL:928112; and many others.

39. One Soviet refugee interviewed as part of the Harvard Project on the Soviet Social System recounts "a little song that the urki sing in the concentration camps which goes something like this: 'We know that we don't go to work on Saturday and we have Saturday every day' " (HPSSS Schedule A, Vol. 3, Case 27 [interviewer H.D., type A2], page 47: http://nrs.harvard.edu/urn-3:FHCL:939725?n=47).

40. Gorodnitsky, "Istoriya odnoy pesni."

41. Ibid. This statement is a play on Bulat Okudzhava's oft-cited (but not uncontroversial) dictum that "guitar poetry was born in Moscow kitchens in the early 1960s, and it died there, too, leaving only a few names." One example of an ex-*zek*'s song that "became folklore" with the help of guitar poetry is Yuz Aleshkovsky's "Pesnya o Staline" (1959; "Song About Stalin"), which circulated as an anonymous camp folk song for many years—performed by Vysotsky, among others—before Aleshkovsky was identified as its author.

42. Kim, *Sochineniya,* 535.

43. Kovner, "Zolotoy vek magnitizdata [part 2]"; G. S. Smith, *Songs to Seven Strings,* 96; Yevgeny Yevtushenko, "Magnitofonnaya glasnost'," *Nedelya* 18, no. 9 (1988): 16.

44. Aleksandr Gorodnitsky, *Sochineniya* (Moscow: Lokid, 2000), 602; Gorodnitsky, interview by Rachel S. Platonov.

45. Gorodnitsky, *Sochineniya,* 602.

46. In this respect, Gorodnitsky's camp-themed songs cleave close to genuine camp songs like "Ya pomnyu tot Vaninskiy port" (1951?; "I Remember

Vanino Port"), which depicts with chilling poignancy the misery and hopelessness of prisoners being transported through the evil-omened port of Vanino, the "capital of the Kolyma region," and a major depot for transshipment of prisoners to the labor camps of the Soviet Far East. This song circulated widely in the post-Stalin period, variously attributed as anonymous camp folklore or as the work of Yuz Aleshkovsky. V. S. Bakhtin has traced the song's authorship (not uncontroversially) to one G. M. Aleksandrov, who was an inmate at Tayshetlag (Ozerlag) in the early 1950s. See V. S. Bakhtin, "'Ya pomnyu tot Vaninskiy port': Avtor i pesnya," in *Fol'klor i kul'turnaya sreda GULAGA*, ed. V. F. Lur'ye (St. Petersburg: Fond "Za razvitiye i vyzhivaniye chelovechestva," 1994).

47. Gorodnitsky, *Sochineniya*, 37–38.

48. A. M. Gorodnitsky, "Untitled recording from the audioarchive of N. F. Kurchev (AVCh-116)," (n.d.), track 16.

49. Gorodnitsky, *Sochineniya*, 42.

50. A. G. Bronnikov and V. A. Mayer, eds., *Rossiyskiye viyony* (Moscow: Izdatel'stvo AST, Geya iterum, 2001), 6.

51. Nelli Pospelova, "Chelovek dvukh stikhiy," *Nezavisimaya gazeta* (March 21, 2003), www.ng.ru/printed/saturday/2003–03–21/13_gorodnitskiy.html.

52. See, e.g., Babenko, "Svoyeobraziye," 202–3; Anatoly Kulagin, "Chetyre chetverti puti: O tvorcheskoy evolyutsii V. S. Vysotskogo," in *Genus Poetarum: Sbornik nauchnikh trudov* (Kolomna: Ministerstvo obrazovaniya Rossiyskoy federatsii; Kolomenskiy pedagogicheskiy institut, 1995), 77–79. Offering a somewhat more subtle analysis, N. Shafer argues that while Vysotsky "was being ironic and was unmasking [his protagonists], he also sympathized a little bit with his spiritually limited characters, because he endowed them with his own yearning for independence" ("O tak nazyvayemykh 'blatnykh pesnyakh' Vladimira Vysotskogo [nachalo]," *Muzykal'naya zhizn'* 20 [1989]: 14).

53. See Terts, "Otechestvo," 81.

54. The specific locales to which the protagonist refers are the Kola Peninsula (Murmansk region) and Tmutarakan, which is an ancient site that corresponds roughly to modern-day Taman' (Krasnodar region). While the city of Tmutarakan no longer exists, however, its name is commonly used to signify a faraway and inaccessible place.

55. Yekaterina Yefimova, *Sovremennaya tyur'ma: Byt, traditsii i fol'klor* (Moscow: OGI, 2004), 32.

56. Hugh McLean, "Walls and Wire: Notes on the Prison Theme in Russian Literature," in *Slavic Linguistics and Poetics: Studies for Edward Stankiewicz on His 60th Birthday*, ed. Kenneth E. Naylor et al. ([Columbus, Ohio]: Slavica, 1982), 263.

57. "Politics in the Poetry of the Great Bards: Vladimir Vysotsky," *Russian Studies in Literature* 41, no. 1 (2004–5): 65. The original version of this article is available from the following source: Georgy Chernyavsky, "Politika v poezii ve-

likikh bardov: 3. 'Ne nadeytes':—ya ne uyedu': Vladimir Vysotsky," *Kaskad,* no. 198 (September 24, 2003), http://kackad.com/kackad/?p=3984.

58. According to Vadim Gorsky, Vysotsky explained that the coinage *soveyskiy* is derived from the fact that everyone and everything in the Soviet Union "is stupefied [*soveyet*] by heavy drunkenness and fatigue" ("Lui Armstrong yevreyskogo razliva: Filerskaya zapis' razgovorov Vysotskogo," *Ural,* no. 8 (2000), http://magazines.russ.ru/ural/2000/8/ural10.html).

59. Kevin Windle, "Yuz Aleshkovskii's 'Pesnya o Staline' and 'Sovetskaya paskhal'naya': A Study of Competing Versions," *Slavonic and East European Review* 74, no. 1 (1996): 19.

60. Kim, *Sochineniya,* 55.

61. Ibid., 55–56.

62. Ibid., 535.

63. G. S. Smith, *Songs to Seven Strings,* 198.

64. The time frame (twenty years) is an allusion to Galich's cousin Victor, who spent twenty-four years in the camps (Galich, *Aleksandr Galich,* 562).

65. *Aleksandr Galich,* track 1. According to A. E. Krylov, this reference also hints at the narrator's social status, as "in the USSR drinking cognac indicated a high level of prosperity" and even belonging to the political leadership (*nachal'stvo*) (*Ne kvasom zemlia polita . . .* , 58).

66. See also G. S. Smith, *Songs to Seven Strings,* 195.

67. Borzenko, "Neudachlivyi antikhrist," 59.

68. At the 20th Party Congress, which was held in February 1956, Nikita Khrushchev made his "secret speech" denouncing the "cult of personality" and the violent "excesses" of Stalin's leadership.

69. Compare Chernyavsky, "Politika v poezii velikikh bardov: 4. 'Smeyesh' vyyti na ploshchad' v tot naznachennyi chas?': Aleksandr Galich"; Georgy Chernyavsky, "Politika v poezii velikikh bardov: 'On vret, on ne znayet, kak nado,'" *Kaskad,* no. 201 (November 6, 2003), http://kackad.com/kackad/?p=4200.

70. There are echoes here of Yevtushenko's "Babi Yar" (1961), which begins as follows: "Nad Bab'im Yarom pamyatnikov net./Krutoy obryv, kak gruboye nadgrob'ye" ("There are no monuments above Babi Yar/A steep bluff, like a crude headstone") (Yevgeny Yevtushenko, *Stikhotvoreniya i poemy,* 3 vols. [Moscow: Sovetskaya Rossiya, 1987], 1:309–11).

71. Svyatoslav Pedenko, "'Erika' beryot chetyre kopii': Vozvrashcheniye A. Galicha," *Voprosy literatury* 4 (1989): 97.

72. D. Andreyeva, "Rossii serdtse ne zabudet . . . (O tvorchestve Aleksandra Galicha)," *Grani* 109 (1978): 219.

73. E. Dvornikov, "'Yeshchyo v litavry rano bit'. . . ,'" *Pravda,* September 23, 1988, 104.

CHAPTER SIX

1. Chernyavsky, "Politika v poezii velikikh bardov: 'Neistov i upryam, gori, ogon', gori': Bardovskaya pesnya protiv vlastey"; Kim and Soroka, "Lyuboy bard—grafoman"; Gorodnitsky, "Concert." See also Cherniyavskiy, "Politics in the Poetry of the Great Bards: Vladimir Vysotsky," 62–63.

2. Popkin, *Pragmatics of Insignificance,* 11, 113.

3. Ibid., 122.

4. Vail' and Genis, *60–e,* 324–25.

5. A. A. Zhdanov, "Soviet Literature—The Richest in Ideas, the Most Advanced Literature," in *Problems of Soviet Literature,* ed. H. G. Scott (New York: International, 1935?), 22. This commitment to didacticism in literature and art is reiterated frequently; see, e.g., "S"yezd stroiteley kommunizma," *Sovetskaya muzyka* 3 (1959): 3; KPSS, *Road to Communism,* 112.

6. Zhdanov, "Soviet Literature," 21.

7. Quoted in Khubov, "Muzyka i sovremennost'," 7.

8. Popkin, *Pragmatics of Insignificance,* 66.

9. Katerina Clark, *The Soviet Novel: History as Ritual,* 3rd ed. (Bloomington: Indiana University Press, 2000), 136.

10. Jeffrey Brooks, *Thank You, Comrade Stalin!: Soviet Public Culture from Revolution to Cold War* (Princeton, N.J.: Princeton University Press, 1999), 83, compare 109, 115; Kharkordin, *The Collective and the Individual,* 234–35.

11. Svetlana Boym, "'Za khoroshiy vkus nado borot'sya!': Sotsrealizm i kitch," in *Sotsrealisticheskiy kanon,* ed. Hans Günther and Yevgeny Dobrenko (St. Petersburg: Akademicheskiy proyekt, 2000), 94; KPSS, *Road to Communism,* 112.

12. Boym, "'Za khoroshiy vkus nado borot'sya!'," 94; Clark, *Soviet Novel,* 183.

13. Vladimir Kharitonov, "Moy adres—Sovetskiy Soyuz" (1971; "My Address Is the Soviet Union") (V. A. Shoshin, ed., *Zdravstvuy, strana geroyev! (sovetskiye pesni)* [Leningrad: Lenizdat, 1985], 178).

14. Khubov, "Muzyka i sovremennost'," 6.

15. Solov'yov-Sedoy, "Za podlinnuyu massovost'," 34. See also Oshanin, "Iz pesni slova ne vykinesh'," 25.

16. Khrennikov, "Sostoyaniye i zadachi," 34; Novikov, "O pesne," 17. See also Zakharov, "O sostoyanii," 10; Pavlova, "Pesni, rozhdyonnye v vuzakh," 4; Kabalevsky, "Muzyka i sovremennost'," 15–16.

17. "Dostoyno vstretit' XXII s"yezd KPSS," *Sovetskaya muzyka* 3 (1961): 4. See also Kabalevsky, "Muzyka i sovremennost'," 19.

18. Mal'tsev, "Menestreli," 305; S. N. Russova, "Avtor i tekst u Vladimira Vysotskogo," in *Mir Vysotskogo: Issledovaniya i materialy III.1* (Moscow: GKTsM V. S. Vysotskogo, 1999), 231.

19. V. A. Red'kin, "Khudozhestvennyi yazyk poeta v oppozitsii k ofitsial'noy ideologii," in *Mir Vysotskogo: Issledovaniya i materialy III.2* (Moscow: GKTsM V. S. Vysotskogo, 1999), 126; G. S. Smith, *Songs to Seven Strings,* 102.

20. Katerina Clark, "Socialist Realism and the Sacralizing of Space," in *The Landscape of Stalinism: The Art and Ideology of Soviet Space,* ed. Evgeny Dobrenko and Eric Naiman (Seattle: University of Washington Press, 2003), 6.

21. G. S. Smith, *Songs to Seven Strings,* 101; Hans Günther, "Poyushchaya rodina (Sovetskaya massovaya pesnya kak vyrazheniye arkhetipa materi)," *Voprosy literatury* 4 (1997): 53.

22. Günther, "Poyushchaya rodina," 53.

23. "Sovetskaya muzyka," http://www.sovmusic.ru/text.php?fname=moskvav.

24. "Sovetskaia muzyka," http://www.sovmusic.ru/text.php?fname=prostor.

25. On the motif of "breadth" in Soviet song, and on semantic links between *shirokiy* and other relevant terms, see also Günther, "Poyushchaya rodina," 54–55.

26. Vasily Lebedev-Kumach, "Moskva mayskaya" (1937; "May-Time Moscow"), Mikhail Vershinin, "Moskovskaya pesnya" (1948; "Moscow Song") ("Sovetskaya muzyka," http://www.sovmusic.ru/text.php?fname=moscmay and http://www.sovmusic.ru/text.php?fname=gimnmsk).

27. Viktor Gusev, "Kolkhoznaya pesnya o Moskve" (1939; "Collective Farm Song About Moscow"); Vershinin, "Moskovskaya pesnya"; Lev Kondyrev, "Moskva-krasavitsa" (1950; "Moscow the Beauty") ("Sovetskaya muzyka," http://www.sovmusic.ru/text.php?fname=kolhmsk and http://www.sovmusic.ru/text.php?fname=moskvakr).

28. Gusev, "Kolkhoznaya pesnya."

29. Hans Günther, "'Broad Is My Motherland': The Mother Archetype and Space in the Soviet Mass Song," in *The Landscape of Stalinism: The Art and Ideology of Soviet Space,* ed. Evgeny Dobrenko and Eric Naiman (Seattle: University of Washington Press, 2003), 89. For an extensive discussion of the mother archetype in Soviet mass song, see both this article and Günther, "Poyushchaya rodina."

30. Gusev, "Khorosho na moskovskom prostore."

31. Lebedev-Kumach, "Moskva mayskaya."

32. Gusev, "Kolkhoznaya pesnya." Hans Günther argues that "in the majority of cases we are dealing with a lyric 'we,' . . . that signifies the whole Soviet people, understood as a 'common body,' as a 'superorganism'" ("Poyushchaya rodina," 52).

33. E. Petrushanskaya, "Pesnya dostayotsya cheloveku: O 'misticheskoy' prirode sovetskikh massovykh pesen," *Literaturnoye obozreniye* 2, no. 286 (1998): 57. See also Günther, "Poyushchaya rodina," 52.

34. The song was composed for the film *Svinarka i pastukh* (1941; *The* [*Female*] *Swineherd and the Shepherd*).

35. Gusev, "Khorosho na moskovskom prostore."

36. Kondyrev, "Moskva-krasavitsa."

37. See, e.g., Vysotskaya, "Moskva—velikiy gorod"; Lebedev-Kumach, "Moskva mayskaya." See also Gusev, "Kolkhoznaya pesnya"; Vershinin, "Moskovskaya pesnya"; Matusovsky and Kukso, "Bol'shaya Moskva" (1964; "Big Moscow") ("Sovetskaya muzyka," http://www.sovmusic.ru/ text.php?fname=bigmsk).

38. Lebedev-Kumach, "Moskva mayskaya."

39. Günther, "'Broad Is My Motherland,'" 89.

40. "Val's, posvyashchyonnyi ustavu karaul'noy sluzhby" (1966; "Waltz Dedicated to the Regulations for Guard Duty"), "Nochnoy dozor" (1964; "The Night Watch") (Galich, *Sochineniya*, 41–42, 89–90).

41. Levina, *Grani zvuchashchego slova*, 82.

42. Quoted in Sosin, "Magnitizdat," 279.

43. Bulat Okudzhava, *Stikhotvoreniya* (St. Petersburg: Akademicheskiy proekt, 2001), 200. All quotations from Okudzhava's song lyrics and poems are from this source; hereafter, all such references will be given parenthetically.

44. Bittner, *Many Lives*, 15–16.

45. Okudzhava's explanation of this song's origins ties it to the Arbat: "There were these kids in the Arbat courtyards, ringleaders [*zavodily*], so to speak. And they could help out in a difficult spot. The image is a collective one, of course. But the name, the name is specific, for me at least. On the Arbat we had [a kid named] Lyon'ka Gavrilov, a red-haired, very likeable lad" (*Stikhotvoreniya*, 615).

46. There are interesting echoes here of Yevgeny Vinokurov's "Moskvichi" (1953; "Muscovites"), a patriotic lyric about two young men killed in battle that begins as follows: "V polyakh za Visloy sonnoy/Lezhat v zemle syroy/Seryozhka s Maloy Bronnoy/I Vit'ka s Mokhovoy" ("In the fields beyond the sleepy Vistula/In the moist earth are lying/Seryozhka from Malaya Bronnaya/And Vit'ka from Mokhovaya") (Shoshin, ed., *Zdravstvuy, strana geroyev!*, 162). In addition to subverting the canonical presentation of Moscow, Okudzhava's "Korol'" also subverts the canonical (heroic) presentation of war, which is epitomized in Vinokurov's song by the assertion that, while life goes on without Seryozhka and Vit'ka, the "saved world [*mir spasyonnyi*]" remembers them.

47. This song was published in *Literaturnaya Gruziya* (*Literary Georgia*) in 1962. As Okudzhava recounted to Vladimir Frumkin, however, the editors initially opposed its publication because of the mention of "religion" in its seventh line (Vladimir Frumkin, personal communication to Rachel S. Platonov, August 20, 2003).

48. Vera S. Dunham, *In Stalin's Time: Middleclass Values in Soviet Fiction*, enlarged and updated ed. (Durham, N.C.: Duke University Press, 1990), 29. As Katerina Clark summarizes, "however modest [the positive hero] may be, the phases of his life symbolically recapitulate the stages of historical progress as described in Marxist-Leninist theory" (*Soviet Novel*, 10).

49. Ada Yakusheva, *Pesnya—lyubov' moya* (Moscow: Lokid-Press, 2001), 11–12.

50. See also G. S. Smith, *Songs to Seven Strings,* 128.

51. See also R. Pletnyov, "O pesenkakh B. Okudzhavy," 265.

52. Bittner, *Many Lives,* 17, see also 16, 25–26.

53. For a more detailed analysis of this song, see Rachel S. Platonov, "Bad Singing: *Avtorskaya Pesnya* and the Aesthetics of Metacommunication," *Ulbandus* 9 (2005–6): 95–97.

54. See also G. S. Smith, *Songs to Seven Strings,* 125.

55. Gorodnitsky, *Sochineniya,* 205.

56. Okudzhava dedicated this poem to local schoolchildren, whom he credited with inventing the word *arbatstvo* ("Arbatness").

57. "O tom, kak veselilis' rebyata v 1934 godu, ili Kak inogda oblegchayet zhizn' vysokiy esteticheskiy printsip: 'Vazhno ne 'Chto?' a 'Kak?' " *Voprosy literatury* 6 (1995): 49, 54.

58. Ibid., 48.

59. Shoshin, ed., *Zdravstvuy, strana geroyev!* 32–33.

60. Clark, *Soviet Novel,* 183.

61. "Sovetskaya muzyka," http://www.sovmusic.ru/text.php?fname=tostzaly.

62. G. S. Smith, *Songs to Seven Strings,* 22.

63. "Sovetskaya muzyka," http://www.sovmusic.ru/text.php?fname=oytsvety.

64. Shoshin, ed., *Zdravstvuy, strana geroyev!* 45–46.

65. Ibid., 61.

66. "Sovetskaya muzyka," http://www.sovmusic.ru/text.php?fname=katyusha. See also Lebedev-Kumach's "Pesnya o Rodine" (1936; "Song of the Motherland"): "Kak nevestu, Rodinu my lyubim,/Berezhyom, kak laskovuyu mat'!" ("We love our Motherland like a bride,/We protect her like a tender mother!") (http://www.sovmusic.ru/text.php?fname=shstrana).

67. Zakharov, "O sostoyanii," 17; Khrennikov, "Sostoyaniye i zadachi," 33.

68. Korzhavin, "O tom, kak veselilis' rebyata," 54.

69. G. S. Smith, *Songs to Seven Strings,* 21.

70. "Sovetskaya muzyka," http://www.sovmusic.ru/text.php?fname=svals; G. S. Smith, *Songs to Seven Strings,* 23. Dorizo's lyrics were originally published in *Literaturnaya gazeta* and, according to Lev Oshanin, numerous composers immediately set them to music. For several years, however, all of these settings remained unpublished and the artistic council of Muzfond specifically prohibited the composer and singer Lyudmila Lyadova "from performing this song during her concerts" ("Iz pesni slova ne vykinesh'," 32). It was only in 1957 that a musical setting of Dorizo's lyrics was finally deemed suitable for public ears, featuring in the film *Delo bylo v Pen'kove* (*It Happened in Pen'kovo*).

71. Kabalevsky, "Muzyka i sovremennost'," 16.

72. Zakharov, "O sostoyanii," 18; G. S. Smith, *Songs to Seven Strings,* 22.

73. Kukin, *Dom na polputi,* 128.

74. Yevgeny Klyachkin, *Zhivy, pokuda lyubimy* (St. Petersburg: Lan', 2000), 87.

75. Ibid., 100.

76. Ibid.

77. Yury Vizbor, *Sochineniya v dvukh tomakh,* 2 vols. (Moscow: Lokid, 1999), 1:371–72.

78. See Galich, *Sochineniya,* 449–50.

79. G. S. Smith, *Songs to Seven Strings,* 192.

80. Boym, *Common Places,* 3.

81. Gudoshnikov, *Russkiy gorodskoy romans,* 30.

82. Vysotsky, *Pesni lyubimye narodom,* disc 2, track 26.

83. K. Rudnitsky, "Pesni Okudzhavy i Vysotskogo," *Teatral'naya zhizn'* 14, 15 (1987): 15.

84. Yevgeny Klyachkin, *Luchshiye pesni* (Muzykal'noye izdatel'stvo M.O., 2000), track 9.

85. Klyachkin, *Zhivy,* 40.

86. Ibid., 276.

87. Gorodnitsky, *Sochineniya,* 42.

88. Ibid., 616.

89. Ibid., 150.

90. Popkin, *Pragmatics of Insignificance,* 122.

91. Quoted in Argus, "Zoshchenko v stikhakh," 324.

CHAPTER SEVEN

1. Wislawa Szymborska, "Feet and Fate," in *Nonrequired Reading* (New York: Harcourt, 2002), 28.

2. Jim Collins, *Architectures of Excess: Cultural Life in the Information Age* (London: Routledge, 1995), 126, 31.

3. Ibid., 126.

4. A. Morozov, "Parodiya kak literaturyni zhanr," *Russkaya literatura* 1 (1960): 68. Similar issues are underlined by Yury Tynyanov's distinction between parodic form (*parodichnost'*) and parodic function (*parodiynost'*) (see "O parodii," in *Poetika, Istoriya literatury, Kino* [Moscow: Nauka, 1977]).

5. Klaus Roth, "Narrating in Socialist Life: Observations on Strategies of Life Management in Southeast Europe," in *Creativity and Tradition in Folklore: New Directions,* ed. Simon J. Bronner (Logan: Utah State University Press, 1992), 128.

6. Ibid., 130.

7. Ibid.

8. Aleksey Mazalov, Yelena Mazalova, and Mikhail Semenenko, discussion with Rachel S. Platonov, June 14, 2001.

9. Renate Lachmann, *Memory and Literature: Intertextuality in Russian*

Modernism, trans. Roy Sellars and Anthony Wall, Theory and History of Literature (Minneapolis: University of Minnesota Press, 1997), 105, 104.

10. Ibid., 105.

11. Julia Kristeva, *Desire in Language: A Semiotic Approach to Literature and Art,* trans. Alice Jardine, Thomas Gora, and Leon S. Roudiez (New York: Columbia University Press, 1980), 65–66.

12. Gerard Genette, *Palimpsests: Literature in the Second Degree,* trans. Channa Newman and Claude Doubinsky (Lincoln: University of Nebraska Press, 1997), 1–2; Kristeva, *Desire in Language,* 36.

13. John Frow, "Intertextuality and Ontology," in *Intertextuality: Theories and Practices,* ed. Michael Worton and Judith Still (New York: Manchester University Press, 1990), 45.

14. Laurent Jenny, "The Strategy of Form," in *French Literary Theory Today: A Reader,* ed. Tzvetan Todorov (Cambridge, Eng.: Cambridge University Press, 1982), 42.

15. As noted in chapter 5, for example, the melodic accompaniment to Kim's "Monolog p'yanogo Brezhneva" is based on a spirited Gypsy song. On Galich's use of musical allusions and citations, see Frumkin, "Ne tol'ko slovo," 18–20.

16. Hodge, *Double Garland,* 69.

17. B. V. Asaf'yev, *Putevoditel' po kontsertam (Slovar' naiboleye neobkhodimykh terminov i ponyatii),* 2nd ed. (Moscow: Sovetskiy kompozitor, 1978), 115; Stites, "Domestic Muse," 189.

18. Ogarkova, "Avtorskaya pesnya," 53.

19. Galich, *Sochineniya,* 431.

20. Vishevsky, *Soviet Literary Culture,* 55.

21. See also ibid.

22. Aleksandr Galich, *Literatorskiye mostiki* (Aprelevka Sound Production, 1998), CD, track 6.

23. On the relationship between the ballad and the romance, see, e.g., Soboleva, *Russkiy romans,* 5, 15; Yu. V. Keldysh, ed., *Muzykal'naya entsiklopediya,* 6 vols., vols. 1, 4 (Moscow: Sovetskaya entsiklopediya, 1973–82), 4:695.

24. I. A. Sokolova asserts that Ancharov was the first bard to employ "long, playful titles," as well as the first to compose "nontraditional" character songs (*rolevaya lirika*), using inanimate objects as narrators, for example; these traditions were later developed by Galich, Vysotsky, and others ("V nachale byl Ancharov," 365–68).

25. Ancharov, *Sochineniya* (Moscow: Lokid-Press, 2001), 69.

26. Lamont, "Subcontinent," 41. See also Galich's "Ballada o pribavochnoy stoimosti" (1964; "Ballad About Surplus Value"), which likewise features an ordinary Soviet citizen whose life takes an absurd and unexpected turn (179–82).

27. Frumkin, "Ne tol'ko slovo," 20, 18.

28. Jack Zipes, *Happily Ever After: Fairy Tales, Children, and the Culture*

Industry (New York: Routledge, 1997), 3, 34; Bruno Bettelheim, *The Uses of Enchantment: The Meaning and Importance of Fairy Tales* (New York: Alfred A. Knopf, 1977), 25. See also William R. Bascom, "Four Functions of Folklore," in *The Study of Folklore,* ed. Alan Dundes (Englewood Cliffs, N.J.: Prentice-Hall, 1965), 292–94; M. Nikolajeva, "Fairy Tales in Society's Service," *Marvels & Tales* 16, no. 2 (2002): 179; Jack Zipes, *Breaking the Magic Spell: Radical Theories of Folk & Fairy Tales,* revised and expanded ed. (Lexington: University Press of Kentucky, 2002), 181.

29. Nikolajeva, "Fairy Tales," 171.

30. On the historical evolution of the fairy tale into a predominantly children's genre, see Zipes, *Happily Ever After,* 3–5.

31. V. Ya. Propp, *Russkaya skazka* (Leningrad: Izdatel'stvo Leningradskogo universiteta, 1984), 40; Bettelheim, *Uses of Enchantment,* 37. See also Nikolajeva, "Fairy Tales," 171.

32. Bettelheim, *Uses of Enchantment,* 37, 147.

33. Catriona Kelly, "Riding the Magic Carpet: Children and Leader Cult in the Stalin Era," *Slavic and East European Journal* 49, no. 2 (2005): 204. Often cited in this regard is P. German's well-known song "Aviamarsh" (1921; "March of the Aviators"), which opens with the line, "We were born to make fairy tales come true"; as Svetlana Boym observes, during the Thaw a parody of this "circulated among the urban intelligentsia," which ran "we were born to make Kafka come true" (*Common Places,* 115).

34. Felix J. Oinas, "Folklore and Politics in the Soviet Union," *Slavic Review* 32, no. 1 (1973): 46–47. Catriona Kelly observes that, significantly, "the point when the *skazka* was given the official seal of approval as a children's genre—the First Congress of Soviet Writers—coincided with the beginning of the entrenchment of the Stalin cult" ("Riding the Magic Carpet," 211).

35. Felix J. Oinas, *Essays on Russian Folklore and Mythology* (Columbus, Ohio: Slavica, 1984), 166, 178.

36. Frank J. Miller, *Folklore for Stalin: Russian Folklore and Pseudofolklore of the Stalin Era* (Armonk, N.Y.: M. E. Sharpe, 1990), 11.

37. Ibid., 78.

38. Quoted ibid., 79. As Miller observes, Kovalyov's new Soviet tales preserve "much of the narrative ceremonialism of the traditional folktale," including "introductory and concluding formulas, three-fold repetitions, rhymed speech, formulaic expressions, and noun-epithet combinations" (79).

39. Richard Stites and James von Geldern, eds., *Mass Culture in Soviet Russia* (Bloomington: Indiana University Press, 1995), 327.

40. Ibid.

41. Kelly, "Riding the Magic Carpet," 211.

42. G. S. Smith, *Songs to Seven Strings,* 110.

43. *Pesni russkikh bardov. Teksty,* 4 vols. (Paris: YMCA, 1977), 116.

44. In Russian folklore, this role is normally associated with the sea-king.

45. Klyachkin, *Zhivy,* 163.

46. Ibid.

47. Jack Zipes, ed., *Beauties, Beasts and Enchantment: Classic French Fairy Tales* (New York: New American Library, 1989), 60.

48. As M. V. Antonova argues, this technique produces a "Beyond-the-Looking-Glass effect" ("Osobennosti sozdaniya," 48).

49. In Lagin's *Starik Khottabich,* the young and virtuous hero Volka Kostylkov teaches a bumbling and backward old genie named Hassan Abdurrakhman ibn Khottab both about the wonders of Soviet modernity (by introducing him to everything from public transportation to vacuum cleaners) and about the virtues of the ordinary Soviet citizen (by rejecting the genie's gifts to him, including glittering palaces, as unnecessary and inappropriate). See Lazar Lagin, "The Old Genie Khottabych: A Story of Make-Believe (Excerpts)," in *Politicizing Magic: An Anthology of Russian and Soviet Fairy Tales,* ed. Marina Balina, Helena Goscilo, and Mark Lipovetskii (Evanston, Ill.: Northwestern University Press, 2005).

50. For a more detailed analysis of this song, focusing on its relationship to Russian high literary culture, see Platonov, "Bad Singing," 97–103. Other discussions of this song include Anatoly Kulagin, "'Lukomor'ya bol'she net . . .' ('Antiskazka' Vladimira Vysotskogo)," in *Literatura i fol'klornaya traditsiya: Sbornik nauchnykh trudov* (Volgograd: Peremena, 1997); Lamont, "Horace's Heirs," 223; G. S. Smith, *Songs to Seven Strings,* 158–59; Vishevsky, *Soviet Literary Culture,* 55.

51. Kulagin, "'Lukomor'ya bol'she net . . . ,'" 118. Kulagin refers to the work of folklorist V. S. Bakhtin, who cites an early parody in which—as in Vysotsky's song—the oak is chopped down and the gold chain is taken to the Torgsin (a store run by the All-Union Association for Trade with Foreigners, which conducted sales for hard currency and exchange for gold). See Vladimir Bakhtin, "'U lukomor'ya dub srubili . . .': Malen'kaya shkol'naya Pushkiniana," *Neva* 1 (1993). Other literary sources alluded to in this song include Pyotr Yershov's *Konyok-Gorbunok* (1834; *The Little Humpbacked Horse*) (my thanks to Tomas Venclova for this observation) and Valentin Katayev's Stalin-Prize-winning play *Syn polka* (1945; *Son of the Regiment*).

52. Rudnitsky, "Pesni Okudzhavy i Vysotskogo," 15. On carnivalesque aspects of Vysotsky's songs, see Kikhney, "K voprosu," 75–76. See also N. Krimova, "My vmeste s nim posmeyomsya," *Druzhba narodov,* no. 8 (1985): 252; Kulagin, "'Lukomor'ya bol'she net . . . ,'" 115.

53. A. S. Pushkin, *Poemy: Dramaticheskiye proizvedeniya* (Moscow: Novator, 1996), 180–81.

54. N. I. Kopylova observes that changing the (magical) numbers associated with various folkloric figures is "an individual authorial technique of [Vysotsky's]

work with folklore" ("Fol'klornaya assotsiatsiya v poezii V. S. Vysotskogo," in *V. S. Vysotsky: Issledovaniya i materialy* (Voronezh: Izdatel'stvo Voronezhskogo universiteta, 1990), 80.

55. Vysotsky, *Pesni lyubimye narodom,* disc 1, track 8.

56. M. V. Kitaigorodskaya and N. N. Rozanova, "Tvorchestvo Vladimira Vysotskogo v zerkale ustnoy rechi," *Voprosy yazykoznaniya* 1 (1993): 103.

57. G. S. Smith, *Songs to Seven Strings,* 157, 59.

58. Kulagin, "'Lukomor'ya bol'she net . . . ,'" 113; Lamont, "Horace's Heirs," 223; Vishevsky, *Soviet Literary Culture,* 55.

59. The riddle here revolves around the fact that *I* is both a letter of the alphabet and the conjunction "and." In translation, unfortunately, this crucial ambiguity is lost.

60. Compare Vishevsky, *Soviet Literary Culture,* 51.

61. Cherniyavskiy, "Politics in the Poetry of the Great Bards: Vladimir Vysotsky," 74. The translation of the song lyrics used here is loosely adapted from this source.

62. N. I. Kopylova observes that the wild boar (*vepr'*), who is also called Chudo-Yudo here, is not a member of the Russian or East Slavic folkloric pantheon ("Fol'klornaya assotsiatsiya," 82).

63. Vysotsky's mathematical focus is strikingly similar to the technique employed by Daniil Kharms in "Million." As Lev Loseff observes, this poem was "regarded by Soviet critics (and by the ideological censorship) as a tribute paid . . . to the Leninist youth movement"; but Kharms's "inordinate preoccupation with arithmetic" (beginning with, and then moving beyond, "simple word play on the march command 'Step, two, three, four!'") removes "any semantic burden" from what seems to be an "outwardly logical and . . . propagandistic poem" (*On the Beneficence of Censorship: Aesopian Language in Modern Russian Literature,* vol. 31, Arbeiten und Texte zur Slavistik [Munich: Verlag Otto Sagner, 1984], 207–8).

64. Kopylova, "Fol'klornaya assotsiatsiya," 90.

65. Vladimir Semichastnyi (1924–2001) headed the KGB from 1961 to 1967 and played a key role in the 1964 ouster of Nikita Khrushchev.

66. Shoshin, ed., *Zdravstvuy, strana geroyev!* 161.

67. Kukin, *Dom na polputi,* 55.

68. Georgy Chernyavsky interprets the last lines of Kukin's song as a self-critical statement, through which Kukin scolds himself "for meekness . . . for the 'kitchen' character of his musical-poetic criticism" ("Politika v poezii velikikh bardov: 'Neistov i upryam, gori, ogon', gori': Bardovskaya pesnya protiv vlastey.")

69. Kukin, *Dom na polputi,* 77. Yury Kukin, *Luchshiye pesni* (Muzykal'noye izdatel'stvo M.O., 1999), track 6.

70. Kikhney and Safarova, "K voprosu," 82.

71. It has been observed that Vysotsky, in particular, adapted folkloric characters that are "known from childhood"; and that his "folkloric style" of presentation was familiar to "his contemporary Soviet audience" (A. V. Abramova, "Introduction," in *V. S. Vysotsky v kontekste russkoy kul'tury,* ed. A. A. Abramov, A. Gostev, et al. [Moscow: ?, 1990], 4; Barbara Nemchik, "Narodno-literaturnye traditsii v tvorchestve Vysotskogo," in *Mir Vysotskogo: Issledovaniya i materialy III.1* [Moscow: GKTsM V. S. Vysotskogo, 1999], 100).

72. G. S. Smith, *Songs to Seven Strings,* 4.

73. Felix Oinas notes that the ballad was "neglected during the first forty years of Soviet rule," likely because, "with their emphasis on the purely personal problems of their protagonists, ballads did not lend themselves readily to Marxist-Leninist interpretation"; but that they became "the object of intensive investigation" after the late 1950s ("Folklore and Politics," 56–57).

74. Tannen, "Oral/Literate Continuum," 1.

75. Ibid., 2–3.

CONCLUSION

1. Pyotr Mezhiritsky, "Muzyka i slovo: Beseda s muzykovedom Vladimirom Frumkinym," *Vestnik Online* 12 (297) (June 12, 2002), http://www.vestnik.com/issues/2002/0612/win/ mezhritsky.htm.

2. Gorodnitsky, "'I zhit' yeshchyo nadezhde . . .' (concert)."

3. Konstantin Tarasov, "Novyi Grushinskiy," in *Grushinskiy: Festival'naya letopis' 1968–2000* (St. Petersburg: Boyanych, Litsey, 2001), 11.

4. D. A. Sukharev, ed., *Avtorskaya pesnya: Antologiya* (Ekaterinburg: U-Faktoriya, 2002).

Bibliography

Abramova, A. V. "Introduction." In *V. S. Vysotsky v kontekste russkoy kul'tury*, edited by A. A. Abramov, A. Gostev, et al., 3–12. Moscow: 1990.

Abramsky, A. "Puti muzykal'noy samodeyatel'nosti." *Sovetskaya muzyka* 5 (1959): 79–82.

Adams, Arthur E. "Informal Education in Soviet Agriculture." *Comparative Education Review* 11, no. 2 (1967): 217–30.

Aizenberg, Mikhail. "'. . . I novyi plashch odenu.'" *Literaturnoye obozreniye* 3 (1998): 17–18.

Akkuratova, Natal'ya. Interview by Rachel S. Platonov. May 30, 2002.

Aksyuk, S. "O sovremennoy russkoy pesne." *Sovetskaya muzyka* 11 (1953): 30–32.

Alexeyeva, Liudmila, and Paul Goldberg. *The Thaw Generation: Coming of Age in the Post-Stalin Era.* Boston: Little, Brown, 1990.

Almazov, Boris. *Ne tol'ko muzyka k slovam: Memuary pod gitaru.* Moscow: Tsentropoligraf, MiM-Del'ta, 2003.

Ancharov, Mikhail. *Sochineniya.* Moscow: Lokid-Press, 2001.

Andreyev, Yu. A. "Chto poyut?" *Oktyabr'* 1 (1965): 182–92.

———. *Nasha avtorskaya . . . Istoriya, teoriya i sovremennoye sostoyaniye samodeyatel'noy pesni.* Moscow: Molodaya gvardiya, 1991.

———. "Problemy molodyozhnoy pesni." *Oktyabr'* 1 (1967): 213–18.

Andreyeva, D. "Rossii serdtse ne zabudet . . . (O tvorchestve Aleksandra Galicha)." *Grani* 109 (1978): 215–28.

Anninsky, Lev. *Bardy.* Moscow: Soglasiye, 1999.

———. "Shepot i krik." In *Natyanuty nerv struny: Stikhi i pesni bardov 50–80 godov,* edited by Aleksandra Nikolashina and Maria Shmakova, 5–12. [Khabarovsk]: Khabarovskoye knizhnoye izdatel'stvo, 1991.

———. "Togda ya yemu sovsem drugoye skazal." *APArt* 2 (1996): 4–6.

Antonova, M. V. "Osobennosti sozdaniya skazochnogo mira v poezii V. S. Vysotskogo." In *Vysotskovedeniye i vysotskovideniye: Sbornik nauchnykh statey,* edited by M. V. Antonova, V. P. Izotov, et al., 48–55. Orel: Ministerstvo obrazovaniya Rossiyskoy federatsii; Orlovskiy gosudarstvennyi pedagogicheskiy universitet, 1994.

Applebaum, Anne. *Gulag: A History*. New York: Doubleday, 2003.

Arendt, Hannah. *The Origins of Totalitarianism*. New York: Harcourt, Brace and World, 1966.

Argus. "Zoshchenko v stikhakh." In *Mir Vysotskogo: Issledovaniya i materialy III.1,* 320–24. Moscow: GKTsM V. S. Vysotskogo, 1999. Reprint of *Novoye russkoye slovo* (May 18, 1968).

Asaf'yev, B. V. *Putevoditel' po kontsertam (Slovar' naiboleye neobkhodimykh terminov i ponyatii)*. 2nd ed. Moscow: Sovetskiy kompozitor, 1978.

Babel, Isaac. *The Complete Works of Isaac Babel*. Translated by Peter Constantine. New York: Norton, 2002.

Babenko, V. N. "Svoyeobraziye rolevoy liriki Vysotskogo." In *Mir Vysotskogo: Issledovaniya i materialy III.1,* 201–6. Moscow: GKTsM V. S. Vysotskogo, 1999.

Baburin, Vladimir. "25 let so dnya smerti Aleksandra Galicha: Interv'yu s Yuliyem Kimom." *Radio Svoboda* (December 17, 2002), http://www.svobodanews.ru/content/ transcript/24199562.html.

Bakhnov, Leonid. "V kontekste sovetskoy deystvitel'nosti." In *Tvorchestvo Bulata Okudzhavy v kontekste kul'tury XX veka: Materialy Pervoy mezhdunarodnoy nauchnoy konferentsii, posvyashchyonnoy 75–letiyu so dnya rozhdeniya Bulata Okudzhavy,* 31–33. Moscow: Sol', 2001.

Bakhtin, V. S. "'Ya pomnyu tot Vaninskiy port': Avtor i pesnya." In *Fol'klor i kul'turnaya sreda GULAGA,* edited by V. F. Lur'ye, 196–204. St Petersburg: Fond "Za razvitiye i vyzhivaniye chelovechestva," 1994.

Bakhtin, Vladimir. "'U lukomor'ya dub srubili . . .': Malen'kaya shkol'naya Pushkiniana." *Neva* 1 (1993): 375–77.

Barker, Adele Marie, ed. *Consuming Russia: Popular Culture, Sex, and Society Since Gorbachev*. Durham, N.C.: Duke University Press, 1999.

Barthes, Roland. "The Grain of the Voice." In *The Responsibility of Forms*, 267–77. Berkeley: University of California Press, 1985.

Bascom, William R. "Four Functions of Folklore." In *The Study of Folklore,* edited by Alan Dundes, 279–98. Englewood Cliffs, N.J.: Prentice-Hall, 1965.

Bekreneva, R., et al. "Istoriya sozdaniya i deyatel'nosti kluba pesni 'Vostok.'" *Klub pesni Vostok* (2009), http://ksp-vostok.spb.ru/history.par.

Belen'ky, L. P. *Voz'myomsya za ruki, druz'ya! Rasskazy ob avtorskoy pesne*. Moscow: Molodaya gvardiya, 1990.

Ben-Tsadok, Mikhael'. "Trubadury protiv obskurantov: Zametki o sovremennoy sovetskoy pesennoy poezii." In *Mir Vysotskogo: Issledovaniya i materialy III.1,* 311–19. Moscow: GKTsM V. S. Vysotskogo, 1999.

Berestov, Valentin. "Vesyolyi barabanshchik." *Literaturnoye obozreniye* 3 (1998): 13–16.

Bettelheim, Bruno. *The Uses of Enchantment: The Meaning and Importance of Fairy Tales.* New York: Alfred A. Knopf, 1977.

Beumers, Birgit. *Pop Culture Russia!: Media, Arts, and Lifestyle,* Popular Culture in the Contemporary World. Santa Barbara, Calif.: ABC-CLIO, c2005.

Bhabha, Homi. *The Location of Culture.* London: Routledge, 1994.

Biryukova, Svetlana. *Spasite nashi dushi.* Tambov: Tambovskiy filial Serpukhovskogo otdeleniya Fonda Akademii tvorchestva SSSR, 1990.

Bittner, Stephen V. *The Many Lives of Khrushchev's Thaw: Experience and Memory in Moscow's Arbat.* Ithaca, N.Y.: Cornell University Press, 2008.

Blanc, Helene. *Les Auteurs du printemps russe: Okoudjava, Galitch, Vyssotski.* Montriche: Les Éditions Noir sur Blanc, 1991.

Blyum, Arlen. *A Self-Administered Poison: The System and Functions of Soviet Censorship.* Translated by I. P. Foote, European Humanities Research Centre Special Lecture Series. Oxford: Legenda, 2003.

Bogomolov, N. "Bulat Okudzhava i massovaya kul'tura." *Voprosy literatury* 3 (2002): 4–14.

Bogomolov, N. A., et al. "Ot redkollegii." In *Golos nadezhdy: Novoye o Bulate Okudzhave,* 3. Moscow: Bulat, 2004.

Borisov, Aleksandr. "K godovshchine konchiny Bulata Shalvovicha Okudzhavy." *Literaturnoye obozreniye* 3 (1998): 29–30.

Borzenko, A. V. "Neudachlivyi antichrist: Stalin-bog v poezii Aleksandra Galicha." In *Galich: Novye stat'i i materialy,* edited by A. E. Krylov, 53–61. Moscow: Yupaps, 2003.

Bourdieu, Pierre. *Distinction: A Social Critique of the Judgement of Taste.* Translated by Richard Nice. London: Routledge, 2010.

———. *The Logic of Practice.* Translated by Richard Nice. Stanford, Calif.: Stanford University Press, 1990.

Boyko, S. S. "'Novoyaz' v poezii Bulata Okudzhavy i Vladimira Vysotskogo." In *Mir Vysotskogo: Issledovaniya i materialy III.1,* 269–78. Moscow: GKTsM V. S. Vysotskogo, 1999.

Boym, Svetlana. *Common Places: Mythologies of Everyday Life in Russia.* Cambridge, Mass.: Harvard University Press, 1994.

———. "'Za khoroshiy vkus nado borot'sya!': Sotsrealizm i kitch." In *Sotsrealisticheskiy kanon,* edited by Hans Günther and Yevgeny Dobrenko, 87–100. St. Petersburg: Akademicheskiy proyekt, 2000.

Bronnikov, A. G., and V. A. Mayer, eds. *Rossiyskiye viyony.* Moscow: Izdatel'stvo AST, Geya iterum, 2001.

Brooks, Jeffrey. *Thank You, Comrade Stalin!: Soviet Public Culture from Revolution to Cold War.* Princeton, N.J.: Princeton University Press, 1999.

Brown, Deming. "'Loud' and 'Quiet' Poets of the Nineteen Sixties." In *Papers in Slavic Philology,* edited by Benjamin A. Stolz, 18–26. Ann Arbor: University of Michigan Press, 1977.

"Bulat Okudzhava." http://www.bokudjava.ru.

Burshtein, A. I. "Rekviyem po shestidesyatym, ili Pod znakom integrala." In *Nauchnoye soobshchestvo fizikov SSSR: 1950–1960–e gody,* edited by V. P. Vizgin and A. V. Kessenikh, 575–618. St. Petersburg: Izdatel'stvo Russkoy Khristianskoy gumanitarnoy akademii, 2005.

Bykova, E. V., A. S. Zubatkin, and N. G. Mikhailova, eds. *Sotsial'nye i tvorcheskiye problemy khudozhestvennoy samodeyatel'nosti.* Moscow: Nauchno-issledovatel'skiy institut kul'tury, 1981.

Cherednichenko, Tat'yana. "'Gromkoye' i 'tikhoye' v massovom soznanii: Razmyshlyaya o klassikakh-bardakh." *Sovetskaya muzyka* 11 (1991): 18–26.

Cherniyavskiy, G. I. "Politics in the Poetry of the Great Bards: Vladimir Vysotsky." *Russian Studies in Literature* 41, no. 1 (2004–5): 60–82.

Chernyavsky, Georgy. "Politika v poezii velikikh bardov: 3. 'Ne nadeytes':—ya ne uyedu': Vladimir Vysotsky." *Kaskad,* no. 198 (September 24, 2003), http://kackad.com/kackad/?p=3984.

———. "Politika v poezii velikikh bardov: 4. 'Smeyesh' vyyti na ploshchad' v tot naznachennyi chas?': Aleksandr Galich." *Kaskad,* no. 200 (October 23, 2003), http://kackad.com/kackad/?p=4099.

———. "Politika v poezii velikikh bardov: 'Neistov i upryam, gori, ogon', gori': Bardovskaya pesnya protiv vlastey." *Kaskad,* no. 195 (August 6, 2003), http://kackad.com/kackad/?p=3727.

———. "Politika v poezii velikikh bardov: 'On vret, on ne znayet, kak nado.'" *Kaskad,* no. 201 (November 6, 2003), http://kackad.com/kackad/?p=4200.

Chubukov, Vsevolod. *Vysotsky: Vova, Volodya, Vladimir.* Moscow: GKTsM V. S. Vysotskogo, 2000.

Clark, Katerina. "Socialist Realism and the Sacralizing of Space." In *The Landscape of Stalinism: The Art and Ideology of Soviet Space,* edited by Evgeny Dobrenko and Eric Naiman, 3–18. Seattle: University of Washington Press, 2003.

———. *The Soviet Novel: History as Ritual.* 3rd ed. Bloomington: Indiana University Press, 2000.

Collins, Jim. *Architectures of Excess: Cultural Life in the Information Age.* London: Routledge, 1995.

Connor, Walter D. *Deviance in Soviet Society: Crime, Delinquency, and Alcoholism.* New York: Columbia University Press, 1972.

Cullen, Bradley T., and Michael Pretes. "The Meaning of Marginality: Interpretations and Perceptions in Social Science." *Social Science Journal* 37, no. 2 (2000): 215–29.

Cushman, Thomas. *Notes from Underground: Rock Music Counterculture in Russia,* SUNY Series in the Sociology of Culture. Albany: State University of New York Press, 1995.

D'yakov, Boris. "Povest' o perezhitom." *Oktyabr'* 7 (1964): 49–142.

Daughtry, James Martin. "The Intonation of Intimacy: Ethics, Emotion, Metaphor and Dialogue Among Contemporary Russian Bards." Ph.D. thesis, University of California at Los Angeles, 2006.

de Certeau, Michel. *The Practice of Everyday Life.* Translated by Steven Rendall. Berkeley: University of California Press, 1988.

Del Pilar, Jose A., and Jocelynda O. Udasco. "Marginality Theory: The Lack of Construct Validity." *Hispanic Journal of Behavioral Sciences* 26, no. 1 (2004): 3–15.

Derrida, Jacques. *The Truth in Painting.* Translated by Geoff Bennington and Ian McLeod. Chicago: University of Chicago Press, 1987.

Dickie-Clark, H. F. "The Marginal Situation: A Contribution to Marginality Theory." *Social Forces* 44, no. 3 (1966): 363–70.

"Diskussiya o pesne." *Sovetskaya muzyka* 3 (1954): 49–58.

Dobrovol'sky, B. M. "Sovremennye bytovye pesni gorodskoy molodyozhi." In *Fol'klor i khudozhestvennaya samodeyatel'nost'*, edited by N. V. Novikov, 176–200. Leningrad: Nauka, 1968.

Dobson, Miriam. "Contesting the Paradigms of De-Stalinization: Readers' Responses to 'One Day in the Life of Ivan Denisovich.'" *Slavic Review* 64, no. 3 (2005): 580–600.

Dol'sky, Aleksandr. "Gitary protiv meshchanstva." *Za industrial'nye kadry* (December 28, 1967), http://bard-cafe.komkon.org/Ural/text/Dolsky/t002.html.

———. "Ya ne chervonets, chtoby vsem nravit'sya!" *Rossiyskaya gazeta* (2002), http://www.rg.ru/Anons/arc_2002/0205/hit.shtm.

"Dostoyno vstretit' XXII s"yezd KPSS." *Sovetskaya muzyka* 3 (1961): 3–6.

Douglas, Mary. *Purity and Danger: An Analysis of the Concepts of Pollution and Taboo.* London: Ark Paperbacks, 1984.

Dowdy, Michael. "Live Hip Hop, Collective Agency and 'Acting in Concert.'" *Popular Music and Society* 30, no. 1 (2007): 75–91.

Dunham, Vera S. *In Stalin's Time: Middleclass Values in Soviet Fiction.* Enlarged and updated ed. Durham, N.C.: Duke University Press, 1990.

Duranti, Alessandro. "The Audience as Co-Author: An Introduction." *Text* 6, no. 3 (1986): 239–47.

Dvornikov, E. "'Yeshchyo v litavry rano bit'. . .'" *Pravda*, September 23, 1988, 4.

Dzhagalov, Rosen. "Avtorskaya pesnya kak zhanrovaya laboratoriya 'sotsializma s chelovecheskim litsom.'" *Novoye literaturnoye obozreniye*, no. 6 (2009): 204–15.

Etkind, Efim. "Sovetskiye tabu." *Sintaksis* 9 (1981): 3–20.

Fedina, N. V. "O sootnoshenii rolevogo i liricheskogo geroyev v poezii V. S. Vysotskogo." In *V. S. Vysotsky: Issledovaniya i materialy*, 105–17. Voronezh: Izdatel'stvo Voronezhskogo universiteta, 1990.

Fomenko, Viktoriya. "Iosif Brodsky i avtorskaya pesnya." In *Iosif Brodsky i mir: Metafizika, antichnost', sovremennost'*, 221–27. St. Petersburg: Zvezda, 2000.

Fraser, Nancy. "Rethinking the Public Sphere: A Contribution to the Critique of Actually Existing Democracy." In *Habermas and the Public Sphere*, edited by Craig Calhoun, 109–42. Cambridge, Mass.: MIT Press, 1996.

Frith, Simon. *Music For Pleasure: Essays in the Sociology of Pop*. Cambridge, Eng.: Polity, 1988.

———. *Performing Rites: On the Value of Popular Music*. Cambridge, Mass.: Harvard University Press, 1996.

Frizman, L. G. *"C chem rifmuyetsya slovo istina . . .": O poezii A. Galicha*. St. Petersburg: Oreol, 1992.

Frow, John. "Intertextuality and Ontology." In *Intertextuality: Theories and Practices*, edited by Michael Worton and Judith Still, 45–55. New York: Manchester University Press, 1990.

Frumkin, Vladimir. "Liberating the Tone of Russian Speech: Reflections on Soviet *Magnitizdat*." In *The Soviet Union and the Challenge of the Future, Volume 3: Ideology, Culture, and Nationality*, edited by Aleksandr Shtromas and Morton A. Kaplan, 277–98. New York: Paragon House, 1989.

———. "'Mezhdu schast'yem i bedoy . . .'" *Vestnik Online*, no. 19 (330) (September 17, 2003), http://www.vestnik.com/issues/2003/0917/koi/v_frumkin.htm.

———. "Ne tol'ko slovo: Vslushivayas' v Galicha." *Obozreniye* 9 (1984): 15–22.

———. Personal communication to Rachel S. Platonov. August 20, 2003.

———. *Pevtsy i vozhdi*. Nizhny Novgorod: Dekom, 2005.

Frumkin, Vladimir, and Boris Kushner. "Tsvetok ili sornyak na skale? Sud'ba pesni pri totalitarizme." *Zametki yevreyskoy istorii*, no. 5 (96) (May 2008), http://berkovich-zametki.com/2008/Zametki/Nomer5/Frumkin1.php.

Furniss, Graham, and Liz Gunner. "Introduction: Power, Marginality and Oral Literature." In *Power, Marginality and African Oral Literature*, edited by Graham Furniss and Liz Gunner, 1–19. Cambridge, Eng.: Cambridge University Press, 1995.

Fürst, Juliane. "The Arrival of Spring? Changes and Continuities in Soviet Youth Culture and Policy Between Stalin and Khrushchev." In *The Dilemmas of De-Stalinization: Negotiating Cultural and Social Change in the Khrushchev Era*, edited by Polly Jones, 135–53. London: Routledge, 2006.

———. "Friends in Private, Friends in Public: The Phenomenon of the *Kompaniia* Among Soviet Youth in the 1950s and 1960s." In *Borders of Socialism: Private Spheres of Soviet Russia*, edited by Lewis H. Siegelbaum, 229–49. New York: Palgrave Macmillan, 2006.

Gabai, Il'ya, Pyotr Yakir, and Yuly Kim. "K deyatel'yam nauki, kul'tury i iskusstva SSSR." *Radio Liberty Research Paper* 21 (1968): 1a–7.

Galich, Aleksandr. *Aleksandr Galich,* Antologiya Satiry i Yumora Rossii XX veka. Moscow: Eksmo, 2003.

———. *Aleksandr Galich:* Moroz Records, 2001.

———. *Literatorskiye mostiki:* Aprelevka Sound Production, 1998. CD.

———. *Pesni, Stikhi, Poemy, Kinopovest', P'yesa, Stat'i.* Ekaterinburg: U-Faktoriya, 1998.

———. *Sochineniya v dvukh tomakh.* 2 vols. Vol. 1. Moscow: Lokid, 1999.

Garzonio, Stefano. "Tyuremnaya lirika i shanson: Neskol'ko zamechaniya k teme." *Toronto Slavic Quarterly,* no. 14 (2005), http://www.utoronto.ca/tsq/14/garzonio14.shtml.

Genette, Gerard. *Palimpsests: Literature in the Second Degree.* Translated by Channa Newman and Claude Doubinsky. Lincoln: University of Nebraska Press, 1997.

Germani, Gino. *Marginality.* New Brunswick, N.J.: Transaction Books, 1980.

Gershkovich, Alexander. "The Alternative Messages in Recent Soviet Art and Literature." In *The Soviet Union and the Challenge of the Future, Volume 3: Ideology, Culture, and Nationality,* edited by Alexander Shtromas and Morton A. Kaplan, 249–76. New York: Paragon House, 1989.

Ghandi, Leela. *Postcolonial Theory: A Critical Introduction.* New York: Columbia University Press, 1998.

Gladarev, Boris. "Zhiznennye miry 'osoboy' leningradskoy molodyozhi." *Neprikosnovennyi zapas* 4, no. 36 (2004), http://magazines.russ.ru/nz/2004/4/glad6.html.

Glebkin, V. V. *Ritual v sovetskom obshchestve.* Moscow: Yanus-K, 1998.

Goffman, Erving. *The Presentation of Self in Everyday Life.* New York: Anchor/Doubleday, 1990?

Golovensky, D. I. "The Marginal Man Concept—An Analysis and Critique." *Social Forces* 30, no. 3 (1952): 333–39.

Gordon, Boris. "Prosto pesnya." *Ogonek* 23 (2002): 37–40.

Gorodnitsky, A. M. "Concert." Kontsertnyi zal u Finlyandskogo vokzala (St. Petersburg, Russia), May 16, 2002.

———. *I zhit' yeshchyo nadezhde . . .* Moscow: Vagrius, 2001.

———. "'I zhit' yeshchyo nadezhde . . .' (concert)." Temple Israel (Boston), March 16, 2002.

———. "Istoriya odnoy pesni." 2001. http://writer.fio.ru/news.php?n=6950&c=1351.

———. "'. . . Nam ne khvatalo Okudzhavy.'" In *Golos nadezhdy: Novoye o Bulate Okudzhave,* edited by A. E. Krylov, 70–88. Moscow: Bulat, 2005.

———. "Untitled recording from the audioarchive of N. F. Kurchev (AVCh-116)." n.d.

Gorodnitsky, Aleksandr. Interview by Rachel S. Platonov. June 10, 2002.

———. *Sochineniya.* Moscow: Lokid, 2000.

———. "Tol'ko Avtor i Slushatel'." *APArt* 3 (1996): 10–13.

Gorsky, Vadim. "Lui Armstrong yevreyskogo razliva: Filerskaya zapis' razgovorov Vysotskogo." *Ural,* no. 8 (2000), http://magazines.russ.ru/ural/2000/8/ural10.html.

Green, A. W. "A Re-Examination of the Marginal Man Concept." *Social Forces* 26, no. 2 (1947): 167–71.

Gregg, Richard B. "The Ego-Function of the Rhetoric of Protest." *Philosophy and Rhetoric* 4, no. 2 (1971): 71–91.

Groys, Boris. "The Art of Totality." In *The Landscape of Stalinism: The Art and Ideology of Soviet Space,* edited by Evgeny Dobrenko and Eric Naiman, 96–122. Seattle: University of Washington Press, 2003.

Gudoshnikov, Ya. I. *Russkiy gorodskoy romans.* Tambov: Tambovskiy Ordena "Znak pocheta" gosudarstvennyi pedagogicheskiy institut, 1990.

Gunew, Sneja. "Framing Marginality: Distinguishing the Textual Policies of the Marginal Voice." *Southern Review* 12, no. 2 (1985): 142–56.

———. *Framing Marginality: Multicultural Literary Studies.* [Carlton, Victoria]: Melbourne University Press, 1994.

Günther, Hans. "'Broad Is My Motherland': The Mother Archetype and Space in the Soviet Mass Song." In *The Landscape of Stalinism: The Art and Ideology of Soviet Space,* edited by Evgeny Dobrenko and Eric Naiman, 77–95. Seattle: University of Washington Press, 2003.

———. "Poyushchaya rodina (Sovetskaya massovaya pesnya kak vyrazheniye arkhetipa materi)." *Voprosy literatury* 4 (1997): 46–61.

Halliday, M. A. K. "Antilanguages." In *Language as Social Semiotic: The Social Interpretation of Language and Meaning,* 164–82. London: University Park Press, 1978.

Harman, Lesley D. *The Modern Stranger: On Language and Membership,* Contributions to the Sociology of Language 47. New York: Mouton de Gruyter, 1988.

Harper, Phillip Brian. *Framing the Margins: The Social Logic of Postmodern Culture.* New York: Oxford University Press, 1994.

Hawkins, Peter. *Chanson: The French Singer-Songwriter from Aristide Bruant to the Present Day.* Burlington, Vt.: Ashgate, 2000.

Heller, Mikhail, and Aleksandr M. Nekrich. *Utopia in Power: The History of the Soviet Union from 1917 to the Present.* Translated by Phyllis B. Carlos. New York: Summit, 1986.

Henderson, Mae G. "Introduction: Borders, Boundaries, and Frame(work)s." In *Borders, Boundaries, and Frames: Essays in Cultural Criticism and Cultural Studies,* edited by Mae G. Henderson, 1–30. New York: Routledge, 1995.

Herbst, Susan. *Politics at the Margin: Historical Studies of Public Expression Outside the Mainstream.* New York: Cambridge University Press, 1994.

Hodge, Thomas P. *A Double Garland: Poetry and Art-Song in Early-Nineteenth-Century Russia,* Studies in Russian Literature and Theory. Evanston, Ill.: Northwestern University Press, 2000.

Hodnett, Grey, ed. *Resolutions and Decisions of the Communist Party of the Soviet Union.* Vol. 4: *The Khrushchev Years, 1953–1964.* Toronto: University of Toronto Press, 1974.

hooks, bell. "Marginality as a Site of Resistance." In *Out There: Marginalization and Contemporary Cultures,* 341–43. Cambridge, Mass.: MIT Press, 1995.

Istomin, S., and D. Denisenko. *Samye znamenitye bardy Rossii.* Moscow: Veche, 2002.

Jenny, Laurent. "The Strategy of Form." In *French Literary Theory Today: A Reader,* edited by Tzvetan Todorov, 34–63. Cambridge, Eng.: Cambridge University Press, 1982.

Jones, Polly, ed. *The Dilemmas of De-Stalinization: Negotiating Cultural and Social Change in the Khrushchev Era.* London and New York: Routledge, 2006.

———. "Introduction: The Dilemmas of De-Stalinization." In *The Dilemmas of De-Stalinization: Negotiating Cultural and Social Change in the Khrushchev Era,* edited by Polly Jones, 1–18. London: Routledge, 2006.

Jones, Ruby Jean. "Echoing Their Lives: Teaching Russian Language and Culture Through the Music of Vladimir S. Vysotsky." Ph.D. thesis. University of Texas, 2008.

"K novomu pod"yomu muzykal'nogo obrazovaniya." *Sovetskaya muzyka* 8 (1950): 3–8.

Kabalevsky, D. "Muzyka i sovremennost'." *Sovetskaya muzyka* 3 (1960): 7–27.

———. "Poiski i zabluzhdeniya." *Sovetskaya muzyka* 2 (1963): 10–16.

Kagansky, Vladimir. *Kul'turnyi landshaft i sovetskoye obitayemoye prostranstvo.* Moscow: Novoye literaturnoye obozreniye, 2001.

Kalinin, Sergey. "Diskussiya kluba samodeyatel'noy pesni 'Poisk' g. Vladivostok (16 noyabrya 1982 goda)." http://www.bards.ru/press/press_show.php?id=335&page=1.

Kalinin, Sergey [webmaster]. *Bards.* www.bards.ru.

Kamburova, Yelena. "On zashchishchal nas ot grubosti i nevezhestva." In *Golos nadezhdy: Novoye o Bulate Okudzhave,* edited by A. E. Krylov, 5–9. Moscow: Bulat, 2005.

Karimov, Igor'. *Istoriya Moskovskogo KSP: Sub"yektivnyi vzglyad na ob"yektivnuyu real'nost'.* Moscow: Yanus-K, 2004.

Karimov, Igor', Nikolai Lisunets, and Galina Khomchik. "Opros ofitsial'nogo sayta Yuriya Vizbora." http://www.vizbor.ru/index.php?chrazdel=9&chmenu=18&r=opros.

Karlin, A. N. "Tri vzglyada na nyneshneye sostoyaniye bardovskoy pesni." http://gondola.zamok.net/021/21karlin1.html.

Karyakin, Yu. "O pesnyakh Vladimira Vysotskogo." *Literaturnoye obozreniye* 7 (1981): 94–99.

Kazbek-Kaziyev, Z. A. "Vospominaniye." *Literaturnoye obozreniye* 3 (1998): 7–10.

Keldysh, Yu. V., ed. *Muzykal'naya entsiklopediya.* 6 vols. Vols. 1, 4. Moscow: Sovetskaya entsiklopediya, 1973–82.

Kelly, Catriona. "Riding the Magic Carpet: Children and Leader Cult in the Stalin Era." *Slavic and East European Journal* 49, no. 2 (2005): 199–224.

Kharkordin, Oleg. *The Collective and the Individual in Russia: A Study of Practices.* Berkeley: University of California Press, 1999.

Khomutova, E. N. "Avtorskaya pesnya kak kul'turno-istoricheskiy fenomen v Rossii XX veka." In *Nauchnye trudy Nizhnevartovskogo gosudarstvennogo pedagogicheskogo instituta: Seriya "Kul'turologiya" 1,* 167–74. Nizhnevartovsk: Izdatel'stvo Nizhnevartovskogo pedagogicheskogo instituta, 2000.

Khrennikov, T. "Bol'shoy i slavnyi put'." *Sovetskaya muzyka* 2 (1969): 2–18.

———. "Muzykal'no-esteticheskoye vospitaniye detey i yunoshestva." *Sovetskaya muzyka* 5 (1961): 12–20.

———. "Na puti k muzykal'noy kul'ture kommunizma." *Sovetskaya muzyka* 6 (1962): 3–26.

———. "Sostoyaniye i zadachi sovetskogo muzykal'nogo tvorchestva." *Sovetskaya muzyka* 5 (1957): 24–51.

Khubov, G. "Muzyka i sovremennost' " *Sovetskaya muzyka* 3 (1953): 3–12.

Kikhney, L. G., and T. V. Safarova. "K voprosu o fol'klornykh traditsiyakh v tvorchestve Vladimira Vysotskogo." In *Mir Vysotskogo: Issledovaniya i materialy III.1,* 72–82. Moscow: GKTsM V. S. Vysotskogo, 1999.

Kim, Yuly. *Na sobstvennyi motiv.* Moscow: Lokid, 1998.

———. *Sochineniya.* Moscow: Lokid, 2000.

Kim, Yuly, and Valentina Soroka. "Lyuboy bard—grafoman." *Gazeta po-kiyevski Online* (November 15, 2007), http://www.pk.kiev.ua/interview/2007/11/15/090052.html.

Kiselyov, Yevgeny. "Nashe Vsyo." *Ekho Moskvy* (June 8, 2008), http://www.echo.msk.ru/programs/all/519168–echo/

Kishkovsky, Sophia. "Notes from a Russian Musical Underground: The Sounds of Chanson." *New York Times,* July 16, 2006, 1+.

Kitaigorodskaya, M. V., and N. N. Rozanova. "Tvorchestvo Vladimira Vysotskogo v zerkale ustnoy rechi." *Voprosy yazykoznaniya* 1 (1993): 97–113.

Klyachkin, Yevgeny. *Luchshiye pesni.* Muzykal'noye izdatel'stvo M.O., 2000.

———. *Zhivi, pokuda lyubimy.* St. Petersburg: Lan', 2000.

Kolmanovsky, E. "Sovetskaya pesnya—nashe ideynoye oruzhiye." *Sovetskaya muzyka* 11 (1979): 44–48.

Konstantinov, F. V., ed. *Lichnost' pri sotsializme.* Moscow: Nauka, 1968.

"Kontsert 40–letiya 'Vostoka.'" http://www.dkgaza.spb.ru/cocert%2040%20let.html.

Kopelev, Lev. "Pamyati Aleksandra Galicha." *Kontinent* 16 (1978): 334–43.

Kopylova, N. I. "Fol'klornaya assotsiatsiya v poezii V. S. Vysotskogo." In *V. S. Vysotsky: Issledovaniya i materialy,* 74–95. Voronezh: Izdatel'stvo Voronezhskogo universiteta, 1990.

Korotich, Vitaly. "Slushat' i slyshat' vremya." *Sovetskaya muzyka* 12 (1987): 2–7.

Korzhavin, N. "O tom, kak veselilis' rebyata v 1934 godu, ili Kak inogda oblegchayet zhizn' vysokiy esteticheskiy printsip: 'Vazhno ne 'Chto?' a 'Kak?'" *Voprosy literatury* 6 (1995): 33–56.

Kotlyar, El'mira. "Pamyati Bulata Okudzhavy." *Literaturnoye obozreniye* 3 (1998): 16–17.

Kovner, Vladimir. "Zolotoy vek magnitizdata [part 3]." *Vestnik Online,* no. 9 (346) (April 28, 2004), http://www.vestnik.com/issues/2004/0428/koi/kovner.htm.

Kozlov, V. A. *Massovye bezporyadki v SSSR pri Khrushcheve i Brezhneve (1953—nachalo 1980–kh gg.).* Novosibirsk: Sibirskiy khronograf, 1999.

KPSS. *The Road to Communism: Documents of the 22nd Congress of the Communist Party of the Soviet Union (October 17–31, 1961).* Moscow: Foreign Languages Publishing House, 1961.

Krasil'nikov, S. A. *Na izlomakh sotsial'noy struktury: Marginaly v poslerevolyutsionnom rossiyskom obshchestve (1917–i-konets 1930–kh godov).* Novosibirsk: Novosibirskiy gosudarstvennyi universitet, 1998.

Krimova, N. "My vmeste s nim posmeyomsya." *Druzhba narodov,* no. 8 (1985): 242–54.

Kristeva, Julia. *Desire in Language: A Semiotic Approach to Literature and Art.* Translated by Alice Jardine, Thomas Gora, and Leon S. Roudiez. New York: Columbia University Press, 1980.

Krylov, A. E. "Bytovaniye i transformatsiya krylatykh vyrazheniy Vysotskogo v gazetno-zhurnal'nykh zagolovkakh." In *Mir Vysotskogo: Issledovaniya i materialy IV,* 217–28. Moscow: GKTsM V. S. Vysotskogo, 2000.

———. *Galich—"Soavtor."* Moscow: Blagotvoritel'nyi fond Vladimira Vysotskogo, 2001.

———. *Ne kvasom zemlya polita . . . : Primechaniya k 'chelovecheskoy tragedii' Aleksandra Galicha.* Uglich: Promdizayn, 2001.

Kukin, Yury. *Dom na polputi.* Moscow: Sovetskiy fond kul'tury, 1991.

———. *Luchshiye pesni:* Muzykal'noye izdatel'stvo M.O., 1999.

———. *Traktat o pesnyakh.* Moscow (?): MP "Bit," 1999.

Kulagin, Anatoly. "Chetyre chetverti puti: O tvorcheskoy evolyutsii V. S. Vysotskogo." In *Genus Poetarum: Sbornik nauchnikh trudov,* 76–92. Kolomna: Ministerstvo obrazovaniya Rossiyskoy federatsii; Kolomenskiy pedagogicheskiy institut, 1995.

———. "'Lukomor'ya bol'she net . . .' ('Antiskazka' Vladimira Vysotskogo)." In *Literatura i fol'klornaya traditsiya: Sbornik nauchnykh trudov,* 113–22. Volgograd: Peremena, 1997.

———. *Poeziya V. S. Vysotskogo: Tvorcheskaya evolyutsiya.* Moscow: Knizhnyi magazin Moskva, 1997.

———. "'Snachala on, a potom my . . .': Krupneyshiye bardy i naslediye Aleksandra Vertinskogo." In *Golos nadezhdy: Novoye o Bulate Okudzhave,* 335–56. Moscow: Bulat, 2005.

Kurilov, D. N. "Avtorskaya pesnya kak zhanr russkoy poezii sovetskoy epokhi (60–e–70–e gg.)." Literaturnyi institut im. Gor'kogo, 1999. http://www.bard.ru/kurilov/04.htm.

Kuteynikova, N. E. "Iskusstvo bardov kak organichnoye yedinstvo fol'klora i literatury." In *Natsional'naya dukhovnaya kul'tura i obrazovaniye,* 69–86. St. Petersburg: ?, 1994.

Kuznetsov, Feliks. "K zrelosti: Konets 'chetvyortogo pokoleniya.'" *Yunost'* 11 (1966): 83–88.

Lachmann, Renate. *Memory and Literature: Intertextuality in Russian Modernism.* Translated by Roy Sellars and Anthony Wall, Theory and History of Literature. Minneapolis: University of Minnesota Press, 1997.

Lagin, Lazar. "The Old Genie Khottabych: A Story of Make-Believe (Excerpts)." In *Politicizing Magic: An Anthology of Russian and Soviet Fairy Tales,* edited by Marina Balina, Helena Goscilo, and Mark Lipovetskii, 165–96. Evanston, Ill.: Northwestern University Press, 2005.

Lamont, Rosette C. "Horace's Heirs: Beyond Censorship in the Soviet Songs of the Magnitizdat." *World Literature Today* (Spring 1979): 220–27.

———. "The Subcontinent of the 'Magnitizdat': The Soviet Bards." In *New Literary Continents,* 40–48. Whitestone, N.Y.: Griffon House, 1984.

Lazarski, Christopher. "Vladimir Vysotsky and His Cult." *Russian Review* 51 (1992): 58–71.

Lebedev, Valery. "Blazhen muzh, ne idushchiy na sobraniye nechestivykh (K 20–letiyu so dnya smerti A. Galicha)." http://www.bard.ru/galich/galich3.html.

Lebedeva, Yekaterina. "Traditsii i istoki pesen Bulata Okudzhavy." In *Tvorchestvo Bulata Okudzhavy v kontekste kul'tury XX veka: Materialy Pervoy mezhdunarodnoy nauchnoy konferentsii, posvyashchyonnoy 75–letiyu so dnya rozhdeniya Bulata Okudzhavy,* 77–80. Moscow: Sol', 2001.

Lebedewa, Katja. *Komm Gitarre, mach mich frei! Russische Gitarrenlyrik in der Opposition.* Berlin: Collection BuchPlus, 1992.

———. "Russische Gitarrenlyrik und die Tonbandrevolution des 'Magnitizdat' nach 1956—kulturelle Voraussetzungen und Quellen." *Zeitschrift fur Slawistik* 36, no. 2 (1991): 229–37.

Leonidov, Pavel. "Do svidaniya, Volodya!" *Novoye russkoye slovo,* August 14, 1980, 3.

Lepsky, Georgy. "V flibust'erskom dal'nem sinem more . . ." *Vol'nyi veter,* no. 40 (1999), http://veter.turizm.ru/40/lepskiy.shtml.

Lerner, David. "Vysotsky: The Revival of a Russian Pop Icon." *Mother Jones,* November 1987, 20–24, 42–43.

Levina, L. A. *Grani zvuchashchego slova: Estetika i poetika avtorskoy pesni.* Moscow: Neft' i gaz, 2002.

Levitan, A., and M. Levitan, eds. *Ot kostra k mikrofonu: Iz istorii samodeyatel'noy pesni v Leningrade.* St. Petersburg: Respeks, 1996.

Lianskaya, Ye. Ya. "A. N. Vertinsky i predystoriya bardovskoy pesni: Vzglyad muzykanta." In *Mir Vysotskogo: Issledovaniya i materialy III.2,* 390–99. Moscow: GKTsM V. S. Vysotskogo, 1999.

Loseff, Lev. *On the Beneficence of Censorship: Aesopian Language in Modern Russian Literature.* Vol. 31, Arbeiten und Texte zur Slavistik. Munich: Verlag Otto Sagner, 1984.

MacFadyen, David. *Red Stars: Personality and the Soviet Popular Song 1955–1991.* Montreal: McGill-Queen's University Press, 2001.

———. *Songs for Fat People: Affect, Emotion, and Celebrity in the Russian Popular Song, 1900–1955.* Montreal: McGill-Queen's University Press, 2002.

Mal'tsev, Yury. "Menestreli." In *Mir Vysotskogo: Issledovaniya i materialy III.1,* 296–310. Moscow: GKTsM V. S. Vysotskogo, 1999. Reprint of *Vol'naya russkaya literatura: 1955–1975.*

Marginal'nost' v sovremennoy Rossii: Kollektivnaya monografiya. Moscow: Moskovskiy obshchestvennyi nauchnyi fond, 2000.

Marinicheva, O. "Chtob dushi i glaza svetali." *Komsomol'skaya pravda,* October 22, 1986, 4.

Marinina, Kseniya, dir. *Monolog.* [Moscow]: [Gosteleradiofond], 2002.

Marran. "Bulat Okudzhava i yego vremya." *Kontinent* 36 (1983): 329–54.

Mazalov, Aleksey, Yelena Mazalova, and Mikhail Semenenko. Discussion with Rachel S. Platonov. June 14, 2001.

McLean, Hugh. "Walls and Wire: Notes on the Prison Theme in Russian Literature." In *Slavic Linguistics and Poetics: Studies for Edward Stankiewicz on His 60th Birthday,* edited by Kenneth E. Naylor et al., 253–65. [Columbus, Ohio]: Slavica, 1982.

McMichael, Polly. "'After All, You're a Rock and Roll Star (At Least, That's What They Say)': *Roksi* and the Creation of the Soviet Rock Musician." *Slavonic and East European Review* 83, no. 4 (2005): 664–84.

Mezhiritsky, Pyotr. "Muzyka i slovo: Beseda s muzykovedom Vladimirom Frumkinym." *Vestnik Online* (June 12, 2002), http://www.vestnik.com/issues/2002/0612/win/mezhritsky.htm.

Mikhailova, N. G. "Kriterii otsenki khudozhestvennoy samodeyatel'nosti i rabota zhyuri smotrov i konkursov (Osnovnye rezul'taty i prakticheskiye vyvody issledovaniya)." In *Problemy otsenki khudozhestvennoy samodeyatel'nosti (v praktike raboty zhyuri),* edited by N. G. Mikhailova, 7–31. Moscow: Nauchno-issledovatel'skiy institut kul'tury, 1980.

———. "Perspektivy izucheniya khudozhestvennoy samodeyatel'nosti kak sotsial'no-kul'turnogo yavleniya." In *Sotsial'nye i tvorcheskiye problemy khudozhestvennoy samodeyatel'nosti,* edited by E. V. Bykova, A. S. Zubatkin, and N. G. Mikhailova, 5–18. Moscow: Nauchno-issledovatel'skiy institut kul'tury, 1981.

———, ed. *Problemy otsenki khudozhestvennoy samodeyatel'nosti (v praktike raboty zhyuri).* Moscow: Nauchno-issledovatel'skiy institut kul'tury 1980.

Miller, Frank J. *Folklore for Stalin: Russian Folklore and Pseudofolklore of the Stalin Era.* Armonk, N.Y.: M. E. Sharpe, 1990.

Miller, Heather Lynn. "'Vysotsky's Soul Packaged in Tapes': Identity and Russianness in the Music of Vladimir Vysotsky." Ph.D. thesis, University of Maryland, 2006.

Mirzayan, Aleksandr. "Avtorskaya pesnya kak baza russkoy natsional'noy idei." http://www.bard.ru/esse.htm.

———. "V nachale byla pesnya." *ApArt* 1 (1996): 2–4.

Mizruchi, Ephraim H. *Regulating Society: Marginality and Social Control in Historical Perspective.* New York: Free, 1983.

Moore, Allan. "Authenticity as Authentication." *Popular Music* 21, no. 2 (2002): 209–23.

Morov, A. "O durnykh vkusakh i nedostatkakh vospitaniya." *Sovetskaya muzyka* 7 (1955): 115–20.

Morozov, A. "Parodiya kak literaturyni zhanr." *Russkaya literatura* 1 (1960): 48–77.

Nemchik, Barbara. "Narodno-literaturnye traditsii v tvorchestve Vysotskogo." In *Mir Vysotskogo: Issledovaniya i materialy III.1,* 100–107. Moscow: GKTsM V. S. Vysotskogo, 1999.

Nest'yev, I. *Zvyozdy russkoy estrady (Panina, Vyal'tseva, Plevitskaya): Ocherki o russkikh estradnykh pevitsakh nachala XX veka.* 2nd ed. Moscow: Sovetskiy kompozitor, 1974.

Nichiporov, I. B. *Avtorskaya pesnya v russkoy poezii 1950–1970–x gg. Tvorcheskiye individual'nosti, zhanrovo-stilevye poiski, literaturnye svyazi.* Moscow: Maks-Press, 2006.

Nikanorova, E. B., and S. A. Prokhvatilova, ed. *Russkiy romans.* St. Petersburg: Lenizdat, 1993.

Nikolajeva, M. "Fairy Tales in Society's Service." *Marvels & Tales* 16, no. 2 (2002): 171–87.

Novikov, A. "O pesne." *Sovetskaya muzyka* 4 (1957): 14–22.

Novikov, Aleksandr. "'Zritelyu podsovivayut voinstvuyushchikh pederastov.'" *Chto napisano perom* (2008), http://bardnovikov.narod.ru/pressa_novikov/zritel.htm.

Novikov, V. [I.]. *Vladimir Vysotsky: Zhizn' i tvorchestvo.* Moscow: [Vagant], 2000.

Novikov, V. [I.], and E. N. Basovskaya. *Avtorskaya pesnya.* Moscow: Olimp, 2000.

Novikov, Vladimir. "Avtorskaya pesnya kak poeziya soprotivleniya." *Vestnik Online* (February 28, 2002), http://www.vestnik.com/issues/2002/0228/koi/novikov.htm.

———. *Roman s literaturoy.* Moscow: Intrada, 2007.

Oganov, A. A. "Fenomen marginal'nosti v kul'ture." In *Marginal'noye iskusstvo,* 64–65. Moscow: Izdatel'stvo Moskovskogo universiteta, 1999.

Ogarkova, A. "Avtorskaya pesnya: Istoriya, sovremennost', budushcheye." In *Gorizonty kul'tury,* 50–65. St. Petersburg: Institut, 1992.

Oinas, Felix J. *Essays on Russian Folklore and Mythology.* Columbus, Ohio: Slavica, 1984.

———. "Folklore and Politics in the Soviet Union." *Slavic Review* 32, no. 1 (1973): 45–58.

Okudzhava, Bulat. *Stikhotvoreniya.* St. Petersburg: Akademicheskiy proekt, 2001.

———. *Ya nikomu nichego ne navyazyval.* Moscow: Knizhnyi magazin "Moskva," 1997.

Ol'khovich, E. "Kogda molodyozhi interesno . . ." *Sovetskaya muzyka* 8 (1966): 119–27.

Ong, Walter. *Orality and Literacy: The Technologizing of the Word.* New York: Routledge, 1997.

Orlov, Aleksandr. "Avtorskaya pesnya: Vchera, segodnya . . . zavtra (po materialam sotsiologicheskikh issledovanii)." In *Voprosy sotsiologii muzyki: Sbornik trudov III,* 77–86. Moscow: Gosudarstvennyi muzykal'no-pedagogicheskiy institut imeni Gnesinykh, 1990.

Oshanin, L. "Iz pesni slova ne vykinesh'." *Sovetskaya muzyka* 2 (1954): 23–37.

"Ot golosa Vysotskogo damy padali v obmorok." *Interfax* (2008), http://www.rambler.ru/news/culture/inmemoriam/554772566.html.

Palczewski, Catherine Helen. "Cyber-Movements, New Social Movements, and Counterpublics." In *Counterpublics and the State,* edited by Robert Asen and Daniel C. Brouwer, 161–86. Albany: State University of New York Press, 2001.

Park, Robert E. "Human Migration and the Marginal Man." *American Journal of Sociology* 33, no. 6 (1928): 881–93.

Pavlova, G. "Pesni, rozhdyonnye v vuzakh." *Muzykal'naya zhizn'* 10 (1959): 4–5.

Pedenko, Svyatoslav. "'Erika' beryot chetyre kopii': Vozvrashcheniye A. Galicha." *Voprosy literatury* 4 (1989): 80–112.

Perevozchikov, Valery. *Neizvestnyi Vysotsky.* Moscow: Vagrius, 2005.

———. *Pravda smertnogo chasa: Posmertnaya sud'ba.* Moscow: Politburo, 2000.

———. "Vladimir Vysotsky: 'Vot esli by magnitofony byli pri Pushkine.'" *Izvestiya* (January 24, 2008), http://www.izvestia.ru/news/332667.

Pesni russkikh bardov: Teksty. 4 vols. Paris: YMCA, 1977.

Petrov, Nikolai. "Sovest' rossiyskoy kul'tury." *Literaturnoye obozreniye* 3 (1998): 39.

Petrushanskaya, E. "Pesnya dostayotsya cheloveku: O 'misticheskoy' prirode sovetskikh massovykh pesen." *Literaturnoye obozreniye* 2, no. 286 (1998): 55–60.

Pilkington, Hilary. *Russia's Youth and Its Culture: A Nation's Constructors and Constructed.* London: Routledge, 1994.

"Pisateli-dissidenty: Biobibliograficheskiye stat'i." *Novoye literaturnoye obozreniye,* no. 66 (2004), http://magazines.russ.ru/nlo/2004/66/pisat29–pr.html.

Platonov, Rachel S. "Bad Singing: *Avtorskaya Pesnya* and the Aesthetics of Metacommunication." *Ulbandus* 9 (2005–6): 87–113.

Pletnyov, R. "O pesenkakh B. Okudzhavy." In *Golos nadezhdy: Novoye o Bulate Okudzhave,* edited by A. E. Krylov and O. Ya. Batrakova, 263–67. Moscow: Bulat, 2004.

Popkin, Cathy. *The Pragmatics of Insignificance: Chekhov, Zoshchenko, Gogol.* Stanford, Calif.: Stanford University Press, 1993.

Popova, I. P. *Marginal'nost': Sotsiologicheskiy analiz.* Moscow, 1996.

Pospelova, Nelli. "Chelovek dvukh stikhiy." *Nezavisimaya gazeta* (March 21, 2003), www.ng.ru/printed/saturday/2003–03–21/13_gorodnitskiy.html.

Prokhorov, Aleksandr. "Cinema of Attractions versus Narrative Cinema: Leonid Gaidai's Comedies and El'dar Ryazanov's Satires of the 1960s." *Slavic Review* 62, no. 3 (2003): 455–72.

Propp, V. Ya. *Russkaya skazka.* Leningrad: Izdatel'stvo Leningradskogo universiteta, 1984.

Pushkin, A. S. *Poemy: Dramaticheskiye proizvedeniya.* Moscow: Novator, 1996.

Pystina, L. I. "'Spetsy' kak sotsial'naya gruppa v strukture rossiyskogo obshchestva 1920–nachala 1930–x gg. (problemy izucheniya)." In *Marginaly v sovetskom obshchestve 1920–1930–x godov: Istoriografiya, istochniki: Sbornik nauchnykh trudov,* 49–68. Novosibirsk: Rossiyskaya akademiya nauk, Sibirskoye otdelenyie; Institut istorii, 2001.

Rasputina, S. P. "Sotsial'naya motivatsiya sovetskogo bardovskogo dvizheniya: Filosofsko-sotsiologicheskiy aspekt." In *Mir Vysotskogo: Issledovaniya i materialy III.2,* 375–79. Moscow: GKTsM V. S. Vysotskogo, 1999.

Rassadin, Stanislav. "Vremya Okudzhavy?" *Novaya gazeta* (January 14, 2002), http://www.novayagazeta.ru/data/2002/02/26.html.

Razzakov, Fyodor. *Vladimir Vysotsky: Po lezviyu britvy.* Moscow: Yauza, Presskom, 2004.

Red'kin, V. A. "Khudozhestvennyi yazyk poeta v oppozitsii k ofitsial'noy ideologii." In *Mir Vysotskogo: Issledovaniya i materialy III.2,* 124–29. Moscow: GKTsM V. S. Vysotskogo, 1999.

Rogatskina, M. L. "Obraz liricheskogo *ya* v poezii Vysotskogo." In *Mir Vysotskogo: Issledovaniya i materialy III.1,* 207–11. Moscow: Komitet po kul'ture Moskvy; GKTsM V. S. Vysotskogo, 1999.

Romanska, Magdalena. "Bulat Okudzhava: Bard and Voice of a Waking Russian Nation." Ph.D. thesis, McGill University, 2003.

Roshin, Vadim, dir. *Vsenarodnyi Volodya.* Edited by Yelena Roshina. Moscow: Soyuz-Video, 2000.

Roth, Klaus. "Narrating in Socialist Life: Observations on Strategies of Life Management in Southeast Europe." In *Creativity and Tradition in Folklore: New Directions,* edited by Simon J. Bronner, 127–39. Logan: Utah State University Press, 1992.

Rothstein, Robert A. "Popular Song in the NEP Era." In *Russia in the Era of NEP: Explorations in Soviet Society and Culture,* edited by Sheila Fitzpatrick, Aleksandr Rabinowitch, and Richard Stites, 268–94. Bloomington: Indiana University Press, 1991.

Rudnitsky, K. "Pesni Okudzhavy i Vysotskogo." *Teatral'naya zhizn'* 14, 15 (1987): 22–23, 14–15.

Rumyantsev, S. Yu. "Lyubitel'skiy muzykal'nyi teatr: Avtorskaya pesnya." In *Samodeyatel'noye khudozhestvennoye tvorchestvo v SSSR: Ocherki istorii, Konets 1950–kh—nachalo 1990–kh godov,* 19–76. St. Petersburg: Gosudarstvennyi institut iskustvoznaniya, 1999.

———. "Muzykal'naya samodeyatel'nost' poslevoyennykh let." In *Samodeyatel'noye khudozhestvennoye tvorchestvo v SSSR: Ocherki istorii, 1930–1950 gg.,* 118–61. Moscow: Gosudarstvenyi institut iskustvoznaniya, Ministerstvo kul'tury RF, 1995.

Rumyantsev, S. Yu., and A. P. Shul'pin. "'Nizovoy' sloy narodnogo tvorchestva." In *Samodeyatel'noye khudozhestvennoye tvorchestvo v SSSR: Ocherki istorii, 1930–1950 gg.,* 77–103. Moscow: Gosudarstvennyi institut iskustvoznaniya, Ministerstvo kul'tury RF, 1995.

———. "Samodeyatel'noye tvorchestvo i 'gosudarstvennaya' kul'tura." In *Samodeyatel'noye khudozhestvennoye tvorchestvo v SSSR: Ocherki istorii, 1930–1950 gg.,* 7–52. Moscow: Gosudarstvennyi institut iskustvoznaniya, Ministerstvo kul'tury RF, 1995.

Russova, S. N. "Avtor i tekst u Vladimira Vysotskogo." In *Mir Vysotskogo: Issledovaniya i materialy III.1,* 227–32. Moscow: GKTsM V. S. Vysotskogo, 1999.

"S"yezd stroiteley kommunizma." *Sovetskaya muzyka* 3 (1959): 3–7.

Sanneh, Kelefa. "The Sweet Sounds of Really Bad Singing." *New York Times,* January 18, 2004, 2.1+.

Savchenko, B. A. *Aleksandr Vertinsky.* Vol. 6, Novoye v zhizni, nauke, tekhnike: Seriya "Iskusstvo." Moscow: Znaniye, 1989.

———. *Avtorskaya pesnya.* Vol. 7, Novoye v zhizni, nauke, tekhnike: Seriya "Iskusstvo." Moscow: Znaniye, 1987.

Seemann, Klaus Dieter. "Bulat Okudzavas 'Cernyj kot' als antistalinistische Parodie." *Welt der Slaven-Halbjahresschrift fur Slavistik* 31, no. 1 (1986): 139–46.

Segal, Boris M. *The Drunken Society: Alcohol Abuse and Alcoholism in the Soviet Union.* New York: Hippocrene, 1990.

Selivanov, F. M. "Introduction." In *Gorodskiye pesni, ballady, romansy,* 5–28. Moscow: MGU, 1999.

Sergeyev, M. "I sporit' i deystvovat': Vmesto otchyota." *Sovetskaya muzyka* 2 (1963): 17–25.

Shafer, N. "O tak nazyvayemykh 'blatnykh pesnyakh' Vladimira Vysotskogo [nachalo]." *Muzykal'naya zhizn'* 20 (1989): 11–14.

Shelest, Georgy. "Kolymskiye zapisi." *Znamya* 9 (1964): 162–80.

Shipov, R. A., ed. *Pyat'desyat rossiyskikh bardov: Spravochnik.* Moscow: Vagant, 2001.

Shoshin, V. A., ed. *Zdravstvuy, strana geroyev! (sovetskiye pesni).* Leningrad: Lenizdat, 1985.

Shulezhkova, S. G. *Krylatye vyrazheniya russkogo yazyka, ikh istochniki i razvitiye.* Moscow: Azbukovnik, 2001.

Sibley, David. *Geographies of Exclusion: Society and Difference in the West.* New York: Routledge, 1995.

Sinel'nikov, Sergey. Personal communication to Rachel S. Platonov. June 23, 2001.

Skobelev, Andrey V., and Sergey M. Shaulov. "Menestreli nashikh dney." *Literaturnaya Gruziya* 4 (1986): 154–69.

———. *Vladimir Vysotsky: Mir i slovo.* Voronezh: MIPP Logos, 1991.

Small, Christopher. *Musicking: The Meanings of Performing and Listening.* Edited by George Lipsitz, Susan McClary, and Robert Walser, Music/Culture. Hanover, N.H.: University Press of New England, 1998.

Smirnov, I. P. "Mikrorevoliutsiya, ili Traktat o neformal'nykh kollektivakh (Pochti vospominaniya)." *Zvezda* 11 (2001): 215–21.

Smith, Gerald Stanton. "The Metrical Repertoire of Russian Guitar Poetry." *International Journal of Slavic Linguistics and Poetics* 30 (1984): 131–50.

———. "Modern Russian Underground Song: An Introductory Survey." *Journal of Russian Studies* 28 (1974): 3–12.

———. "Polyusa russkoy poezii 1960–1970–kh: Brodsky i Vysotsky." In *Mir Vysotskogo: Issledovaniya i materialy III.2,* 288–91. Moscow: GKTsM V. S. Vysotskogo, 2000.

———. *Songs to Seven Strings: Russian Guitar Poetry and Soviet "Mass Song."* Bloomington: Indiana University Press, 1984.

Smith, Hedrick. "Intellectual Life: The Archipelago of Private Culture." In *The Russians,* 410–16. [New York]: Quadrangle/New York Times, 1976.

Smolitsky, V. G., and N. V. Mikhailova, eds. *Russkiy zhestokiy romans: Sbornik.* Moscow: Gosudarstvennyi respublikanskiy tsentr russkogo fol'klora, 1994.

"Smotr muzykal'noy samodeyatel'nosti." *Sovetskaya muzyka* 8 (1950): 66–67.

Smyth, Terry. "Marginality and the Role of the Clinical Teacher." *Journal of Advanced Nursing* 13 (1988): 621–30.

Soboleva, G. G. *Russkiy romans.* Moscow: Znaniye, 1980.

Sokhor, A. "Massovaya, bytovaya, estradnaya . . ." *Sovetskaya muzyka* 10 (1965): 18–23.

———. "Nashe oruzhiye—nashi pesni." *Sovetskaya muzyka* 10 (1957): 13–19.

Sokolov, D. "Klub samodeyatel'noy pesni (KSP)." In *Neformal'naya Rossiya: O "neformal'nykh" politizirovannykh dvizheniyakh i gruppakh v RSFSR (opyt spravochnika),* edited by V. Berezovsky and N. Krotov, 265–71. Moscow: Molodaya gvardiya, 1990.

———. "Samodeyatel'naya (avtorskaya) pesnya v SSSR i Rossii; Kluby samodeyatel'noy pesni (KSP)." http://www.progressor.ru/stas/aboutksp.htm.

Sokolova, I. A. "Avtorskaya pesnya: Opredeleniya i terminy." In *Mir Vysotskogo: Issledovaniya i materialy IV,* 429–49. Moscow: GKTsM V. S. Vysotskogo, 2000.

———. *Avtorskaya pesnya: Ot fol'klora k poezii.* Moscow: GKTsM V. S. Vysotskogo, 2002.

———. "Mnogogolos'ye Yuriya Vizbora: Zhanry, formy, stilistika." In *Mir Vysotskogo: Issledovaniya i materialy III.2,* 404–16. Moscow: GKTsM V. S. Vysotskogo, 1999.

———. "V nachale byl Ancharov . . . O poeticheskom tvorchestve Mikhaila Ancharova i yego vklade v razvitiye zhanra avtorskoy pesni." In *Mir Vysotskogo: Issledovaniya i materialy II,* 354–75. Moscow: GKTsM V. S. Vysotskogo, 1998.

Sokolovskaya, T. D. "Zhanrovo-stilevoye mnogoobraziye rechevykh sredstv poezii Vladimira Vysotskogo." In *Mir Vysotskogo: Issledovaniya i materialy,* 315–18. Moscow: Komitet po kul'ture Moskvy; GKTsM V. S. Vysotskogo, 1997.

Soldatenkov, Pyotr. *Vladimir Vysotsky.* Moscow: Olimp, 1999.

Solov'yov-Sedoy, V. "Za podlinnuyu massovost'." *Sovetskaya muzyka* 5 (1956): 34–37.

Sosin, Gene. "Aleksandr Galich: Russian Poet of Dissent." *Midstream* 20, no. 4 (1974): 29–37.

———. "Magnitizdat: Uncensored Songs of Dissent." In *Dissent in the USSR: Politics, Ideology, and People,* edited by Rudolf L. Tokes, 276–309. Baltimore: Johns Hopkins University Press, 1975.

Sovetskaya muzyka. www.sovmusic.ru.

Spitzer, Leo. *Lives In Between: The Experience of Marginality in a Century of Emancipation.* New York: Hill and Wang, 1989.

Steinholt, Yngvar B. "You Can't Rid a Song of Its Words: Notes on the Hegemony of Lyrics in Russian Rock Songs." *Popular Music* 22, no. 1 (2003): 89–108.

Stites, Richard. "The Domestic Muse: Music at Home in the Twilight of Serfdom." In *Intersections and Transpositions: Russian Music, Literature, and Society,* edited by Andrew Baruch Wachtel, 187–205. Evanston, Ill.: Northwestern University Press, 1998.

———. *Soviet Popular Culture.* New York: Cambridge University Press, 1992.

Stonequist, Everett V. *The Marginal Man: A Study in Personality and Culture Conflict.* New York: Charles Scribner's Sons, 1937.

Stroinska, Magda. "Forbidden Reality: The Language and Function of Propaganda." In *Secret Spaces, Forbidden Places: Rethinking Culture,* edited by Fran Lloyd and Catherine O'Brien, 121–32. New York: Berghahn Books, 2000.

———. "Introduction: Beyond Language and Culture: Relative Points of View." In *Relative Points of View: Linguistic Representations of Culture,* edited by Magda Stroinska. New York: Berghahn Books, 2001.

Sukharev, D. A., ed. *Avtorskaya pesnya: Antologiya.* Ekaterinburg: U-Faktoriya, 2002.

———. "Vvedeniye v sub"yektivnuyu bardistiku." *Znamya* 10 (2000): 183–200.

Suslov, Il'ya. "Pesni, nashedshiye svoikh avtorov." *Yunost'* 11 (1963): 94–95.

Suvorov, Dmitry. "Ocherki o Vysotskom." *Ural,* no. 7 (2002), http://magazines.russ.ru/ural/2002/7/suv-pr.html.

Szymborska, Wyslawa. "Feet and Fate." In *Nonrequired Reading,* 27–28. New York: Harcourt, 2002.

Tannen, Deborah. "The Oral/Literate Continuum in Discourse." In *Spoken and Written Language: Exploring Orality and Literacy,* edited by Deborah Tannen, 1–16. Norwood, N.J.: Ablex, 1982.

Tarasov, Konstantin. "Novyi Grushinskiy." In *Grushinskiy: Festival'naya letopis' 1968–2000,* 8–11. St. Petersburg: Boyanych, Litsey, 2001.

Tarlysheva, E. A. "Avtorskaya pesnya: Problema zhanra." In *Problemy slavyanskoy kultury i tsivilizatsii,* 80–82. Ussuriysk: Ministerstvo obshchego i professional'nogo obrazovaniya Rossiyskoy Federatsii; Ussuriyskiy gosudarstvennyi pedagogicheskiy institut, 1999.

———. "Vertinsky i bardy shestidesyatykh." In *Mir Vysotskogo: Issledovaniya i materialy III.2,* 400–403. Moscow: GKTsM V. S. Vysotskogo, 1999.

Terts, Abram. "Otechestvo: Blatnaya pesnya . . ." *Sintaksis* 4 (1979): 72–118.

Tetzlaff, David. "Music for Meaning: Reading the Discourse of Authenticity." *Journal of Communication Inquiry* 18, no. 1 (1994): 95–117.

Tilipina, T. P. "O sootnoshenii rolevogo i liricheskogo geroyev." In *Mir Vysotskogo: Issledovaniya i materialy III.1,* 212–17. Moscow: GKTsM V. S. Vysotskogo, 1999.

Timofeyev, A. "Pesni Vikhoreva." In *Ya by skazal tebe mnogo khoroshego . . . ,* edited by A. Levitan and M. Levitan, 5–7. St. Petersburg: Boyanych, 1996.

Tolczyk, Dariusz. *See No Evil: Literary Cover-Ups and Discoveries of the Soviet Camp Experience.* New Haven, Conn.: Yale University Press, 1999.

Toporkova, I., ed. *Blatnye pesni: Tsyplyonok zharenyi,* Zolotaya seriya poezii. Moscow: Eksmo, 2005.

Treml, Vladimir G. *Alcohol in the USSR: A Statistical Study.* Durham, N.C.: Duke Press Policy Studies, 1982.

Turner, Victor. "Betwixt and Between: The Liminal Period in Rites de Passage." In *The Forest of Symbols: Aspects of Ndembu Ritual,* 93–111. Ithaca, N.Y.: Cornell University Press, 1967.

———. *Dramas, Fields, and Metaphors: Symbolic Action in Human Society.* Ithaca, N.Y.: Cornell University Press, 1974.

———. *The Ritual Process: Structure and Anti-Structure.* London: Routledge, 1969.

Tyazhel'nikova, V. S. "Sovetskaya pesnya i formirovaniye novoy identichnosti." *Otechestvennaya istoriya* 1 (2002): 174–81.

Tynyanov, Yu. N. "O parodii." In *Poetika, Istoriya literatury, Kino,* 284–310. Moscow: Nauka, 1977.

Urban, Michael. *Russia Gets the Blues: Music, Culture, and Community in Unsettled Times.* Ithaca, N.Y.: Cornell University Press, 2004.

Vail', Pyotr, and Aleksandr Genis. *60–e—mir sovetskogo cheloveka.* Moscow: Novoye literaturnoye obozreniye, 2001.

———. "Shampanskoye i politura." *Vremya i my* 36 (1978): 134–42.

Venclova, Tomas. "Two Russian Sub-Languages and Russian Ethnic Identity." In *Ethnic Russia in the USSR: The Dilemma of Dominance,* edited by Edward Allworth, 249–59. New York: Pergamon, 1980.

Vertinsky, Aleksandr. *Dorogoy dlinnoyu.* Moscow: Pravda, 1991.

Vikhorev, Valentin. Interview by Rachel S. Platonov. July 6, 2001.

———. "Raznoobrazny i samobytny." In *Bereg nadezhd: Pesni leningradskikh avtorov: 1950–1960–e,* edited by A. Levitan and M. Levitan, 5–6. St. Petersburg: Boyanych, 2002.

Vishevsky, Anatoly. *Soviet Literary Culture in the 1970s: The Politics of Irony.* Gainesville: University Press of Florida, 1993.

Vizbor, Yury. *Monologi so stseny: O sebe, o kino, o pesne.* Moscow: Gud'yal-Press, 2000.

———. *Sochineniya v dvukh tomakh.* 2 vols. Vol. 1. Moscow: Lokid, 1999.

"Vladimir Vysotsky: People Shone When They Stood Next to Him." *Spotlight with Al Gurnov* (January 25, 2008), http://www.russiatoday.com/spotlight/release/1066/video.

Vladyshevskaya, T., et al. *Istoriya russkoy muzyki.* Moscow: Muzyka, 1999.

von Geldern, James, and Richard Stites, ed. *Mass Culture in Soviet Russia.* Bloomington: Indiana University Press, 1995.

Voronova, M. V. "Stilisticheskiye sredstva markirovki liricheskogo i rolevykh geroyev V. S. Vysotskogo." In *V. S. Vysotsky: Issledovaniya i materialy,* 117–28. Voronezh: Izdatel'stvo Voronezhskogo universiteta, 1990.

Vysotskaya, Irena. *Moy brat Vysotsky: U istokov.* Moscow: Rizalt, 2005.

Vysotsky, Vladimir. "Khorosho by zazhech' svet." *Pskovskaya guberniya,* no. 322 (2007), http://gubernia.pskovregion.org/number_322/12.php.

———. *Monologi so stseny.* Moscow: AST, 2000.

———. *Pesni lyubimye narodom.* Retro, 2000. 3 CDs.

———. *Sobraniye sochineniy v chetyryokh tomakh, Tom 4: Proza.* e-book ed. Moscow: Vremya, 2010.

———. *Sochineniya v dvukh tomakh.* 2 vols. Vol. 1. Moscow: Lokid-Press, 2001.

———. *Vladimir Vysotsky* (32-CD collection). [Moscow]: Moroz Records, 2000.

Weisberger, Adam. "Marginality and Its Directions." *Sociological Forum* 7, no. 3 (1992): 425–46.

White, Stephen. *Russia Goes Dry: Alcohol, State and Society.* Cambridge, Eng.: Cambridge University Press, 1996.

Windle, Kevin. "Yuz Aleshkovskii's 'Pesnya o Staline' and 'Sovetskaya paskhal'naya': A Study of Competing Versions." *Slavonic and East European Review* 74, no. 1 (1996): 19–37.

Wolff, Janet. *Resident Alien: Feminist Cultural Criticism.* New Haven, Conn.: Yale University Press, 1995.

Yakusheva, Ada. *Pesnya—lyubov' moya.* Moscow: Lokid-Press, 2001.

Yans, Georgy. "Neistov i upryam." *Odintsovo Info* (May 8, 2008), http://www.odintsovo.info/news/?div_id=54&id=16735.

Yefimova, Yekaterina. *Sovremennaya tyur'ma: Byt, traditsii i fol'klor.* Moscow: OGI, 2004.

Yevtushenko, Yevgeny. "Magnitofonnaya glasnost'." *Nedelya* 18, no. 9 (1988): 16.

———. *Stikhotvoreniya i poemy.* 3 vols. Vol. 1. Moscow: Sovetskaya Rossiya, 1987.

Yurchak, Alexei. *Everything Was Forever, Until It Was No More: The Last Soviet Generation.* Princeton, N.J.: Princeton University Press, 2006.

"Za ideynuyu chistotu i podlinnuyu massovost'." *Sovetskaya muzyka* 7 (1966): 6–21.

Zakharov, V. "O sostoyanii i zadachakh pesennogo tvorchestva." *Sovetskaya muzyka* 2 (1954): 3–22.

Zhdanov, A. A. "Soviet Literature—The Richest in Ideas, the Most Advanced Literature." In *Problems of Soviet Literature,* edited by H. G. Scott, 15–24. New York: International, 1935?

Zhitomirskaya, M. "Avtorskaya pesnya i fol'klor." *Menestrel'* 2 (1981).

Zipes, Jack, ed. *Beauties, Beasts and Enchantment: Classic French Fairy Tales.* New York: New American Library, 1989.

———. *Breaking the Magic Spell: Radical Theories of Folk & Fairy Tales.* Revised and expanded ed. Lexington: University Press of Kentucky, 2002.

———. *Happily Ever After: Fairy Tales, Children, and the Culture Industry.* New York: Routledge, 1997.

Zubrilina, S. N. *Vladimir Vysotsky: Stranitsy biografii.* Rostov-on-Don: Feniks, 1998.

Zygulski, Kazimierz. "Leisure and Personality." In *Personal Activity in the Socialist Society,* edited by N. S. Mansurov et al., 425–50. Moscow: Institute for Sociological Research (Academy of Sciences of the USSR), Institute of Philosophy and Sociology (Polish Academy of Sciences), 1974.

Index

About the Author

Rachel S. Platonov is a lecturer in Russian Studies at the University of Manchester.